MUSIC OF THE SPHERES
AND THE DANCE OF DEATH

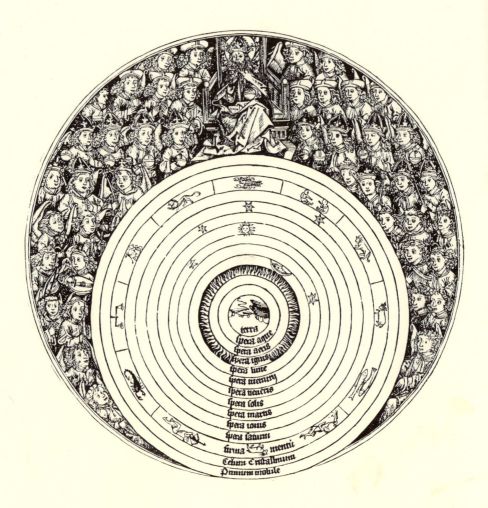

Music of the Spheres
and the Dance of Death

Studies in Musical Iconology

BY KATHI MEYER-BAER

PRINCETON UNIVERSITY PRESS, PRINCETON, NEW JERSEY, 1970

Copyright © 1970 by
PRINCETON UNIVERSITY PRESS

ALL RIGHTS RESERVED

L.C. Card: 68-15768

I.S.B.N. 0-691-09110-2

Publication of this book has been aided by
the Whitney Darrow Publication Reserve
Fund of Princeton University Press

This book has been composed in
Linotype Caslon Old Face

PRINTED IN THE UNITED STATES OF AMERICA
BY VAIL-BALLOU PRESS
BINGHAMTON, NEW YORK

To Curtis, Olga and George

Preface

"THUS with each special and single problem there arises the difficulty that the scholar—aside from his whole theological and philological training—should know the literature, language, and tradition of the different civilizations. . . . It cannot be helped that, according to his character and his education, one will regard too much as Egyptian, another as Babylonian, a third everything as Persian, and that each scholar will be affected by a certain color-blindness, making him indifferent to important shadings.

Only the collaboration of many can enable us to achieve the aim of elucidating Hellenistic mysticism."

R. Reitzenstein, *Poimandres*, 1904.

This passage from *Poimandres* describes the scope and intention of the present study. The subject, the symbolism of music, has recently attracted the interest of several scholars and musicologists, and a number of books and articles have been written on particular aspects of it. But few have set the problem in full perspective. The tendency, rather, has been to focus so sharply on a single facet that not only have other aspects been obscured, but the intricate pattern of the diverse threads of the historical development has been blurred.

A few specific studies might be mentioned here to illustrate the difference between other recent work and my undertaking in this book. Two of these focus on the images and metaphors used for music in literature. John Hollander's *The Untuning of the Sky* (Princeton, 1961) has as its aim—in his own words—"the interpretation of the working of music and of musical language," particularly in English literature of the period between 1500 and 1700. As the title indicates, the central theme is the idea of the music of the spheres. The author deals also with the concept of mood and mode and gives us a wealth of quotations and interpretations. With subtle scrutiny he investigates the different shades of words and the great influence which the poets had on the formation of images. In explaining the different metaphors, Hollander demonstrates how their meaning changed from the Renaissance to the Baroque period. Although in the introduction he traces the tradition back to antiquity, the story of its development is not a major concern in his book. My primary interest lies in the ways these ideas were formed and developed. But in his chosen range, as to the specific period and the specific wordings, his study is of the greatest value. G. Finney, in her essays *Musical Background for English Literature* 1580–1630 (Newark, N.J.), begins with the interpretation of musical images in English literature, but from there she proceeds to general ideas. In "A World of Instruments" (*English Literary History*, xx, 1953) she includes visual images. Her article "Music the Breath of Life" (*The Centenary Review*, Vol. 4 [1960]) deals with problems similar to those in the second part of my book. The author uses much the same method, connecting specific facts with general ideas.

R. Hammerstein, in his book *Die Musik der Engel* (Bern, 1962), has concentrated on one topic, the music-making angels. The comparison of the ideas of the liturgies in heaven and on earth is the subject of his study, and he investigates the whole problem from this point of view. He gives us an abundance of information; his quotations from the Church Fathers and the medieval writers on the theory of music are especially valuable, as are his descriptions of the representations of angel musicians in the visual arts. Here his discussion of the musical instruments is particularly useful. The chapter on the different kinds of "trumpets" used in the representations of the Last Judgment is a little masterpiece. However, through his restriction on the Christian thinking, many concepts are left out which for my book are vital: the structure of the heavens, the exact location of the angels, why they appear in a certain order, and what their duties are in addition to making music. The concept of the motion of the spheres and the angels' task of perfecting this motion are left aside—and therewith the connection to the prime mover in the highest heaven, the cause and foundation of the whole hierarchy. Hammerstein does not consider the pagan writers, even such an important source as Martianus Capella is not mentioned. With these limitations, he cannot give us the whole story, but he illuminates the one splendid vision of the Christian heaven with its angel musicians.

It is the aim of my study to provide a broad outline of the chief traditions, tracing their origins and phases over a long span of time. The materials drawn upon range widely among written sources and works of art, and the endeavor is to treat the visual musical symbols in their appropriate intellectual context. This is, thus, really neither a book about purely pictorial symbols of music nor simply an illustrated book about ideas, but rather an effort at an integrated study of both. Needless to say, no outline pretends to be exhaustive. Indeed, it is hoped that it might prove to be simply the starting point for the many further studies that are needed in this field.

I want to express my sincerest thanks to the many scholars who have given me generously of their information. Their contributions are acknowledged in the footnotes. I am especially indebted to Professor Edward Lowinsky for his advice. He pointed out to me in the first draft of my text the many places where it was not comprehensive. With the help of my editor, Mrs. Elisabeth Bass, I have tried to improve the wording. Through a wonderful empathy she has been able to grasp my intended meaning and to help me present the problems convincingly. I owe a debt also to my colleague Edmund Bowles, who assisted me in verifying the names of the musical instruments.

I further wish to express my deep gratitude to the American Philosophical Society, which gave me a grant to assemble the material for the illustrations, and to the American Council of Learned Societies, which gave me a grant to make the editing possible.

The actual plan for this work originated in a discussion with Professor H. W. Janson on some problems connected with Donatello's musician *putti*. Ultimately, the question arose: when and how did angel orchestras originate? I did not know, and could not subsequently find the answer anywhere in existing sources. In my quest for an answer, I became involved in the problems which form the topic of my study. To Professor Janson and many other scholars in many fields of research go my warmest thanks for advice and help.

Photographic Sources

A.C.L. Brussels, 90a, 90b, 173, 174

Alinari, 14, 25, 27, 59, 62, 63, 94, 95, 136, 146

Anderson, 26, 54, 70, 79, 84, 113, 117, 130, 133

Antiquarium, Munich, 140

Archives Photographiques, 83, 147

Bencini e Savioni, 24

Biblioteca Apostolica, 5, 15, 20, 21, 61

Bibliotheque Nationale, 22, 23, 31, 41, 74, 75, 100

Brisighelli, Udine, 69

British Museum, 10, 17, 38, 115, 116, 119, 120, 127, 152

Brogi, 58, 71, 91, 92

Byzantine Museum, 144

Deutsches Archaeologisches Institut, Athens, 121, 126

Deutsches Archäologisches Institut, Rome, 7, 129, 131, 141

Devinoy, 39, 51, 52

Foto MAS, 42, 44, 45, 46, 76, 171

Foto Villani-Bologna, 78

Gabinetto Fotografico Nazionale, 33, 34, 65

Giraudon, 49, 64, 73

Hermitage Museum, 9, 156

Hessisches Landesmuseum, 77

Isabella Stweart Gardner Museum, 55

Kingsley Porter Photograph Collection, 43, 50

Landesbibliothek, Wiesbaden, 40

Landesdenkmalamt, 89

Marburg, 3, 4, 53, 66, 145, 150, 151

Metropolitan Museum of Art, 106, 107, 154

Museo Archeologico Gela, 12

Museo Civico, Piacenza, 30

Museum of Fine Arts, Boston, 114, 123, 138

The National Gallery, London, 80

National Gallery of Art, 82

National Monuments Record, 86, 87

New York Public Library, 1, 2, 29, 93, 96, 97, 98, 99, 103, 105, 155, 157, 158, 159, 160, 163, 164, 165, 166, 168, 172

Oesterreichisches Archäologisches Institut, 124

The Oriental Institute, University of Chicago, 18

The Pierpont Morgan Library, 35, 36, 37, 68, 167

J. B. Pritchard, *The Ancient Near East in Pictures*, 108

Rijksmuseum, Amsterdam, 81

Soprintendenza alle Antichità, Florence, 118

Soprintendenza Antichità, Rome, 132

Staats-Bibliothek, Munich, 32, 169

Steinkopf, Berlin-Dahlem, 56

Technische Hochschule, Stuttgart, 88

Walters Art Gallery, 122

Contents

Preface vii

List of Illustrations xvii

PART ONE

Introduction to Part I 3

I. THEORIES OF THE COSMOS IN ANTIQUITY 7

The Structure and Motion of the Cosmos · The Abode of the Dead
and the Problem of the Highest Heaven · The Movers of the Spheres
and the Figure of the Angel

II. THE HELLENISTIC PERIOD 20

Plato's Successors · Gnostic Writings · Neoplatonists and Stoics

III. THE EARLY CHRISTIAN CENTURIES 29

Non-Christian Theories · Martianus Capella · The Church Fathers
· Dionysius's Angel Hierarchy

IV. THE EARLY WORKS OF ART 42

Representations of the Cosmos · The Movers of the Spheres and the
Figure of the Angel · Representations of the Angel Orders ·
Symbols of Music

V. TONAL THEORIES OF MUSIC OF THE SPHERES 70

Early Variants · Medieval Theory · Reflections in Visual Art

VI. THE EMERGENCE OF CELESTIAL MUSICIANS IN
CHRISTIAN ICONOGRAPHY 87

The Beatus Manuscripts · Emergence of Musicians and Dancers ·
Elders and Angels

VII. LATE MEDIEVAL WRITINGS AND DANTE'S PARADISE 116

Mystics and Scholastics · The Transition to Dante · Dante's Vision

VIII. MUSICIAN ANGELS 130

Dancing Angels and the Dance of the Blessed · Singing Angels · Angel Orchestras · Angels of the Psalter · Angels' Instruments—Real or Imaginary?

IX. RENAISSANCE AND HUMANISM 188

X. TWO OFFSHOOTS OF THE IDEA OF THE MUSIC OF THE SPHERES 203

PART TWO

Introduction to Part II 219

XI. MUSIC AS A SYMBOL OF DEATH IN ANTIQUITY 224

Ancient Non-Greek Civilizations · Harpies, Sirens, and Muses in Homer's Greece

XII. LATER GREEK CONCEPTS AND THE HELLENISTIC PERIOD 242

The Benevolent Siren · The Psychopomp Muse · The Figure of Orpheus

XIII. THE CHRISTIAN ERA & THE DEVELOPMENT OF EARLY MEDIEVAL IMAGES 270

Changed Concepts of Life after Death · The Survival of Orpheus · The Concept of the *Pneuma* · Sirens and Harpies · The Figure of Satan · The Symbolism of Particular Instruments

XIV. LATER MEDIEVAL IMAGES: THE DANCE OF DEATH 291

The Figure of the Skeleton · Fifteenth-Century Examples of the Dance of Death · Holbein's *Totentanz* · Origins of the Dance of Death

XV. THE FIFTEENTH-CENTURY MYSTICS 313

XVI. SURVIVALS OF EARLIER IMAGES 320

Later Versions of the Dance of Death · Survivals of Ancient Figures in Fairy Tales · Music and Death: A Summary

Contents

CONCLUSION: SURVIVALS IN CONTEMPORARY MUSICAL CONCEPTS 337

Appendix I. 349

Excerpts from First Chapter of Letter on Harmony Addressed to Archbishop Rathbod of Treves by Regino of Prüm

Appendix II. 351

Excerpts from the Hymn "Naturalis Concordia vocum cum planetis"

Appendix III. 352

The Music in Dante's Cosmos

Appendix IV. 357

A Note on the Singers of the Ghent Altar

Appendix V. 360

Real or Imaginary Instruments: An Examination of the Beatus Manuscripts and the Utrecht Psalter

Index. 365

List of Illustrations

1. *The Lord as ruler of the cosmic harmony.* Woodcut from Hartmann Schedel, *Buch der Chroniken*, Nuremburg, 1493. *Photo:* New York Public Library   2

2. *Imago Mortis.* Woodcut from Hartmann Schedel, *Buch der Chroniken*, Nuremburg, 1949. *Photo:* New York Public Library

3. The monument for Frederick, Archbishop of Magdeburg. *Photo:* Marburg   4

4. *Chorus angelorum,* from the monument for Frederick, Archbishop of Magdeburg. *Photo:* Marburg   6

5. Mount Zion rising into the sphere of the cosmos. Vatican Ms. gr. 699. *Photo:* Biblioteca Apostolica Vaticana   10

6. Drawing after the fresco at Dendera, Egypt. *Photo:* from W. Grüneisen, *Sainte Marie Antique,* 1911   43

7. Bronze spindle with eight discs. Museo Archeologico Naples. *Photo:* Deutsches Archäologisches Institut, Rome   44

8. The cosmos supported by four sirens. *Photo:* from L. Curtius, "Musik der Sphaeren," *Deutsches Archäologisches Institut, Römische Abteilung Mitteilungen,* 50 (1935-36), p. 36   46

9. The deified king, ruler of the cosmos; silverplate. Hermitage Museum, Leningrad. *Photo:* Hermitage Museum, Leningrad   47

10. Hybrid winged figure, huge stone sculpture. *Photo:* By courtesy of the Trustees of British Museum   48

11. Ivory plate overlaid with golden foil from Nimrud. Ashmolean Museum, Oxford. *Photo:* from A. Parrot, *The Arts of Asia,* tr. by S. Gilbert, New York, Golden Press, 1961, Fig. 330   49

12. Winged Eros with lyre. Navarra Collection at Terranuova. *Photo:* Museo Archeologico Gela   49

13. Mosaic in the Koimesis Church at Nicaea. *Photo:* from O. Wulff, *Die Koimesiskirche zu Nicäa,* 1903, Pl. II   50

14. Joshua before a wingless angel. Mosaic, Rome, Santa Maria Maggiore. *Photo:* Alinari   52

15. Joshua before a winged angel. Vatican MS.gr.31. *Photo:* Biblioteca Apostolica Vaticana 52

16. The highest heaven with a bust of Christ. *Photo:* from W. Grüneisen, *Sainte Marie Antique*, 1911 53

17. The winged male figure Assur. Fresco, British Museum. *Photo:* By courtesy of the Trustees of The British Museum 53

18. Throne relief on east jamb of western doorway at Persepolis. *Photo:* Oriental Institute, The University of Chicago 54

19. Two stone slabs from the ruins of the Visigoth church at Quintanilla de las Viñas. *Photo:* from J. Pijoan, *Summa Artis*, 1942, VIII, 381 55

20. Christ as ruler of the cosmos. Vatican Ms.gr.699. *Photo:* Biblioteca Apostolica Vaticana 56

21. King David on a throne. Vatican Ms.gr.699. *Photo:* Biblioteca Apostolica Vaticana 58

22. Illumination from the eleventh-century manuscript of the Homilies on the Virgin. Paris, Bibliothèque Nationale Ms.gr.1208, f.8. *Photo:* Bibliothèque Nationale 59

23. Illumination from the eleventh-century manuscript of the Homilies on the Virgin. Paris, Bibliothèque Nationale Ms.gr.1208, f.109v. *Photo:* Bibliothèque Nationale 60

24. Detail from the twelfth-century fresco in the Chiesa di San Pietro at Civate. *Photo:* Bencini e Savioni, Florence 61

25. The Madonna with angels. *Photo:* Alinari 63

26. The blessed entering the City of God. *Photo:* Anderson 64

27. Saint Michael holding a sign with the Thrice Holy. *Photo:* Alinari 65

28. Reconstruction after the description by John of Gaza. *Photo:* from R. Hinks, *Myth and Allegory in Ancient Art, Warburg Institut, Studien*, Vol. 6 (1939) 66

29. Drawing after the original ceiling painting in Hadrian's villa by N. Ponce, *Arabesques antiques*, 1789. *Photo:* New York Public Library 67

30. Second-century Italian mosaic floor. Museo Civico, Piacenza. *Photo:* Museo Civico, Piacenza 69

31. Flyleaf of the eleventh-century manuscript of Boethius's *De Institutione Musicae*. Paris, Bibliothèque Nationale Ms.lat.7203. *Photo:* Bibliothèque Nationale 82

32. Illumination from the Uta Evangeliary. Staats-Bibliothek,

Munich, Codex Monacensis lat.13601, fol.3v. *Photo:* Staats-Bibliothek, Munich   84

33. Twelfth-century ceiling painting in the Cappella Palatina, Palermo. *Photo:* Gabinetto Fotografico Nazionale, Rome   88

34. Detail from the ceiling painting in the aisle of the Cappella Palatina, Palermo. *Photo:* Gabinetto Fotografico Nazionale   89

35. Adoration of the Lamb, from the Divagations on the Apocalypse by Beatus de Libiena. The Pierpont Morgan Library, New York, Ms.644, fol.87. *Photo:* The Pierpont Morgan Library, New York   91

36. The Lamb on Mount Zion, from the Divagations on the Apocalypse by Beatus di Libiena. The Pierpont Morgan Library, New York, Ms.644, fol.174v. *Photo:* The Pierpont Morgan Library   93

37. The Lamb on Mount Zion, from the Divagations on the Apocalypse by Beatus di Libiena. The Pierpont Morgan Library, New York, Ms.429, fol.112. *Photo:* The Pierpont Morgan Library   94

38. The Lamb on Mount Zion, from the Divagations on the Apocalypse by Beatus di Libiena. British Museum Ms. 11695. By courtesy of the Trustees of the British Museum. *Photo:* The British Museum   95

39. The Lord in Glory, the twelfth-century tympanon of the south portal at Moissac. *Photo:* P. Devinoy, Paris   97

40. Illumination from the twelfth-century Hildegard Codex. Wiesbaden Landesbibliothek, Codex No. 1, fol.38r. *Photo:* Landesbibliothek, Wiesbaden   99

41. King David playing on a harp and dancing. Paris, Bibliothèque Nationale Ms.lat.1. *Photo:* Bibliothèque Nationale   101

42. Detail from the west portal of the cathedral at Toro. *Photo:* Foto MAS, Barcelona   102

43. Detail of the musician Elders on the roof of the Amiens Cathedral. *Photo:* Kingsley Porter Photograph Collection, Fogg Art Museum, Harvard University   104

44. Portico de la Gloria, from the cathedral at Santiago di Compostella. *Photo:* Foto MAS   105

45. Portico de la Gloria, from the cathedral at Santiago di Compostella. *Photo:* Foto MAS   105

46. Portico de la Gloria, from the cathedral at Santiago di Compostella. *Photo:* Foto MAS   106

47. Detail from the Portail Royal of the Chartres Cathedral. *Photo:* Courtauld Institute of Art, London   107

48. A pillar on the south portal of Chartres Cathedral. *Photo:* from Et. Houvet, *Cathédrale de Chartres, Portail Sud,* Vol. II   108

49. Detail from west façade of Notre Dame, Paris. *Photo:* Giraudon, Paris   109

50. Capital from Saint Pons de Thomières (Herault). *Photo:* Kingsley Porter Photograph Collection, Fogg Art Museum, Harvard University   111

51. Detail from the twelfth-century portal, La Lauda, at Fronzac. *Photo:* P. Devinoy, Paris   112

52. Portal of Sainte Marie, Oloron-Sainte-Marie. *Photo:* P. Devinoy, Paris   113

53. Musician angels on the tympanon of the Cathedral of Saint Jean at Lyons. *Photo:* Marburg   115

54. Fresco by Andrea da Firenze in the Spanish Chapel of Santa Maria Novella in Florence. *Photo:* Anderson   131

55. Detail from Fra Angelico, *Death and Assumption of the Virgin.* Isabella Stewart Gardner Museum, Boston. *Photo:* Isabella Stewart Gardner Museum, Boston   132

56. Detail from Fra Angelico, *Last Judgment.* Ehemalige Staatliche Museen, Berlin-Dahlem. *Photo:* Steinkopf, Berlin-Dahlem   133

57. Botticelli, illustration for Dante's *Paradiso.* Drawing. Staatliche Museen, Berlin, Kupferstichkabinet. *Photo:* from F. Lippmann, *Drawings by Sandro Botticelli for Dante's Divina Commedia,* 1896 135

58. Luca della Robbia, detail from the so-called Cantoria in the Cathedral of Florence. Museo del Duomo, Florence. *Photo:* Brogi 135

59. Detail from Botticelli, *Coronation of the Virgin.* Uffizi, Florence. *Photo:* Alinari   136

60. Greek vase, Munich Glyptothek. *Photo:* from C. Lenormand, *Élite des monuments céramographiques,* 1844-61   137

61. Apollo seated on a throne. Vatican Ms.reg.lat.1290. *Photo:* Biblioteca Apostolica Vaticana   138

62. Giulio Romano, *Il Ballo d'Apollo con le Muse.* Pitti Gallery, Florence. *Photo:* Alinari   139

63. Mary in Glory, from the *Caleffo dell'Assunta.* Archivio di Stato, Siena. *Photo:* Alinari   140

64. Pol de Limbourg, Nativity, from *Les très riches Heures du Duc de Berry,* fol.44v. Musée Condé, Chantilly. *Photo:* Giraudon   142

65. Detail of the vault of Santa Maria della Bocca, at Offida. *Photo:* Gabinetto Fotografico Nazionale   144

66. The Lord in Glory in the Celestial Jerusalem, from Saint Augustine's *Civitas Dei*. Laurenziana, Florence, Plut. 12, cod. 17. *Photo:* Marburg   146

67. The Lord in Glory in the Celestial Jerusalem, from Saint Augustine's *Civitas Dei*. Bibliothèque Macon, France, Ms.1. *Photo:* from A. de Laborde, *Les manuscrits à peinture de la Cité de Dieu*, Paris, 1909   148

68. The Lord in Glory. The Pierpont Morgan Library, New York, Ms. 742. *Photo:* The Pierpont Morgan Library   149

69. Coronation of the Virgin, fresco in the Cathedral of Venzone. *Photo:* Brisighelli, Udine   150

70. Masolino, *Assumption of the Virgin*. Museo Capodimonte, Naples. *Photo:* Anderson   152

71. Leonardo da Bisuccio, Coronation of the Virgin, a fresco in San Giovanni a Carbonara at Naples. *Photo:* Brogi   153

72. Paolo Veneziano, *Coronation of the Virgin*. The Frick Collection, New York. *Photo:* The Frick Collection, New York   157

73. Etienne Chevalier adoring the Virgin, from the *Heures d'Etienne Chevalier*. Musée Condé, Chantilly, Ms.71. *Photo:* Giraudon   159

74. Pol de Limbourg, Saint Jerome in his study, from the *Bible moralisée*. Paris, Bibliothèque Nationale Ms.fr.166. *Photo:* Bibliothèque Nationale   159

75. Saint Denis at his desk, from Saint Dionysius's *De Hierarchia;* Bibliothèque Nationale Ms.fr.2090, fol.107v. *Photo:* Bibliothèque Nationale   160

76. Hieronymus Bosch, roundel from the painting *The Seven Cardinal Sins*. Prado, Madrid. *Photo:* Foto MAS   161

77. Detail from the Ortenberger Altar. Hessisches Landesmuseum, Darmstadt. *Photo:* Hessisches Landesmuseum, Darmstadt   162

78. Lodovico Carracci, *Paradise*. San Paolo Maggiore, Bologna. *Photo:* Foto Villani-Bologna (Italy)   164

79. Gaudenzio Ferrari, *Assumption of the Virgin*, Saronno. *Photo:* Anderson   165

80. Matteo di Giovanni, *Madonna with the Girdle*. Reproduced by courtesy of the Trustees, The National Gallery, London. *Photo:* The National Gallery, London   167

81. Geertgen tot Sint Jans, *Mary in Glory*. Museum Boymans-van Beuningen, Rotterdam. *Photo:* Rijksmuseum, Amsterdam   168

82. Master of the Saint Lucy Legend, *Mary, Queen of Heaven.*
National Gallery of Art, Washington, D.C. (Samuel H. Kress
Collection). *Photo:* National Gallery of Art, Washington, D.C.   169

83. Detail from Tintoretto, *Coronation of the Virgin.* Louvre,
Paris. *Photo:* Archives Photographiques   170

84. Jacobello del Fiore, *Coronation of the Virgin.* Accademia,
Venice. *Photo:* Anderson   172

85. Illumination from the Utrecht Psalter for the 150th Psalm.
Facsimile edition, London 1875, fol.83a   174

86. Bosses in the north transept of Westminster Abbey. *Photo:*
National Monuments Record, London   175

87. Detail of the minstrels' gallery in Exeter Cathedral. *Photo:*
National Monuments Record, London   176

88. Genesis window in Saint Theobald at Thann, Alsace. *Photo:*
Technische Hochschule Stuttgart. Institut für Kunstgeschichte   178

89. Fragment from a fourteenth-century glass window from
Mark, Westphalia. C. Lübke Museum, Hamm, Westphalia. *Photo:*
Landesdenkmalamt Westphalen, Münster   179

90a and 90b. Memling, Christ and angel musicians, Koninklijk
Museum, Antwerp. *Photo:* Copyright A.C.L. Brussels   180–81

91. Luca della Robbia, detail from the so-called Cantoria. Museo
del Duomo, Florence. *Photo:* Brogi   182

92. Detail from Gaudenzio Ferrari, *Assumption of the Virgin,*
Saronno. *Photo:* Brogi   184

93. Zeus in his two aspects. Woodcut in Vincenzo Cartari, *Imagini
delli dei degli antichi,* 1571. *Photo:* New York Public Library   189

94. Agostino di Duccio, detail from the portal of the Church of
Saints Andrea and Bernardino, Perugia. *Photo:* Alinari   190

95. The Muse Clio. Agostino di Duccio, relief from the Tempio
Malatestiano at Rimini. *Photo:* Alinari   190

96. A woodcut from Franchino Gafori, *Practica Musicae utriusque cantus,* Brescia, 1508. *Photo:* New York Public Library   192

97. Diagram from Robert Fludd, *Historia utriusque cosmi,* 1617.
Photo: New York Public Library   196

98. Diagram from Robert Fludd, *Historia utriusque cosmi,* 1617.
Photo: New York Public Library   198

99. Diagram from Robert Fludd, *Philosophia sacra et vere Christiana seu Meteorologia Cosmica,* 1622. *Photo:* New York Public
Library   200–201

100. Engraving by Colignon after G. J. Bernini. Bibliothèque Nationale, Paris. *Photo:* Bibliothèque Nationale   208

101. Engraving by Hoffman & Hermundt after Waginger. *Photo:* from R. Haas, *Die Musik des Barocks, Handbuch der Musikwissenschaft,* 1929   210

102. Engraving of the twenty-four Elders on title page of Heinrich Schütz, *Kleine geistliche Concerte,* Erster Theil, 1636. *Photo:* from R. Haas, *Die Musik des Barocks, Handbuch der Musikwissenschaft,* 1929   211

103. Frontispiece engraving by F. Baronius after Paul Schor for Athanasius Kircher, *Musurgia,* 1650. *Photo:* New York Public Library   213

104a and 104b. Eton Choirbook. Illuminations in the initials to the composition of the *Salve Regina* by Robert Wilkinson. *Photo:* Professor Frank Harrison, Oxford   215

105. Frontispiece engraving for J. Rist, *Musikalische Kreuz-Trost-Lob und Dankschule,* Lüneburg, 1659. *Photo:* New York Public Library   218

106. Clay figures from a Chinese tomb. The Metropolitan Museum of Art, New York, Rogers Fund, 1923. *Photo:* The Metropolitan Museum of Art   225

107. Drawing by C. Wilkinson after fresco in the tomb of Djeser-Ka-Re-souhe. The Metropolitan Museum of Art, New York. *Photo:* The Metropolitan Museum of Art   226

108. Relief, Cairo Museum. *Photo:* Marburg   227

109. Small Egyptian ash urn. Louvre, Paris. *Photo:* M. Chuzeville, Paris   229

110. Mural in the Tomba del Morto a Corneto. *Photo:* from J. Martha, *L'art Étrusque,* 1889   230

111. Drawing after painting in the Tomba del Morto a Corneto. *Photo:* from F. Weege, *Etruskische Malerei,* 1921   231

112. Mural in Tomba del Triclinio at Tarquinii. *Photo:* from F. Weege, *Etruskische Malerei,* 1921   231

113. "Season" sarcophagus. Formerly Palazzo Barberini, now Dumbarton Oaks. *Photo:* Anderson   233

114. Drawing after Corinthian vase. Museum of Fine Arts, Boston. *Photo:* Courtesy of Museum of Fine Arts, Boston, Pierce Fund   236

115. Red-figured amphora. By courtesy of the Trustees of the British Museum. *Photo:* The British Museum   236

116. Black-figured Lekythos. By courtesy of the Trustees of the British Museum. *Photo:* The British Museum   238

117. Roman sarcophagus. Museo Nazionale, Rome. *Photo:* Anderson   238

118. Etruscan ash urn. Museo Archeologico, Florence. *Photo:* Soprintendenza alle Antichità d'Etruria, Florence   239

119. Red-figured amphora. By courtesy of the Trustees of the British Museum, London. *Photo:* The British Museum   240

120. Drawing from a fourth-century Greek vase. By courtesy of the Trustees of the British Museum, London. *Photo:* The British Museum   241

121. Greek stele. National Museum, Athens. *Photo:* Deutsches Archaeologisches Institut, Athens   244

122. Detail of Greek stele. The Walters Art Gallery, Baltimore, Md. *Photo:* The Walters Art Gallery   245

123. Cup. Museum of Fine Arts, Boston. *Photo:* Courtesy, Museum of Fine Arts, Boston, Pierce Fund   246

124. Detail of a sarcophagus from Belevi, Asia Minor. Antikensammlung, Vienna. *Photo:* Oesterreichisches Archäologisches Institut, Vienna   247

125. Frieze from a tomb. Antikensammlung, Berlin. *Photo:* from *Mitteilungen des deutschen Archaeologischen Instituts,* Athens, 1888   247

126. Mourning sirens on a Greek stele, National Museum, Athens. *Photo:* Deutsches Archaeologisches Institut, Athens   248

127. Detail from the so-called Monument of the Harpies from the Mausoleum at Xanthos. By courtesy of the Trustees of the British Museum, London. *Photo:* The British Museum   249

128. Drawing after a fresco in the so-called Synagogue at Dura Europos. *Photo:* from M. E. du Mesnil du Bouisson, *Les peintures de la synagogue de Doura Europos,* 1939   251

129. Front of a third-century sarcophagus. Vatican Museum, Rome. *Photo:* Deutsches Archäologisches Institut, Rome   254

130. Roman-Christian sarcophagus. Museo Laterano, Rome. *Photo:* Anderson   254

131. Roman sarcophagus. Palazzo Barberini, Rome. *Photo:* Deutsches Archäologisches Institut, Rome   255

132. Front of a third-century sarcophagus. Museo Nazionale, Rome. *Photo:* Soprintendenza Antichità, Rome   255

133. Second-century sarcophagus. Vatican Museum, Rome. *Photo:* Anderson   256

134. Drawing after fresco in the Temple of Marasa-Locris. *Photo:* from C. Picard, "Néréides et sirènes," *Annales de l'école des hautes études de Gand,* No. 2 (1938)   258

135. Seal cylinder. Kaiser Friedrich Museum, Berlin. *Photo:* from R. Eisler, *Orpheus the Fisher,* 1921   261

136. First-century Roman mosaic floor. Palazzo dell'Università, Perugia. *Photo:* Alinari   262

137. Drawing after frieze from a border-stone in the Temple of Bel at Nippur. *Photo:* from *Mémoires de la délégation en Perse,* Paris, 1905, VII   263

138. Illumination from a sixteenth-century Rajasthani manuscript. Museum of Fine Arts, Boston. *Photo:* Courtesy, Museum of Fine Arts, Boston, Ross-Coomaraswamy Collection   264

139. Drawing after a fresco in the so-called Synagogue at Dura Europos. *Photo:* from M. E. du Mesnil du Bouisson, *Les peintures de la synagogue de Doura Europos,* 1939   265

140. Greek vase found in southern Italy, now in Antiquarium, Munich. *Photo:* Antiquarium, Munich   265

141. Mural in the Casa di Orfeo at Pompeii. *Photo:* Deutsches Archäologisches Institut, Rome   266

142. Mosaic floor from a Roman villa in Chebbe Tunisia, now Museo del Bardo, Tunis. *Photo:* from G. Guidi, "Orfeo, Liber Pater Oceano" in Mosaici della Tripolitania, *Africa Italiana,* VI (1935)   267

143. Roman cameo. Collection Roger, Paris. *Photo:* from G. Lippold, *Gemmen und Kameen,* 1922   269

144. Alabaster flask. Byzantine Museum, Athens. *Photo:* Byzantine Museum, Athens   274

145. Romanesque capital at Torsac-en-Charente. *Photo:* Marburg   275

146. Luca della Robbia, Orpheus the musician, Campanile del Duomo, Florence. *Photo:* Alinari   276

147. Illumination from Pontifical Manuscript, school of Reims. Chapitre de Notre Dame, Reims. *Photo:* Archives Photographiques   280

148. Illumination in a *bestiaire.* Bibliothèque de l'Arsenal, Paris, Ms.3516, fol.202v. *Photo:* from D. Jalabert, "De l'art antique et l'art roman," *Bulletin monumental,* II, 95 (1936)   282

149. Drawing after a stained glass window, Lyons Cathedral. *Photo:* from E. Mâle, *L'art religieux du XIIIᵉ siècle,* 1919   283

150. Romanesque capital at Sainte Madeleine in Vézelay. *Photo:* Marburg   285

151. Tympanon of west portal of the cathedral at Conques. *Photo:* Marburg   286

152. Engraving after Mantegna. By courtesy of the Trustees of the British Museum. *Photo:* The British Museum   287

153. Silver cups found in Boscoreale near Pompeii. *Photo:* from *Monuments et Mémoires,* Fondation Piot, v, Paris, 1899   293

154. Jan or Hubert van Eyck, *The Last Judgement.* The Metropolitan Museum of Art, New York, Fletcher Fund, 1933. *Photo:* The Metropolitan Museum of Art   295

155. Woodcut from Savonarola, *Ars Moriendi,* Florence, 1494. *Photo:* New York Public Library   296

156. Ivory cask. Hermitage Museum, Leningrad. *Photo:* Hermitage Museum   297

157. Woodcut from Guyot Marchand, *Danse macabre,* Paris, 1486. *Photo:* New York Public Library   300

158. Woodcut from the *Heidelberger Totentanz.* Printed by Knoblochzer, Heidelberg, 1485. *Photo:* New York Public Library   301

159. Woodcut from the *Heidelberger Totentanz.* Printed by Knoblochzer, Heidelberg, 1485. *Photo:* New York Public Library   301

160. Woodcut from the *Heidelberger Totentanz.* Printed by Knoblochzer, Heidelberg, 1485. *Photo:* New York Public Library   301

161. Fresco Klein-Basler Totentanz. Klingenthal, Switzerland. *Photo:* from G. Buchheit, *Der Totentanz,* 1926   302

162. Woodcut from Holbein, *Les Simulachres et Historiées Faces de la Mort,* Lyons, 1538. *Photo:* New York Public Library   303

163. Woodcut from Holbein, *Les Simulachres et Historiées Faces de la Mort,* Lyons, 1538. *Photo:* New York Public Library   303

164. Woodcut from Holbein, *Les Simulachres et Historiées Faces de la Mort,* Lyons, 1538. *Photo:* New York Public Library   303

165. Woodcut from Holbein, *Les Simulachres et Historiées Faces de la Mort,* Lyons, 1538. *Photo:* New York Public Library   303

166. Woodcut from Holbein, *Les Simulachres et Historiées Faces de la Mort,* Lyons, 1538. *Photo:* New York Public Library   303

167. Woodcut border from a *Livre d'Heures,* Paris, Pigouchet, 1498. *Photo:* The Pierpont Morgan Library, New York   306

168. Skeleton dance from E. F. Knight, *Where Three Empires Meet,* 1893. *Photo:* New York Public Library   311

169. Single-leaf woodcut *Christus und die minnende Seele,* Munich, 1501. Staats-Bibliothek, Munich, Einblatt III, 52. *Photo:* Staats-Bibliothek, Munich   314

170. Pieter Breughel the Elder, *Christ in Limbo*. Engraving by H. Cock. *Photo:* from R. V. Baestelaer, *Les estampes de Pierre Brueghel l'ancien,* 1907   320

171. Hieronymus Bosch, "Music in Hell," detail from the *Garden of Lust.* Prado, Madrid. *Photo:* Foto MAS   323

172. Frontispiece for J. W. Valvasor, *Theatrum mortis tripartitum,* 1682. Engraving after And. Trost by J. Koch. *Photo:* New York Public Library   324

173. Jan van Eyck, detail from the Ghent Altar. Eglise de S. Bavon, Gand. *Photo:* Copyright A.C.L. Brussels   358

174. Jan van Eyck, detail from the Ghent Altar. Eglise de S. Bavon, Gand. *Photo:* Copyright A.C.L. Brussels   358

ONE

MUSIC OF THE SPHERES

FIG. 1. The Lord as ruler of the cosmic harmony; woodcut from Schedel, *Buch der Chroniken* (1493). INSTRUMENTS: lutes and harp

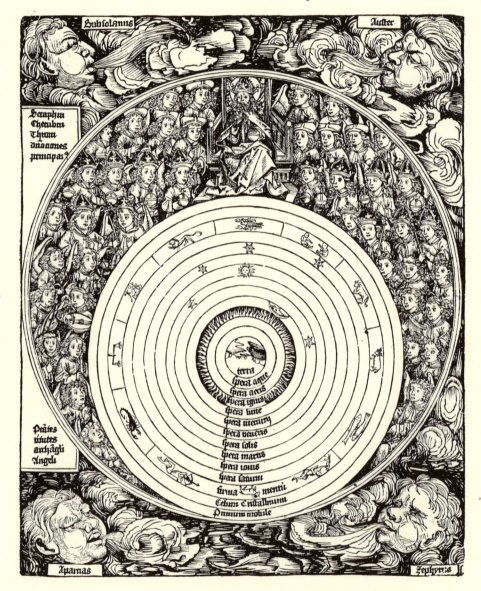

Introduction to Part One

In 1493, Hartmann Schedel of Nuremberg published his *Buch der Chroniken*. It is one of the earliest attempts at a history of the world and is illustrated with 1,809 woodcuts by Michael Wolgemut and Wilhelm Pleydenwurff.[1] Musical instruments are depicted in six of the many illustrations. In one, four couples perform a quiet dance to the accompaniment of flute and drum. In two others, Tubal, the mythical inventor of music according to the Bible, and King David are shown with instruments, a portable organ and a harp, as signs and emblems that they are musicians. In the other three woodcuts, however, music is used in a wider symbolic sense. The illustration for the seventh day of creation shows an image of the Lord atop the spheres of the universe and surrounded by angels, some of whom are playing on musical instruments (Fig. 1). Another woodcut shows a bridge collapsing under a party of sinners who have insulted a priest and the symbols of the Sacrament. A young man in the party is playing a lute. In the woodcut illustrating the seventh age and things to come —Schedel has divided his chronicle into seven ages of mankind— there are dancing skeletons, one of whom is playing on a wind instrument (Fig. 2). Thus in these three woodcuts music is shown and used allegorically as a symbol of harmony, as a symbol of sin, and as a symbol of death.

We have a similar combination of these three aspects in one of the monuments in the cathedral of Halberstadt, the monument for Frederick, archbishop of Magdeburg, dated 1552.[2] To the left of the archbishop's effigy, Christ appears rising from the tomb, with his right hand holding a chain binding Death and Satan together (Fig. 3), and a second devil further along the chain. To the right is a fig-

---

[1] Hartmann Schedel, *Buch der Chroniken*, Nuremberg, Ant. Koberger (1493); F. Stadler, *Michael Wolgemut und der Nürnberger Holzschnitt* (*Studien zur deutschen Kunstgeschichte*), CLXI (1913); A. Schramm, *Der Bilderschmuck der Frühdrucke*, Vol. 17 (1934), Figs. 412, 546, 567; *Handbuch der Bibliothekswissenschaft*, I (1931), 379.

[2] S. Kozaky, *Danse macabre* (Budapest, 1935–44), Vol. I, Pls. 5–7.

3

FIG. 2. *Imago Mortis*; woodcut from Schedel, *Buch der Chroniken* (1493). INSTRUMENTS: rebec and shawms

FIG. 3. The monument for Frederick, Archbishop of Magdeburg (1552) in the Cathedral of Halberstadt

ure of Death, a skeleton, holding Adam and Eve enchained, and again a devil, here playing a lute. Above, at the height of the head of the effigy, there is a frieze of angels dancing a round (Fig. 4). On the lower part of the monument, hell is clearly represented, with symbols of death and sin. On a level with the feet of the effigy is the figure of Christ as victor over death, and on the higher level is the dance of the angels, representing heaven, or Elysium. This juxtaposition of heaven and hell appears in many representations, especially in those of the Last Judgment; and, from the fourteenth century on, many of them use dancing and musical instruments to illustrate paradise.

The relationship of this heavenly dance of the blessed to the Dance of Death and the origin of these two concepts will be the topic of this study. Both ideas, that bliss as well as death is related to music, arose in antiquity and gradually gained the form that became familiar in the fourteenth and fifteenth centuries. The image of angels singing, playing, and dancing to praise the Lord may be traced back to early concepts of the music of the spheres, as well as to the idea of harmony in the universe expressed through music. The connection of death to music is less familiar, but I shall try to show that it, too, has a continuous tradition.

Both ideas are rooted in the ancient beliefs of the Near East and Greece, and it is there that this study must begin.[3] The first part will focus on music as a symbol of "harmony"—a word whose double meaning of "fitting together" in general as well as specifically in music is so familiar that the term almost seems a tautology. It is, in part, the history of the association of the two kinds of harmony that will be traced, along paths leading from ancient theories of an orderly cosmos, through ancient and medieval concepts of multiple heavens and of celestial music and dance, to the ultimate evolution of the angel orchestras that became prevalent in Renaissance painting and sculpture. In a sense, this will also be an account of the transmutation of the early pagan figures of the movers of the spheres into Christian angels, as well as of their association with music.

The chief images with which the first part will be concerned are the

---

[3] In works of the Far East, representations of music sometimes seem to have connotations similar to their Western counterparts, but their actual underlying meaning is different. See, for instance, A. K. Coomaraswamy, "Indian Bronzes," *Burlington Magazine*, Vol. 17 (1910), p. 88, Pl. II, n. 7. The bell in the hand of Mataraja, the dancing Siva, is a fertility symbol.

music of the spheres, and the visions of the dance of the blessed and
of angel musicians. Some of the specific questions relevant to following the paths of their development are: in which heaven is music
being performed; who are the figures that make music or dance to it;
what kind of music is being made?

FIG. 4. *Chorus angelorum*, from the monument for Frederick, Archbishop of
Magdeburg (1552)

I Theories of the Cosmos in Antiquity

FOR THE BASIC FRAMEWORK or background of the majority of the images and symbols on which this study will touch, it is essential to sketch the cosmologies of some of the ancient peoples. The ideas of the Babylonians, Persians, and Greeks, quite as much as those of the Old Testament authors, provided the original structure and population of the cosmos from which later concepts and figures related to music were derived. Hence, we begin with a brief account of how they envisaged the universe, the number of spheres or heavens they presumed it to contain, the order in which the heavens were arranged, and how, or by whom, the spheres and stars were thought to be moved.

THE STRUCTURE AND MOTION OF THE COSMOS

For the Babylonians, astronomy was the basis of religion,[1] and they logically assumed seven heavens, corresponding to the seven planets. Each planet was thought to move on a sphere, and this sphere was thought to be ruled and moved by one god. The highest god was the sun god, with whom Ashur was identified, and the power of the other astral entities was graded on the basis of their distance from the sun, with the star nearest the sun considered the most powerful.[2] Seven was the sacred number for the Babylonians,

---

[1] J. B. Dupuis, *Abrégé de l'origine de tous les cultes* (Paris, 1822); article on "Babylonians-Assyrians" in James Hastings' *Encyclopedia of Religions and Ethics*, I, 309; P. Duhem, *Le système du monde* (Paris, 1917), V, 541; P. Jensen, *Die Kosmologie der Babylonier* (Strasbourg, 1890); A. Jeremias, *Babylonien im Neuen Testament* (1908); H. Winckler, "Himmels- und Weltenbild der Babylonier," *Der Alte Orient*, III (1901), 2/3.

[2] In the period before 2800 B.C., the ruling constellation was Taurus and the bull was therefore the sacred animal. After about 2800 B.C., Aries became the constellation nearest the sun, and the ram gradually became the sacred animal. This change was also noticeable among the people of Ur and of the Bible. The ram or the lamb, interchangeably, remained the sacred animal not only in Exodus but also in the Gospels and Saint John's Revelation.

and the seven planets were believed to move on solid tracks or rails. Corresponding to the duration of the orbits of the stars, these tracks were visualized as spheres of different sizes, arranged one on top of the other or in concentric circles, with the smallest, earth's, forming the lowest or innermost part. In early Babylonian theory the gods who ruled and moved the spheres were thought to change their abode from one planet to another. In later theory, each ruled a particular planet, and it, in turn, had a certain character. The relation of these characters to men, especially with regard to the time of their birth, became part of the medieval theory of *musica humana,* and is still alive in astrology.[3] At the time when it was thought each god remained on one planet, people believed there were messengers who transferred the ruling power from one star or god to the other every tenth day. These genii were supposed to be winged and were called in Greek *angeloi*—messengers—angels.[4]

Cosmic temples, the towering ziggurats, were built to exemplify the construction of the universe. Herodotus describes such a tower in Babylon with seven stories or tiers. There, the person to be initiated had to climb from the bottom to the top, undergoing purification rites on each level. Possibly the Tower of Babel in the Bible was such a ziggurat. There were also towers with three or four levels or floors. Symbolism of the numbers seven, three, and four was also expressed in the number of steps which led from one part of the sanctuary to the next. Certain hymns had to be sung on each step or grade; this is the origin of the songs called graduals in the liturgy of the Church.[5]

In the biblical history of creation, the vision of the universe is different.[6] Heaven is visualized as a canopy or bell-like lid over the earth, and the stars are fixed to this dome. In the psalms the Lord appears to have His throne at the apex. The throne is supported by cherubim, and He is ministered to by seraphim. This heaven is stable,

---

[3] Dupuis, *Abrégé de l'origine, chap.* XII.

[4] O. Wulff, *Cherubim, Throne und Seraphim* (1904); Diodor, as quoted in Winckler, "Himmels- und Weltenbild," 2/3; Winckler, "Babylonische Welt-schöpfung," *Der Alte Orient,* VIII (1906), Part I, 15.

[5] H. P. L'Orange, *Studies on the Iconography of Cosmic Kingship in the Ancient Orient* (Oslo, 1953), p. 12, Fig. 4; Herodotus's description of the sanctuary of the Medes at Egbatana, and description of the seven walls and the seven portals in Babel; Herodotus, *Historiae,* lib. I in Loeb Classics, pp. 129, 225; *The Histories,* trans. by A. de Selincourt (Penguin Classics, 1954), p. 54.

[6] Ezekiel, 10; Psalms, 18, 10; Daniel, 6, 18.

is the firmament. It is only later, in the period after the Captivity, especially in the Book of Ezekiel, that different ideas turn up. Ezekiel opposed Babylonian religion, but did not escape its influence. He writes of winged spirits, described as having two, four, or six wings, and of the tetramorphs.[7] These figures have four faces (man, eagle, bull, and lion), and are clearly modeled after the Babylonian deities for the four corners of the universe—the gods of the winds.[8] Huge wheels move with or beside them, and these wheels are highly reminiscent of the seven spheres of the Babylonians.

The Persian or Iranian cosmology is described in their sacred book, the *Avesta*.[9] In the earlier version, supposedly completed before the seventh century B.C., the universe is believed to consist of three parts, or heavens: one from the stars to the moon, a second from the moon to the sun, and a third from the sun to paradise. Later versions of the *Avesta* refer to seven heavens, a change which probably can be attributed to Babylonian influences. The Persians came into contact with Babylonian—or, as they were then called, Chaldean—ideas in the Hellenistic period. In the Mithraic cult, which was related to both Chaldean and Persian culture, there are sometimes three, sometimes seven heavens. The Persian creed says nothing about moving forces, but the order of the heavens corresponds, as shall presently be seen, to a moral scale.[10]

The Greeks imagined the universe yet again differently. In the

---

[7] Ezekiel, 1 and 15, *passim*; L. Dürr, *Die Stellung des Propheten Ezechiel* (*Alttestamentliche Abhandlungen*, IX, 1) (Münster, 1923); Wulff, *Cherubim, Throne und Seraphim*.

[8] The figures of the Babylonian gods for the four winds are: Marduk, the winged bull; Nebo, a human form; Nergal, a winged lion; and Nimurta, the eagle. Their heads became the faces of the tetramorph in Ezekiel, and later became the symbols of the Evangelists. See the article "Nebo," by A. Jeremias, in Roscher's *Lexikon der Mythologie*; *Jewish Encyclopedia*, Art. "Cherubim" (to the Babylonians . . . cherubim symbolized the winds); for illustrations, see the following by A. Layard: *Nineveh and its Remains* (1849), II; *Discoveries in the Ruins of Nineveh and Babylon* (1853), pp. 600ff.; *Nineveh and Babylon* (1882), p. 121.

[9] J. Schefeltowitz, *Altpersische Religion und Judentum* (1920); E. Herzfeld, *Iran in the Ancient East* (Oxford, 1941); E. Herzfeld, *Zoroaster and His Work* (Princeton, 1947), p. 622.

[10] D. W. Bousset, "Die Himmelsreise der Seelen," *Archiv für Religionswissenschaft*, IV (1901), 136, 229ff.; N. Söderblom, *La vie future d'après le Mazdéisme: Études d'eschatologie comparée* (Paris, 1901) (*Annales du Musée Guimet*, 9).

Homeric period, the earth was seen as a flat disc, surrounded by the river Oceanus. The gods lived on top of a mountain, Olympus.[11] The tradition of such a mountain, based on earth and rising through the spheres, was evidently still alive in the sixth century, for an illumination in the Vatican Kosmas manuscript shows the cosmos with a mountain reaching from the center to the outer spheres (Fig. 5). The outermost circle has twelve compartments, each containing the figure of an angel. This tradition also seems to have influenced Dante's idea of purgatory as a mountain reaching from the inferno to paradise.

The Greek gods moved from one place to another freely, not on fixed paths or spheres. No technical devices are mentioned, except Hermes' winged shoes (*talaria*) and Eos's chariot, drawn by winged horses. At the end of the world, across the Oceanus, was the island of Elysium, where those humans favored by the gods were allowed to live after death. This island is described as a kind of paradise. The

[11] O. Gruppe, *Griechische Mythologie* (1906); W. Otto, *Die Götter Griechenlands,* translated as *The Homeric Gods* (New York, 1954); K. S. Guthrie, *The Pagan Bible* (1925); C. Fries, "Babylonische und griechische Mythologie," *Jahrbuch für das klassische Altertum* (1902), v, 9/10.

FIG. 5. Mount Zion rising into the sphere of the cosmos, from the sixth-century Greek manuscript of Kosmas Inidikopleustes

Greeks also believed that the few humans elevated to the rank of demigods were transferred to or transfigured into stars.[12] This would imply that the stars were alive and would make the demigods identical with celestial bodies.

These Homeric ideas had changed by the time of Pythagoras and Plato (fourth century B.C.). Foreign ideas began to intrude, though the question of their origin, whether Egypt or India, has not been settled.[13] Plato gives two different versions of the cosmos, one in his *Republic* and one in *Phaedrus*.[14] In *Phaedrus*, heaven seems to be seen as a bell-like dome. Inside, the gods hold processions along the galaxy, riding in chariots drawn by winged horses. Human souls, as yet unborn, take part in these processions. They, too, are conveyed in chariots with two winged horses, but only one of these horses is good, courage; the other, lust, is evil, and stands for libido. It tries to hamper the flight of the soul to the outer atmosphere, which is the realm of ideas. The outer atmosphere is set in swirling motion by Eros—inspiration. In this *Phaedrus* version of the cosmos, neither heaven nor the stars move, but Eros agitates the outer realm and affects the movement of the heavenly horses which drive the gods and the souls. It may thus be said that in *Phaedrus* Plato set the cosmos in motion, in contrast to the stable universe of the Homeric period; and this involved forces to move the spheres. The idea that Eros, who is inspiration as well as love, is the moving force of the universe was adopted by later writers and poets, such as Dionysius the Areopagite, and it is the *amore che tutto muove* of Dante.[15]

---

[12] A. Dieterich, *Nekyia, Beiträge zur Erklärung der neuendeckten Petrusapokalypse* (1913); E. Trumpp, *Das Hexameron des Pseudo Epiphanius (Bayerische Akademie, phil. hist. Abhandlungen*, Vol. 16, No. 2 [1882], pp. 167ff.); Söderblom, *La vie future.*

[13] L. Rougier, *L'origine astronomique de la croyance pythagorienne* (Cairo, 1937).

[14] Plato, *Phaedrus*, in Loeb Classics (1953), I, 495; Plato, *Republic*, in Loeb Classics, II, 404–405; K. Reinhardt, *Platons Mythen* (Bonn, 1927).

[15] See Chapter III, p. 29 below, and C. Baeumker, "Witelo, ein Philosoph und Naturforscher des 13. Jahrhunderts," *Beiträge zur Geschichte der Philosophie des Mittelalters*, III/2 (Münster, 1908); Philo, *De gigant.*, II, 8, in *Loeb Classics*, II, 448; Plotinus, *Enn.*, II, 95 and V, 1.12; Proclus, *In Timaeum* (ed. E. Diehl), 1903, V, 320 a; Dante, *Paradiso*, XXXIII, 145; C. Baeumker, *Das pseudo-hermetische Buch der 24 Meister, Liber XXIV philosophorum*, in *Abhandlungen aus dem Gebiet der Philosophie . . . Georg v. Hertling gewidmet* (Freiburg, 1913), pp. 17ff.

Plato's description in the *Republic* is quite different; here he takes the important step of relating the motion of the spheres to music and grading the spheres according to the tones of the musical scale—a vision that ultimately led to the idea of a highest heaven and to the concept of *musica mundana.* The description of the cosmos in the *Republic* occurs toward the end, in the tale told by an Armenian or Iranian from Pamphily, that is, Asia Minor.[16] The narrator is supposed to represent Pythagorean ideas. His description of the cosmos is part of the account of the soul's fate before and after death. His story mentions two portals in heaven and two beneath the earth. Heaven seems to be visualized as a huge globe, ringed by a shining band similar to the rainbow. Running between two points along this band is an axis or spindle, which apparently passes through the globe and turns, at one of its ends, in the lap of Ananke, the goddess of necessity. Attached to this spindle are eight discs of four different sizes, which form a double cone, with the apexes at the two ends of the spindle. These discs are of different colors, and on the edge of each of them a siren sits, singing one note of the scale. Their voices result in harmony, and this harmony is the harmony of the universe. The spindle is kept moving by the three Fates: past, present, and future. In the air around the spindle, the souls move.

Among the souls of the dead, some have come from the nether world, where they have to spend a thousand years in purification. Once purified, they rise, and the mouth of the nether world lets them pass into the meadow of delight. If they have not yet attained purity, the mouth roars, and the souls return for another thousand years. Saved souls stay for seven days in the meadow of delight. Here they undergo a test by the Fate Lachesis. They must determine their future life, partly by lot and partly by their own decision. Once the decision is made, they must lead this life for another thousand years. Some of the souls who have reached heaven are sent back down again, while those who have achieved and retained a state of complete purification may stay in heaven. New arrivals have to submit to the same kind of tests as those coming from the underworld.[17]

[16] Duhem, *Le système du monde*, i, 64. Bousset, "Die Himmelsreise," p. 155.

[17] Plato, *Republic*, in *Loeb Classics*, ii, 404–405; A. Döring, "Wandlungen in der pythagoräischen Lehre," *Archiv für Geschichte der Philosophie*, v (1892), 12; A. Rivaud, "Le système astronomique de Platon," *Revue d'histoire de la philosophie*, ii (1928); B. de Roffignac, "Les anges moteurs et l'iconographie du moyen-âge," *Société des Antiquitaires du Centre, Mémoires* (1935), Vol. 46,

THE ABODE OF THE DEAD AND THE PROBLEM
OF THE HIGHEST HEAVEN

In addition to Plato's introduction of music to the cosmos, an important aspect of each of his versions is the impact of moral implications, of moral judgments. While the grimmer side of life after death is essentially the subject of the second part of this book, the fate of the soul is also important for charting the place in the cosmos where the blessed are assembled, for outlining the highest heaven. Again, one goes back to the Babylonians and Persians, not merely to shed light on the contrast between Plato and his Homeric predecessors, but also to understand why certain forces and figures later became identical or interchangeable, why in the Middle Ages the souls of the blessed, the angels, the muses, and the sirens became interrelated, and why certain groups of spirits were identified with certain heavens.

The Babylonians conceived of two places where souls lived after death, two islands somewhere to the west.[18] One island was described as surrounded by a stream. The goddess of hell, a monster, was said to guard the entrance to the castle of the underworld situated on this island, which was further protected by seven walls with seven or fourteen towers. The second island was also toward the west, in the midst of the ocean. To reach it, a soul had to travel through darkness for twelve or twenty-four miles. Then the soul would arrive at an entrance guarded by the nereid (or siren) Eridu who submitted the soul to judgment. Once the soul was admitted, Eridu would convey it in a boat across the river of gall, into the garden of bliss, with its fountain of youth and tree of life, according to

---

p. 13; S. Reinach, *Orpheus* (4th edn., 1941), p. 63; M. Müller, *Lectures on the Origin and Growth of Religion, as Illustrated by the Religions of India* (1878).

It should be mentioned that Aristotle had a completely different explanation of the cosmos. He assumed 55 spheres were necessary to explain the motion of the celestial bodies. Though this theory is not relevant to our study, it might be noted that the number 55 contains, as a fraction, the number eleven, sacred to the Hindu cosmology. In Western culture, this number acquired no significance.

[18] A. Jeremias, Hölle und Paradies bei den Babyloniern," *Der Alte Orient*, 1 (1900); P. Jensen, *Die Kosmologie der Babylonier* (1890), pp. 23ff., 140ff.; Dieterich, *Nekyia*; A. Jeremias, *Babylonisches im alten Testament* (1905); S. H. Langdon, *Le poème sumérien du Paradis, du Déluge et de la Chute* (1919).

the myth of Gilgamesh. However, in the myth of Ishtar, when the daughter of the moon goddess journeys to the place of hell, she is accompanied "by spirits like birds, all garbed in cloaks of feathers." This would suggest that the journey takes place through the air and not over water, and such a vision would be more in keeping with the symbols of the tower and the seven tiers, and the purification rites on seven levels. The location of the islands is vague, and it remains unclear whether the direction "toward the west" is along the plane of the earth, downward under the earth, or on an ascent to heaven. But the idea of islands and the judgment of the soul after death are concepts encountered in Plato, as noted above, and do recur in later stories.

In the classic version of the Persian or Iranian religion, that is, in the period before the seventh century B.C., after death the soul traveled through the three heavens of the Persian cosmos. A good man's soul was accompanied by three angels, an unjust man's soul by four demons—making, once again, a total of seven spirits. At the start, judgment was given by weighing the soul, to find if it was light enough to pass into heaven,[19] a view directly opposite to the official Christian version under which a soul cannot enter heaven if it is found too light.[20] Above the highest heaven was paradise, the place destined for the blessed. There the creator, with the sun and moon and stars, would honor the soul with songs of praise.

This story was later incorporated into the Mithraic cult, a later form of the Persian creed and the religion of the late Roman emperors, notably of Julian the Apostate (A.D. 361–363).[21] The cult, which spread to the Rhine and the British Isles, merged a number of Greek and Babylonian ideas.[22] In the Persian *Apocalypse* of Arda Viraf (third century),[23] the soul travels through seven heavens, accompanied by two spirits, Srosh and Atar. Judgment is passed on the border from the second to the third heaven. The fourth heaven contains the paradise, described as a beautiful garden similar to the para-

---

[19] Bousset, "Die Himmelsreise." Herzfeld, *Zoroaster*; Söderblom, *La vie future*.

[20] E. Panofsky, *Early Netherlandish Painting* (1953), I, 270.

[21] Origen, *Contra Celsum*, translated in Ante Nicene Fathers (New York, 1925), IV, 395ff.; F. Cumont, *Mystère de Mithra* (1890–96); F. Lajard, *Recherches . . . Mithra* (1867); Bousset, "Die Himmelsreise."

[22] Herzfeld, *Iran in the Ancient East*, p. 275.

[23] Bousset, "Die Himmelsreise."

dise of the Bible (in fact, the very word in Persian means an enclosed garden, and this has been a pervasive image). According to Origen, this myth was symbolized in rites by pictorial representation of the heavens and the stars; there was a sanctuary with seven doors and a flight of seven steps—each made of a particular metal corresponding to the character of each of the seven planets—leading to an eighth platform on top.[24]

THE MOVERS OF THE SPHERES AND THE FIGURE OF THE ANGEL

As long as the earth was regarded as the stable center of the cosmos, that is, until the time of Pythagoras, the movement of the stars was explained as their movement around the earth. Once their courses were understood to follow certain rules, the stars were thought to move on spheres. Only the Babylonian creed, based on astronomical observation, took motion of the spheres into consideration. The *Avesta* is not explicit on this subject. The heaven of the Bible's early books was stable, and the stars were fixed to the firmament. The idea of motion occurs only later, and through Babylonian influence, in Ezekiel's wheels.[25] In Greek mythology of the Homeric period, the heaven did not move, the gods lived on a stable mountain, Olympus. Nor did the gods move the spheres; [26] they themselves moved about freely, and only Eos and later Helios had prescribed paths.

In both of Plato's versions, however, motion is an important factor in the universe, and in each case we are given detailed facts as to what moves and what are the moving forces. The *Phaedrus* tells of the whirl in the outer realm of ideas, with Eros the moving force. More motion is represented in the chariots drawn by two winged horses, with courage as the upward force of the good horse and lust the downward force of the bad one. These forces are moral and intellectual values and as such outside the scope of this narrative, except for noting that the good forces drive upward and the bad downward.

The description of the universe in Plato's *Republic* is relevant in many respects. It provides the first reference to music in connection with the motion of the cosmos. As mentioned above, the narrator of

---

[24] Origen, *Contra Celsum*, vi, 22.   [25] Ezekiel, 1:15–21; 10:9–13.
[26] Reinhardt, *Platons Mythen*, pp. 78ff., 103ff.

the myth in the *Republic* is supposed to represent Pythagorean ideas,[27] and Pythagoras is credited with having discovered a correlation between the ratios of musical intervals and the ratios of the orbits of the celestial bodies. Part of the Pythagorean creed was based on the belief that this correlation originated from as well as resulted in the harmony of the universe. In the version in the *Republic,* the discs around the spindle are the spheres which constitute the universe. Each sphere is guided by a siren singing one tone of the musical scale. Though nothing is said about different values of the spheres, the tones of the musical scale might imply a grading. However, since the discs on the spindle seem to form a double cone, none of the discs is characterized as the highest, and Elysium is not yet transferred to the highest heaven. The spindle is driven by the Fates, personifying motion and time. In addition to this new connection of motion to time and to music, there is the new number nine; there are eight discs plus the surrounding globe. Nine was a sacred number for the Greeks [28] —not, incidentally, for the Pythagoreans; [29] there were nine muses, and nine was to become the number for heavenly choirs. In the *Republic's* account, souls move outside the spindle. Later they came to be included in the motion of the cosmos and partly identified with the sirens.

Plato's sirens are particularly interesting. Sirens sang in earlier Greek legends, but their song did not mean harmony; it represented the luring and seductive aspects of music.[30] In the period between

[27] Bousset, "Die Himmelsreise"; Döring, "Wandlungen," pp. 512, 516. See also Aristotle, *De Coelo,* in Loeb Classics, p. 192n.

[28] Aristotle, *Metaphysica,* 1, 5, and Hippolytos, *Philos.* (ed. Diels, p. 555), quoted by C. Jan in "Die Harmonie der Sphaeren," *Philologus,* Vol. 52 (1894), pp. 13ff.; Baeumker, "Witelo"; F. Dornseiff, *Das Alphabet in Mystic und Magie* (Stoicheia, *Studien zur Geschichte und Kultur des Altertums,* 1922, Vol. 7); F. X. Kugler, *Die Symbolik der Neunzahl bei den Babyloniern* (Hilprecht Anniversary Volume, 1909), pp. 304ff.; W. H. Roscher, "Bedeutung der Siebenzahl im Kultus und Mythus der Griechen," *Philologus,* Vol. 60 (1901), pp. 360ff.; Roscher, *Die enneadischen Fristen der ältesten Griechen, Sächsische Akademie, phil. hist. Abhandlungen,* Vols. 21/4, 24/1, 26/1 (1903, 1904, 1906); Roscher, *Hebdomadenlehre der griechischen Philosophen und Ärzte, ibid.* (1906); Roscher, "Die hippokratische Schrift von der Siebenzahl," *Studien zur Geschichte und Kultur des Altertums,* Vol. 6 (1913), from MS. Bibl. Nat. gr. 2142.

[29] Döring, "Wandlungen in der pythagoräischen Lehre," p. 512; Winckler, "Himmels- und Weltenbild"; Jeremias, *Babylonisches im Alten Testament.*

[30] *Odyssey,* XIII, 37–54, 166–200.

the *Odyssey* and the *Republic,* their character apparently underwent
a basic change, from that of evil spirits to angelic and savior-like
beings. The figure of the siren has since retained a dual aspect,
though today evil predominates. There are numerous forerunners
and relatives to such winged spirits. Some have been mentioned as
the messengers between the stars and their rulers in the Babylonian
religion.[31] The Egyptians had a soul-bird which carried the soul of
the dead or into which the soul of the dead was transformed.[32] The
Hittites had the winged lion, a figure also adopted by the Babylonians. In the excavations at Megiddo (Israel), today attributed
to the Hittite civilization, winged lions were found dating from the
second millennium B.C.,[33] and it is supposed that these figures represented cherubim, the beings that carry the throne of God. In Persia,
winged figures drove the sacred bulls that drew the celestial chariot
on which the deified king rode.[34] It seems probable that the role
assigned to winged figures in the Egyptian, Babylonian, Hittite, Hebrew, and Persian representations had an influence on the transformation of the Greek siren.

If the Megiddo ivories represent cherubim, this would imply that
some of the angels in the Old Testament were visualized with wings.
However, this would contradict the evidence of the Bible stories, because, up to the Books of Ezekiel, the angels appear as an aspect or
an emanation of God (to Abraham, Jacob, Moses) and seem consistently to appear in human form. They are taken by Abraham for
men. In Jacob's dream they have to climb a ladder[35] to heaven. In
the Psalms, the cherubim carry the throne of God and act as guard-

---

[31] Messengers are sent every tenth day, Diodor II/30 and II/47.2, as quoted
in Winckler, "Himmels- und Weltenbild"; for the form of the cherubim, see
G. Loud, *The Megiddo Ivories,* University of Chicago, Oriental Institute Publications, LII (1939), Pls. 1, 2, 3, and 7; for the etymology of the term "cherub,"
see F. Lugt, "Man and Angel," *Gazette des Beaux-Arts* (May 1944): "In the
light of recent discoveries the etymologists will now perhaps concede that the
Hebrew word *K'rub* could be of the same stem as the Sanscrit *gribh,* the gothic
gripan, the Persian *griftan,* the German *Greif,* and the English *griffin*"; *Kirubu*
is the name of the Assyrian bull deity whose name may also be related to
"cherub." See also Reinach, *Orpheus.*

[32] *Aegyptisches Totenbuch, übersetzt und kommentiert von Grégoire Kol-
paktchy* (1955), Figs. 10, 25, 36; E.A.W. Budge, *The Papyrus of Ani* (1913).

[33] Loud, *The Megiddo Ivories;* Lugt, "Man and Angel," p. 268.

[34] L'Orange, *Studies on the Iconography of Cosmic Kingship.*

[35] Genesis, 28:12.

ians of men and as messengers, but no wings are mentioned.[36] In
Ezekiel's visions, however, they appear as spirits, beings of their own,
and have three forms. Is one perhaps entitled, then, to see Ezekiel's
winged spirits as Babylonian genii, now surrounding the Lord and
living in heaven? The three angels who have the status of individual-
ity in the Old Testament are the archangels Michael, Raphael, and
Gabriel. No mention is made of wings on any of these, even in the
late tale of Tobias, or, indeed, in the story of the Annunciation, nor
does the Bible mention any connection of angels with music. The
angels acquired this faculty only later, in the Hellenistic period, the
era of Alexander's empire, where the Greek and Oriental cultures
met.

Plato's use of the figures of sirens to turn the discs of the cosmic
spindle was an innovation. The goddesses of the celestial dances had
previously been the Charites or the Graces, and the guardians of the
cosmic order were the Muses.[37] All had established connections with
dance and music. The nine Muses sang alternating songs at the
funeral of Achilles.[38] But none of these goddesses was ever described
as winged. Is it, therefore, too much to assume that Plato chose the
sirens because they were the only figures related to music and at the
same time winged, and that the use of winged figures as moving
forces of the spheres reflects the influence of Oriental belief? I feel
that the use of the figures of the sirens represents such a fusion.
Hitherto, the Greek cosmos did not turn; now, in order to move it
along spheres in the air, it needed winged spirits, and the sirens had
wings. They were, further, the only winged figures who, with their
faculty of singing, embodied music. The representatives of music and
harmony had hitherto been the Muses. All this suggests that the

---

[36] Moses, 2:25; Isaiah, 7:1; Enoch, tr. A. Dillmann (1851), 14:8ff., 38:12;
Gregor, *Homil. in Evang.*, 34:12 (*Patrol. lat.*, 76:1251); Ephrem of Edessa,
Scrutat. L. I, *serm.* IV t. iii, p. 8, and *Scrutat.* L. II, *serm.* I, p. 166, quoted in
Dictionnaire Catholique, "Anges," Chapter V; Wulff, *Cherubim, Throne und
Seraphim*, pp. 2, 6.

[37] Virgil (*Georgica*, II, 475ff.) asks the Muses to teach him the rules of the
heavens and the stars. The Greek Charites are the Latin Graces; their name is
first mentioned by Hesiod; they live together with the Muses. The Muses are
invoked for inspiration, the Charites for performance, often together with the
Horae. They are also related to the Moirae and are generally represented as
three. See Roscher's *Lexikon der Mythologie*.

[38] *Odyssey*, XXIV, 47.

sirens were elevated in Plato's Republic to the rank of Muses, due to their combination of being winged creatures and of having the faculty of song.

Whatever the exact sources of Plato's work, it contained much of the germ of later development. His spheres corresponded to a moral scale, their motion was related to music, indeed to a musical scale, and was associated with the winged figure of the siren. It should, however, be noted that the concept of the structure of the cosmos had not yet been combined with ideas of moral judgment, and that it was this merger, in the first centuries B.C. and A.D., which ultimately turned the spheres into a sequence of lower and higher heavens, and moved Elysium from the end of the world into the highest heaven.[39]

---

[39] Proclus, *In polit.* (ed. G. Kroll, 1899, II, 255); Lucian, *Vera historia*, English tr. by A. Church (1880), ch. x; Porphyrius as quoted by Proclus, *In Timaeum* I, 47 D (ed. Diehl, I, 152) and by Saint Augustine, *De civit.*, x, 9, *Patrol. lat.* 41, 287; Claudianus Mamertius, *De statu animae*, I, 12; *Corpus scriptorum ecclesiasticorum latinorum*, Vol. XI, ed. Engelbrecht (Vienna, 1885); Bonaventura, *Breviloquia*, II, 3; *II. Sententiae; In categoriis* (ed. Marius Victorinus); *Opera Omnia*, ed. Fratres minores (1882–1902), Vol. v; E. Rohde, *Der griechische Roman* (Leipzig, 1876), p. 193; Porphyrius, *On the Life of Plotinus* (Library of Philosophical Translations, 1917); J. Bidez, "Boèce et Porphyre," *Revue belge de philologie et d'histoire*, Vol. 2 (1913); F. Cumont, *Recherches sur le symbolisme funéraire des Romains* (1942).

II The Hellenistic Period

ALEXANDER'S CONQUESTS spread Greek ideas to all the countries of the Near East, where they were variously adapted to the idiosyncracies of surrounding cultures. Virtually all Plato's images recur, often singly and never all together, in the writings of quite different authors—Jewish, Gnostic, and Stoic, not to mention Neoplatonic. Among the fruit of this new cross-fertilization was a variety of images of music in the heavens which ranged from the purely pagan to those in Gnostic and early Christian works. Judging by the surviving literature, the Hellenistic era also produced many early elaborations of the orders of angels—ultimately codified in Dionysius' influential hierarchy—and the first concepts of the angels as the makers of heavenly music, albeit in the still relatively limited role of singing the praise of the Lord.

PLATO'S SUCCESSORS

First, mention should be made of two works once ascribed to Plato himself, but actually written by later followers of his school: *Epinomis* [1] and *Axiochus*.[2] The author of *Epinomis* postulated eight powers that caused the revolutions of the heavenly bodies. Three of them, the sun, the moon, and the fixed stars, were revolved by the gods. (Later, in the Hellenistic period, the chief author of heavenly movement became the divine intelligence, the *nous* or *logos*, which was also to appear as the authentic power in the Gospel of Saint John.) *Epinomis*, further, mentions music of the spheres as "a gift from the blessed choir of the Muses [which] has imparted to man the services of measured consonance with a view to the enjoyment of rhythm and harmony." The passage in *Axiochus* is yet more explicit. In the words of Spenser's translation: "Then they which in their lifetime were inspired and led with good angels are received into the

---

[1] Plato, *Epinomis*, tr. J. Harvard (Oxford, 1928).
[2] Plato, *Axiochus*, tr. Ed. Spenser, ed. Fr. M. Padelford (Baltimore, 1934).

household of the blessed where [there are] sorts of dauncers, heavenly Musicke . . . in this place and in the Elysian fields. . . ."[3] Pindar, also, spoke of the blessed dancing on the isle of Elysium.[4]

These pseudo-Platonic dialogues, further, give the numbers three and eight for the number of spheres or heavens. The eight evolved from the seven Babylonian spheres, plus one surrounding or topping heaven; subsequently nine spheres evolved from these eight, with one more surrounding, to comply with the number of Muses. These works also place the highest heaven side by side with Elysium and describe both as abodes of the blessed. Here the blessed pass the time in singing and dancing, with the Muses leading the dances.

The idea of incessant song occurs in the description of the town of the mythical Hyperboreans written by Hekateios of Abdera, who lived under the first Ptolemies. In his *Utopia,* the Hyperboreans worship Apollo with continuous song and dance, which becomes a sign of eternal and heavenly bliss.[5]

Many Greek ideas were also taken over by the Roman authors in the first centuries B.C. and A.D. in virtually pure form. Cicero speaks in his *Somnium Scipionis,* a work which had a tremendous influence on later writers, of nine heavens.[6] Virgil, too, has nine heavens, and the souls of the blessed dance around the lyre of Orpheus.[7] The Stoic Cornutus (first century), in his *De natura deorum,* enumerates nine spheres.[8] Philo,[9] the great Jewish philosopher, though neither a Neoplatonist nor a Gnostic, was strongly influenced by Greek ideas. He visualized nine heavens (sometimes seven) and spheres that were moved not only by angels but also by Muses. The Muses sang and

---

[3] *Ibid.,* pp. 56ff.

[4] Pindar, quoted in E. Rohde, *Der griechische Roman* (Leipzig, 1876), p. 215.

[5] A. Dieterich, *Nekyia* (1913), pp. 21ff.; Rohde, *Der griechische Roman.*

[6] Cicero, *Somnium Scipionis,* in *Aurelii Macrobii . . . Opera quae extant omnia* (Patawii, 1736); and *De natura deorum,* 1.5.10, II, Ch. 11; A. Döring, "Wandlungen in der pythagoräischen Lehre," *Archiv für Geschichte der Philosophie,* v (1892), 503, 512.

[7] Virgil, *Aeneid,* VI, 439.

[8] Cornutus, *De natura deorum,* cap. 14, quoted in W. Roscher, *Die enneadischen . . . Fristen, Sächsische Akad. phil. hist. Abhandlungen,* Vol. 26 (1908), p. 110.

[9] Philo, *De congressu quaerendae eruditionis gratia,* 19, with English translation by F. H. Colson, 1929, in Loeb Classics, IV; see also II, 4 of the Loeb Classics edition.

taught mankind harmony modeled on their heavenly music. The first
or chief mover was God; his chariot (identical with his throne) was
guided by *logos* and supported by the cherubim, whose name signifies
intelligence. The Jewish apocryphal books of Enoch and Pseudo-
Enoch,[10] probably written in the first century, relate the soul's journey through seven heavens, characterized by seven classes or ranks of
angels. In these works the sacred numbers of seven and nine were
combined, for in each of the seven heavens there are nine legions of
angels. In two of Enoch's heavens, the angels' duty is to praise God
with music and song. In another apocryphal Jewish book from the
first century, Baruch's *Apocalypse,* there are five heavens—a number
which reflects the number ten, sacred to the Jews and to the Pythagoreans.[11] Paul mentions seven heavens and eight or eleven
choirs of angels.[12]

Gnostic Writings

A yet more complex merger of the various trends was effected by
the Gnostic writers in the first centuries B.C. and A.D.[13] The Gnostic
visions or apocalypses not only give the number of heavens, but in
recounting the journeys of the soul after death describe the structure
of the heavens, their qualities, and their inhabitants. Some Gnostic
books have come down to us intact, but most of the doctrine is known
only from quotations by the Church Fathers, who inveighed against
these creeds as falsifying the Gospels.[14] Gnostic ideas nevertheless
penetrated into Christian visions and descriptions, and depending on

---

[10] *The Book of the Secrets of Enoch,* tr. Ch. Morfill (Oxford, 1896), ed, by
N. Bonwetch in *Göttinger Akad. der Wissenschaften, phil. hist. Abhandlungen,*
N. F. (1896); German translation by A. Dillmann (1856), xiv, 8ff., quoted by
O. Wulff, *Cherubim, Throne und Seraphim* (1904), pp. 6ff.; Bousset, "Die
Himmelsreise der Seelen," *Archiv für Religionswissenschaft,* iv (1901).

[11] Baruch quoted by Origen, *De principiis,* ii, 3.6 (*Die griechischen Christl.
Schriftsteller der ersten drei Jahrhunderte*), *Corpus Berolinensis,* Vol. 5;
Bousset, "Die Himmelsreise," p. 141.

[12] I Corinthians 2:6; II Corinthians 12, 2:4; O. Everling, *Die Paulinische
Angelologie* (1908); G. Kurze, *Der Engelsglaube des Paulus* (1915).

[13] Their name derives from the Greek *gnosis,* meaning knowledge. Alternately,
they are called Mandeans, based on *manda,* the Persian word for knowledge.

[14] Origen, *Contra Celsum,* ed. P. Kötschau (*Preussische Akad. der Wissenschaften,* Kirchenväter Commission, die griechischen Schriftsteller, 1/ii,
1899); translated in Ante Nicene Fathers (New York, 1935), iv, 395ff,;
Augustine, *Civitas, lib.* x. *Patrol. lat.* 41, pp. 287ff.; Clement, *Eclogae
Prophetarum, Patrol. gr.* 9, 697.

the degree of influence from Persian, Babylonian, or Greek beliefs, one finds three, seven, or nine heavens. As noted with regard to the Books of Enoch, these numbers sometimes appeared in combination.[15]

The *Ascensio Jesaiae* is a Gnostic story in which Ethiopian, Jewish, and Christian ideas can be traced.[16] It describes the journey of Jesaia, or Isaiah, through seven heavens whose characteristics are indicated by differences in the angels who sing in each. In the story of Joseph the Carpenter, by a Christian author, Christ sends two angels to protect the soul of Joseph during its journey through seven eons of darkness.[17] (The distances from one heaven or sphere to the other were measured in time, and the periods were termed eons.) A relation of time to space was also visualized in the Greek mythology; Zeus, the son of time (Chronos), was the ruler of the cosmos. In the Mithraic cult the highest god, Ormazd, was the son of time; and in the Roman version of Mithraism, Ormazd was called *Coelus*, or heaven.[18]

In the course of development, Gnostic writings describing the fate of the soul after death showed predominantly Christian, Jewish, or Babylonian (or Chaldean) influences.[19] Some of these writings have recently been rediscovered, and for our topic the most relevant are the Christian *Petrus Apocalypse* [20] and the Jewish-Christian *Adam Apocalypse*.[21] The *Petrus Apocalypse*, a book mentioned by Clement of Alexandria,[22] was found in a manuscript in Upper Egypt. It contains the so-called *Petrus Evangelium*, which describes the abode

---

[15] A. Kohut, *Über die jüdische Angelologie und Daemonologie in ihrer Abhängigkeit vom Parsismus* (*Deutsche morgenländische Gesellschaft, Abhandlung* 4, 1866); article "Angelology" signed K. in *Jewish Encyclopedia*.

[16] Bousset, "Die Himmelsreise," p. 141; *Neutestamentliche Apokryphen in deutscher Übersetzung und mit Einleitung hersg. v. E. Hennecke* (1904), "E."

[17] Bousset, "Die Himmelsreise," p. 150.

[18] E. Herzfeld, *Iran in the Ancient East* (1941), p. 275.

[19] W. Kroll, *De oraculis Chaldaicis* (*Breslauer Philologische Abhandlungen* 7, 1, 1894); M. R. James, *Testament of Abraham* (Texts and Studies), II (1892); for the *Logia Chaldaea*, see Bousset, "Die Himmelsreise"; for the views of the Gnostics—Basilides, Valentin, and Marcon—see J. Lebreton, *Histoire de l'église* (1935), II.

[20] Dieterich, *Nekyia*.

[21] E. Trumpp, *Das Hexameron des Pseudo Epiphanius*. German translation in *Abhandlungen der Bayerischen Akad. der Wissenschaften, phil. hist.*, XVI (1882), 2.

[22] Clement, *Stromata*, lib. 6, cap. 3, *Patrol. gr.* 9, 249.

of the souls in bliss, as well as the place of the condemned. In it we read that two angels appear before Christ in heaven—angels noted for their shining light; such light had become in addition to music another major characteristic of angels and of the state of bliss. In the region of the blessed, "the angels abide among them . . . with a dress of sparkling light . . . and in this place they extol the Lord with praising voices." Avenging angels are dressed in dark clothing. Dieterich, the modern editor of the *Petrus Apocalypse*, has emphasized the Greek origin of the images, but, as has been noted, the similar ideas that appeared in Greek stories by the time of Pythagoras and Plato probably came originally from Persian and Babylonian sources.

The *Adam Apocalypse*,[23] a manuscript signed by Epiphanius, bishop of Cyprus, is a yet more important source for our topic, because the description of the heavens is explicit and provides many of the details which were to become basic in later writings and works of art: "In the beginning, on the first day, God created heaven and earth, water, air, and fire, the invisible spirits, that is, the angels: the Thrones, the Dominations, Principalities and Powers, the Cherubim and Seraphim, all castes and orders of the spirits . . . and on the second day the Lord created the lower heaven and called it firmament. That implies that it has not the quality of the higher heaven, which is fire. And this second heaven is light . . . while the dense watery element is called firmament." The third heaven is described as constructed in the form of a tent or canopy which is attached to the higher heaven, an idea later found in many pictorial representations. After the creation of this third heaven, the angels were formed out of fire. "Angels, burning spirits. And God took them and brought them into the heavens, and divided them into different hosts, according to quality." This image appears in later descriptions and representations as a stream of fire emerging from beneath the throne of God.

The *Adam Apocalypse* describes the three castes or dignities of angels as comprising ten hosts. The first and highest are the "beautiful," the second the cherubim, the third the seraphim, who carry the throne of God in this version. These three castes reside in the first

---

[23]There are two manuscripts of the *Hexameron* containing the *Adam Apocalypse*, one in Ethiopian: British Museum MS: Orient. 751; and one in Arabic: Munich, cod. arab. 203. Quotations are my translation from the German version provided by Trumpp, pp. 217, 220, 221, 226, 241.

heaven. There is a fourth caste, the powers, of which Michael is the leader; this caste seems to belong to the highest heaven and later to the second heaven, possibly to form the bridge between the first and the second. In the second heaven, three more dignities dwell, each again composed of ten hosts. The three dignities in the second heaven are the dominions, led by Gabriel, the thrones, led by Raphael, and the sultans, whose leader is Syrial, who blows the trumpet. The ten hosts of the sultans are said to be chosen by God "that they might blow the trumpets, as it is described in the vision of John, that is, the Apocalypse." In the third heaven, the first caste of angels is led by the angel of death, the second caste by the angel responsible "for the bodies of all the just and for their souls on the day of judgment . . . that is, the day of resurrection . . . the day of the wedding feast of the year thousand which John in his poem, the Apocalypse, mentions." The angel who leads the third caste in the third heaven is the guardian of the plants, the weather, and the seasons, and "each dignity residing in the three heavens has hundreds of hosts, so that tens of thousands and myriads and myriads may praise the Lord." After the fall of Satan, God closes the doors of heaven so that the angels can leave it only by a central path. The Trinity floats above the throne of God and "the angels started at once to praise the Trinity; the dignity of the sovereigns began, and then . . . the cherubim, the seraphim, the powers, the masters [*Artab*], the thrones, the sultans, the judges, the archangels, the angels followed . . . offering continuous praise. And they offered praise in unison from one end of the heaven to the other until the paean reached the beautiful angel who was set above the dignities of the heaven as master of the hosts. He was to take the praises and convey them to the heavenly Jerusalem to offer them to the Trinity."

The beautiful angel took them, but arrogance led him to keep them, and on the fourth day at evening, the downfall of the beautiful angel occurs. The angels never see the Trinity directly but only through the medium of mirrors. "And when the angels look [into the mirrors] they see written the name of the Holy Trinity. They exult . . . and speak, holy . . . holy . . . holy, and they raise their voices in exultation." The seraphim caste, especially, is called upon to perform the songs of praise, but the other hosts must also join in this duty. After the fall of the beautiful angel, that is, of Satan, the Lord says to him, "I had set you above all the praises of the angels and raised you to the highest position." Later there is a battle between the angels subdued by Satan and the angels loyal to the Lord, who bring their praises to the heavenly Jerusalem.

The *Adam Apocalypse*, the oldest source known to date for the elaborate hierarchy of the angels, has come down to us in an Arabic and in an Ethiopian manuscript, the Arabic being the older. It is obvious that such a complex theory was not completely an original invention, and it is easy to detect ideas drawn from very different earlier cultures. The organization of the heavens combines the Persian concept of three heavens with the Greek nine, in that three castes of angels are specified for each heaven. Cherubim and seraphim are Hebrew names and indicate the Bible as a source, a suggestion which is confirmed when the author, Epiphanius refers to the *Torah*. Oriental influence appears in the name of the third caste in the second heaven, the sultans, and it is also recognizable in several Oriental names for leaders, as well as in the image of the sultans blowing trumpets for the Day of Judgment. The Christian element is clear in the figures of the Holy Trinity and in the references to the Revelation of Saint John.

The references to John in the *Adam Apocalypse* are not idle quotations, but imply that the author wished to include the Book of Revelation in his interpretation. It is more than probable that there were other similar attempts to weld the old creeds into one religion, and one more complete Gnostic book of this kind has come down to us, though from a somewhat later period. It is the *Book of Ginza* ("highest god").[24] Persian and Babylonian influences appear even more strongly in this book, and it has been thought to be related to the Mithraic cult. It describes a cosmos arranged in seven spheres and introduces the number seven into the Persian structure, which had previously comprised three tiers or heavens. Of these Gnostic books, written in the first centuries before and after Christ, only the *Adam Apocalypse* is obviously written by a Christian author.

The detailed order of the angels that the *Adam Apocalypse* provides was adapted, with slight variations, to the canonic hierarchy of angels. The castes of the masters, judges, and sultans were dropped or changed, presumably because they represented Oriental, autocratic state dignitaries with which the Hellenistic and Roman worlds were less familiar. The choirs of the angels are visualized as singing in every part of heaven; they either alternate and answer each other,

[24] M. Lidzbarski, *Ginza* (1925); Lebreton, *Histoire de l'église*, II, 316.

passing the praise upward until it reaches the Trinity, or they join in united chorus. There is a similar image in the Book of Job,[25] written not much earlier, where the stars perform a song in praise of God. Both sources seem to suggest singing performed without interruption, continuously and eternally. And it might be noted that the angels' sparkling light in the *Adam Apocalypse* is clearly akin to the light of Job's stars.

NEOPLATONISTS AND STOICS

The images of the *Adam Apocalypse* recur in many later writings, developed in variations according to the authors' creeds. Writers of the Hellenistic world, the Neoplatonists and Stoics, all described nine spheres. Singing was either reserved to one heaven, the highest, or else each sphere was governed by one of the Muses, who then led the chorus. Starting in the second century, it was said to be the souls of the immortals who made the music in the highest heaven, which had come to be called Elysium. The nine spheres were identified with the nine Muses by the Stoic Cornutus (first century),[26] by Plutarch (second century),[27] and by Poseidonius (first century).[28] The abode of the blessed was located in the highest heaven or the scene of singing in honor of the gods was placed on an island whose location was left vague. Lucian (second century) [29] had the souls of the blessed dancing and the sirens singing on an island of the blessed that had been transferred to the stars.[30]

Two poems of the Hellenistic period recount souls singing in chorus and dancing. As noted above, Hekateios of Abdera (ca. 300

[25] Job 38:7.

[26] Cornutus, *De natura deorum, cap.* 14, quoted in Roscher, *Die enneadischen . . . Fristen,* Vol. 26, p. 110.

[27] Eisele, "Zur Daemonologie Plutarchs v. Chäronea," *Archiv für Geschichte der Philosophie,* 17, 1 (1903), pp. 28ff.; Plutarch, *De anima procreatione in Timaeum,* 32, p. 1029 D, quoted in Cumont, *Recherches sur le symbolisme funéraire,* Ch. IV.

[28] K. Reinhardt, *Poseidonius, Orient und Antike* (1928); W. Roscher, *Die hippokratische Schrift von der Siebenzahl,* p. 99, where it is proved that this manuscript (MS. Bibl. Nat. gr. 2142) is pre-Pythagorean.

[29] Lucian, *Vera historia,* II, 5 and II, 13 in Loeb Classics, I, 302, 311, 317ff., 325; II, p. 357; *A Traveler's True Tale after Lucian of Samosate,* ed. A. Church (New York, 1880).

[30] In an earlier version, that of Euripides, they are described as shining with light as a symbol of their eternal life. Eurypides, *Hippolytos,* v. 732; *Ion,* v. 1078.

B.C.) described in his *Utopia* the mythical ideal Hyperborean nation. In their capital everyone acts as a priest of Apollo, "because this god is praised daily in continuous songs." Most of the inhabitants of this city play the kithara, and "without interruption they sing hymns to the accompaniment of the kithara in the temple of the god and glorify his works." [31] A similar description of a mythical island appears in a poem by an unknown author who is presumed to have been a Stoic.[32] On a trip from Arabia to India, Jambulus, the hero of the poem, is captured by the Ethiopians and taken by ship to an island of the blessed,[33] which is one of a group of seven such islands. Their inhabitants honor the gods with hymns. In this cosmology the sun is the god of the highest sphere; then follow the all-encircling heaven and all the worlds (*ouraniae*).

It is characteristic that in both of these Hellenistic poems the songs recounted have words, whereas in the accounts typical for the Gnostics the songs are described as consisting only of the thrice Holy derived from the threefold Alleluia of Jewish temple rites. In the description of Jambulus's island there are traces of the Mithraic cult, which considered the sun to be the highest deity and had, by that time, adopted the Babylonians' sevenfold cosmos. Jambulus lives for seven years on the island; the writing of the inhabitants has seven characters, of which each has four variations, an allegory of the lunar month. The musical instruments used on the island are typically Greek, the aulos and the kithara. Both descriptions are regarded as descriptions of real rites as performed by adherents of the cult of Mithras and by the Pythagoreans, who honored Apollo Helios as their patron.[34]

[31] Fragments only of Hekateios of Abdera have come down. C. Müller, *Fr. Hist. Gr.*, II, 386–88, quoted by Rohde, *Der griechische Roman*, pp. 208ff.

[32] Diodor, *Bibliotheca historica* II, 55/60. See Rohde, *Der griechische Roman*, p. 224; Lucian, *Vera historia*, I, 3.

[33] Among the blessed are Homer, Ulysses, etc.

[34] Dieterich, *Nekyia*, pp. 36ff.; Rohde, *Der griechische Roman*.

III The Early Christian Centuries

THE IDEAS OF THE MUSICAL COSMOS and the angel orders were woven into all the beliefs of the ensuing period, into Jewish, Pagan, and Christian thought; and the first five or six centuries of the Christian era saw the crystallization of systematic concepts in both fields, concepts which were to influence thought and art throughout the Middle Ages and beyond. The orders of angels were further elaborated by authors of different creeds, and the Christian version was finally, in effect, codified in Dionysius's treatise, *The Celestial Hierarchy*. The idea of music in the cosmos underwent more or less parallel development, particularly by pagan authors, which may be said to have culminated in Martianus Capella's encyclopedic *De Nuptiis Philologiae et Mercurii et de Septem Artibus Liberalibus Libri Novem*.

NON-CHRISTIAN THEORIES

The *Talmud* elaborated classes of angels praising the Lord, and it, too, began by citing nine castes.[1] Among their names only "cherubim" and "seraphim" are used later in Dionysius the Areopagite's definitive hierarchy. Their number in the *Talmud* is a thousand times a thousand, alternately ten thousand times ten thousand, and later ninety thousand myriads. In one place it is said that the angels sing during the night only, to replace the Jewish community, which sings during the day. The *Talmud's* angels understand and know only Hebrew. Seven spirits appear before the throne of the Lord, and there are seven heavens. The singing angels are located in the fifth heaven, Maon, and their choir is composed of 694 myriads of

---

[1] Earlier versions of the *Talmud* mention three or seven classes of angels; A. Kohut, *Über die jüdische Angelologie und Daemonologie in ihrer Abhängigkeit vom Parsismus* (Deutsche morgenländische Gesellschaft, Abhandlung 4, 1966), pp. 19ff.; Ferd. Weber, *Jüdische Theologie auf Grund des Talmud* (1897), Ch. 12, pp. 162ff.; J. B. Frey, "L'angélologie juive au temps de Jésus-Christ," *Revue des sciences philosophiques et théologiques*, Vol. 5 (1911).

singers.[2] Here they sing "from the rising sun till night 'the name of His beautiful realm be praised,' they answer each other and alternate in the hymm of praise."

One important feature of the *Talmud's* account is the description of paradise. This is located in the heaven Arabo, the highest of the seven and the abode of Mechiza. Here stands the figure of the Lord, attended by the Just Ones and by angels, who are not identical with the blessed. There are two kinds of angels: the eternal ones, who are archangels, and those born anew every day out of a stream of fire [3] which is part of the Empyreum. The angels sing hymns of praise, the Just Ones perform a dance in which the Lord takes part; but the Just Ones also vie with the angels in singing the praise of the Lord. The angels and the Just Ones form concentric circles, an arrangement which recurs later in maps of the universe in the early manuscripts that show musician angels, as well as in Dante's *Paradise*. The red-colored angels of many later paintings are the fiery seraphim.

The pagan authors of the early Christian era elaborated the idea of music in the cosmos. Poseidonius,[4] Plotinus,[5] and his followers Proclus [6] and Porphyrius [7] emphasized the connection between the Muses and the spheres. The Muses sing while turning the spheres,

[2] This number seems to have no symbolic explanation; the Revelation of Saint John tells of 144, that is, 12 × 12 singers.

[3] Kohut, *Über die jüdische Angelologie*, p. 9; his sources are Enoch and Midrasch Rabba.

[4] Hippolytos of Rome, *Commentary to the Book of Daniel, lib.* vi, *cap.* 41, ed. N. Bonwetch; N. Bonwetch, "Studien zu den Kommentaren Hippolyts zum Buch Daniel und Hohen Lied," *Texte und Untersuchungen zur Geschichte der christlichen Literatur*, N.F., Vol. 1 (1897); W. Roscher, "Die hippokratische Schrift von der Siebenzahl," *Studien zur Geschichte und Kultur des Altertums*, Vol. 6 (1913), from MS. Bibl. Nat. gr. 2142, pp. 99ff.; K. Reinhardt, *Poseidonius, Orient und Antike* (1928).

[5] Porphyrius, περὶ ἀγαλματων, ed. Bidez; *Vita Plotini*, 22 (ed. Didot, p. 115), μουσάων ἱερὸς χορός . . . καὶ ἐν . . . εχὸ φοῖβος; Plotin, *Enn.*, ii, 9.5 and v, 1.2; H. Mackenna, *Plotinus on the Nature of the Soul*, tr. from the Greek (1924); C. Baeumker, "Witelo, ein Philosoph und Naturforscher des 13. Jahrhunderts," *Beiträge zur Geschichte der Philosophie des Mittelalters*, iii/2 (1908), 523ff.; F. Cumont, "L'oracle sur la mort de Plotin lui-même transmis par Porphyrius," *Recherches*, p. 260.

[6] Proclus, *In polit.* (ed. Kroll, i, 255); H. F. Müller, "Dionysos, Proklos, Plotinus," *Beiträge zur Geschichte der Philosophie des Mittelalters*, Vol. 20, Heft 3/4 (1922).

[7] Porphyrius as quoted by Proclus in his commentary *In Timaeum*, i. 47. D (ed. Diehl, i, 152); Cumont, *Recherches*; Bidez, *Vie de Porphire*, 1913.

and their song *is* the harmony of the universe. Whereas in Plato's *Republic* the sirens replaced the Muses, two Neoplatonic writers, Proclus and Lucian [8] (second century), had the sirens sing in the island of bliss, Elysium, which had been transferred to the stars, while the souls of the blessed dance and sing, in an image similar to that in the poem about Jambulus. Porphyrius identified the society of Apollo and the Muses with the harmony of the world. There are similar descriptions (omitting Apollo) by Chalcidius,[9] Macrobius,[10] Claudianus Mamertius,[11] Fulgentius,[12] and, last but not least, Martianus Capella,[13] whose *De Nuptiis* will be analyzed in detail later. Jamblicus (fourth century) also described the dance of the blessed on an island. That the Muses move the nine spheres was mentioned by Claudianus,[14] Macrobius (fourth century),[15] and Simplicius (sixth century),[16] though Zeus (*Jovis custos*) is the moving force in the

[8] Proclus, *In Timaeum*, I. 47. D; Lucian, *Vera historia*, II, 5 and II, 13 in Loeb Classics, pp. 64, 68.

[9] Commentary *In Timaeum* (ed. J. Wrobel, 1876); B. W. Switalski, "Des Chalcidius Kommentar zu Plato's Timaeus," *Beiträge zur Geschichte der Philosophie des Mittelalters*, II/6 (1902). Almost nothing is known concerning the personality of Chalcidius; the chief source on him is Theo of Smyrna; H. Martin, *Études sur le Timée*.

[10] *Ambrosii Theodori Macrobii Opera* (Biponti, 1788), I, 129–35 and III; *Conviviorum primi diei Saturnaliorum, ed. Fr. Eyssenhardt* (1868); G. Paré, A. Brunet, P. Trembley, *La renaissance du XIIᵉ siècle*, publ. de l'Institut d'études médiévales d'Ottawa (1933); T. Whittaker, *Macrobius* (1923).

[11] Claudianus Mamertius, *De statu animae*, I, 12; *Corpus scriptorum ecclesiasticum latinorum*, Vol. XI, ed. Engelbrecht (Vienna, 1885); E. Gilson, *La philosophie du moyen-âge* (1947), p. 215; Baeumker, "Witelo," pp. 523ff.

[12] H. Liebeschütz, "Fulgentius Metaforalis," *Warburg Institut, Studien*, Vol. 4 (1926).

[13] First edition Vicenza in 1499, fol. B. VIII, "*Elementorum quoque praesides, angelicique populi pulcherrima multitudo animaeque praeterea beatorum veterum quae iam caeli templa meruerant . . .*", ed. Walthardt (Bern, 1763) p. 75; Notker des Teutschen *Werke*, Vol. 2 (*Denkmäler des M. A.*, ed. H. Hattemer, 3, 1), 1849, p. 369; E. R. Curtius, *Europäische Literatur und lateinisches Mittelalter* (1948), p. 46.

[14] See n. 11 above.

[15] Jamblique, *Les mystères des Égyptiens*, tr. Pierre Quillard (1948), pp. 85, 162.

[16] *Simplicii . . . Commentaria in Aristotelis de Physico-audito*, in *Commentaria in Aristotelis De coelo*, ed. I. L. Heiberg, *Preussische Akad. der Wissenschaften*, Vol. VII (1894); D. J. Allan, *Medieval Versions of Aristotle*, "*De caelo*" and of the Commentary of Simplicius, *Medieval and Renaissance Studies*, eds. R. Hunt and R. Klibanski (London, 1950), II, 82ff.

commentary to *Timaeus* by Chalcidius.[17] The idea that each Muse
corresponds to one sphere and to one musical tone, and that the
harmony results from their music, was outlined by Sidonius Apollinaris,[18] and again by Martianus Capella. From the Persian orbit
there is the *Apocalypse* of Arda Viraf, where the soul travels through
seven heavens; [19] and Mani, the reformer of the *Avesta,* who is the
link between Persian and Roman beliefs and one-time teacher of
Saint Augustine, told of three heavens through which the soul had
to pass.[20]

One further idea found in these writings bears noting: the concept
of the duality of gods or forces in the cosmos. This idea is not in itself
directly related to music, but there is an analogy between this duality
and the interplay of the macrocosmos and the microcosmos in the
human soul, and hence a link to music as a means for establishing the
harmonious correspondence of both. The important work in this context is the *Asclepius* attributed to Apuleius,[21] a book based on the
Logia Chaldea,[22] which remained influential as late as the thirteenth
century. Musical harmony was regarded as a simile for the harmony
of soul with the universe by Plotinus,[23] and this view was also ex-

[17] See n. 9 above.

[18] *Monumenta Germaniae Historica Auctores Antiquissimi,* 8, 79, 5; Sidonius
Appolinaris, *Carmina. Epistola,* ed. Luetjohann (Berlin, 1887); R. Meissner,
Dein Clage ist one Reimen, Festschrift Oskar Walzel (Potsdam, 1924), pp. 32ff.

[19] Bousset, "Die Himmelsreise der Seelen," *Archiv für Religionswissenschaft,*
IV (1901), 136.

[20] Saint Augustine, *Contra Manichaeos, Patrol. lat.* 34, 219; s.a. *Patrol. lat.*
42; J. Lebreton, *Histoire de l'église* (1935).

[21] Apuleii, *Opera quae supersunt,* ed. Helm (1913); W. A. Oldfather, *Index
Apuleianus, Philological Monographs,* III (1934); S. Müller, "Das Verhältnis des
Apuleius de Mundo zu seiner Vorlage," *Philologus,* Suppl. Vol. XXXII, No. 2
(1939); J. Festugière, "Les dieux ousiarques de l'Asclepius," *Recherches de
science religieuse,* XXIII (1938), 175ff.; Curtius, *Europäische Literatur,* pp. 120,
125.

[22] Not to be confused with the *Oracula Chaldea,* which are attributed to Julian
Theurgicos, who lived in the second century under Marcus Aurelius. The *Oracula*
are mentioned by Proclus, Suidas, John the Damascene, and Wilhelm of Moerbecke, *ca.* 1260; there is a commentary by Psellus in *Patrol. lat.* 122, 1123ff.;
first edition by Franc. Patric. Zoroastris (Ferrara, 1591); the *Logia Chaldaea,* a
fusion of Mithraic and Greek teachings, are related to but not identical with
the *Oracula;* in the *Logia* Ananke is the chief ruler of the cosmos; R. Reitzenstein,
Poimandres (1904); F. Cumont, *L'Égypte des astrologues* (Brussels, 1937);
Festugière, "Les dieux ousiarques," pp. 175ff.

[23] See n. 4 above.

pounded in detail by Saint Augustine [24] in the sixth book of his *De Musica*. It was this relationship that Boethius (early sixth century) called *musica humana*. The validity of this correspondence is the basis for the double meaning of the term "motion," used in music as well as for emotions in the human soul. However, extensive discussion of the subject must be reserved to the last chapter of this book.

MARTIANUS CAPELLA

Pagan images of music in the cosmos were systematically articulated in Martianus Capella's long poem or treatise *De Nuptiis Philologiae et Mercurii et de Septem ArtibusLiberalibus Libri Novem*. It was written about 500 in North Africa, supposedly as a textbook for his son. The book was widely read, as evidenced by numerous surviving manuscripts and frequent references to it, and was republished many times, well into the eighteenth century.

De Nuptiis is cast as one of the tales of travel through the spheres that were popular in the first centuries B.C. and A.D.; it is also essentially a *summa* of all the pagan allegorical figures related to the arts. It is not a complete theory, but Capella succeeded in demonstrating the relationships and connections of these figures in a story which recounts Mercury's courtship of and marriage to Philologia. The couple travels up through the spheres, to the castle of Zeus, where the wedding takes place. As a wedding present, Zeus gives them the seven liberal arts. The story follows the journey through the heavens, which are identified with the gods of the planets. The guides on the trip are the Muses, who, for the first time, have individual character. They turn the spheres and make them emit different sounds. Urania, the leader, spins the outermost sphere of fixed stars, which revolves the fastest and has the highest pitch. Then come the other Muses and their spheres, in descending order:

URANIA	FIXED STARS
POLYHYMNIA	SATURN
EUTERPE	JUPITER
ERATO	MARS
MELPOMENE	SUN
TERPSICHORE	VENUS
CALLIOPE	MERCURY (Capella calls this sphere Cyllenium)
CLIO	MOON
THALIA	EARTH

[24] Saint Augustine, *Retractiones, Patrol. lat.* 32, 591 and 603; Saint Augustine, *De immortalitate animae, cap.* 15 and 24, *Patrol. lat.* 32, 1033; C. Baeumker, *Das pseudo-hermetische Buch der 24 Meister.*

Thalia is left to guard the vegetation, for the earth's sphere does not rotate and does not give a sound. It might be noted that nothing is said in this context about the distances between the planets.

In the chapter on arithmetic, one of the liberal arts, ratios are explained by using the example of musical intervals; [25] and though the connection with the spheres is not made here, the report of the journey relates the space between the spheres to musical intervals: the greater the interval, the wider the distance, the more fatiguing the journey. The consonance of the music is said to be perfect. The sphere of Jupiter follows the Doric scale and has the brightest light. It is called *pyrois*, the fiery one, or, in Latin, the Empyreum.[26] During the procession and the ceremony, in Jupiter's castle at the sacred wedding, the chorus of the Muses sings with sweet sound. Their song is accompanied by various instruments—trumpets, flutes, and the organ. This music is said to blend in perfect harmony, because the song follows the rules of the sacred numbers. In the castle, Philologia is dazzled by the shining light of seven candles. In addition to the chorus of the Muses, the bride is welcomed by the heroes, the "rulers of the elements, the most beautiful multitude of angels . . ." and the souls of the blessed elders: Linus, Homer, Mantuanus (Virgil), Orpheus, and many of the philosophers. The story ends with a kind of prophecy: whosoever proceeds to the Empyreum will experience metaphysical bliss.

Martianus, then, speaks of two perfect harmonies: one is the harmony of the spheres, and the other is the dulcet chorus of the Muses. The order of the Muses corresponds to the order of the spheres, the liberal arts to the Muses. The harmonies are based on the order of

[25] H. Deiters, *Über das Verhältnis des Martianus Capella zu Aristides Quintilianus*, Posener Gymnasial Programm (1881) (later ed. with *Studien zu den griechischen Musikern*); the commentary by Remigius of Auxerre to the musical problems in Capella, in M. Gerbert, *Scriptores ecclesiastici de musica* (1784), i.

[26] The term "Empyreum" means the heaven of fire; the vision is taken from Ezekiel and from the Revelation of Saint John; the term "Elysium" is derived from the Elysian Fields, the abode of the blessed in Greek mythology; Empyreum is sometimes identified with the crystal heaven; Bonaventura, *Breviloquia*, ii, 3, mentions the crystal heaven together with Empyreum and the firmament: "Tres caelos principales, empyreum, crystallum, et firmamentum"; s.a. Saint Thomas, *Sent.*, ii, d. 14 q; *Baeumker*, "Witelo," p. 439. For the Empyreum as the abode of the angels, see Saint Augustine, *Civ.*, x. 9, *Patrol. lat.* 41, 287, quoting as his source Porphyrius.

the sacred numbers. It should also be noted that some of Capella's allegories were influenced by Christian ideology. The Empyreum was not known to pagan mythology as the highest heaven. Also, Capella has the angels, the elders, and the multitude—all inhabitants of the heaven of John's Revelation—living in complete harmony with the heroes of the Olympic heaven.

Capella blended his parallel elements into a charming vision, into a cosmos where all work in harmony. He does not say whether the perfect harmonies of the spheres and of the Muses' song are the same. By touching on motifs only, he offers a solution that combines all the allegorical parallels. Yet he circumvents the problem of specifically identifying the nine Muses and the eight spheres and the seven liberal arts with exact musical intervals. Perhaps this is precisely the reason why his book was so influential.

THE CHURCH FATHERS

The writings of the Church Fathers reflect all the traditions mentioned so far: the sounding cosmos of pagan ideology, the manifold structure of the heavens from the Neoplatonists and the Gnostics, and the hosts and choirs of singing angels and the blessed from the Bible. Saint Ambrose,[27] quoting Origen, stated that through the motion of the stars, a marvelous sweet harmony is established and that Plato was its discoverer. Saint Augustine [28] noted that the cosmos "in spiritual and intellectual vision" is composed of seven, eight, nine, or ten heavens. Clement of Alexandria [29] described the journey of the soul through seven heavens which represent steps of purification in a way similar to that recounted in the apocryphal *Apocalypse* of Abraham.[30] In Clement we find, too, reference to the apocryphal Acts of Saint John, which contained a hymn relevant to our topic:

> The Grace dances. I shall play the aulos,
> The number eight dances with us
> The number twelve dances above

[27] Ambrose, *De Abraham, Patrol. lat.* 14, 480; Ambrose, *Enarrat. in XII psalmis Davidicis, Patrol. lat.* 14, 922.

[28] *De Genesi, Patrol. lat.* 34, *cap.* 29.

[29] Clement, *Eclogae prophetarum,* as quoted by Bousset, "Die Himmelsreise," p. 148; *Neutestamentliche Apokryphen,* p. 424.

[30] M. R. James, *Testament of Abraham* (Texts and Studies), II (1892); the meaning of the term "Testament" is identical with "Apocalypse."

The whole cosmos takes part in the dance
Whosoever does not take part in the dance
does not know what shall come.

All these remarks and texts show the survival of older ideas. It is
not surprising that the Church Fathers, many of whom were brought
up in the classic tradition, accepted them without debate, though
they were strongly opposed to the pagan rites. Yet the text of the
hymn also reflects change and transition. The Greek dancing Graces
are replaced with a single dancing Grace; the harmony of the cosmos
becomes the harmony which the blessed shall find in after life. In the
highest heaven, the blessed souls are dancing. This hymn was apparently admitted to the early Christian liturgy, for in the fourth century Saint Augustine [31] mentions it and rejects it, significantly
enough, for reasons of detail.

In the early Church writings a decisive shift occurred toward
greater emphasis on the elaboration of the angel orders. It appears
that it was especially the Fathers of the Eastern Church who brought
about this change.[32] In the third century, Hippolytos of Rome, the
author of the *Canon*, wrote a commentary to the *Book of Daniel* in
which he still identified the nine heavens with the nine Muses, and
the Muses with the planets.[33] But Cyril of Jerusalem (third century) [34] mentions nine hosts of singing angels; and Ephrem of
Edessa (third century) [35] has the seraphim sing and extol the Lord,
while the cherubim have the duty of carrying the throne of God (a
distinction mentioned also by Philo,[36] who identified the throne with
the chariot of the Lord).

---

[31] Letter to Cerebrius, No. 237, *The Fathers of the Church. A New Translation* (New York, 1956), Vol. 32, p. 182.

[32] Justin, *Apologia pro Christianis, Patrol.* gr. 6, 336; G. Bareille, "Le culte
des anges à l'époque des pères de l'église," *Revue Thomiste*, Vol. 8 (1900), p. 41.

[33] See n. 4 above.

[34] Cyrillus, *Catechesis VI de uno Deo, Patrol. gr.* 33, 545ff. (90) "Angeli in
varios coelos et ordines . . . alios aliis excellentiores divisi . . . diversis in
coelis . . . angelorum ordinem numerus et ordo. Angeli et archangeli . . . in
inferiorem omnium ordine et coelo." Cherubim and seraphim are mentioned as
the highest orders by Basilius, *Liturgiae, Patrol gr.* 31, 1678.

[35] *Dictionnaire de théologie catholique* (Paris, 1909), "Anges," *cap.* 2,
d'après les Pères; Wulff, *Cherubim, Throne und Seraphim*, pp. 8ff.; Jerome,
Patrol lat. 22, 280.

[36] Philo, with an English translation by F. H. Cobson, in Loeb Classics, ii

In the liturgy of the Eastern Church, Syrian as well as Byzantine, the nine hosts of angels were represented in processions.[37] The different castes are mentioned in the *Praefationes*, with the seraphim and the cherubim forming the rear of the procession. The Apostolic Constitutions list the nine orders in the seventh and ninth books and state that "the holy seraphim and cherubim sing the song of victory and shout with never-ceasing voice, 'Holy.' "[38] Basilius of Caesarea provides the text of this hymn. The choir sang: "Taking mystically the part of the cherubim and singing the thrice Holy for the Trinity which grants us everlasting life, let us wait for the King of the Universe who is invisibly accompanied by the heavenly hosts." The priest sang: "You dwell on the throne of the cherubim, Master of the seraphim, because you are praised by the angels, archangels, and the crowns [thrones?], dominations, virtues, forces, powers, and the many-eyed cherubim. Around you in a circle stand the seraphim; with never-ceasing voice and never-ceasing praise they answer each other with the victory hymn, singing and shouting 'Holy.' "[39]

This certainly is evidence that a cult of angels was incorporated into the liturgy of the Eastern Church of the fourth century. Opposition to this cult was reflected in the decisions of the Councils of Laodicea in 375 and 492.[40] It is understandable that adoration of angels would have been forbidden in the early Christian era, because the Fathers were afraid that the sirens and victories, *nikes*, invoked in pagan Greek and Oriental funeral rites, might have too much influ-

---

(1929), 23: "He has set each star (i.e., cherub) in its proper zone as a driver in a chariot"; P. Heinisch, "Der Einfluss Philos auf die altchristliche Exegese," *Alttestamentliche Abhandlungen*, Heft 1/2 (1908).

[37] W. Neuss, "Das Buch Ezechiel," *Beiträge zur Geschichte des alten Mönchstums*, Heft 1/2 (1912).

[38] *Constitutiones Apostolicae*, ed. E. Bunsen in *Analecta Ante-Niceana*, Vol. II (1854); the Apostolic Constitutions are a collection of rules for the early Christian communities; Books 1–3 are especially important for a knowledge of customs; the Cherubic Hymn is part of the liturgy set up by Basilius, Jacobus, and Chrysostome. See *Bibliothek der Kirchenväter*, v, 19, ed. Kroll (1895).

[39] "The Liturgies of the Eastern Church," in I. F. Hapgood, *Servicebooks of the H. Orthodox Church* (2nd ed., 1922); the cherubic song is alluded to in the hymn πρὸς τριάδας v. 27, in A. Daniel, *Thesaurus hymnologicus*, III (1846), 137, No. 27; the full text in *Bibliothek der Kirchenväter*, v, 19, 12; Wulff, *Cherubim, Throne und Seraphim*, pp. 15ff.; Neuss, "Das Buch Ezechiel."

[40] F. Lugt, "Man and Angel," *Gazette des Beaux-Arts* (May 1944). When Lugt speaks of dates "as early as the IVth century," one should read "as late as."

ence. After the fourth century, the restrictions were eased, and the castes of angels acquired special characteristics.

The text of the hymn quoted above, from the apocryphal Acts of Saint John, does not refer to any place or particular heaven where this praising is performed, though angel choirs are assigned to specific locations in many later works of art. Choirs representing angels must have remained popular also in the liturgy of the Western Church. On this there are two interesting reports from the ninth century, one from the Saint Riquier monastery at Centula (France) and another from Corvey (Westphalia, Germany). The chroniclers speak of three groups of singers, including one composed of boys, forming a *chorus angelicus* which is said to sing the Gloria from the western gallery of the church.[41]

DIONYSIUS'S ANGEL HIERARCHY

Dionysius's famous treatise, *The Celestial Hierarchy*, is regarded as the source of the vision of the nine classes of angels.[42] This book, ascribed to Dionysius the Areopagite, was first mentioned at the Council of Constantinople in 533. The author wrote it as a secret treatise for an initiated group of clergy and did not intend it for the common reader. Indeed, its teaching is cloaked in mystic language to

[41] K. Meyer, "Der Einfluss der gesanglichen Vorschriften auf die Chor . . . Anlagen in den Klosterkirchen," *Archiv für Musikwissenschaft* (1922), p. 2.

[42] *Patrol. gr.* 3; the *scholiae* to Dionysius by Maximus Confessor are published in the same volume. The book was translated by John Erigina and used in his *De praedestinatione.* For the commentaries by Hilduin and Jean Gerson (*ca.* 1390), see A. Combes, *Jean Gerson Commentateur Dionysien* (1940); B. F. Westcott, *Essays in the History of Religious Thought in the West* (1891), pp. 148ff.; Müller, "Dionysos, Proklos, Plotinus"; H. Grabmann, *Die mittelalterlichen Übersetzungen des Pseudo-Dionysos Areopagita* (Mittelalterliches Geistesleben, 1926). A copy of the *Hierarchia* was sent in 827 by the Byzantine Emperor Michael Balbus to Louis I of France.

COMMENTARIES:

Maximus Confessor, *ca.* 580–662, printed with Dionysos in *Patrol. gr.* 3, and not in *Patrol. lat.* 190/191

Johannes Scotus, transl.	851
Johannes Saracenus	twelfth century
Hugue of Saint Victor	*ca.* 1120
Grosseteste	*ca.* 1235
Saint Thomas	*ca.* 1255
Albert the Great	*ca.* 1260
Jean Gerson	*ca.* 1390
Ambrosius Camaldulensis	fifteenth century

make it accessible only to the initiated. The philosophy propounded by Dionysius is based on a theory that a light mystically emanates from the Lord and is transmitted through the hierarchy, the holy order of the angels, to mankind. While this treatise on the hierarchy is accepted as the source of the many later descriptions and representations of musician angels and orchestras, the text itself says nothing, or almost nothing, concerning music; its emphasis is on the other duties of the angels.

Dionysius divides the celestial hierarchy into nine "choruses," using the term not in its musical sense but to mean "group" or "class." The nine orders are arranged in a scale. They are divided into three groups, each of which is subdivided into three classes. The author's terminology is full of symbolic meanings. The number nine, the result of multiplying 3 by 3, is clearly a symbol of the Trinity. The purposely obscure writing has necessitated many commentaries elaborating on the special tasks of the orders. The highest group is described as "standing" around the Lord, and it is their duty to teach heavenly wisdom to the middle sections, who in turn must teach the lowest orders, until the heavenly wisdom reaches some initiated members of mankind. This is there chief duty. In addition, all the orders must praise the Lord with the Thrice Holy, the number three again mystically referring to the Trinity. It should, however, be noted that the term used ($\nu\mu\nu\epsilon\iota\nu$) means spoken praise and acclamation, rather than singing ($\psi\alpha\lambda\mu\epsilon\iota\nu$), and that none of the angels' emblems refers to music. Another major characteristic of the angels is their shining appearance, and the higher the order, the greater the radiance. Their sense of hearing is explained as their faculty to accept heavenly spiritual inspiration. The following list of correspondences has been drawn from the commentaries: [43]

Angels with six wings, the Counsellors:

Seraphim	Flames	Love
Cherubim	Eyes	Knowledge
Thrones	Wheels	Devotion

Angels with four wings, the Rulers:

Dominations	Royal insignia	Nobility
Virtues	Scale	Calmness
Powers	Arms	Activity

[43] E. v. Drival, L'iconographie des anges," *Revue de l'art chrétien*, x (1886), 272ff.; B. de Roffignac, "Les anges moteurs et l'iconographie du moyen-âge," *Société des Antiquitaires du Centre, Mémoires* (1935).

Angels with two wings, the Servants:

Principalities	Sceptre	Law
Archangels	Crozier	Work
Angels	Censer	Prayer

Although Dionysius's description of a celestial order of angels did not mention music, it influenced later visions in which music came to have a prominent place; and it seems probable that the very elaboration of a Christian angelic order more or less parallel to pagan concepts of cosmic order should be regarded as providing the vital link to the musical images that ultimately emerged.

In Dionysius's treatise on the celestial hierarchy, the angels rotate in wheels unrelated to the circumferences of the spheres. The cosmos is not constructed of spheres, and the wheels on which the angels move are fire. To the order of the seraphim, the highest and nearest to the Lord, belongs the emblem of flames, and their allegorical epithet is love. The cosmos as a whole is ruled by love, an especially happy formula for reconciling earlier concepts with Christian ethics [44] and the origin presumably of Dante's *amore che tutto muove*, the force that moves the cosmos.[45]

The treatise is one of the early attempts to combine Greek and Gnostic concepts with Christian ideology. In its original form, it has not much to contribute directly to this study's particular problem, that is, the integration of music into the vision of the Christian cosmos.

By the eleventh century, the various traditions of cosmic and angelic orders had merged, and the vision had assumed an aspect famil-

---

[44] Dionysius's idea that "manifestation of the nature of God is a glorious hymn in which we celebrate his love" also occurs in pagan writings, including those of: Aristoxenos, quoted by Cicero, *Tusc.*, I, 19 and 41; Nikomachus, *Arithm.*, II; Philo, *De gigant.*, 3, 8; *De somniis*, I, 37; Plotinus, *Enn.*, II, 9.5 and V, 1.2; Proclus, *In Timaeum*, V, 320 A.

Also in Christian writings: Saint Augustine, *De immortalitate animae*, *Patrol. lat.* 32, 1033ff.; *Enchiridion de fide, spe et caritate*, *Patrol. lat.* 40, 154ff.; translated in *Fathers of the Church*, Writings of Saint Augustine, 4, pp. 357ff.; *De musica*, Vol. 2, pp. 324ff.; Claudianus Mamertius (see n. 11 above); Boethius, *De musica*, *Patrol. lat.* 63. See also Baeumker, *Das pseudo-hermetische Buch der 24 Meisters*; Baeumker, "Witelo," pp. 525ff.; Combes, *Jean Gerson Commentateur Dionysien*.

[45] M. A. Gaetani di Sermoneta, *La materia della 'Divina Commedia' ecc. in sei tavole* (1865); K. Vossler, *Die Göttliche Komödie* (1907–19).

iar today: the blessed sing and dance in the highest heaven, be it Elysium or Empyreum. There are nine spheres or heavens and nine choirs of angels. The spheres are moved by angels or the Muses. Their song results in the harmony of the universe, and this harmony can be transmitted, through music, to the human soul. The idea of correspondence of heavenly and human harmony through music was first formulated by St. Augustine, later by Boethius, and subsequently adopted by many poets and philosophers.

IV The Early Works of Art

The developments we have followed in written sources were reflected as well in painting and sculpture, but there are curiously few direct references to music in the works surviving from the period prior to the tenth century. Since a profusion of relevant works and manuscripts have come to light in recent years, this chapter will concentrate on a relatively small number of typical examples, with cursory mention of the more important of the others. The discussion will focus largely on four points: how the structure of the cosmos was imagined and depicted; how angels were visualized, especially their grouping; what place in the cosmos was assigned to them; and what role, if any, was allocated to musicians and music.

REPRESENTATIONS OF THE COSMOS

Concerning the picture of the cosmos, two different approaches are discernible: one might be called the scientific or naturalistic approach, and the other, the symbolic or mythical viewpoint. There are, further, two notably different images of heaven: as a single location, or as manifold heavens in a cosmos constructed of different layers of spheres. Heaven was seen as one big vault or firmament in the Old Testament, as well as in Egyptian myth.[1] An example of this version is found in a painting at Dendera (Fig. 6) which shows a standing figure, representing Schou (air) supporting a curved figure representing Nouit (heaven), who forms an arch. This image did not survive in such pure anthropomorphic form, but it may be recognized in later vaults where no division between the spheres is shown, e.g.,

[1] W. Grüneisen, *Sainte Marie Antique* (1911), Figs. 192–93; G. Maspero, *L'archéologie égyptienne* (2nd edn., 1887); a ceiling with a more elaborate form of the cosmos is found in Grüneisen, Fig. 198; in Maspero, p. 188; and in K. Lehmann, "The Dome of Heaven," *Art Bulletin*, Vol. 27, No. 1 (1945), Fig. 7.

FIG. 6. Egyptian vision of the cosmos as a cupola; drawing after the second-century fresco at Dendera, Egypt

where stars are scattered in no special design over a dark blue ceiling (as at Ravenna, Galla Placidia tomb).[2]

The Chaldeans or Babylonians saw a cosmos structured in seven spheres, to which sometimes an eighth was added as the highest heaven. This Chaldean image of seven heavens is represented in architecture by seven tiers or steps in a spiral, as, for instance, in the tower of Babel as described by Herodotus,[3] who reported that it had seven stories and that the initiated had to perform certain rites of purification at each level. Other Babylonian sanctuaries, however, had three or four stories. In Persia, similar towers of a later period had eight layers, or else their floor plan was divided into eight segments, as in the sanctuaries at Darabzird and Firuzabad. In Baghdad, a cosmic sanctuary with eight parts, dedicated under the new Sassanian dynasty in A.D. 762, is supposed to have been the model for many later buildings.[4]

[2] O. Wulff, *Altchristliche und byzantinische Kunst, Handbuch der Kunstwissenschaft,* I, 347, Fig. 310.

[3] Herodotus, *Historiae,* I, in Loeb Classics, pp. 98, 181.

[4] H. P. L'Orange, *Studies on the Iconography of Cosmic Kingship in the Ancient Orient* (Oslo, 1953), p. 10.

FIG. 7. Bronze spindle with eight discs, found in southern Italy

In the south of Italy, a number of bronze *vortices*, or spindles, have been found which consist of eight discs on an axis, their circumferences forming a kind of double cone (Fig. 7).[5] It is probable that these, like the golden tablets found in the same area, were used in the rites of the Pythagoreans, a sect which had several centers in southern Italy and Sicily. Although the details of these rites have remained a secret, it is known that the idea of the cosmos constructed in eight layers was a basic dogma of Pythagorean belief. The image of the seven or eight spheres was derived from the Babylonians, but the Pythagoreans added a new concept of numbers as a ruling principle of the cosmos and also identified them with musical intervals.[6] The *vortices* may well have been symbolic ceremonial instruments, like rosaries in Buddhistic and Christian creeds. Possibly, the discs would sound a scale of tones if struck, though, as far as I know, this has not been tried.

In two-dimensional frescoes or mosaics, the cosmos was represented in concentric circles or in stripes. Such pictures have been found in mosaics in the vaults or ceilings and on the floors of sanctuaries.[7] The cosmos became the most popular motif for decorating the ceilings of Oriental domes or cupolas and their later Christian transformations, as well as for ceilings in secular houses. In the cupola paintings, the heaven regarded as the highest forms the center. When a picture of the cosmos decorates the half-vault of an apse or a triumphal arch, the spheres more often appear as layers or strips of out-rolled scrolls.[8] In most of these cases—cupolas or arches—it is not easy to

[5] O. Brendel, "Symbolik der Kugel," *Deutsches Archäologisches Institut, Römische Abt. Mitteilungen*, 51 (1936), p. 75.

[6] Döring, "Wandlungen in der pythagoräischen Lehre," *Archiv für Geschichte der Philosophie*, v (1892).

[7] Lehmann, "The Dome of Heaven."

[8] E. Tea, *La basilica di Santa Maria Antiqua*, Publ. della Univ. Cattolica del Sacro Cuore (1937), Ser. 5, Sc. stor. 14, Pls. v, x, *passim*; Grüneisen, *Sainte Marie Antique*; W. Weidlé, *Mosaici Paleocristiani e Byzantini* (Milan, 1954), Pl. 64, from San Prassede, Rome, ninth century.

decide the exact number of the spheres, because ornamental borders may or may not be included, or they could be counted as one or several, depending on the design. But it might be noted that the number of circles is definitely greater in the domes of the Far East, perhaps due to the greater number of deities in the Hindu hierarchy.[9]

To understand the significance of the circles and layers, it is necessary to interpret the figures and signs shown as their movers and inhabitants. The appearance of actual musician angels is rare prior to the tenth century, possibly because of the difficulty of depicting people singing, possibly due to reluctance to associate the numerous figures of musicians with instruments common to pagan work. Be that as it may, only angels blowing "trumpets" for the Last Judgment are depicted with any frequency in the early work, and they are not making music, but giving a signal to wake the dead, to summon them to judgment, and thus functioning, in effect, as the descendants of the heralds of the Sumerians.[10] Nevertheless, the development that ultimately led to angel orchestras can be traced and their antecedents discerned by following the evolution of images with reference to the concepts outlined in the previous analysis of the written sources.

For a start, there is the famous ceiling of the Temple of Bel at Palmyra from the second century (Fig. 8). It has three layers. In a central hexagon there is the bust of Bel, the highest god and *primus movens*, in the highest heaven. He is surrounded by six planets, and in the corners there are four figures with human heads and wings. The latter are designated by Curtius, who was the first to draw attention to this work, as sirens.[11] With his usual great intuition, he saw in the design of the Palmyra ceiling an allegory of the music of the spheres and the model for many later representations of the Lord or Christ in glory. He called the winged figures sirens in the Platonic sense, that is, spirits with wings who sing and support and move the spheres. Though I agree in general with Curtius's interpretation, I feel the winged figures might equally well represent the winged messengers or genii or movers from the myths of Babylonian culture, to which this work otherwise belongs.

[9] A. C. Soper, "The Dome of Heaven in Asia," *Art Bulletin* (1947).

[10] S. Kozaky, *Danse macabre* (Budapest, 1935–44), I, 65.

[11] L. Curtius, "Musik der Sphaeren," *Deutsches Archäologisches Institut, Römische Abt. Mitteilungen*, 50 (1935–36), pp. 348ff.

FIG. 8. The cosmos supported by four sirens; drawing after the ceiling painting in the Temple of Bel at Palmyra

There is another example from about the same period on a slab surviving from the Mithraic cult (now in the Museum of Treves).[12] This shows a youth, not specifically depicted as Mithras, holding a globe in one hand and with his other hand turning a wheel on which the signs of the zodiac are inscribed. Thus it symbolizes the motion of celestial bodies with a wheel rather than with winged figures. Yet a third work of this period is a clay disc (now in the Museum of Brindisi) [13] on which two of the Fates and a chariot drawn by horses appear in an inner circle. The horses are led by Mercury and a deity which may be Helios or Eros, or the god to whom the sanctuary in which the disc was used was dedicated. The Fates occurred in combination with a chariot drawn by winged horses in one of Plato's cosmic myths, in *Phaedrus*. There, as mentioned above, the Fates turned the spindle and the gods and the human souls proceeded on chariots with winged horses.

[12] L'Orange, *Studies on the Iconography of Cosmic Kingship*, p. 32.
[13] Brendel, "Symbolik der Kugel," Fig. 10.

The Movers of the Spheres and
the Figure of the Angel

The relation of wheel, chariot, and winged spirit is important, for they were all used to depict motion. The celestial chariot is a motif common to several religons and was, further, often identified with the throne of God. While the Psalms mention only the throne on which the Lord sits attended by cherubim, Ezekiel and Philo identified the throne with a chariot and had the cherubim carry the throne, and, later, drive the chariot.[14] Christian iconography adheres almost exclusively to the throne. A Persian work from the Sassanian period, on the other hand, shows a celestial chariot as the vehicle of the deified king. In one Persian example (Fig. 9), there is a chariot drawn by the sacred bulls, who are driven by winged spirits with whips.[15] In this representation, the mortal king's identity with the

---

[14] Ezekiel, i, 5; x, 20; Philo, *De congressu quaerendae eruditionis gratia*, ii, 23, *De Cherubim.*

[15] L'Orange, *Studies on the Iconography of Cosmic Kingship*, Fig. 19.

FIG. 9. The deified king, ruler of the cosmos; Persian silverplate from the seventh century

heavenly king is made explicit by a motif which came to be used in later works to show Christ as Pantocrator.

Among the various motion images, the winged figure is of special interest in the context of music. From the winged cherubim and winged genii of the Babylonian and Hittite mythologies, there evolved the Greek sirens whom Plato used to turn the spheres. The sirens in their positive aspect were related to the Muses and hence

FIG. 10. Hybrid winged figure from the palace of Ashurnasirpal II at Nimrud; ninth century B.C.

FIG. 11. Ivory plate overlaid with gold foil, showing a female figure with wings; Assyrian, early first millennium

FIG. 12. Winged Eros with lyre; detail from Lekythos found at Gela, Sicily; fourth century B.C.

form a link in the progression toward the ultimate appearance of the musician angel.[16]

There are, however, only scanty traces of this development before the tenth century. The figure of the winged animal appears in many Oriental religions, and this may also have been the early form of the cherubim (Fig. 10). Human figures with wings have been found during the recent excavations at Nimrud, including several female figures explained as the demon Lilu or Lilith (Fig. 11).[17] In Greek mythology Eros (Fig. 12) and Nike appeared in this form, and the

[16] Philo, *De congressu, De Cherubim*, i, 143.22 and 142.27. "Logos as the king of the angels and charioteer"; P. Heinisch, "Der Einfluss Philos auf die Altchristliche Exegese," *Alttestamentliche Abhandlungen*, Heft 1/2 (1908); W. Neuss, "Das Buch Ezechiel," *Beiträge zur Geschichte des alten Mönchstums*, Heft 1/2 (1912), pp. 63, 107, 158, with quotations from Jerome and Gregory the Great; Neuss mentions the mandorla as a reflection of the celestial chariot; angels on wheels, e.g., on the ciborium columns at Saint Mark's in Venice and in the Kosmas MS., in Chartres, the Athos Book for Painters, etc.

[17] A human being with four wings also appears on an Assyrian seal, from the period of Sargon; L. Curtius, *Antike Kunst* (*Handbuch der Kunstwissenschaft*, i), 256, Pl. VIII; Lilith in A. Parrot, *The Arts of Asia* (1961), Fig. 330; M.E.L. Mallowen, *Nimrod and its Remains* (1966), Fig. 133.

FIG. 13. Ninth-century mosaic in the Koimesis Church at Nicaea, showing angels with wings, halos, and the names of their orders: archangels and potentates

sirens had human faces set on bird-like bodies. Amor, too, is represented with wings, and the *putti,* the winged children, are descendants of Amor or Eros, Amoretti or Eroti. They can be found in monuments of the Augustan period.[18] In the period when Hellenistic and Oriental ideas merged in the countries of the Near East, the figures of Nike, of Eros, and of the cherubim, were summed up in the figure of the angel as it is known today. Thus, it begins to appear as a winged youth in the earliest Christian works, such as those in the catacombs of Nicaea (Fig. 13),[19] in the frescoes of Baouit,[20] and in a somewhat later fresco from a catacomb, at the Naples Museum.[21] Yet in the Vienna Genesis the angels are bearded men without wings.[22]

Angels were not, in fact, consistently winged until many centuries later. In the Old Testament neither the angels nor the archangels Michael and Raphael are visualized as having wings. Gabriel in the text of the Annunciation is not described as a winged angel, and in the earliest representations he is wingless. The angel who appears to Joshua has no wings in the fifth-century mosaic in Santa Maria Maggiore (Fig. 14), but he does have them in the ninth-century illumination of the Joshua scroll (Fig. 15).[23]

In addition to the question of their outward appearance, the angels' duties and the representation of their roles posed many problems. While the scholastics were still conducting controversies as to whether the angels were to be considered the movers of the spheres,[24]

[18] F. Cumont, *Mystères de Mithra* (1890–96), pp. 332ff. See also Part II of this book.

[19] Weidlé, *Mosaici Paleocristiani,* Pls. 50 and 51; O. Wulff, *Die Koimesiskirche zu Nicäa* (1903), p. 209; P. A. Underwood, "The Evidence of Restoration in the Sanctuary Mosaics of the Dormition at Nicaea," *Dumbarton Oaks Papers* (1959), p. 235.

[20] M. Bernath, *Die Malerei des Mittelalters* (1916), p. 17, Fig. 19.

[21] Wulff, *Altchristliche und byzantinische Kunst,* I, 51, Fig. 38.

[22] F. Wickhoff, *Die Wiener Genesis,* Jahrbuch der Kunstsammlungen des allerhöchsten Kaiserhauses, Suppl. to Vol. 15/16 (1895); F. Lugt, "Man and Angel," *Gazette des Beaux-Arts* (May 1944), Fig. 13; A. Goldschmidt, *Die Elfenbeinskulpturen* (1914), I, p. 54, Fig. 123.

[23] Lugt, "Man and Angel," p. 267, Figs. 3 and 4.

[24] Saint Thomas, *Summa Theologiae,* Ia, 99, 50/64 and 106/114; *De Substantiis separatis seu de angelorum natura opusculum* (quoted in Duhem, *Le système du monde,* V, 541; *Quodlibet,* XII, Art. IX, *Utrum coelum sit animatum,* in Duhem, V, 559; *Scriptum in II^m librum sententiarum,* Dest. XIV, quaest. I, Art. III, *Utrum motus coeli sit ab intellegentiis;* Bonaventura, *Breviloquia;* F. Tinello, Art. "Angeli, la teologia scolastica," in *Enciclopedia Cattolica.*

FIG. 14. Joshua before a wingless angel with halo; from a fifth-century mosaic in the Basilica S. Maria Maggiore in Rome

FIG. 15. Joshua before a winged angel with halo; from the ninth-century Joshua scroll

painters and sculptors had to solve the problem of how to show the angels as movers and, even more difficult, of how to show them singing. The movers were sometimes represented as spokes of a wheel or a sphere, as in the mosaic ceiling of the San Zeno chapel in San Prassede in Rome (Fig. 16).[25] This type of picture expresses

FIG. 16. (LEFT) The highest heaven with the bust of Christ supported by winged angels with halos; drawing after the ninth-century mosaic in the cupola of the San Zeno Chapel of San Prassede in Rome

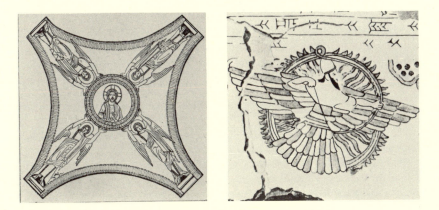

FIG. 17. (RIGHT) The winged male figure, Assur, the god of the sun in the "aura"; a drawing after the fresco from Nimrud; ninth century B.C.

the intrinsic and long-standing connection between the movers and the supporters of the heavens, and such wheels are found in pagan, Christian, and Oriental works.

The idea that the world, the heaven, and the sun had to be supported as well as moved is found in some of the oldest works related to our topic, and the role of winged figures moving the spheres is closely related to supporting the heavens. Among the recent excavations at Nimrud is a fresco of a male figure with wings in a circle (Fig. 17). It has been explained as Assur, god of the sun. Babylonian sculptures show the disc of the sun supported or carried by two flying

[25] Grüneisen, *Sainte Marie Antique*, Fig. 200; for the form of the wheel in Oriental ceilings, see Soper, "The Dome of Heaven in Asia," Fig. 19; Yün-Kang cave 9; Lugt, "Man and Angel," Fig. 11; O. Siren, *Chinese Sculpture* (London, 1915), Pl. 82.

spirits, as if the disc were emerging from two great wings (Fig. 18).
A sun disc supported by two winged flying figures appears on one of
the Megiddo ivories of the second millennium B.C.[26] These winged
figures have been recognized as forerunners of Ezekiel's spirits [27]
and, ultimately, of Christian angels. In a very early Christian work,
for example, on the door of Koja-Kalessi in Isauria [28] and on a number of sarcophagi, one finds the sun disc again, sometimes with a cross
or a bust of Christ, carried by winged figures, which now represent
angels.

The disc supported by winged figures proved a persistent motif.
On the wall of the Visigoth Church (seventh to eighth centuries)
at Quintanilla de las Viñas (Burgos, Spain) there are two sculptures
which use this design (Fig. 19).[29] One of these shows the bust of
"Sol," the other the bust of the Savior. One could not wish for a better demonstration of how pagan idols were transformed into Chris-

[26] Parrot, *The Arts of Asia*, Fig. 282; Mallowen, *Nimrod*, p. 250, original
now in British Museum. G. Loud, *The Megiddo Ivories* (1939), Pl. 11.

[27] L. Dürr, *Die Stellung des Propheten Ezechiel* (*Alttestamentliche Abhandlungen*, XI, 1) (Münster, 1923)

[28] On the portal of Koja-Kalessi, two angels with six wings carry a circle with
a bust of the bearded Christ (fifth century); T. W. Headlam, "Ecclesiastical
Sites in Isauria," *Journal of Hellenistic Studies*, Suppl. Vol. of Papers (1892),
pp. 10ff.; Wulff, *Altchristliche und byzantinische Kunst*, I, 136, Fig. 126.

[29] J. Pijoan, *Summa Artis*, VIII (Madrid, 1942), 381, Figs. 535–36, Quintanilla de las Viñas in Burgos, where the bust of the sun god is carried by
angels with two wings (eighth century).

FIG. 18. Throne relief on the east jamb of the western doorway at Persepolis,
showing a winged sun disc

FIG. 19. Two stone slabs from the ruins of the Visigoth Church at Quintanilla de las Viñas, Burgos, Spain

tian symbols over these centuries. The sun is replaced by Christ holding the cross, and one of the winged figures is now carrying a cross. A similar motif was used on a number of sarcophagi, both pagan and Christian. There is, for example, one on which a disc with a portrait-bust of the deceased is being held by two figures, as on Etruscan monuments—human figures with long and mighty wings (see Fig. 132). The motif of the disc with the portrait supported by angels or *putti* survived far into the eighteenth century. One finds the same

FIG. 20. Christ as ruler of the cosmos; from the sixth-century Greek manuscript of Kosmas Inidikopleustes

winged figures supporting mandorlas with the Lord, or Christ or the Virgin, or sometimes the bust of the saint to whom a cathedral is dedicated.

For the physical appearance of the single angel, reference must again be made to Ezekiel's vision. He described three kinds of angels, some with two, some with four, and some with six wings, as well as spirits with four faces, tetramorphs. The latter have one face like a human being, the other faces are like the lion, the bull, and the eagle.[30] These faces have become the symbols of the evangelists. The six-winged angel is sometimes referred to as a tetramorph and sometimes as a cherub. Generally, he is virtually covered with wings, under which hands or arms often appear. These six-winged angels are often depicted standing on wheels that signify the spheres, as in the illumination of Ezekiel's vision in the Vatican Kosmas manuscript of the sixth century, where Christ appears in glory supported by four six-winged cherubim on wheels (Fig. 20).

REPRESENTATIONS OF THE ANGEL ORDERS

The writings of the first centuries B.C. and A.D., in which the theory of the hierarchy of angels was elaborated, often described angels praising the Lord as grouped in nine choirs or orders and located in nine heavens. The word "host" or "army" might be used instead of "choir" or "chorus," because the term appears to have been used not only in the musical sense but also to mean a group in general, a crowd.[31] Thus, the Itala fragment refers to the chorus of prophets. The companions of David, depicted, interestingly, in the form of wheels,[32] are called "chori" in a Greek manuscript from the Vatican (Fig. 21).

Yet, though the figure of a winged youth as the image of an angel was accepted in Christian iconology from the second century on, representations of the chorus of angels do not seem to have appeared until considerably later. John of Damascus (eighth century) refers in several places to representations of hosts of angels attending Christ and the Virgin, but none of these is known to have survived. The earliest extant examples appear in the Kosmas manuscript and in the

[30] Ezekiel, I, 14–21; X, 21.

[31] Weidlé, *Mosaici Paleocristiani*, Pl. 153, Cefalù; W. Temple, "The Song of the Angelic Hosts," *Annuale Mediaevale, Duquesne Studies*, II (1961).

[32] H. Degering and A. Boeckler, *Die Quedlinburger Italafragmente* (1932).

FIG. 21. King David on a throne; from the sixth-century Greek manuscript of Kosmas Inidikopleustes

homilies of the monk Jacob. One early style seems to have been to depict the angelic orders as clusters of heads (Figs. 22 and 23).[33]

[33] Joannes Damascenus, *Oratio adversus Constantinum Cabalinum*, *Patrol. gr.* 95, 323ff.; *Epistola ad Theophilum imperatorem*, *Patrol. gr.* 95, 362; *Veneranda Dei Genetricis Figura*, *Patrol. gr.* 95, 636; C. Storniajolo, *Le Miniature della*

Topografia Cristiana di Cosmo Indicopleuste (Milan, 1908), Cod. Vat. gr. 699, Pl. 26, *Davide e cori*; G. La Piana, "The Presentation of the Virgin," in *Late Classical and Medieval Studies in Honor of M. Friend* (1955), MS. Vat. gr. 1162, Homilies of Jacobus, fol. 8a; an almost identical illumination in a manuscript of the sermons on the Virgin by Jacobus in the MS. gr. 1208, Bibliothèque Nationale, Paris; see A. Grabar, *Byzantine Painting* (1953), p. 183; C. Bayet, *L'art byzantin* (Paris, 1883); M. Bernath, *Die Malerei*, Pl. 29, Fig. 66; a similar arrangement in Bayet, *op. cit.*, p. 165, Fig. 51, from an eleventh-century manuscript in the Bibliothèque Nationale; six dense rows of angels behind the "lit de repos du Christ" appear in Bayet (p. 163, Fig. 50), with lances, and one with a shield, from an eleventh-century manuscript, also in the Bibliothèque Nationale.

FIG. 22. Illumination from the eleventh-century manuscript of the Homilies on the Virgin by the monk Jacobus. The Virgin appears in the middle of the top row. The group on the left are saints, those on the right are the prophets

FIG. 23. Illumination from the eleventh-century manuscript of the Homilies on the Virgin by the monk Jacobus

Sometimes a single angel can be recognized as representative of a certain order by a *titulus*, or groups are identified by inscriptions (Fig. 24).[34] Sometimes the group is shown as a dense crowd with only the front figures fully visible, as in the group of Powers in the Rabula Codex.[35] Here lances and shields are used to indicate the caste of the Powers. In her book, *The Angel in Art*, H. Mendelsohn states that one of the front columns of the ciborium in San Marco in Venice

[34] "Archai" on the Limburg Staurothek; Jac. Rauch, "Die Limburger Staurothek," *Das Münster*, 8, Heft 7/8 (1955); Weidlé, *Mosaici Paleocristiani*, Pls. 50–51, from Nicaea; S. Bettini, *Mosaici antichi di San Marco* (Bergamo, 1946), Pl. 108.

[35] *Rabula Codex*, Florence, Laurenziana, MS. Plut. 1, 56.

shows the nine orders.[36] These columns date from about the fifth or sixth century, but they do not, on examination, constitute an exception here. Their style has been related to works of the Near East. Each column is composed of nine tiers and one, the top row, divided into nine arcades, shows six angels with two wings, their hands covered with cloths. This latter designates them as servants, as ministers to Christ, who is shown on a throne in one of the remaining arcades,[37] flanked by two tetramorphs standing on wheels. According to the inscription, this group represents the nine orders (*ordines*) or choirs of the angels. The inscription, however, was added in the

[36] H. Mendelsohn, *Die Engel in der bildenden Kunst* (1907); Wulff, *Altchristliche und byzantinische Kunst*, p. 128, Fig. 115.

[37] Following A. Grabar, "Recherches sur les influences orientales dans l'art balkanique," *Orient et Byzance, Études d'art*, 1 (1928), 78, and Grabar, *La peinture religieuse en Bulgarie* (1928), Pl. IV; this gesture has been described as typical for burial scenes and such figures are thought to represent psychopomps or guides for the souls. This may be true for a certain period, but usually in Oriental art it indicates servants in general, or represents other services.

FIG. 24. Detail from the twelfth-century fresco in the Chiesa di San Pietro at Civate, showing three of the angelic orders: *Virtutes, Principatus,* and *Potestates*

twelfth century.[38] The orders are not clearly represented, the six serving angels are not distinguished in their functions, and the total number of angels is only eight.

The two most explicit representations of the orders of angels prior to the tenth century, though not of all nine of the orders, occur on the triumphal arches in Santa Maria Antiqua and San Prassede in Rome.[39] At Santa Maria Antiqua, one finds distinct groups allotted to distinct spheres, and the use of different colors makes it possible to distinguish the groups. In the center of the arch there is a figure of the Virgin, to whom the church is dedicated. She is surrounded or flanked in three strips or layers by the following figures: tetramorphs in the top row, one on each side; then, in the middle row, groups of angels, a double row of nine angels on each side. One of these groups is designated by an inscription as archangels; they wear red robes. The other group, the seraphim, have white robes and red and amber wings; they stand with their feet in flames, depicting the theory that there are two kinds of angels, eternal angels and angels born anew every day out of a stream of fire issuing from beneath the throne of of the Lord. The groups of angels on the arch are characterized as day and night angels by the color of the background, pink to symbolize day and green for the night. The two groups also wear different footgear, the angels of the day sandals, the angels of the night boots. Seen through the opening of the Virgin's arch, in the tribuna or apse, there is a representation of the crucifixion which includes two tetramorphs who have the usual appearance, with six wings covering the entire body. The angels on the arch are represented as moving forward toward the Madonna and toward Christ. Their hands, without emblems and not covered, are held in a gesture of adoration. There is no indication that they are singing or playing; but they are located in a specific heaven, in the middle one near the Virgin and and near Christ. They are lower than the tetramorphs (who may be regarded as identical with cherubim, who support or stand beside

[38] A. Gayet, *L'art byzantin* (Paris, 1901), 1, 21; Lehmann, "The Dome of Heaven," p. 3; O. Demus, *Die Mosaiken von San Marco in Venedig* (Vienna, 1935), p. 84, says that the inscriptions have not yet been deciphered and studied.

[39] Weidlé, *Mosaici Paleocristiani*, Pl. 62. In this representation from San Prassede in Rome, 817–24, on the triumphal arch, "gli eletti s'aviando alla Gerusaleme Celeste," the faithful have no wings; they are led by angels with wings. Weidlé, *Mosaici Paleocristiani*; Grüneisen, *Sainte Marie Antique*; Tea, *La basilica di Santa Maria Antiqua.*

FIG. 25. The Madonna with angels; from the ninth-century mosaic in San Prassede in Rome

the throne of God), yet higher than the multitude of the faithful or blessed, who are grouped in the lowest strip.

In an ninth-century mosaic on the apse of San Prassede in Rome, Mary is seated in glory on a throne, flanked by two groups of angels, of which four in each front row are wholly visible, while of the crowd in the back only the heads can be seen (Fig. 25). The angels have wings and halos, and they are in the posture of adoration, with hands folded and without emblems. They wear sandals. The mosaic on the left side of the triumphal arch in the same church represents the entry of the faithful into paradise (Fig. 26). The blessed are shown without wings and without halos, their hands covered with cloths. They are led by two angels with wings and halos. The angels have sandals, the blessed wear low shoes. Paradise is visualized as a walled

FIG. 26. The blessed entering the City of God; from the ninth-century mosaic in San Prassede in Rome

city, a celestial Jerusalem, in an image which recurs later, especially in the illuminations on fourteenth-century manuscripts of Saint Augustine's *Civitas Dei*.

These are the earliest instances I have found in which the group of the "faithful" or "just" is depicted in the hierarchy, reflecting concepts found in Revelation.[40] This represents a change from the vision of a natural cosmos to the vision of a structured order of heavens.

Symbols of Music

Direct references to heavenly music were notably rare before the tenth century in both pagan and Christian art. In all the many works of this period that depict groups of angels, there is only one feature that can be said to allude to musical activity. That is, there are angels carrying small tablets inscribed with the Thrice Holy, indicating that it is the duty of these angels to sing continuous praise of the Lord (Fig. 27).[41] Such tablets may well have been carried in the processions of the Byzantine Church, and they are reminiscent of the

[40] Grüneisen, *Sainte Marie Antique*; Tea, *La basilica di Santa Maria Antiqua*; Weidlé, *Mosaici Paleocristiani*, Pl. 64.

[41] Weidlé, *Mosaici Paleocristiani*, Figs. 50–51; Grabar, *Byzantine Painting*, p. 174, Archangel Michael from Menologion of Saint Basilius, MS. Vat. gr. 1613; Underwood, "The Evidence of Restoration in the Sanctuary Mosaics."

golden tablets with sacred texts found in the south of Italy, on Crete, and in Libya.[42]

In the pagan world of the first centuries, representations of the cosmos were popular, but the reference to music in their imagery was limited. There were, reportedly, mechanical devices and elaborate paintings. Origen describes a picture of the cosmos in a Mithraic temple,[43] and John of Gaza (fifth century) provides an interesting description of such a painting, listing pagan symbols side by side with Christian signs.[44] Several interpretations have been proposed for his

[42] Roscher, *Lexikon der Mythologie*, "Orpheus," col. 1124. Tablets have been found in southern Italy, in Kroton, Thurioi, Petelia; *Hymni Orphici*, ed. A. Dieterich (1891); O. Kern, "Die Herkunft des orphischen Hymnen Buches," in *Graecia Halensis, Genethiakon Carl Robert zum 8. März* (1910), pp. 89ff.

[43] Origen, *Contra Celsum*; Bousset, "Die Himmelsreise der Seelen," *Archiv für Religionswissenschaft*, IV (1901), 163.

[44] R. Hinks, *Myth and Allegory in Ancient Art, Warburg Institute, Studien*, Vol. 6 (1939), p. 31, Pl. 2; P. Friedlaender, *Spätantiker Gemäldezyklus in Gaza, Studi e testi*, 89 (1939).

FIG. 27. Saint Michael holding a sign with the Thrice Holy; from the ninth-century mosaic in San Apollinare in Classe, Ravenna

FIG. 28. Reconstruction after the description by John of Gaza, showing figures of Greek mythology beside Christian symbols. The cosmos appears three times: on top a human male is crowned by a winged figure; at the bottom on the left an orb is carried by Atlas, supported by Sophia; at the bottom, at right, a cupola is supported by Iris. Inside this arch an orb with the Cross, beside it Gaea with two children and a winged figure *Karitas*

description (Fig. 28 shows one example). All of these suggestions include a kind of globe with the cross inside, and Atlas or Heracles carrying a second orb. Angels with wings are described as drawing a chariot. Leaving precise interpretation open to question, John of Gaza's description may nonetheless be cited as an example of the fusion of pagan and Christian figures and symbols in approximately the fifth century. However, representations of music and musicians, otherwise numerous in pagan work of the time, appear in pictures of the cosmos only in connection with dancing. Many ceiling paintings, including those in secular houses, were arranged in several layers, suggesting an allegory of the spheres in the cosmos, and frequently in one or more of these layers there are figures of dancers, as in Fig. 29. The dancers are youths or maidens,[45] who are often holding gar-

[45] N. Ponce, *Description des bains de Titus* (1786); Ponce, *Arabesques antiques* (1789); Ponce, *Collection des tableaux et arabesques trouvés à Rome* (1805).

lands or veils. Sometimes they alternate with kneeling and supporting figures, sometimes with winged and flying figures. Sometimes
they appear only in the corners of the painting. Sometimes they hold
musical instruments, and sometimes they form a circle. Scholars have
speculated as to the meaning of these figures.[46] A likely possibility is
that they are wingless descendants of the sirens, figures intended to

[46] Lehmann, "The Dome of Heaven."

FIG. 29. Drawing after the original ceiling painting in Hadrian's villa at
Tivoli; second century. In the center, the orb of the cosmos is supported by
four Atlantes; near the outer frame, maidens, holding ribbons or garlands, dance
a round

symbolize by their dancing the musical motion of the spheres, and that they are, hence, forebears of the angel musicians. They are not assigned to any particular stratum, as it were, to the highest sphere or the center. This indicates that, in the Augustan period, Elysium was not yet recognized as part of the highest heaven, as was later to become the case.

Besides the above type of example, there appear to be only one or two other works expressing a relation between the cosmos and music. A mosaic floor in Algeria shows the figure of a maiden, supposedly the personification of one of the seasons, holding an instrument similar to the mandolin—an instrument with four strings for plucking, a long neck, and a comparatively small body, a form usual in Roman works.[47] As there is no other known representation of a season with a musical instrument, this may well be a casual motif. The other instance is a mosaic floor, now in the Museum of Piacenza,[48] which shows a lyre in the center, with an outer circle of eight flying swans (Fig. 30). This floor has been construed as a representation of the constellation Lyra, but it might be better understood as representing, with the lyre, the music of the spheres. The eight swans might be related to eight of the Muses or sirens, hence to the spheres; or they may be the sacred swans of Apollo. In Plato's *Phaedo*, Socrates tells the legend of these swans:[49] they start to sing before their death to express their joy at being released from their bodily prison and allowed to enter heaven.

The lyre ultimately became a popular symbol of the harmony of the cosmos. It appears in the hands of the Muses, or Eros, or Orpheus; when it appears in the hands of Christ, as it did frequently, the relation of the symbols is reversed. The lyre becomes the means for harmonizing the cosmos, and the figure that governs the cosmos rules it by playing the seven strings of the lyre, harmonizing the seven spheres.[50] (The relation of Orpheus with the lyre to the figure

---

[47] *Inventaire des mosaïques, Gaule* (Paris, 1909–11), Fig. 203.

[48] M. E. Blacke, *The Pavements of the Roman Buildings of the Republic and Early Empire*, Mem. of the Am. Academy in Rome, VIII (1930), 116, Pl. 38.

[49] Plato, *Phaidon*, in Loeb Classics, I, 295.

[50] This idea will be elaborated in the second part of this book; it occurs in Synesius, *De somniis*, cap. 3 (quoted in Duhem, *Le système du monde*, IV, 359); Athanasius, *Contra Helenos*, cap. 38, *Patrol gr.* 25; Censorinus, *De die natali*, "Dorylaus scripsit esse mundum organum dei, alii addiderunt esse id heptachordon quia 7 sunt vagae stellae."

of Christ with the lyre has yet to be investigated. Possibly the figure of Orpheus playing the lyre or the kithara expressed the idea of immortality in the Orphic rites, and the figure of the risen Christ holding the lyre in the earliest catacomb paintings replaced Orpheus, the prophet or god of immortality.) The allegory of Christ governing the cosmos while playing on the celestial lyre became a favorite simile in the writings of the Church Fathers.[51] On a mosaic over the northern portal of San Marco, an inscription (from a later period, the twelfth century) relates the Evangelists to celestial music: "These four guard the harmony of the world, they sing and their song results in the harmony of the world." [52]

[51] An edition of Synesius's work was published in Paris in 1612; his major works are available as *Opera omnia*, ed. Krabinger (Landshut, 1850); see Heinisch, "Der Einfluss Philos"; for mention of the idea in the works of Clement, Sedulius, Prudentius, Alanus, Paulinus of Nola, see E. R. Curtius, *Europäische Literatur und lateinisches Mittelalter* (1948), p. 249; also mentioned by Proclus in *De sacrificio*, available in the volume collected by Marsilio Ficino, *Opus Procli . . .* Aldus, 1516, fol. 44 r°.

[52] Gayet, *L'art byzantin*, p. 21.

FIG. 30. Second-century Italian mosaic floor, showing the spheres of the cosmos; the swans and the kithara are both emblems of Apollo

V Tonal Theories of Music of the Spheres

THE IDEA OF MUSIC of the spheres was also the foundation for the semi-mythological theories of music that evolved in the early centuries of the Christian era and became one of the preoccupations of medieval writings on music. During the centuries preceding 1100, considerable intellectual energy was lavished on elaborating systems of musical scales and harmonics with reference to planetary orbits and mythical figures. It is, however, perhaps the measure of the complexity and abstract quality of this theorizing that its direct reflection in art was rare.

EARLY VARIANTS

The starting point for most theories was, again, Plato. In this instance, the basis was provided by his *Timaeus,* which expounded the mathematical ratios of the spheres and provided the following sequence of numbers: 1 2 3 4 9 8 27.[1] This series has aroused some puzzlement,[2] but becomes clear if it is separated into two orders:

$$1 < {2\text{-}4\text{-}8 \atop 3\text{-}9\text{-}27}$$

Starting from the number one, which belongs to both orders, we have the geometric progression of the numbers 2 and 3; and if these numbers are then connected, what we obtain are ratios of the musical intervals. These are 1:2 for the octave, 1:3 for the octave plus fifth, 2:3 for the fifth, 3:4 for the fourth, and 8:9 for the whole tone. Although the *Timaeus* does not refer directly to music, these are the intervals that appear in the music treatises of Greek authors insofar

---

[1] Plato, *Timaeus,* tr. R. G. Bury, in Loeb Classics, Vol. 7, II, *cap.* 3; A. E. Taylor, *A Commentary on Plato's Timaeus* (Oxford, 1928).

[2] J. Handschin, "Ein Mittelalterlicher Beitrag zur Lehre von der Sphaeren-musik," *Zeitschrift für Musikwissenschaft,* 9 (1927), p. 195.

as they have come down to us.[3] Further, the *Timaeus,* in excerpts and translations, was the most popular of Plato's dialogues from the early Middle Ages to the Renaissance,[4] and is a legitimate ancestor of the medieval treatises.

A number of early theories arose out of the difficulty of reconciling the *Timaeus* ratios with the *Republic's* vision of the spheres. The solutions were various and, as may readily be understood, arbitrary. There were three predominant variants. One endeavored to adapt the diatonic scale, the second the chromatic system, the third a selection of intervals, to the ratios of the planets. The theory of Greek music was based on the tetrachord, that is, a group of four tones.[5] These tetrachords were composed of the intervals of two whole tones and one half-tone. If the half-tone was at the end, the tetrachord was called diatonic; if the half-tone was in the middle, chromatic. The octave or scale was composed of two tetrachords. If these in turn were composed so that the middle tone was identical to both tetrachords, such as

f g a b
c d e f

the system was called connected, *synemenon.* If the tetrachords did not overlap, the system was called separated, or *diazeugmenon.* The Greek system of tones comprised two octaves and had a fixed name for each tone, unlike our method of repeating the names or letters after one octave.

Before considering detailed examples of the musical theories of the spheres, it is well to touch on one related problem. This concerns the qualification of "high" and "low" which we are accustomed to apply

---

[3] M. Meibom, *Antiquae Musicae Auctores Septem* (1652); C. E. Ruelle, *Collection des auteurs grecs relatifs à la musique* (1895).

[4] B. W. Switalski, "Des Chalcidius Kommentar zu Plato's Timaeus," *Beiträge zur Geschichte der Philosophie des Mittelalters,* III, 6 (1900), 5, 60; M. Baumgartner, "Die Philosophie des Alanus de Insulis," *Beiträge zur Geschichte der Philosophie des Mittelalters,* II, 4 (1896), 69, school of Chartres; E. Gilson, *La philosophie du moyen-âge* (1947), pp. 258ff.; Gilson, "La cosmogonie de Bernardus Silvestris," *Archives de l'histoire doctrinale . . . du moyen-âge,* Vol. 13 (1928), p. 7; for the commentary on *Timaeus* by William of Conches, see P. Duhem, *Le système du monde* (Paris, 1917), III, 44; and H. Liebeschütz, "Fulgentius Metaforalis," *Warburg Institut, Studien,* Vol. 4 (1926); for Jerome, see E. R. Curtius, *Europäische Literatur und lateinisches Mittelalter* (1948), pp. 445ff.

[5] G. Reese, *Music in the Middle Ages* (1940), chap. 1–2.

to musical tones. Plato [6] knew that the place of a tone in the system depended on the length of the string of the kithara. But he did not call one tone "longer" and another "shorter," because these terms were used for the rhythmic qualities of sound. He related the pitch of a sound to a faster or slower motion of the sound. The faster the motion, the shriller the tone. The words Plato used to characterize pitch are ὀξύς and βάρος. They can be translated in various ways: the faster sounds as shrill, harsh; the "middle" sounds as even, smooth (ὅμοιος); and the slow sounds as soft, deep. Plato objected to their designation as "below" or "above" on grounds that this corresponded to heavy (βάρος) and sharp (ὀξύς). In many translations, however, Plato's terms are rendered throughout as "high" and "low," the terms used today. This leads to confusion because Plato held the sounds with the fastest motion to be "low" and the sounds with the slowest motion to be "high," the reverse of modern usage, and he did so because for him the celestial bodies with the shortest orbits, e.g., the moon, corresponded to the fast motion. Today the sound wave is decisive, but it was not so for Plato.

Early treatises on the theory of corresponding spheres and musical intervals listed the spheres under the names of the ruling deities and expressed the intervals with the Greek names of the tones. Hypothetically, the original order is supposed to have been: [7]

Phaion	Kronos	Hypate	E
Phaeton	Zeus	Parhypate	f
Pyroeis	Ares	Hypermese	g
Stilbon	Mercury	Mese	a
Phosphoros	Venus	Paramese	b
Helios	Sun	Paranete	c
Selene	Moon	Nete	d

The first column gives the older version of the names of the gods, the second the more modern name, the third the names of the tones, and the last column, which is added here, gives a modern designation of the tones. This system is found in Nikomachus (second cen-

[6] Plato, *Timaeus*, in Loeb Classics, Vol. 7, II, *cap.* 3.
[7] C. Jan, "Die Harmonie der Sphaeren," *Philologus*, 52 (1894), pp. 13ff.

tury) and was adopted by Boethius.[8] The scale is diatonic and the "lowest" tone corresponds to the highest or outermost sphere.

Alexander of Ephesos (second century),[9] on the other hand, used the chromatic scale and reversed the order, so that the highest sphere corresponds to the "highest" tone:

Fixed stars	d
Saturn	d flat
Jupiter	c
Mars	b flat
Sun	a
Venus	g flat
Mercury	f
Moon	e
Earth	D

The same scale, but in opposite order, was used by Censorinus (third century),[10] who expounded his theory by naming the intervals rather than citing the names of the notes.

A third theory did not use a continuous scale, but went back to the ratios given in Plato's *Timaeus* for a selection of notes. This appears in several manuscripts attributed to Ptolemaeus,[11] and the system may have been elaborated in the school at Alexandria. It was supplemented later, notably in the fourteenth century, by Nikephoros Gre-

---

[8] *Ibid.*; Nikomachus, in Ruelle, *Collection des auteurs grecs*; Baeumker, *Das pseudo-hermetische Buch der 24 Meister, Liber XXIV philosophorum*; R. Bragard, "Boetius' *De Musica*," *Speculum*, IV (1929).

[9] Jan, "Die Harmonie der Sphaeren," where he quotes Alexander of Ephesus and Adrast, *Astronomia*; Achilles Tatios commentary to Theon's *Astronomia* and Aratos's *Phaenomena*; *Theon of Smyrna* (fl. second century), Liber de *Astronomia*, with Latin translation by Th. H. Martin (1849).

[10] Censorinus, *De die natali, cap.* 13; for editions see *Katalog der Musik Bibliothek Paul Hirsch* (1928), I, No. 112–13; A. v. Thimus, *Die harmonikale Symbolik des Altertums* (1868), p. 76.

[11] Two manuscripts ascribed by Jan, in "Die Harmonie der Sphaeren," to Ptolemaeus are Naples, MS. III, c. 2 Chart. 4° (cat. Cyrilli II, p. 342) and MS. III, *c.* 3 Chart. 8° (cat. Cyrilli II, p. 344), both from the sixteenth century.

goras [12] (who, in his turn, was attacked by the monk Barlaam). The
system reads:

Fixed stars	36	b′	
			9/8
Saturn	32	a′	
			4/3
Jupiter	24	e′	
Mars	21	d′	(4/3)
Sun	18	b	
			9/8
Venus	16	a	
			4/3
Mercury	12	e	
			4/3
Moon	9	B	
			9/8
Earth	8	A	

Thus the system is composed of the intervals of fourths and whole
tones, with the ratios of 4/3 and 9/8, and the nearest or lowest
sphere corresponds to the lowest tone. The compass of the sounds is
here a double octave, which was the compass of Greek music.

Such are the three basic approaches to a theoretical concept of the
music of the spheres; that is, we have either the diatonic or the
chromatic scale, or we have selected intervals forming a double octave. The scales or orders corresponding to the spheres are either
such that the "lowest" tone, *Proslambanomenos*, corresponds to the
earth or the moon, or to the opposite pole, the fixed stars. It has not
yet been possible to determine exactly when Plato's order was reversed, but this seems to have been brought about by scholars of the
Alexandrian school. The three different systems reflect approaches to
the problem from three different points of view: acoustics, astronomy, and astrology. Alexander of Ephesos wrote on music and math-
ematics; Censorinus on astrology, Ptolemaeus on astronomy.[13]

The parallel of spheres to tones was so popular that it was used as
the image of harmony by non-technical writers, such as Cicero,[14]
among others. The description of music of the spheres in his *Somnium Scipionis* was especially influential; for example, similar de-

[12] *Nikephoros Gregoras*, ed. Wallis, the commentary to *Ptolemaeus* by Barlaam,
see Jan, "Die Harmonie der Sphaeren," and Handschin, "Ein Mittelalterlicher
Beitrag," pp. 200–203.

[13] See n. 9 above.

[14] Cicero, *Somnium Scripionis*, in *Aurelii Macrobii . . . opera . . . quae
extant omnis* (Biponti, 1788).

scriptions can be found in two passages by Marius Victorinus.[15] His version of the cosmos had nine spheres. The outermost sphere was the place of the fixed stars and was moved by the highest deity. Its movement was fastest and corresponded to the highest pitch. After that, the spheres of the seven planets followed in graduated order down to the moon, which had the lowest pitch. The earth was immobile and silent. Cicero's account contains discrepancies, but these need not be discussed here.

Two commentators on the *Somnium*, who wrote about 400, also touched on the problem of music of the spheres, and their accounts diverge somewhat from Cicero's. Favonius Eulogius,[16] a pupil of Saint Augustine's, was even more inconsistent concerning order and numbers. He assumed eight spheres, which he graded like Censorinus, but had nine tones. At one point he gives the scale with diatonic intervals, and at another the double octave is cited as corresponding to a double cone of the spheres, with the sun in the middle of this double-cone structure. It appears probable that Censorinus was less concerned with explaining the exact ratios than with building an image, and an image that seems influenced by Plato's *Republic*. In any event, many of the earlier theories, that is, up to Boethius, had the sun correspond to the middle tone of the system, the Mese or A. The other commentator on the *Somnium*, Macrobius,[17] adopted the double order of numbers from Plato's *Timaeus*, but hesitated to list the exact tones. In addition, he made one very informative remark, saying that he did not intend to consult all the current treatises on the subject, "quos quantum mea fert opinio, terminum habere non estimo" ("there are so many that I would never finish studying them").

MEDIEVAL THEORY

The third of the methods outlined above is the one most often referred to by the writers of the Middle Ages. By the sixth century, the direction of the scale was settled so that the outermost sphere of the

---

[15] A. Warburg, *Gesammelte Schriften* (1932), p. 413; E. Panofsky, "Hercules am Scheidewege," *Warburg Institute, Studien,* Vol. 18 (1930), pp. 12ff.; see also n. 25 below.

[16] See Handschin, "Ein Mittelalterlicher Beitrag."

[17] Macrobius, *Opera;* Macrobius, *Conviviorum primi diei Saturnaliorum,* ed. Eyssenhardt (1868), II, 3, 11; T. Whittaker, *Macrobius* (1923).

fixed stars corresponded to the "highest" tone, although the theory which followed the opposite direction was still known as late as the tenth century.[18]

The medieval writers distinguished three kinds of music, *musica mundana, musica humana,* and *musica instrumentalis,* of which only the latter refers to what we regard as music today. In these treatises, the music of the spheres is the subject of the sections on *musica mundana,* while *musica humana* refers to the connection or correspondence between the music of the spheres and the human reactions to music.[19]

Medieval treatises on music typically merged various traditions and sources. Few were as independent as Grocheo [20] (*ca.* 1300). Regino of Prüm,[21] an encyclopedic author who wrote about the year 900, provided a detailed, though not very systematic, explanation of *musica mundana* in the first chapter of his *Letter on Harmony,* of which excerpts are translated in Appendix I. He started with a parallelism of spheres and intervals based on the diatonic scale, then supplemented it from Martianus's *De Nuptiis,* deducing a rather chromatic version. He then proceeded to connect the spheres of the planets, following Boethius, with the Greek names of the tones. In this context, the sun has the Mese, the middle tone. Later, he turned to the different order expounded by Cicero and Macrobius, where Mese is held by the sphere of the fixed stars. Regino's chapter fused the chief methods and sources important in the development of concepts of music of the spheres, citing many of the precursors mentioned above, and quoting Virgil and Cassiodorus.[22] When dis-

[18] M. Gerbert, *Scriptores ecclesiastici de Musica,* I (1784), 230ff.; *Epistula de Harmonica Institutione:* the *Tonale* by Regino, in E. de Coussemaker, *Scriptores de Musica,* II (1867), xiiff.; a detailed analysis of most of the treatises regarding the problem of musician angels and touching also on the theory of the music of the spheres may be found in R. Hammerstein, *Die Musik der Engel* (1962), 122–144.

[19] W. Grossmann, *Die einleitenden Kapitel des Speculum Musicae von Johannes de Muris* (1924); the *Speculum* is today ascribed to Jacques de Liège; Coussemaker, *Scriptores de Musica.*

[20] Johannes de Grocheo, *Musiktraktat,* ed. E. Rohloff (*Media Latinitas Musica,* II), 1943.

[21] Gerbert, *Scriptores ecclesiastici de Musica,* I, 230ff.

[22] Virgil, *Aeneid,* VI, 626, mentioned by Isidore of Seville in his *Sententiae de musica,* and in Notker's *De musica,* see Gerbert, *Scriptores ecclesiastici de Musica,* I, 23, 96; A. Hughes, "Theoretical Writers on Music up to 1400," *Oxford History of Music* (1929), p. 117.

cussing the "proportions," the intervals, so important for medieval writers on the theory of music,[23] he repeated Martianus's theory concerning the relation of the nine Muses to the nine spheres, a topic which will be dealt with presently; he mentioned Martianus's attempts to adapt the nine Muses to eight, the compass of the octave, as well as to seven, the number of tones in the scale. Finally, Regino offered an interpretation of the myth of Orpheus and Euridice which shows how seriously he took the reality of the music of the spheres. By his account, Orpheus failed in his attempt to free Euridice from Hades because he was only a kithara player and did not know the theory of music, which would have enabled him to cope with the cosmic powers. This remark, which seems preposterous to the modern reader, refers to the distinction then drawn between the *musicus,* the musician versed in theory, as opposed to the practical musician, the *cantor,*[24] who was less highly esteemed.

The detailed theory of the musical structure of the cosmos was also expounded in several didactic poems. One such is a ninth-century poem on the liberal arts, which has survived in fragmentary form.[25] As far as one can tell from extant portions, its section on music deals with *musica humana.* However, in the section on Arithmetica, the numbers are listed with their allegorical counterparts. To cite the portions relevant to music of the spheres:

> Three is the perfect number, the Holy Trinity.
> In it several intervals originate.
> Three is the root of music.
> Three consonances are contained in music.
> Three are the aspects of time: present, future, and past. . . .
>
> Six, so many tones has harmony.
> From it the basic intervals originate:
> 6:12 is the *duplex symphonia* (octave);
> 6:9 is called *sesquialtera* (fifth);
> 6:8 is called *diatesseron* (fourth). . . .

[23] R. A. Mynors, *Cassiodori Institutiones LVI* (1937).

[24] Curtius, *Europäische Literatur,* p. 46; this differentiation is already mentioned in the seventh century by Isidor; W. Gurlitt, "Zur Bedeutungsgeschichte von musicus und cantor bei Isidor von Sevilla," *Abhandlungen der Mainzer Akad. d. Wiss, geistes- und sozial-wissensch. Kl.* (1950), p. 7.

[25] *Monumenta Germaniae, Poetae Latini aevi Carolini,* ed. L. Trauke, IV, 249, Anonymus, Cod. Berenensis CCCLVIII, *De Arithmetica,* followed by *De Musica, De Rhetorica,* etc.

Dealing with the number seven, the author lists the planets.

> Nine. The number nine is called the perfect
> one. It is called perfect because through
> its formulas the triads emerge. . . . It forms
> the harmony of the Tone 8:9. Also the nine
> musical spheres which are thought to surround
> the world have attracted the nine Muses. As
> many are the orders of the angels, and the
> noble prophets are said to have as many stones.

Thus the Muses, the spheres, and the orders of the angels and music are explicitly related to each other here.

In church hymns dealing with the sounding cosmos the emphasis was laid on concepts of Christian ideology; the spheres or heavens correspond to the virtues or the angelic orders. There are several hymns which mention the nine orders of angels,[26] and from the ninth century on, these angel choirs are incorporated in the music of the cosmos. There are two such hymns by John Duns Scotus, already mentioned as a commentator on Dionysius's *Hierarchy*.[27] In one, Scotus counts eight spheres and seven intervals between them. Heaven, the eighth and highest sphere governs the cosmic harmony, here ruled by Urania, as in Martianus's work. The hymn ends with *Extremis Rex Mundi*, the highest king of the world, playing on his

---

[26] *Monumenta Germaniae. Poetae latini aevi Carolini*, III, 532;

> Novem hinc perfectus cernitur.
> Idem vocatur inde sed perfectior.
> Quod fit suis triade ducta formulis
> Primique versus prodit iste terminum
> Censetur armonie sed pars ultima.
> Octa de collata novem nam fit tonus.
> Hinc et novem Musas vocarunt musici.
> Spere (sphere) que mundum tot feruntur cingere
> Sic angelorum tot habentur ordines. . . .

Johannes Scotus, *De divisione naturae, Patrol. lat.* 122, 715, 718, 722; *Analecta hymnica*, Vol. 7. *Prosarum Lemovicense* . . . (1889), No. 1, p. 32, from MSS. St. Martial; H. Spanke, *Beziehungen zwischen romanischer und mittelalterlicher Lyrik* (1936); "Aus der Formengeschichte des mittelalterlichen Liedes," *Geistige Arbeit* (1938); Curtius, *Europäische Literatur*, p. 242.

[27] See Chapter III, n. 44.

flute, organizing the harmony of the cosmos. In his work *De divi-sione naturae,* Scotus also mentions facts similar to those described by Regino.[28]

A contemporary of Scotus, one Lios Monocus,[29] probably also of British origin, compares the seven steps of the heavenly court to seven virtues. He lists two somewhat different orders of virtues. (The first: *sanctificatio, dilectio* [*Christi*], *operatio, copia crucis, clementia, discussio veri, pietas;* the second: *pavor domini, Christi dilectio, operatio, delectio* [?], *remissio, conversio, copia crucis.*)

Rathbod (d. 917), to whom Regino's letter on harmony was dedi-cated, wrote a poem entitled "Carmen allegoricum de S. Switberto," [30] which describes how the saint saw heaven open and marveled at the music in the Empyreum. In this instance, the sound of the spheres was produced when one sphere crossed the axis of another. The outermost sphere sings the Nete, the highest note, as a glossary explains; the order of the spheres and their distances, expressed as musical intervals, are listed, and Switbert heard:

> Angelici coetus decies centena chororum
> milia simphoniis commodulando sacris
> Auribus in caelo semper felicibus audi,
> quorum ter sanctus sine fine ora sonant.

---

[28] Regino, in Gerbert, *Scriptores ecclesiastici de Musica,* i.

[29] So far virtually nothing is known about Lios Monocos, except that he is thought to have been English.

[30] *Monumenta Germaniae. Poetae latini aevi Carolini,* iii, 167, "Carmen al-legoricum de S. Switberto," by Rathbod, with glosses from the eleventh century:

> Nonne tuas modulis oblectat dulcibus aures
>   Orbibus aplanes obvius empyriis;
> Mundus ubi adversos cum praecipitatur in axes
>   Atque parallelis cursibus astra fremunt,
> Vera apud aethereos reboat tum musica cyclos
>   Omnicanens, numeris et comitata suis,
> Usque adeo crescens, ut plus quam nete resultet,
>   Ter quoque sive quater bisdiapason agat;
> Qui sonus humanos longo dyastemate sensus
>   Praeterit, at superis nobile chroma canit.
> Hic tibi suavisonum pangit, vir sancte, melodum,
>   Quod due tresque canunt, quattuor, octo, novem.

. . . .

> The angelic round of tens of hundreds of choirs,
>   thousands singing together in sacred harmonies,
> Hear them with happy ears,
>   the three-times Holy which they sound without end.

The thousands and hundreds of singers and the three-times Holy are ideas encountered earlier in the Talmudic and early Christian visions.

The authors of these poems were obviously familiar with the theories of the music of the spheres. It is the theory of selective intervals that is used most frequently and, though the exact theory is not usually explained, there is clear reference to the relation of the courses of the planets and the range and order of the corresponding sounds. It should, however, be noted that the hymns which mention the nine orders of angels assign no specific role to them in relation to the music of the spheres.[31]

There is one particularly interesting record of a hymn, "Naturalis concordia vocum cum planetis," [32] which combines all the different aspects noted above. Both the text and the music have survived; they were written, probably in the eleventh century, on the flyleaves preceding a manuscript of Boethius's *De Musica*. The text (see Appendix II), giving Cicero as its source, explains the music of the spheres. It begins by outlining the arrangement of the order, than goes on to list in detail the specific intervals, following the system of selected intervals. The compass of the sounds is said to be the double octave. It concludes with an enumeration of the objects related to the number seven, which is the nucleus of "almost everything."

The music of this hymn is set down in neumes on lines, of which one or two are scratched into the vellum so that the neumes can be transcribed. (It is the form of the neumes that suggests the eleventh century as the time when the tune was written.) The compass of the melody is a double octave, and the ductus follows exactly the intervals suggested for the distances of the several spheres. The whole inscription occupies two leaves, with the final six verses presented

---

[31] *Analecta hymnica*, Vol. 7; H. A. Daniel, *Thesaurus* (1855–56), Nos. 2–11; the relevant excerpts in O. Wulff, *Cherubim, Throne und Seraphim* (1904), p. 23; six orders are mentioned in a Gallican Mass published by F. J. Mone, *Lateinische Hymnen des Mittelalters*; the nine orders mentioned in the Mozarabic liturgy, see *Patrol. lat.* 35, 150, in the *Te Deum*, in antiphons to the Magnificat in the Roman Breviary, etc.

[32] Handschin, "Ein Mittelalterlicher Beitrag."

without music. On the righthand side of the second leaf, there is, additionally, a chart (Fig. 31), whose content is as follows:

DEUS

Seraphim	Nete yperboleion	(a′)
Cherubim	Paranete yperb(oleion)	(g′)
Tronos	Trite yperb(oleion)	(f′)
Dominatio	Nete diazeugmenon	(e′)
Principatus	Paranete diaz(eugmenon)	(d′)
Potestates	Trite diaz(eugmenon)	(c′)
Virtutes	Paramese	(b)

Abhinc supercelestis armonia

Caelum	Mese	(a)
Saturnus	Lychanos meson	(g)
Jupiter	Parypate m(eson)	(f)
Mars	Ypate m(eson)	(e)
Sol	Lychanos ypaton	(d)
Venus	Parypate yp(aton)	(c)
Mercurius	Ypate yp(aton)	(B)
Luna	Proslambanomenos	(A)
Terra	Silentium	

Thus, reading from the bottom upward, the order of the planets is listed on the left side, from earth to heaven, *caelum*. Above this there begins the supercelestial order of the seven higher classes of the angels. On the right is listed the system of the Greek scale for the double octave. The planets correspond to the lower octave, from A to a; the angel orders to the higher octave, from b to a′. The *mese* (a), the middle of the system, corresponds to heaven, on the border between the visible cosmos and the supernatural heaven. The melody is Gregorian in style, unusual in two respects: in the great compass of a double octave and in that no sections are repeated. Since there are not enough tones to accommodate them, the three lower orders of angels are omitted and not mentioned in the text.

Text, music, and chart combined give a very clear picture of the eleventh-century concept of the music of the spheres. Since it was placed before Boethius's treatise in the manuscript, it seems to have been added as an illustration of the theoretical discussions.

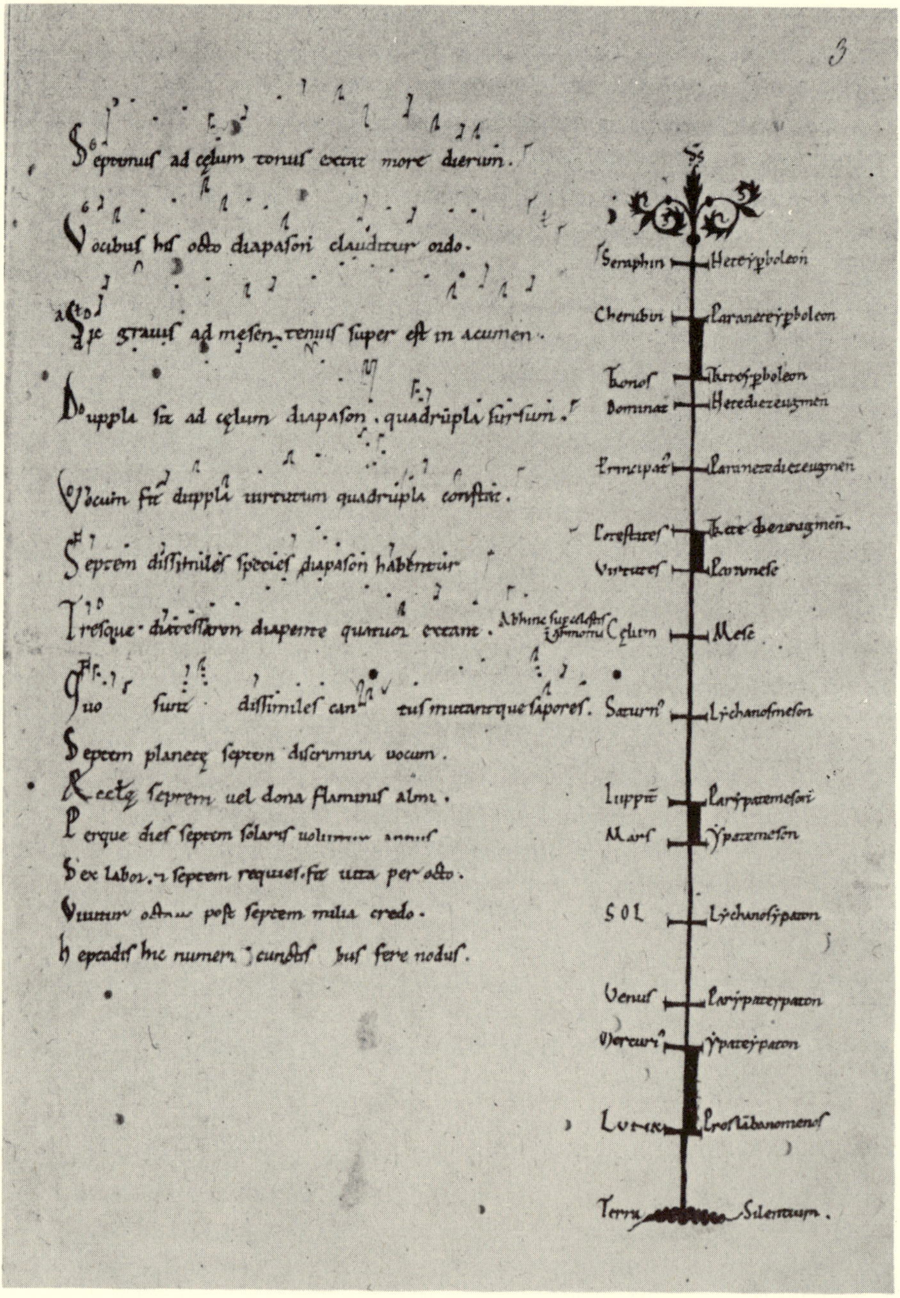

FIG. 31. Flyleaf of the eleventh-century manuscript of Boethius's *De Institutione Musicae*. On the left side appears the end of the hymn discussing the items related to the number seven

REFLECTIONS IN VISUAL ART

Illustrations of the theoretical aspect of the music of the spheres may also be found in pictorial works, though their occurrence seems to have been infrequent. There is, of course, the famous woodcut from Gafurius's *Theatrum instrumentorum,* discussed below, whose rich allegorical content is not surprising in a book on the theory of music of the Renaissance period. More noteworthy, perhaps, is a document from the early eleventh century in which the idea of perfect consonances corresponding to the Trinity is woven into an illumination of the Crucifixion (Fig. 32).[33] The illumination occupies a page in the Evangeliary of the Abbess Uta of Niedermünster, near Regensburg. The whole picture is set in a rectangular frame. The vertical stem of the crucifix divides it in the center from top to bottom. Two oval circles surround the upper and lower halves of the cross. In the upper oval there is Christ on the cross; in the lower, figures of Life and Death. The top corners of the frame show the sun and moon; the bottom corners contain a scene of nine figures, souls being resurrected, and the ripped curtain of the Temple. Halfway along the side borders of the frame there are figures representing Church and, probably, Synagogue. There are inscriptions around, on, and inside the frame referring to the two poles of Life and Death, Death and Resurrection. In the lower part of the illumination are two figures of life and death.

What is of special interest for our topic is that inside the upper oval, under the arms of the cross, there are four squares with inscriptions, two on each side, forming the diagram on page 86.

This is a symbolic diagram of the music of the spheres and the per-

---

[33] Also, one of the tituli from S. Emmeran at Regensburg, preserved in a manuscript at Linz, and in the *Wilheringer Codex* at Munich, begins: "Carmina vicena heroica decem sperarum inter chorum S. Dionysii et corpus ecclesiae semper bina unam speram concernencia;" the relics in the chapel were supposed to have belonged to Saint Dionysius; the ceiling was decorated with ten spheres; A. Endres, "Romanische Deckenmalereien in Regensburg und ihre tituli zu Emmeran in Regensburg," *Jahrbuch für christliche Kunst,* Vol. 15 (1902), pp. 205, 235, 275; the tituli are from before 1166, when the new cathedral was dedicated under Abbot Peringer; see *Chron. mon. Tegernsee,* in B. Pez, *Thesaurus Anectodorum novissimus,* (1721–23), Vol. III, Part III, 576; G. Swarzenski, *Die Regensburger Buchmalerei* (1901), II, 88ff.; *Das Evangeliar der Uta von Niedermünster,* Cod. lat. 13601. Cim. 54 of the Staats-Bibliothek at Munich; S. Kozaky, *Danse macabre* (1935–44), II, 79ff., Fig. 10.

FIG. 32. Illumination from the Uta Evangeliary, eleventh century

fect consonances. The letters on the squares have been solved as standing for *Mors, Mundus, Infernum,* and the last, which is illegible, might have been *Vita.* Under the squares, the Roman numerals IIII, VI, VIII, and XII stand for the ratios of the perfect consonances 1:2, 2:3, and 3:4, representing the octave, fifth, and fourth. On the curved lines connecting the numbers are inscriptions which name the respective intervals: *diapente* (fifth) and *diatesseron* (fourth), and *diapason symphoniarum* (octave). At this time, these three intervals alone were considered consonances and were used as a symbol of the Trinity.

Under the Roman numerals is written: *primus tetrag* [*onus*], *perfectus, primus cubus,* and *symphonicus.* The geometrical references to tetragon and cube are presumably due to the fact that the cube was considered a perfect form because, with its four angles on the six planes, eight corners, and twelve edges, it contains the numbers of the perfect ratios. The word *cubus* may also be construed as a wordplay or pun as the opposite of *incubus,* the *anticubus* or Satan. The diapason leads from Death to Hell, and from the earth (*mundus*) to the harmony of the spheres. The design thus represents the symbolic meaning of the musical intervals, used to enhance this representation of the Crucifixion by expressing the victory of Christ, the perfect consonance, over Satan, the *anticubus.*[34]

The names of the intervals are written in the form of arches, a form found in many later treatises on the musical intervals.[35] Similar *tituli* are described in Udeskalc's report on the decorations of the Church of Saint Afra in Augsburg.[36]

[34] In the circumscribed tituli the relationship is further elaborated, but the text is so cryptic that an exact translation is impossible:

Christus fidem solidans	vincens [anti] tetragonum
Christ faith founding	vanquished Satan
Festa triumphorum	dant celica iubilarum
Feasts triumphal	give heaven jubilation
Ritmus grammarum	servit organa symphoniarum
Rhythm and grammar	serves the works of the musical intervals
Forcior occisus [?]	vicit haec forcia [?] Christus
Stronger than death	Christ vanquished

[35] E.g., in the *Tractatus de musica* by Jerome de Moravia, Coussemaker, *Scriptores de Musica,* I, 20; *Aribonis Scholastici Musica,* Gerbert, *Scriptores ecclesiastici de Musica,* II, 205, in the treatises by Gafori, Fludd, *et al.*

[36] Endres, "Romanische Deckenmalereien."

However, as stated earlier, explicit representation of the theory of music of the spheres in the visual arts seems to have been rare. Perhaps the infrequency of illustration is due to the fact that the medieval preoccupation with the technicalities of *musica mundana* did not prove an enduring field of intellectual endeavor. By the fifteenth century, the whole approach to writing about music had changed. In place of elaborate systems for integrating the orders of angels into a musical structure of the classical spheres, music theory concentrated on *musica instrumentalis* and the problems of the new polyphony.

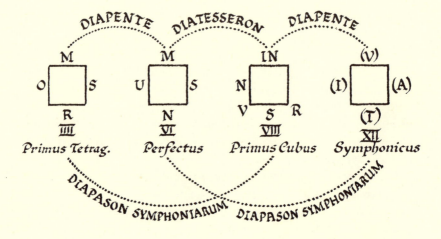

VI

The Emergence
of Celestial Musicians in
Christian Iconography

THE EARLIEST APPEARANCE of celestial musicians in Christian iconography seems to have evolved, paradoxically, neither from the Christian nor from the Graeco-Roman pagan tradition, but as a result of Arab influence, stemming originally from the Near East. Despite the frequent references in medieval poems and hymns to angels in connection with music of the spheres, not to mention many Biblical references to angels in connection with music, the only reflection of this in the visual arts was the occasional representation of angels carrying tablets inscribed with the Thrice Holy.

The earliest pictures of angels with musical instruments are found in the Beatus manuscripts of Revelation, inscribed as having been illustrated by "Saracens." [1] The oldest of the Beatus manuscripts date from the tenth century, but in these angels were the exception rather than the rule. In the new iconography that seems to have originated with the Beatus illuminations, the most prevalent musician figures initially were not angels but the twenty-four Elders of Revelation, and it is with them that this chapter must largely be concerned.

THE BEATUS MANUSCRIPTS

Beatus, a bishop of Libena (Spain) in the seventh century, wrote a commentary on Revelation which has survived in twenty-seven manuscripts. In most cases, the illuminations show a distinctive iconology, and most of them also adhere to a distinctive style. [2] Ten of the manuscripts are from the tenth century; three are explicitly so dated. Four are from the eleventh century, and five from the twelfth; the others were done somewhat later. A number of them have extensive colophons giving information about the illuminators and the time when the commentaries were written. Among the paint-

---

[1] W. Neuss, *Die Apokalypse des hl. Johannes in der altspanischen und altchristlichen Bibelillustration* (Münster, 1931); M. Churruca, *Influjo oriental en los temas iconograficas de la miniatura española* (Madrid, 1939).

[2] Neuss, *Die Apokalypse*, p. 5; Churruca, *Influjo oriental*.

ers, some characterize themselves as "Saracens," a term identical with
what we would call Moors or Arabs and designating the people who
ruled southern Spain from 711 until 1492. (Other illuminators give
their name as Majus or Maius, and it is possible that this means
Persian). [3] There is ample evidence that these Saracens came originally from the Orient, from the Near East, via North Africa.[4] The
connection is made more probable by the fact that Beatus used as
sources for his commentaries the writings of North African Church
Fathers.

In addition to the Beatus manuscripts, there are a few other traces
of Arab influence in depicting musicians. One example is the ceiling
of the Cappella Palatina at Palermo, from the twelfth century (Fig.

[3] "Majus" or "Magus" may be a family name or may mean "Persian."

[4] G. Marçais, "Les figures d'hommes et de bêtes dans les bois sculptés d'époque
fatimite," Institut français d'archéologie orientale, *Mémoires*, Vol. 8, III (1940),
242.

FIG. 33. Twelfth-century ceiling painting in the Cappella Palatina, Palermo,
showing Oriental court musicians

FIG. 34. Busts of musician angels; detail from the ceiling painting in the aisle of the Cappella Palatina, Palermo. INSTRUMENTS: lutes

33). It has a border of Arabic script, and one figure, that of a dancing woman, is identical with a fresco in Samara.[5] Most of the musicians on the ceiling appear in scenes of secular festivities, reflections of life at Oriental courts. However, there are also musician angels, busts with halos, some crowning the columns in the pattern, some at the feet of the columns; some holding chalices with the water of life, and some playing on "lutes" (Fig. 34).

The Beatus manuscripts are worth discussing in detail, since they are an abundant and significant source of musician figures. The text of Revelation mentions five major groups as singing and making music: the four beasts, the seven spirits, the twenty-four Elders, the hundred and forty-four blessed, and, finally, the multitude of ten thousand times ten thousand angels. Their instruments are said to be harps. They are mentioned in Revelation 4, the vision of the Lord, Revelation 5, the vision of the Lamb, Revelation 7, the adoration of the Lord and of the Lamb, Revelation 14, the Lamb standing on Mount Zion. Various of the manuscripts show angel musicians not only in these contexts but also in other illuminations—in the introductory pictures and on the general frontispiece—as well as angels without music in the map of heaven and in the picture of the Heavenly Jerusalem (Rev. 21:22.) Angels do not, however, appear as musicians in all the manuscripts. They usually have halos; they have one, two, or three wings, or none at all, but are designated as angels

[5] E. Herzfeld, *Die Malereien von Samara* (Berlin, 1927), Vol. 3, *Ausgrabungen*, Pl. II.

by the text. It may be noted that this differs from the official tradition whereby angels are represented with two, four, or six wings.

Of the groups mentioned as singing and playing in Revelation, the four beasts are represented either by the symbols of the Evangelists or as cherubim, that is, as figures of angels with six wings. Sometimes "cherub" is inscribed.[6] The seven spirits are generally shown as angels with two wings. The Elders, said to wear their crowns, are represented as kings. In some earlier manuscripts of Revelation not related to the Beatus group, they are shown waving their crowns, about to throw them down in token of adoration.[7] In several of the Beatus manuscripts, Revelation is followed by the Book of Daniel, in which musicians appear in the illuminations showing the adoration of the idol of Nebuchadnezzar.[8] These figures are similar to the Elders and the seven spirits, except that they do not have halos and they play on different kinds of instruments.[9] In most of the Beatus manuscripts, all members of a group play or carry an identical kind of instrument. It is only in the MS. Morgan 429 and in the Berlin MS. (which is in the Carolingian rather than the Catalan style), and once in the British Museum manuscript, that the figures have several kinds of instruments in scenes where they are supposed to play simultaneously.[10]

There are usually three kinds of instruments depicted, all stringed. The most common is a plucked instrument which looks like a kind of lute with three strings.[11] An exact definition is not possible because

---

[6] Thus in *Cod. Albeldense* (976) and *Cod. Emilianense* (992), both in the Escorial; J. Pijoan, *Summa Artis*, VIII (Madrid, 1942), Figs. 733–34; A. Tea, *La Basilica di Santa Maria Antiqua* (1937), p. 181.

[7] Munich, *Codex Aureus*, s. H. Ehl, *Die Buchmalerei des frühen Mittelalters* (Berlin, 1925), Pl. 7; T. Frimmel, *Die Apokalypse in den Bilderhandschriften des Mittelalters* (Vienna, 1885); see also Dürer's *Apokalypse*.

[8] W. Neuss, *Die katalanische Bibelillustration* (1922), p. 89, Pl. 32; W. Neuss, *Die Apokalypse des hl. Johannes* (Münster, 1931), Fig. 100, from the Roda Bible, Bibliothèque Nationale, Paris, MS. lat. 6.

[9] Neuss, *Die Apokalypse*, from the Apokalypse at Seo de Urgel, fol. 213b.

[10] *Ibid.*, I, 252, Fig. 262, from the MS. Berlin, Staats-Bibliothek MS. theol. lat. 561, fol. 77, *Lord in Glory* with eight Elders, and *The Lamb on Mount Zion*; G. King, "Divagations on the Beatus," *Art Studies*, Vol. 8, No. 1 (1930).

[11] F. W. Galpin, *A Textbook of European Musical Instruments* (1937); for wind instruments, see E. Buhle, *Die musikalischen Instrumente in den Miniaturen des frühen Mittelalters* (1903); A. Blasquez, "Los manuscritos de los comentarios al Apocalipsis de San Juan por S. Beato de Libeana," *Revista de Archivos . . .* , XIV (1906), 257ff.; for the lute, K. Geiringer, "Vorgeschichte

FIG. 35. Adoration of the Lamb; illumination from the tenth-century manuscript, Divagations on the Apocalypse, by Beatus di Libiena. Ms. Morgan 644. INSTRUMENTS: long-necked lutes with plectrum

---

der Europäischen Laute," *Zeitschrift fur Musikwissenschaft*, x (1928), 560ff.; F. Saxl, "Beiträge zur Geschichte der Planetendarstellungen," *Islam*, III (1912), 162, Fig. 6, Venus with a lute, from *Cod. Monac. arab.* 464, Staats-Bibliothek, Munich.

the instruments are shown directly from the front, so that the shape of the sound box cannot be recognized. But it is possible to see that one has a curved soundboard and a long neck which usually looks straight. Perhaps it is drawn to look straight so that one might see the three pegs on a crossbar on top of the neck, which would be hidden by the body if the neck were represented bent backward. The finger which plucks the string is often quite elongated, a feature which might suggest the use of a plectrum; but fingers are often elongated in other scenes where a pointing gesture is emphasized. The soundboard generally has an almond shape, but is sometimes indented in a way resembling the viol form, and different forms of sound boxes for the lute-like instrument sometimes appear within one and the same illumination.[12] When there is a bow, it may be strongly curved or it may be almost flat like a modern bow. The way of playing is often depicted accurately and realistically, but sometimes the illuminator does not seem to have understood the technique, and the Elders swing their instruments about like clubs.

The arrangement of the figures in the Adoration of the Lamb is most often in the form of a circle (Fig. 35, though this is not always the case). In the scene of the *Agnus in monte* (Figs. 36, 37), the Elders are usually standing in rows. Their number varies greatly. Sometimes there are only two, sometimes all twenty-four. The arrangement is not always symmetrical, especially if the illumination is spread over two pages.

The musicians in most of the illuminations stand while playing. There is, however, one notable exception in the British Museum's eleventh-century Beatus manuscript, in the *Agnus in monte* illumination (Fig. 38). This shows five musicians on each side of the mountain, all playing fiddles. The position of their hands shows clearly that the illuminator was acquainted with the playing technique, and the positions of their legs and feet indicate beyond doubt that they are dancing. If it were not certain, on the basis of the text, that these figures represent Elders or the blessed in heaven, one would assume from their appearance that they were *jongleurs,* or musicians of an Oriental court. This is not surprising in view of the origins of the Beatus manuscripts and the influence on their style and iconography

[12] The small drum in the form of an hourglass and cymbals occur in the scene of the Adoration of the Idol in the MSS. Madrid, B.V.B. 31, from the cathedrals of Urgel and Valladolid.

FIG. 36. The Lamb on Mount Zion; illumination from a tenth-century manuscript, Divagations on the Apocalypse, by Beatus di Libiena. Ms. Morgan 644. INSTRUMENTS: long-necked oval fiddle

FIG. 37. The Lamb on Mount Zion; illumination from a tenth-century manuscript, Divagations on the Apocalypse. Ms. Morgan 429. INSTRUMENTS: plucked
and bowed rebecs, harp, lute, and cymbals

FIG. 38. (OPPOSITE PAGE) The Lamb on Mount Zion; illumination from an eleventh-century manuscript, Divagations on the Apocalypse. Brit. Museum Ms. 11695. INSTRUMENTS: long-necked, oval fiddles

of Arab illuminators, who evidently imagined the heavenly adoration as a princely feast with music and dance.[13]

It would be difficult to overstate the significance of the Beatus manuscripts for musical iconology. They represent, if they did not indeed directly cause, the development of a whole new tradition. It is noteworthy that earlier or contemporary illuminations of *Revelation* never showed figures of musicians, despite the ample justification for doing so offered by the book's text. Take, for example, the ninth- and tenth-century miniatures of the Adoration of the Lamb. In the first, from the *Codex Aureus* of Regensburg,[14] the Elders are shown rising from their thrones to throw down their crowns in token of adoration. In another, from a manuscript of the Reichenau school,[15] the adoration is presented in two layers, with the adorants in both layers forming two groups, men on the left, women on the right. In each top group, one figure holds a crozier; in each bottom group, one figure swings a censer. Lastly, there is an illumination of the same subject in the Carolingian style.[16] The lower part of the picture represents a large building, a Temple or Ecclesia, with four columns. Above each column there is an emblem of an Evangelist in a circle; and higher in the clouds, there are two groups of figures with halos, making adoring gestures, very much resembling those in the mosaic of Santa Maria Antiqua. Yet, there is no suggestion of music in any of these examples from outside the Beatus tradition.

The Beatus musicians seem to have been highly influential models even in matters of detail. For example, so striking an iconological

---

[13] E. Faral, *Les Jongleurs en France* (Paris, 1910); M. Pidal, *Poesia juglaresca* (Madrid, 1924); Fr. Anton y Casaseca, *Las influencias hispano-arabes en el arte occidentale de los siglos XI y XII* (1926).

[14] Munich MS. lat. 14000, ed. G. Leidinger; A. Goldschmidt, *German Illuminations*, i (1932); Ehl, *Die Buchmalerei*, Fig. 7.

[15] This MS. is erroneously cited as being in the Dombibliothek Cologne (No. 218) by W. Gernsheim, *Die Buchmalerei der Reichenau* (1924), p. 75, and by Ehl in *Die Buchmalerei*, Pl. 17. Dr. Peter Bloch and Dr. E. Reiff of the Rheinische Bildarchiv kindly informed me that the MS. is at Hildesheim MS. U. I, 19, a lectionary, and is identical with the MS. Beverina 688, mentioned by Buhle, *Die musikalischen Instrumente*; see also St. Beissel, "Geschichte der Evangelienbücher in der ersten Hälfte des Mittelalters," *Stimmen aus Maria Laach*, Vol. 23, Heft 92/93 (1906), p. 139; W. Vöge, *Eine deutsche Malerschule* (1891).

[16] Goldschmidt, *German Illuminations*, i, Pl. 32, frontispiece of the Gospel of Saint Medard de Soissons, 827, Bibliothèque Nationale, Paris, MS. lat. 8850.

feature as the postures of the Elders on the portal at Moissac (Fig. 39) seems to have been inspired by a Beatus illumination: Moissac's Elders, twenty-four kings, are seated, but the position of their legs reminds us of the dancers in the British Museum's manuscript. Another apparent influence of the Beatus musicians is the prevalence of the "lute" as the instrument for angels. Traditionally, the lute was a symbol of Venus; thus it appeared in Gardens of Love and as an emblem of Luxuria.[17] How it could have become a favorite instrument for angels and *putti* is inexplicable without reference to the Beatus tradition.

One further point worth noting is that with these dancing Elders, the dancing figures who moved the spheres in the works of antiquity seem to have been revived. In fact, much of the symbolism in the Beatus manuscripts is reminiscent of far earlier times. As noted, the

[17] E. v. Marle, *Iconographie de l'art profane* (1931), Vol. II, *Garden of Love*, Figs. 448, 463; *Roue de Fortune* from Lichtenberg, with Venus and attendants with lute; in the series of the Master of the Tarochi, Venus has no lute, but the Muses have, as does Poesia among the Liberal Arts; in Holbein's *Dance of Death* the lover in the nun's scene has a lute.

FIG. 39. The Lord in Glory; the twelfth-century tympanon of the south portal at Moissac. INSTRUMENTS: plucked and bowed rebecs

illumination of the Adoration of the Lamb is often designed in a circle (see Fig. 35), with the Lamb of the Lord in the center, surrounded by the beasts of the Evangelists, often interspersed with
pairs of angels, one with a musical instrument and one with a vial of
the water of life. Frequently, there is then an outer circle of stars and
sometimes a circle of one- or two-winged angels. Charts and maps of
the world in the Beatus manuscripts open the Book of Daniel, to map
the travels of the apostles. They echo antique forerunners, showing
an earthly paradise off in one corner to the east.[18] The vision of
heaven often follows the traditional cosmological form of concentric
spheres with the Lord enthroned in the center; he is surrounded by
many flying figures, both angels and souls.[19] While the vision of the
cosmos and the idea of angel musicians moving the spheres are never
fully fused in any one of the Beatus manuscripts, there is certainly an
abundance of suggestive material in the illuminations.

Emergence of Musicians and Dancers

The influence which the new musical iconology had on the sculpture and the painting of the Romanesque period rapidly became
apparent. Prior to the eleventh and twelfth centuries, no musicians
were to be found in representations of heaven except those sounding
the trumpets of the Last Judgment. A typical work of this period is
the illumination shown in Fig. 40, from the famous codex of the
twelfth century which contains the writings of Saint Hildegard. Here
the orders of the angels were arranged in nine spheres of the cosmos.
In the two outer circles there are busts of angels with wings and halos;
then follow three circles with heads only; then one circle of busts
where the hands are also visible, but empty; another circle of heads
with wings, and, in the innermost circle, star-like sparkles.

However, starting in the eleventh century scores of musicians
began to appear, though none of these figures, until late in the
twelfth century, were angel musicians. The type which appeared

---

[18] P. Bordona, *Spanish Illuminations* (Firenze, 1930); Neuss, *Die Apokalypse*;
the map of the world belongs to the illuminations of the Book of Daniel; Churruca, *Influjo oriental*.

[19] British Museum MS. 11695, Apocalypse from Silos, Fol. 86b. The scenes
of the Heavenly Jerusalem also foreshadow many later representatives of the
Cité de Dieu. Neuss, *Die Apokalypse*; Churruca, *Influjo oriental*; A. de Laborde,
Les manuscrits à peinture de la Cité de Dieu, Société des bibliophiles français
(Paris, 1909).

FIG. 40. Illumination from the twelfth-century Hildegard Codex, showing the nine spheres of the cosmos

initially were mostly elderly men—the Elders of the Apocalypse. The Elders do not always appear as a group of twenty-four; their number is sometimes reduced to twelve, to eight, six (Parthenay), or four.[20] When there are twelve, they often have the apostles as a

[20] See n. 10 above.

counterpart. At Boscherville they form four groups of three each, and there may have been other combinations of four.[21] Some were a peculiar type, perhaps surprising to find in cathedrals and liturgical manuscripts: acrobats and *jongleurs*.[22] Although these are not attributable to the influence of the Beatus manuscripts, where such figures appear only in the Daniel illumination, they derive from analogous origins. The *jongleurs* or minstrels were, at the time, a new class of musician which had developed in Spain under the influence of Arab culture. For the first time in European history, the players of musical instruments were being admitted to the courts and raised to a socially acknowledged level.[23] The figures in the Beatus manuscripts were copied from Oriental representations,[24] and at the same time were modeled on a reality which also had its sources in the Orient. The new form of music and the new type of musician obviously made a considerable impression on the visual arts, for hereafter, musicians begin regularly to form a part of the heavenly hierarchy.

In examining developments in the Romanesque period, it seems well to start with a work which reflects both the old and the new, where musicians may be seen as part of the whole arrangement and the new characteristics be observed, a work showing traces of Oriental origins, which change the whole aspect and shed light on the peculiarities of the new iconology. The example chosen is the tympanum at Moissac, mentioned above, which represents the Christ of the Apocalypse, sitting on the throne surrounded by the four beasts, two angels, and the Elders (see Fig. 39). The Elders are arranged in three layers, with the upper two flanking the figure of Christ and the rest forming a solid row underneath. This arrangement is like that in one of the Beatus illuminations of the *Agnus in monte;* it is also similar to earlier representations in layer form, as in the Church of Santa Maria Antiqua. The difference is that in Moissac the Elders are musicians, and that the angel standing here as an emblem of Saint John is a dancer. The Elders carry musical instruments which are identical with the lute-like instruments encountered in the

[21] For different cycles of four, see Rodolfus Glaber, *De divina quaternitate*, Book I, 1. *Patrol. lat.* 142, 614.

[22] J. B. Beck, *La musique des troubadours* (1910); H. Focillon, "Apôtres et jongleurs," *Revue de l'art ancien et moderne*, LV (1929).

[23] Faral, *Les Jongleurs en France;* Pidal, *Poesia juglaresca.*

[24] Churruca, *Influjo oriental.*

Beatus illuminations. The Elders are seated, and many hold their legs in positions which can be construed as dancing positions. This seems a clear case of a fusion of the older Christian and the new Beatus tradition. Finally, as already mentioned above, the dancing figures of pagan representations of the dome of heaven have re-emerged here in Christian context.

It is also important to note the type of instrument played. The few earlier surviving representations of musicians are invariably representations of King David and his companions, and the instrument is the harp or the psaltery. In this connection, a comparison of the group of musicians in the Bible of Charles the Bald (Fig. 41) with the

FIG. 41. King David playing on a harp and dancing; illumination from the ninth-century Bible of Charles the Bald. INSTRUMENTS: harp, rattle, horn

Moissac players is informative.[25] In Charles's Bible, a ninth-century
manuscript, David plays a harp, and the four of his companions who
play have instruments which are copied from old Roman sources.
The same tradition may be observed in the Psalter of Saint Gall, a
manuscript of the same period. In the Utrecht Psalter,[26] also from
the ninth century, we find a combination of antique and contemporary instruments. Buhle has suggested that presentation of antique
or modern instruments alternated from period to period, but there
are far too many exceptions to this thesis.

It might be noted here that, unfortunately, it has not been possible
to include the tradition of the musician David in the present study.
Work on the subject is undoubtedly needed.[27] But David is not, in

[25] E. Reuter, *Les représentations de la musique dans les sculptures romanes en
France* (1938), Pl. VIII; G. Schünemann, "Die Musikinstrumente der 24 Alten,"
Archiv für Musikforschung, I (1936).

[26] Latin Psalter in the University Library of Utrecht, facsimile edition,
London, 1875, fol. 25b (Psalm XLII), 27a (Psalm XLVI), 37b, 48a, 63a, 76a,
81b, 83a, *passim*.

[27] H. Steger, "Rex David," *Erlanger Beiträge zur Sprach- und Kunstwissenschaft*, VI (1961).

FIG. 42. Detail from the west portal of the cathedral at Toro, with musicians
Elders in the outer arch and angels, without musical instruments, in the inner
arch. INSTRUMENTS: harp, organistrum, guitar-fiddle (?), bowed fiddle, short-
necked fiddle (?)

any case, connected with the idea of music of the spheres, though he has sometimes erroneously been so assigned.[28] David is never the leader of the dance of the blessed. If he is seen with the harp in heaven, his place is among the patriarchs, as one reads in Dante and sees in many representations (Fra Angelico, *Last Judgment*, Uffizi; the manuscripts of the *Cité de Dieu*, etc.). In the illustrations of the Utrecht Psalter he is always playing on earth, and if elsewhere he is represented dancing, it is to illustrate the dancing before the Ark (Jaca, Spain).

The figures of the Elders as musicians occur frequently, especially on the portals of cathedrals in Spain and southern France. The characteristics of particular interest for this study are: 1) their relationship to other surrounding figures; 2) their number; 3) their gestures and positions; and 4) their instruments and how they handle them.

To take the last first, the chief point of interest is whether the Elders are holding or playing instruments of the same type or different types. When the instruments are identical, it is most often the "lute" seen in the Beatus manuscripts. Identical instruments occur at Fenouillard, Parthenay, and Aulnay.[29] In these instances, the Elders hold their instruments in identical positions. Identical instruments but different positions are found at Anzy-le-Duc, Autun, Saint-Junien, Ripoll, Fronzac, and Moissac.[30] When the instruments differ, with few exceptions they are stringed instruments and are predominantly the three types seen in the Beatus manuscripts: the lute-like instrument to be plucked, the one with the bow, and the harp. These three are found at Etampes, Vermonton, Notre Dame de Paris, Toro (Fig. 42), Carboeiro, and at Amiens, where the figures of the Elders appear between and above the gargoyles on the roof (Fig. 43). At Chartres, in addition to the three instruments mentioned, there is the psaltery, and at Soria and Saint James of Compostella, the organistrum or hurdy-gurdy—an instrument, operated by two

---

[28] Ch. Tolnay, "Music of the Universe," *Journal of the Walters Art Gallery*, VI (1943).

[29] Reuter, *Les représentations de la musique*, lists nineteen French Romanesque sculptures in northern France showing musician elders: Paris, Notre Dame, portail de Sainte Anne, Étampes, Chartres, Angers, Vermenton; Poitou and Saintonge: Aulnay; Parthenay (Basses Pyrénées), "deux fois"; Moissac, Tombe de Saint-Junien (Haute Vienne); Bourgogne: Avallon, Anzy-le-Duc, Aulnay, Saint Pierre, portail du transept sud, Reuter, Pl. VII.

[30] Report of the Eighth Congress, International Musicological Society (1961), Vol. I, Pl. V.

FIG. 43. Detail of the musician Elders on the roof of the Amiens Cathedral.
INSTRUMENTS: psaltery

players, where the sound is made by a wheel rubbed against the
strings.

In all the representations the Elders are either playing on their instruments or just holding them. When they are not playing, they
often hold a vial with the water of life in the other hand. The form
of these vials is sometimes deceptive; they can be confused with some
kind of clapper or rattle. In Oloron-Sainte-Marie, in Carboeiro, some
of the Elders have such vials; they do not have them at Toro [31] or
Notre Dame de Paris.

Let us examine in detail the ensembles in two instances. The
twenty-four Elders on the Portico de la Gloria at Santiago [32] (Figs.
44, 45, 46) have fourteen instruments to be plucked, including two
guitars; four harps, two of which are triangular with straight edges,
two of which have curved boards for the pegs; two psalteries, one

[31] Reuter, *Les représentations de la musique*, Pl. x.
[32] K. Meyer, *Das Konzert* (1927), Fig. 7; A. Gómez-Moreno, *El arte roman-
ico espanol* (Madrid, 1934); Reuter, *Les représentations de la musique*, pp.
23ff., 43, 62.

FIGS. 44–46. The twenty-four Elders; from the twelfth-century Portico de la Gloria of the cathedral at Santiago di Compostella. INSTRUMENTS: oval fiddles, harps, psaltery, guitar-fiddles, organistrum

FIG. 46. Detail from Pontico de la Gloria

organistrum played by two Elders and one wind instrument. (One of
the guitars has been erroneously identified as a plater.) Two have no
instruments. Possibly they are intended to mark the rhythm; it is
hard to tell whether they hold a vial or a rattle in the form of a
pumpkin.

At Chartres, the musician Elders appear three times—once on the
twelfth-century Royal Portal (Fig. 47), then on the pillars of the
south portal, thirteenth century (Fig. 48), and in one of the porticos.
On the Royal Portal the twenty-four are arranged in the two outer
arches around the tympanon. They are seated or standing and have
the following instruments: ten "lutes," five on each side, four psalteries in two forms (one form similar to the instrument of one of the
Cluny figures); the two pairs at the bottom have a psaltery, a
"lute," a vielle (the bow may have been destroyed, the instrument
has a bridge), and a harp with a curved board for the pegs and a big
sound box. The remaining instruments are badly deteriorated, but
some may have been harps. The angels in the inner arch have the
emblems of their orders.

On the south portal the Elders, six on each side, appear on two
pillars separated from the part with the tympanon. The arches
around the tympanon are filled with figures of angels; six hold the

tools of the Passion; of the nine orders the cherubim have six wings, the seraphim flames, the following orders their emblems: scepters, crowns and swords, the Virtues books; at the bottom angels with censers, and on each side, flanking the representation of the Last Judgement, angels with trumpets. These angels are the only ones with musical instruments.

These orchestras or ensembles of different instruments and players were intended to represent heavenly music. The question of whether the instruments are images of real instruments or imaginary ones will be discussed later. However, the usual pattern in the twelfth and thirteenth centuries was a combination of two or three types of instruments. A comprehensive study of these groups might shed important light on the different traditions and sculptors.

The Elders are generally standing or seated. As noted, some of the

FIG. 47. Detail from the Portail Royal of the Chartres Cathedral, showing the seated Elders playing their instruments. INSTRUMENTS: harp, psaltery, lute (?), guitar-fiddle, rebec, nun's fiddle

FIG. 48. A pillar on the south portal of the Chartres Cathedral, with the Elders
holding their instruments. INSTRUMENTS: two guitar-fiddles, psaltery, lute,
rebec, harp

seated Elders at Moissac have their legs, oddly enough, in dancing positions that seem to derive from the British Museum Beatus manuscript. The crossed legs in the sculpture of the Elders on the west façade of Notre Dame de Paris (Fig. 49) seem to be a reflection of this "dancing." In one instance, there is even an acrobat or *jongleur* among the Elders. This is on a capital at Boscherville in Normandy, which is also an exception in respect of its choice of instruments. Its twelve Elders have one "lute," one curved harp, an organistrum played by two, two bowed string instruments, one of which is a knee viol, one drum played by the acrobat, one psaltery, one pan pipe, and one portative organ. Here the acrobat is standing on his head. Dancers and *jongleurs* are found in other cycles or single scenes, for

FIG. 49. Detail from the west façade of Notre Dame, Paris. Two Elders are holding musical instruments, and one of them is stepping on the dragon Satan. INSTRUMENTS: keyboard fiddle or organistrum

example, in the scene of Salome dancing before Herod,[33] as the companions of Luxuria,[34] and in the representation of the eight modes from Cluny. There are dancers in scenes with accompanying musicians and acrobats, and they even appear without any relation to the content in the manuscript of a liturgical book, a tropary.[35] But, interesting as the history of the *jongleurs* and their representation is, it would be a digression here, and further discussion must be reserved for later.

Dancing in heaven is a primary concern for the history of heavenly music. Dancers appeared in a number of the visions and representations of the cosmos in antiquity, and they began to re-emerge in the Romanesque period. They came to be accepted in the heavenly hierarchy just as the *jongleurs* were at the courts. Dancers reappeared at first as Elders or as one of the beasts, and then, ultimately, dancing was transferred to the community of the blessed. Dancing figures that represent blessed souls appear at Cahors on a tympanum of Christ in Glory. Here two angels stand beside Christ in the mandorla, in the ecstatic posture typical of the Beatus manuscripts. At the bottom of the tympanum, Christ appears again with the book of judgment; on his right, in a separate scene, there are three figures dancing. Still farther below are the twelve apostles, in a row corresponding to that of twelve of the Elders at Moissac. At Saint Pons de Thomières [36] dancing figures, now independent on one of the capitals, represent the blessed, as a counterpart to the damned (Fig. 50). The dancers form a ring, with the men in the back and the women in front. It might be noted that they do not appear to move in the ecstatic way seen at Moissac and Cahors, and they have neither halos nor wings. With these twelfth-century works, the dance of the blessed in paradise had definitely entered the scope of Christian iconology.

ELDERS AND ANGELS

When the Elders appear in the tympanum itself, they are arranged in layers or rows (Moissac); if they appear in arches, they usually

[33] Reuter, Pl. xviii. Avallon, Saint Lazare portal.

[34] *Ibid.*, Pl. xxviii, capital of Anzy-le-Duc; Pl. xix, Saint Pierre, Huesca; Pl. xvii, Foussais, Sainte Hilaire portal.

[35] K. Meyer, "The Eight Gregorian Modes on the Cluny Capitals," *Art Bulletin*, Vol. 34 (1952), pp. 75ff.

[36] P. Mesplé, 'Les chapitaux du cloître de Saint Pons de Thomières," *Revue des Arts* (1960), p. 111.

FIG. 50. Capital from Saint Pons de Thomières, showing the round of the blessed

form rays (Santiago, Aulnay, Oloron); sometimes they follow the curving of the voussoirs, as at Fronzac (Fig. 51). In earlier works, when they are placed in one voussoir, ornaments fill the other arches. An exception is Aulnay, where the Elders are placed in the middle voussoir, the apostles in the innermost arch, while the outermost is filled with all kinds of creatures, among them the famous harp-playing donkey.[37] At Santiago there are the signs of the zodiac; at Oloron-Sainte-Marie, the bottom row shows representatives of different trades and crafts (Fig. 52). Later, in the thirteenth century, angels often figure in the voussoirs but are generally in no way connected with the Elders. There are instances where there are only angels in all of the voussoirs and instances where angels appear only in some of them.

A number of authors have cited certain cathedrals as containing ex-

[37] Reuter, *Les représentations de la musique*, Pl. 23B; J. Baltrusaitis, *Art sumérien, art roman* (1934), p. 51.

FIG. 51. Detail from the twelfth-century portal, La Lauda, at Fronzac. INSTRUMENTS: psaltery, bowed rebec, harp

amples of orchestras of angels.[38] They seem, however, to have confused the orders or choirs of angels with orchestras. Certainly there are quite a number of representations of different orders or kinds of angels, but there is, as will be seen, only one example from the twelfth century where angel musicians are represented. From the great number of these angel voussoirs, I have selected six as examples of typical combinations. At Amiens,[39] the central portal on the west façade has eight voussoirs, and of these the two innermost show angels. In one they are in the form of adorants, in the other their hands are covered with cloths, thus designating them as ministers or servants. At Auxerre we have three voussoirs on the central portal, with, again, the two innermost filled with angels. Unfortunately the figures are in such a poor state of preservation that it is impossible to decide what they are carrying. In Bordeaux the south portal at Saint

[38] Thus H. Mendelsohn, *Die Engel in der bildenden Kunst* (1907), p. 44.
[39] For general information, see E. Mâle, *L'art religieux du XIIIᵉ siècle* (Paris, 1919); J. Roussel, *La sculpture française. Époque gothique*, I, II; photographs of Amiens in the Kingsley Porter Collection at the Fogg Museum, Cambridge, Massachusetts.

Seurin is dedicated to the representation of the Last Judgment.[40] In the tympanum, two of the angels have herald trumpets. Of the eight

[40] L. Bégule, *La cathédrale de Lyon* (Paris, 1911), p. 55; Roussel, *La sculpture francaise*, II, 1.

FIG. 52. Seated musician Elders holding their instruments; from the twelfth-century portal of Sainte Marie in Oloron-Sainte-Marie. INSTRUMENTS: figure-eight or guitar-fiddles

voussoirs, the two inner ones are given over to angels, one to adorants and another to figures carrying the instruments of the Passion, or possibly objects used in the liturgy. There are angels on two other voussoirs as well: on an outer one there are ten angels, of which the two central figures are cherubim, not on wheels, and on another there are eight angels of which the central ones wear crowns. Some of their emblems indicate that orders are represented here. Two other churches at Bordeaux, Saint André and Sainte Croix, have voussoirs with angels. At Sainte Croix they appear in conjunction with the Elders, but none of the angels is shown as a musician. At Charlieu,[41] a church where an angel orchestra has been reported, angels do appear in the outer voussoir; however, they do not have wings and musical instruments cannot be recognized. The figures are badly deteriorated; one might be carrying a musical instrument, perhaps a vielle; another is dancing and swinging a kind of scarf.[42] But the objects which they carry are so indistinct that I would not dare to interpret them as musical instruments. Chartres [43] has on the south portal (thirteenth century) a representation of the nine orders of angels. The orders here all have their typical emblems: the cherubim have six wings, the seraphim stand on wheels, others have crowns, lances, and shields, books and censers; but there is no music whatsoever represented. There are, of course, musician Elders and plenty of other musician figures at Chartres.

Prior to the thirteenth century, the most prevalent representations of angels show them as adorants or as carrying the instruments of the Passion or objects commonly used in the service. Among all these numerous representations, I found only one from the twelfth century where the angels are musicians, and that is at Lyons (Fig. 53).[44] Unfortunately most of these figures are so badly damaged that the instruments cannot be recognized. Three angels are relatively intact: one blows a shawm, another holds a psaltery, a third cymbals. It is impossible to identify other instruments, but one is entitled to suppose that all the angels here are making music.

The figures of the angels on the Romanesque cathedrals, then, in

---

[41] *Ibid.*, 1, 4; Kingsley Porter Collection, Fogg Museum, Cambridge, Massachusetts.

[42] Kingsley Porter Collection, Fogg Museum, Cambridge, Massachusetts.

[43] Et. Houvet, *Cathédrale de Chartres* (1926).

[44] Bégule, *La cathédrale de Lyon*, p. 55; A. Sachet, *Le grand jubilé de Saint Jean de Lyon* (1886) (without the figures).

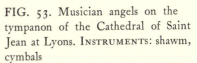

FIG. 53. Musician angels on the tympanon of the Cathedral of Saint Jean at Lyons. INSTRUMENTS: shawm, cymbals

contrast to the Elders, do not follow the Beatus tradition so much as the theory of the Dionysian order and ideas of the cosmic spheres. The voussoirs with angels, however, are so varied that no special trend as to Greek or Persian or Babylonian sources can be traced. The arches are readily interpreted as part of the cosmos, but there is no discernible pattern of voussoirs to suggest that they stand for spheres of the cosmos; hence one must assume that all are meant to represent the highest heaven. For example, the west portal at Chartres would represent the highest heaven, with Christ in the middle served by the nine orders of the angels.

Thus, by the thirteenth century, the two traditions, the Oriental musicians and the Christian order of angels, had met on the portals of the cathedrals. But they appear side by side, not in fusion. The Elders remained musicians, and the angels, with the one exception at Lyons, performed non-musical duties more or less according to the description given in the *Hierarchy* of Dionysius.

VII

Late Medieval Writings and Dante's *Paradise*

EARLIER CHAPTERS HAVE OUTLINED the literary history up to the twelfth century and indicated that for the period from about 500 to 1100 the visions of the cosmos provided by Martianus Capella and Dionysius the Areopagite became predominant in pagan and Christian ideology, respectively. It was possible to trace the influence of both these books in theoretical treatises on music, in Christian writings and hymns, and in secular poetry; and from their frequent use, it may be concluded that they must have been widely known among literate people.

Mention was also made of attempts to merge and integrate pagan and Christian concepts into a coordinated vision of the cosmos, and it is these, especially, that began to be further elaborated in the twelfth century. Defining the role of the angels in moving the spheres and clarifying the nature of the highest heaven were among the major preoccupations of the Scholastics, and the concepts that they and other contemporary writers evolved were ultimately reflected in Dante's enormously influential *Divine Comedy*, as well as in subsequent Renaissance thought and art.

MYSTICS AND SCHOLASTICS

The two schools of thought in this period of transition were represented by the Scholastics and the Mystics,[1] headed by Saint Thomas Aquinas and Saint Bernard of Clairvaux. Actually, the philosophy of the Mystic writers falls more within the scope of the second

---

[1] E. Gilson, *Philosophie du moyen-âge* (1947); E. Panofsky, "Abbot Suger de St.-Denis," *Meaning in the Visual Arts* (1955), pp. 127ff.; though Mâle, *L'art religieux de la fin du moyen-âge en France*, quotes Saint Bernard as saying "Tout ce que sera en Paradis ne sera que liesse que joie que chant. . . ," I found references only to light in the writings of Saint Bernard, *Patrol. lat.* 182, 353 *Epist. ad fratres de Monte Dei, lib.* III, 1, about the earthly and the heavenly paradise; 1225, *De vita eterna vel de coelo et Paradiso; Patrol. lat.* 183, 915 *Sermones in Cantica.*

part of this book. In this period, especially, they were more interested in moral evaluations than in cosmological speculations. When Saint Bernard discussed the celestial Jerusalem he was not indulging in an explicit description of the beauties of the City of God, but was concerned with its moral implications.[2] The Scholastics, on the other hand, consciously endeavored to incorporate the cosmological teachings of ancient pagan theory into Christian theology. They sought to combine the stories of the creation as given in Genesis and Plato's *Timaeus* and therefore produced numerous commentaries on these two works.[3] To understand the force of the urge to integrate pagan and Christian doctrine, it is perhaps enlightening to note how much importance was given to defining the highest sphere. At this time it was called the highest heaven, sometimes the Empyreum, the crystal heaven, but not yet Elysium. Whatever it was called, it was seen as being above or outside the real cosmos.[4]

Odd as it may seem, another problem related to the topic of heavenly music which concerned the writers of the period was the question of when the angels were created.[5] Were the angels created before, at the same time as, or after the spheres? Did the fall of Lucifer occur directly after the creation, or sometime later? The character of the angels and their duties in the cosmos depended on the answers to these questions. It has been noted that in the ancient cosmologies, the regular motion of the celestial bodies was attributed to rational forces, which were imagined to be gods, messengers of the gods, or other winged spirits. These spirits not only moved the spheres, but supported them as well, and it was from these winged spirits that angels were evolved. Dionysius had established the order of angels adopted by Christian theology. From his doctrines on the character of the

[2] R. Klibansky, *The Continuity of the Platonic Tradition during the Middle Ages* (London, 1939); E. R. Curtius, *Europäische Literatur und lateinisches Mittelalter* (1948), p. 116.

[3] Of Arabic philosophers: Algazel, Avicenna, Alfarabi, and Averroes; of Jewish writers: Maimonides and Isaak Israeli; of ecclesiastical writers: Dominicus Gundissalinus, *De proc. mundi*; *Schrift von dem Hervorgange der Welt*, ed. G. Bülow, *Beiträge zur Philosophie des Mittelalters*, 24/3 (1925); Roger Bacon, *Op. maius*, II, *cap.* 5.

[4] The Empyreum mentioned by Saint Augustine, *Civitas Dei*, x, 9; the crystal heaven by Saint Gregory the Great, *Sermons on Ezekiel, Patrol. lat.* 76, 785–1072.

[5] Plato, *Timaeus*, 38 E, 39 E, in Loeb Classics, Vol. 7; Gilson, *Philosophie du moyen-âge*, pp. 9ff.

angels, their duties, and especially their task of moving the spheres, a complicated theory of light was elaborated, as well as a less important theory of sound.[6]

For the Scholastics, Aristotle, in addition to Plato, became the decisive authority. Aristotle termed the movers of the spheres *intelligentiae*. They were thought immanent to the spheres and were energies as well as *materia*. The stars were *astra animata*, animated stars, as well as *vis intellectiva et desiderata*. The *vis desiderata* is "love" as a moving force of the universe; the *vis intellectiva* is the *nous* or *logos*, the intelligence which rules the whole cosmos. Its emanations are the *intelligentiae*, the rulers and movers of the single bodies.[7] Plato's philosophy corroborated the view that the stars have a soul, *anima*.[8] As already noted, these ideas recur in Philo, Plotinus, and Syrianus (fifth century). They are also found in Proclus's commentary on *Timaeus*,[9] where the angels and the *intelligentiae*, both as forces and as figures, become identical with the spheres.

Among the Christian writers, Claudianus Mamertius [10] and Saint Augustine [11] emphasized this identity, while the writers of the East-

---

[6] Panofsky, "Abbot Suger."

[7] The angels or intelligences are related to the stars by Proclus, *In Timaeum*, v, 320; this idea also appears in Origen, *De princ.*, ii, *cap.* 3 and Saint Augustine, *De immort. anim. Patrol. lat.* 32, 1033; *Enchiridion, Patrol. lat.* 40, 260; *Retractiones, Patrol. lat.* 32, 591 and 603; this idea is opposed by Basilius, *Hom. in hexaem., Patrol. gr.* 29, 76; by Jerome, *Epist. 124 ad Avitum, Patrol. lat.* 22, 1062; John the Damascene, *De fide orthod., Partol gr.* 94, 885; C. Baeumker, "Witelo, ein Philosoph und Naturforscher des 13. Jahrhunderts," *Beiträge zur Geschichte der Philosophie des Mittelalters*, iii/2 (Münster, 1908), 523. The stars are animated with *vis intellectiva et desiderativa* in Robert Grosseteste; see L. Baur, "Die Philosophie des Robert v. Grosseteste," *Beiträge zur Geschichte der Philosophie des Mittelalters*, Vol. 18, Heft. 4–6 (1919); Aristotle, *De motu animae*, 2–4, xxviii; *De anima*, tr. J. A. Smith, Book i, 3/4, Book ii, 10/11, in *Collected Works* (1931), Vol. 3; *Aristotle's Psychology* (*De anima*), tr. W. A. Hammond (1902); Aristotle or Ps. Aristotle, *De Coelo*, "Circles of the Stars," ed. W. K. Guthrie, in Loeb Classics, pp. 182ff.

[8] See n. 5 above.

[9] Philo, *De gigant.*, No. 8, in Loeb Classics, ii; Plotinus, *Enn.*, ii, 9.5 and v, 1.2; Syrianus, in *Metaphysica Commentaria*, ed. G. Kroll, ii, 24.6; Proclus, *In Timaeum*, 47.D, (ed. Diehl, i, 152), all quoted by Baeumker, "Witelo," pp. 523ff.

[10] Claudianus Mamertius, *De statu animae*, i, 12; *Corpus scriptorum ecclesiasticorum latinorum*, Vol. xi, ed. Engelbrecht (Vienna, 1885).

[11] Saint Augustine, *De immort. anim.*, c. 15, *Patrol. lat.* 32, 1033; *Retract.*, *Patrol. lat.* 32, cols. 591, 603.

ern Church, Basilius, Jerome, and John of Damascus,[12] were not convinced of it. The latter emphasized only the rule and identity of the numbers, correlating the ratio of the motion to the number (quantity and quality) of the *intelligentiae*.

These theories were revived by Arab writers, such as Avicenna,[13] who greatly influenced cosmological doctrine after *ca.* 1000. Avicenna postulated nine spirits for nine spheres: earth, moon, sun, five planets, the fixed stars. To this an outer heaven without stars was added as a tenth intelligence, the *intellectus agens* or *primus movens*.[14] As for Plato, this highest heaven was the realm of the demiurge. This tenth sphere was referred to by Avicenna and his followers as the Empyreum, the glowing heaven or heaven of light, or as the "crystal heaven," a term taken from Ezekiel and Revelation. The idea of a special outer sphere is important in the iconology of music because in many later works of art and writings it is this heaven alone that is represented as the abode of the hosts of angels, of the angels who dance and make music. Avicenna's ideas are cited by Maimonides,[15] Albert the Great,[16] and Saint Thomas.[17] They were also reflected in pictorial representations, where the *primus movens* is found at the center of the concentric circles or in the top row of the layers which stand for the different spheres or grades of the universe.

The special problems to be solved were, in what way the single bodies, motions, *animae*, or *intelligentiae* were dependent on the *primus movens*, and, further, whether the moving forces, the angels or *intelligentiae*, were to be imagined as spiritual only, or as both spiritual and material. Dionysius's formulation of the order of the

[12] John of Damascus, *De fide orthod.*, *Patrol. gr.* 94, 885, 868; Basilius, *Hom. 3 in Hexaem.*, *Patrol gr.* 29, 76; Jerome, *Epist. 124 ad Avitum*, *Patrol. lat.* 22, 1062.

[13] Baur, "Die Philosophie des R. v. Grosseteste"; C. Baeumker, *Das pseudo-hermetische Buch der 24 Meister*, p. 24; K. Werner, *Die Kosmologie . . . des Mittelalters* (not available), quoted by Baur.

[14] P. Duhem, *Le système du monde* (Paris, 1917), I, 81; O. Brendel, "Symbolik der Kugel," *Deutsches Archälogisches Institut, Römische Abt. Mitteilungen*, 51 (1936), p. 57; Festugière, "Les dieux ousiarques de l'Asclépius," *Recherches de science religieuse*, XXVIII (1938), 175ff.

[15] J. Guttmann, *Die Scholastik in Beziehung zum Judentum* (1902); Baeumker, "Witelo." p. 438.

[16] Bauer, "Die Philosophie des R. v. Grosseteste," p. 199; Albert the Great, *De animalibus*, ed. H. Stadler, in *Beiträge zur Geschichte der Philosophie des Mittelalters*, Vol. 15–16 (1931).

[17] Saint Thomas, *De substantiis*, see n. 24, Chapter IV.

angels was elaborated and commented on by numerous writers, beginning with Maximus (d. 662) and Saint Gregory.[18] It was translated and commented on by, among others, John of Damascus and Duns Scotus, who drew on it for his *De praedestinatione*.[19] In the twelfth and thirteenth centuries, commentaries were written by Hugh of Saint Victor (*ca.* 1120), Robert Grosseteste (*ca.* 1235), Saint Thomas (*ca.* 1255), Albert the Great (*ca.* 1260), and later by Jean Gerson (*ca.* 1390).[20] The two points which particularly stirred discussion were the question of the angels' duty in moving the spheres and statements concerning their order. These problems are interrelated because in the "hierarchy" the angels are supposed to correspond to the grading of the spheres. One issue was whether angels inhabited all the spheres or only the highest heaven. Apart from the commentaries on Dionysius, these problems were also discussed in a number of treatises with the title *De intelligentiis*,[21] such as those by Robert Grosseteste, bishop of Lincoln, Roger Bacon, and Albert the Great.

A detailed examination of all these works is beyond the scope of this study, but let us summarize the problem as expounded by Saint Thomas in his *De substantiis separatis seu de angelorum natura opusculum*.[22] "That the single soul or intelligence moves the spheres has been stated by the philosophers [that is, the Greek writers]. . . . This does not conform with our faith, which teaches that God alone is the creator. Nevertheless, we can grant to the angels which move the heavens an immediate existence and call them movers; for by them only the spheres are moved, though the spheres are not created through the angels. . . . In any case, we can agree that one states the following: the angels of a higher order, those who own a form of greater universality . . . are the outer movers [*motores remoti*] and are separate beings. But the angels of a lower grade, those who have

[18] K. S. Guthrie, *The Pagan Bible* (1925); Br. F. Westcott, *Essays in the History of Religious Thought in the West* (1891), pp. 148ff.; the idea is mentioned by Gregory, and in Adrian's letter to Charlemagne, see Panofsky, "Abbot Suger."

[19] C. H. Haskins, *The Renaissance of the 12th Century* (1927), p. 296.

[20] Westcott, *Essays in the History of Religious Thought.*

[21] C. Baeumker, "Abfassungszeit und Verfasser des *liber de intellegentiis*," *Miscellanea Franc. Ehrle I, Studi e Testi*, 37 (Rome, 1924), *Scritti di Storia*, 1. The book *De intell.* was translated by Gerald de Cremona from the Arabic; the *Liber de causis*, translated by Moerbecke, was used by Witelo and Grosseteste.

[22] Baur, "Die Philosophie des R. v. Grosseteste"; Saint Thomas, see n. 23 below.

more restricted form, are the movers of the spheres nearer to the earth. In this sense, Avicenna declares: the movers who are named intelligences by the philosophers are what the dogma calls angels of higher order. The souls of the spheres on the other hand are called by Christian writers inferior or serving angels." That these angels had an existence *in substantia,* were material beings, was, for Thomas, highly probable. Asked by his colleague Jean de Verceil and by an anonymous writer from Venice whether it was true that the angels were the moving forces of the celestial bodies, Thomas answered: "That the celestial bodies are moved by spiritual beings, I cannot think of one philosopher or saint who would have denied it; and if we admit that the angels move the spheres, no official source, that is, no saint, could deny this proposition. . . . Therefore the conclusion is: Everything that moves in nature is moved by the Ruler; the angels transmit the motion to the spheres." In answer to a question concerning the animation of the spheres, Thomas stated: "The conclusion is that the celestial bodies are either animated and moved by their own souls . . . or that they are moved by the angels. That God moves them through His intermediaries, the angels, conforms best to the order of things as Saint Dionysius affirms it, in a manner that cannot be doubted." [23]

Thus, Thomas strove to solve the problems, quoting from Dionysius and the famous book *Sententiae* [24] and the writings of the Church Fathers. The theory of the angels as movers of the spheres was considered of great importance by the Scholastics, and their discussions were, in effect, an attempt to integrate the doctrine on the hierarchy of the angels into the theoretical system of the spheres. The earlier pagan image of the cosmos with the seven spheres of the planets came to be replaced by a Christian cosmos. With the addition of a ninth and then a tenth heaven, the universe was adapted to a vision that conformed—to use Thomas's term—with the faith. The "philosophers," indeed, had already extended the universe to nine spheres, and it was thus a Greek vision that had captured the imagi-

[23] Saint Thomas, *Commentaria in libros sententiarum,* ed. Migne, in *Summa,* Vol. 1.

[24] The author of the *Sententiae* is Petrus Lombardus; other authors of *Sententiae* are Roland Bandinelli (fl. 1159), Taio, *libri V, Patrol. lat.* 80, 744ff., who used as source Saint Gregory; P. Bliemetzrieder, "Anselms v. Laon systematische Sentenzen," *Beiträge zur Geschichte der Philosophie des Mittelalters,* Vol. 18, Heft 2/3 (1919), pp. 13ff., 49; E. v. Drival, "L'iconographie des anges," *Revue de l'art chrétien,* x (1866), 272ff.

nation of the writers of the first five centuries of our era, though neither the Church Fathers nor the Scholastics realized that they were propagating a pagan cosmos. The Scholastics now added a tenth heaven as the abode of the Lord and of Christ; and this heaven became the abode of the hosts of angels.

The Transition to Dante

Coordination of the order of angels with pagan figures, the Muses, the sirens, and the like, occurred in secular writings. Thus a secular poem from the beginning of the fourteenth century lists, after the orders of the angels, the patriarchs, prophets, and the apostles, the martyrs, confessors, virgins, widows, then the seven liberal arts, and the nine Muses. Among the arts, music appears with a scroll, and among the Muses only Calliope has a musical instrument.[25] In liturgical hymns, in contrast, the Muses seldom figured among the heavenly choruses. I found only one poem, from Saint Martial (*ca.* eleventh century),[26] in which the Muses are called *praeclara chorea* and located in the highest heaven.

Two attempts in the twelfth century to integrate figures of pagan mythology into the Christian cosmos were especially significant, for they proved to have decisive influence on later views. These are contained in *De universitate mundi*, by Bernard Silvestris,[27] and *Anti-claudianus*, by Alanus de Insulis.[28] Both works are a mixture of cosmology and mythology; in form a mixture of prose and poetry. Both offer a peculiar and rich texture of information from a great variety

---

[25] In the illuminations of this manuscript different colors are used to characterize the orders of the angels, carrying on past tradition. The Dominations have scarlet wings and pink robes; the Principalities pink wings and yellow surcoats, and they are armed and have white shields with red crosses; the Powers, with scarlet wings and green surcoats, are fighting and overpowering the Devil; the Virtues have green wings and red crosses on white robes; four Archangels have scarlet wings and blue robes, but only Michael is armed and wears a crown; the Angels have scarlet wings, white and blue robes edged with green. British Museum, Royal 6. E. ix, *ca.* 1335–40.

[26] *Analecta hymnica*, Vol. 7, No. 32.

[27] De universitate mundi, eds. C. Barach and J. Wrobel (1876); Gilson, *Philosophie du moyen-âge*; E. Faral, "Le manuscrit 511 du Hunterian Museum," *Studii Medievali*, N. S. 9 (1936), pp. 69–88.

[28] *Patrol. lat.* 210; M. Baumgartner, "Die Philosophie des Alanus de Insulis," *Beiträge zur Geschichte der Philosophie des Mittelalters*, ii/4 (1896), 69; J. Huizinga, *Über die Verknüpfungen des Poetischen mit dem Theologischen bei Alanus de Insulis* (Amsterdam, 1932); Curtius, *Europäische Literatur*.

of sources, and the influence of *Anticlaudianus*, particularly, is important for Dante's *Divine Comedy*.[29]

Both Silvestris and Alanus were related to the school of Chartres.[30] This school, neither Scholastic nor Mystic, belonged to a circle which has been called Platonic. Its members tried to unite classical themes and visions with the theological ideas of the twelfth century and the interest in the rising modern sciences, combining Christian theology with a revival of classic Greek and Roman authors. The movement has been characterized as a sort of proto-Renaissance. The dual background is clearly demonstrated in the topic of both books, which recounts the myth of the creation of a new and perfect Man, a topic not becoming to an orthodox Christian.[31]

Silvestris wrote his *De universitate mundi* in the middle of the twelfth century. In addition, he wrote a commentary on the *Aeneid*, one more indication of his classical orientation. The form of his cosmological book was inspired by Capella's work. It is divided into two parts, the Megakosmos and the Microkosmos, which describe the creation of the universe and then the creation of a new Man. Nature is the personified force that forms chaotic mass into the cosmos. She is helped in her task by Noys (the *nous,* from Greek philosophy) and by two other assistants: Anima, the soul of the world, and Entelechia, a name derived from Aristotle. They create the firmament, the firmament then creates the stars, the stars then create the world. Above the firmament, and this is important, lives the outer-worldly God. Within the firmament, Noys rules, seated on her throne between the cherubim and the seraphim. Under them, in descending order, are the lower orders of the angels, the fixed stars, the zodiac, and the planets. The earth is described with lists of the twenty-four important mountains, twenty-four rivers, twenty-four animals, and twenty-four trees. For each item one important trait is mentioned. Most are chosen because of their mythological significance, for instance, Helikon as the mountain of the poets. Only one or two in each list are taken from the Bible.

---

[29] *Ibid.*

[30] G. Paré, A. Brunet, P. Trembley, *La renaissance du XIIe siècle*, Publ. de l'Institut d'études médiévales d' Ottawa, 1933; Gilson, *Philosophie du moyen-âge*, p. 258; Haskins, *The Renaissance of the 12th Century*; Haskins, *Studies in the History of Medieval Science* (1924).

[31] E. Wolff, *Die goldene Kette. Die Aurea Catena Homeri in der englischen Literatur von Chaucer bis Wordsworth* (1947); A. O. Lovejoy, *The Great Chain of Being* (1936).

The second part of the book, wherein nature undertakes to crown Megakosmos with the creation of the perfect Man, takes the form of a journey through the spheres. Nature asks the help of Noys, the intellect of the highest god. To find the right inspiration, Noys takes as models the great heroes and representatives of mankind. Again it is typical that, among twelve pairs of models, Christian figures are in the minority. There are but two, the Holy Virgin and Eugenius III, who was pope at the time when Silvestris wrote his poem, and they are the last on the list. Noys advises Nature to ask the help of Physis and of Urania, who was, as may be recalled, the ruling Muse in Capella's poem. Nature travels through the spheres and, in the outer ring of the firmament, in the Aplanon, which is the sphere of the fixed stars, meets Urania, the Usiarch (the highest among the gods of the planets), and his scribe, Genius. Nature and Urania then ascend to the sacred heaven where the highest God reigns and offer prayers for help, which is granted. They descend through the spheres of the planets, each ruled by its own usiarch, who is identical with the planet's Greek god. In addition to these ruling gods, they meet other figures; in the sphere of Venus they meet Cupid and also see the Elysian fields. In the sphere of the moon, they find thousands of spirits; these spirits are angels and ancient pagan gods of the forest and sea. Here Nature and Urania again meet Noys, and they complete their creation of Man.

Though music is not referred to in *De universitate mundi*, this book is an important link in the history of cosmology. Bernard de Silvestris's cosmos is constructed much like Capella's. Both provide a combination of Christian and pagan deities, as well as a cosmos divided into two separate higher and lower heavens. Also, in this cosmos angels are found in the spheres of Venus and Luna, and the Elysian fields are in the lower heaven; thus the final stage, in which Elysium coincides with the highest heaven, has not yet been reached.

Alanus's version, though it was obviously influenced by Silvestris or the sources Silvestris used, is essentially different. Of the two extant works by Alanus, it is *Anticlaudianus* that is relevant here. In the other, *Planctus*, the cosmos is used only as background and angels function as ministers and servants to God, Who rules the cosmos as eternal emperor by transmitting His commands to mankind.

The theme of *Anticlaudianus* is similar to that of Silvestris's work, in that, again, Nature plans the creation of a new and perfect Man.

But Alanus's solution is very different. Nature convokes a committee of heavenly companions, all of whom are representatives or allegories of virtues and positive moral forces. But Intelligence decides that they need the help of God to form the soul of Man. First, however, the older sister of Intelligence, Phronesis or Sophia (i.e., Wisdom), who knows all the sacred mysteries and rites, is asked for advice. Seven maidens, the seven liberal arts, build a chariot for the journey through the spheres to the highest heaven, and music is one of the wheels of the chariot. Nature, Intelligence, and Phronesis ascend through the spheres until they reach the abode of Theologia; this is the halfway point, and they must leave the chariot and Intelligence behind. Then Nature and Phronesis go on their way to the "highest Jupiter" (Dante's *sommo Giove*), ascending through the crystal heaven to the Empyreum, which is the seat of the Holy Virgin, the choirs of angels, and the blessed. Here is the castle of the Lord, adorned with allegorical paintings of the eternal ideas. The majesty of God imagines, and, by this, creates the soul of the perfect Man. This soul is then transmitted to Nature, but Phronesis must cover it with a salve to protect it against bad influences from the spheres through which they must pass on their return to earth. During the journey, the soul of the perfect Man has to fight off the vices, which are ultimately driven into hell, with the aid of virtues. Once they are safely on earth, Phronesis creates the perfect Man's body and joins it to the heavenly soul.

In Alanus's cosmos, the fusion of pagan and Christian elements is more harmonious than in Silvestris's, and represents another step along the way to Dante's vision. For Alanus, the Empyreum is the highest heaven, and in it the highest god, the angels, and the blessed reside together, as they did in the crystal heaven of Revelation and as they were presently to do in Dante's *Paradise*. There is almost no mention of music, but in Alanus's case it is known that he disliked music and thought it appropriate only to make one sleep. It is therefore hardly surprising that he not only excludes *musica instrumentalis*, but *musica mundana* and *humana* as well.

Dante's Vision

From the viewpoint of the iconology of music, Dante's *Divine Comedy* is a climax in its development, for it was here that music and dance finally became an integral part of the Christian paradise. The

Divine Comedy gathers together the earlier trends and, combining them with impressions that Dante drew from his surrounding culture, shapes all into a grandiose vision. And Dante's vision, in turn, became the source and inspiration for most of the later representations of heavenly music in the visual arts.

Dante presented his cosmological ideas earlier in the *Convivio*, then in *Paradiso*, the third section of the *Comedy*. In both, the cosmos is described as constructed of ten spheres. In the *Convivio*, Dante's debt to his forerunners stands out very clearly. The title itself is the same as that of the often imitated work by Athenaeus (*Deipnosophistai*).[32] Also the technique of quoting various testimonials on a given problem is the same. The heroine, "philosophy" (called Beatrice by Dante), is the same as for Boethius.[33] The literary form is like Capella's.[34] Each of the four treatises begins with a poem, then goes on to a commentary in prose. The description of the spheres in the second treatise has clear roots in the past. To cite an example, the well-known first line of the second treatise's introductory poem is *Voi che intendendo il terzo cielo movete* ("You, who . . . are moving the third sphere"), a line quoted in *Paradiso*. Dante comments that "certain intelligences, or to use a more common term, the angels who are movers, turn the heaven of Venus. . . ."

In *Convivio*, Dante's explanation of the motion and meaning of the spheres closely resembles Alanus's version,[35] yet he never cites him, either in *Convivio* itself or in the *Divine Comedy*, despite the frequency with which he refers to other writers, both from antiquity (Plato, Aristotle, Cicero, etc.) and later times (Boethius, Orosius, etc.). Dante does not mention the Muses as rulers of the spheres, but outlines the orders of the angels in the usual way. *Convivio*, however, is more a compendium of quotations on specific problems than a coherent picture, and one does not get the sense that it reflects an underlying vision of a structured cosmos. Indeed, the *Convivio's* signifi-

---

[32] The title is similar to *Symposium*.

[33] Curtius, *Europäische Literatur*, pp. 219ff.

[34] The first edition of Capella was printed in Vicenza in 1499; a German translation in *Denkmäler des Mittelalters* in 1884; A. Warburg, *Gesammelte Schriften* (1932), Vol. 1, 264, A 3; there were eight editions of Capella published from 1499 to 1599; in 1670, P. D. Huet was chosen by Bossuet to prepare an anthology of the Latin classics for the Dauphin, and Leibniz was assigned as editor of Capella. See G. Hess, *Leibniz korrespondiert mit Paris* (1922); see also n. 13, Chapter III.

[35] Curtius, *Europäische Literatur*.

cance would probably be judged quite differently if it had not been succeeded by the *Divine Comedy,* especially *Paradiso.*

The unsurpassed greatness of the *Divine Comedy* is based on Dante's faculty for connecting the realms of extreme poles of experience. In the deepest strata of the inferno, as well as in the loftiest heavens, Dante talks not only to heroes of antiquity and martyrs of the Church, but also to people whom he has met in real life. He discusses complicated theories and also describes the habits of his period. For our essential topic, Dante mentions several musical forms of the thirteenth and fourteenth centuries, and, most important, he was the first to integrate music fully into the description of the heavens, relating it not only to the spheres themselves but to the inhabitants of the heavens.[36] Motion, angels, and the community of the blessed had also appeared in Alanus's cosmos, but there was nothing about music.

The *Divine Comedy* is a late descendant of the tales of the journey through the spheres. In it ideas of antiquity are fused with Christian and contemporary ideas, and the companionship of Dante and his guide Virgil is a symbol of this union. The cosmos has the form of a double cone, as it had for Plato; but one cone is the inferno, the Christian hell. The abode of the dead heroes of antiquity is Elysium, located at the upper rim of the inferno. The patriarchs and the blessed reside in the celestial paradise. Dante's paradise contains all the spheres of the universe, and a union of the pagan and Christian concepts is effected with the highest section of paradise visualized as consisting of three spheres: Empyreum, crystal heaven, and, above, the abode of the Lord, the *primum mobile* or *primus movens,* the pantocrator. The lower spheres are ruled by the deities of the planets. The nine orders of the angels are mentioned, but they have no vital role. The central figure in the highest heaven is the Virgin; around her the hosts of angels sing.

For Dante, music is heard only in paradise, and he describes it in the forms of his own time. A detailed account of this is given in Appendix III, so a brief summary will suffice here. Dante expresses the increase in intensity as he climbs from the lower heavens to the higher ones through different musical forms, as well as through other images. Without the reader being aware of it, the growing intensity

---

[36] A. Scrocca, *Il sistema Dantesca dei cieli* (1895), *cap.* 4, *Degli* angeli; V. Gui, "La musica nella Divina Commedia," *Manifesti di attivita culturale* (1954), II, 19ff.; R. Hammerstein, *Die Musik der Engel* (1962), I, 7.

brings his poem to a climax in the Empyreum. In the lower spheres of paradise Dante hears single voices singing; as he goes higher, a choir, and then solo singing combined with the choir. Then dancers sing, and finally, in the scene with the Eagle, the dancers form figures as in a ballet, and there is polyphonic singing, where the parts of the song have different texts. In the highest heaven nothing is mentioned but motion, light, and sweet singing of unspecified form. But even with these rather general characterizations, the force of Dante's diction lets one visualize the Empyreum quite distinctly. It seems as though one is being guided through a grandiose building full of light and splendor, seeing dancers here and hearing choirs there. If it is true that Dante had studied in Paris, he may well have seen the magnificent cathedrals of Chartres, Saint-Denis, etc. Could not the sculpture of the orders of angels and the music-making Elders on the portals of Chartres and the stained-glass paintings of the rose windows have given him the inspiration for his description of paradise with circles of angels and the court of the saints in the heavenly rose?

Dante's poem was widely read and well known from the very beginning. His vision captured the imagination of painters and illuminators for the representation of paradise. In the later representations, as in Dante's vision, there is less and less emphasis on depicting the cosmos itself. The number of strata is frequently reduced to three, and, ultimately, no indication of single spheres is given. If in the paintings the structure of the cosmos becomes less prominent, other aspects of the old traditions, aspects relevant to music, come to the fore, and are now molded or fused into scenes of Dante's *Divine Comedy*. Thus, among the three scenes from Revelation that involve musicians, the vision of the Lord in glory is fused with the coronation of the Virgin as *regina coelorum*. The terrestrial paradise of Dante comes to be used as the background in the representations of the Adoration of the Lamb, which now takes place on lawns. This beautiful garden appears also in paintings of the Last Judgment, where the angels and the blessed are dancing. Mâle recognized here the combination of the text of Revelation with a quotation from Saint Paul. Dante's vision of the heavenly rose is similarly merged with the idea of the City of God; Augustine's *civitas*, meant as the spiritual community of the faithful, now becomes the celestial Jerusalem, a citadel where the Lord resides surrounded by his court, including the court musicians. Somewhat similarly, in the Beatus illustrations the heavenly Jerusalem was a castle, though without court or musicians, and in Capella's *De nuptiis* the castle was the seat of Zeus.

The popularity of the Virgin as a theme for painters and sculptors may have been enhanced by the leading role she plays in Dante's *Paradiso*, though her legends had already long been in wide currency. The legends had originated in apocryphal Gnostic writings of the first centuries of our era, had been admitted to the liturgy about the fifth century, and became popular by the twelfth century.[37] In the context of this study, the important subjects are the assumption and the coronation of the Virgin. In the earliest versions of the legend, the orders of the angels are mentioned as hailing the Virgin at her entrance into heaven. A Coptic source (fourth century) describes the orders of the angels as preceding the Virgin.[38] In an office of the Gallican liturgy (seventh century), the entrance is described as triumphal, with the apostles offering their services and the angels singing.[39] From the fourteenth century on, most of the paintings with musician angels represent these scenes and show the Virgin as *regina coelorum et angelorum*.[40] In some of these paintings the cosmic structure can still be discerned, but in many others it is taken for granted that the place is the highest heaven, signified by the thrones on which the Virgin and Christ sit.

However, without exaggerating Dante's individual influence, it may be said that his work marks a major turning point in the iconology of music. Whereas the earlier chapters of this study have almost amounted to a negative list of musical figures that had not yet appeared, the opposite is true after 1300. Dante's vivid images of a melodious paradise, presumably aided and abetted by the growing acceptance of the *ars nova*, seemed to have inspired a veritable outburst of representations of celestial music. Indeed, the image of angels making music in the highest heaven became so widespread that Burckhardt could say that in Madonna pictures something seems to be lacking if one does not see angels with musical instruments on the steps of her throne.[41]

[37] Mâle, *L'art religieux du XIIIe siècle* (Paris, 1919).

[38] E. Staedel, *Ikonographie der Himmelfahrt Mariens* (1935).

[39] J. Mabillon, *De liturgia gallicana*, lib. III, 212ff.; Staedel, *Ikonographie*.

[40] *Ibid.*, pp. 59ff.

[41] J. Burckhardt, *Beiträge zur Kunstgeschichte von Italien* (2nd edn., 1911), p. 69, *Das Altarbild*.

VIII   Musician Angels

The angel as a participant in the making of celestial music finally began to be a prevalent figure in works of art in the fourteenth century. Angels appeared first as dancers, joining the dance of the blessed in paradise, and as singers in the heavenly chorus. The angel instrument player, ultimately the most popular image, was the last to join the making of celestial harmony, though angel players had appeared earlier in a rather different role related to the Psalms. The various forms of this development, and possible reasons for its seeming tardiness, will be discussed in this chapter, with a final note on the question of whether or not the celestial concerts depicted can be interpreted as reflections of contemporary reality.

Dancing Angels and the Dance of the Blessed

Figures of angels or blessed souls dancing a round became a new motif to denote paradise in Christian iconography beginning in the first half of the fourteenth century. The many earlier dancing figures connected with the Beatus manuscripts, the *jongleurs* and acrobats who appeared so often on Romanesque and Gothic capitals, usually did not represent heavenly dancers. The one example noted above from the Romanesque period, the dancers on the capitals at Saint Pons de Thomières (see Fig. 50), provides a rare exception.[1] In the fourteenth century, however, the motif of a round danced by angels or the blessed became prevalent, and the site of their dancing was usually understood to be the highest heaven, Empyreum, or paradise. On the other hand, angels forming a circle or semi-circle are not always dancing; it is possible that they illustrate the Dionysic idea of angels moving the spheres, or that they simply correspond to early representations of adorants approaching the Lord or the Virgin from both sides.[2]

[1] P. Mesplé, "Les chapitaux du cloître de Saint Pons de Thomières," *Revue des arts* (1960), p. 111.

[2] R. Hammerstein, *Die Musik der Engel* (1962), p. 237 and Fig. 73, characterizes the two groups of angels in Giotto's fresco *The Lord in Glory* in the Padua Arena as dancing. I would prefer to define them as approaching adorants.

FIG. 54. Fresco by Andrea da Firenze in the Spanish Chapel of Santa Maria Novella in Florence. On the left are the blessed, dancing as they enter Paradise; on the right are representatives of secular music. INSTRUMENTS: fiddle or vielle, tambourine

Dancers in a ring, dancing a round, however, began to be a regular feature of paradise. We see them in Andrea da Firenze's painting of the Last Judgment in the Spanish Chapel in Santa Maria Novella at Florence (Fig. 54).[3] On the upper left, Saint Peter is greeting pairs of dancing girls adorned with wreaths and letting them into paradise; on the lower right, four women are dancing in a ring to the accompaniment of a tambourine and a vielle.

A similar group appears in the picture of *The Good Government* by Ambrogio Lorenzetti in Siena.[4] Here the round is used as a sign of the good and harmonious society, in an allegorical reflection of the state of bliss in heaven. The dancing girls, including, again, a group of four dancing to the accompaniment of a tambourine, look quite different from the very realistic merchants and officials of the Italian town in the rest of the painting. They clearly come from another world, that of heaven and of Dante's *Paradiso*. By the time this was

[3] M. Bernath, *Die Malerei des Mittelalters* (1916), Fig. 370; detail in B. Berenson, *Italian Painters of the Renaissance* (1952), Fig. 127.

[4] E. v. Marle, *The Development of the Italian Schools of Painting* (1923–28), I, 407ff.

painted, the symbolic meaning of figures dancing a round must have been generally understood; it is not likely that girls were usually dancing in the streets, even if the city were well ruled.

By the fifteenth century the figures of the dancing blessed and the dancing angels became quite common. From early in the century there are the delightful celestial rounds in Fra Angelico's [5] two paintings of the Last Judgment and in his *Death and Assumption of the Virgin* (Fig. 55). In the latter, the earliest of the three works, Mary is surrounded by angels on three levels. In the middle layer there are five angels on each side, and again they are dancing a round. Angels with musical instruments appear on the highest of the three levels. In the earlier of the two *Last Judgments*, Christ as the highest judge is seen in a circle in the upper center of the painting. He is surrounded by three rows of angels. The mandorla is supported by cherubim and then by two rows representing the other orders. Then follow, on the right and left, the saints and the patriarchs, seated on two benches, one group headed by the Virgin, the other by Saint John the Baptist. In the group on the right, King David can

[5] F. Schottmüller, *Fra Angelico* (*Klassiker der Kunst*) (1911), Pls. 5, 25, 140.

FIG. 55. Detail from Fra Angelico, *Death and Assumption of the Virgin.* Isabella Stewart Gardner Museum. INSTRUMENTS: tambourine, psaltery, vielle, lute, busine (?)

FIG. 56. Detail
from Fra Angelico,
Last Judgment

be identified by his psaltery. Thus, Fra Angelico has arranged the saints in the same order as Dante did in his heavenly rose.[6] The orders of the angels also appear as in Dante, all stationed in the highest heaven. The cherubim, with bird-like wings, forming the group nearest to Christ, reflect the oldest tradition. Further down and off to the sides, there are scenes of the damned and the blessed. Fra Angelico presents paradise as a charming flower garden in which blessed souls and angels, alternating, are starting a round. At the point where their circle remains open, two clerics, one a Dominican and one a Franciscan, are walking and talking; and again we remember the canto from Dante's *Paradiso* where representatives of these monastic orders play important roles in one realm of heaven. If Fra Angelico did not have this detailed knowledge directly from having read the *Divine Comedy* himself, Dante's ideas must have been commonly known. This is, incidentally, one of Angelico's pictures without a heavenly orchestra.

The *Last Judgment* of the later period, of which a detail is shown here, has a slightly different arrangement. Christ, in the upper middle, is directly surrounded by the three highest orders of the angels, with the cherubim forming the outer frame of the mandorla and the seraphim and the thrones supporting it. In the background the three middle orders appear in rich array, and the minor classes of angels are in the clouds below. On the left, as shown in Fig. 56, the blessed move upward through a flower garden on a sort of mountain path, the mountain being formed by clouds. At the bottom of this left panel, angels with wings, and the blessed, without wings but with a faint halo, again alternate. Farther up there appear groups of three, two of the blessed led by an angel, and still farther up the blessed are forming a kind of procession, not a round but a winding line, as if they were dancing.

In the second half of the fifteenth century such dances became a favorite motif in a variety of scenes and surroundings. Clouds under some of the groups indicate that the dances are supposed to take place in heaven. Only certain important ones shall be mentioned here. Botticelli has angels dance in the illustrations to Dante's *Paradiso* (Fig. 57). Dancing youths appeared on the balconies for the singers in the Cathedral of Florence (Fig. 58). They are less important in Della Robbia's work, though his singers and players will presently

---

[6] *Paradiso*, XXXI, 100; XXXII, 1–39.

FIG. 57. Botticelli's illustration for Dante's *Paradiso*, showing angels dancing around Dante and Beatrice

FIG. 58. Wingless *putti*, dancing and singing. A detail from the so-called Cantoria by Luca della Robbia in the Cathedral of Florence

warrant discussion.[7] In Botticelli's *Nativity* there is a round of angels alternating with blessed in the foreground, and above a charming round of angels.[8] In his *Coronation* (Fig. 59) the group of the Virgin and Christ is surrounded by a similar round of dancing angels. Outside Italy, there is a round of angels in Altdorfer's[9] painting, *Birth of the Virgin*, where the whole scene is set in a cathedral, the Ecclesia, and in this work the cathedral is raised to the heaven of bliss by a crown of dancing *putti*. Dancing angels are sculptured on the foot of the font in the Saint Anthony chapel of Seville's cathedral (*ca.* 1500). Angels dance and also play in a Siennese *Mary in Glory*

[7] *Drawings by Sandro Botticelli for Dante's Divina Commedia*, ed. F. Lippmann (1896), Pls. 21, 28, 29; the drawings are in the Berlin Museum and in the Vatican Library; in the illustration on Pl. 28 the names of the orders are inscribed.

[8] London, National Gallery; K. Escher, *Malerei der Renaissance in Italian* (*Handbuch der Kunstwissenschaft*, 1922), p. 164, Fig. 156.

[9] E. Heidrich, *Die alt-deutsche Malerei* (Jena, 1909), Pl. 154.

FIG. 59. Detail from Botticelli, *Coronation of the Virgin*

FIG. 60. Painting on a fifth-century B.C. Greek vase, showing the nine Muses, only five of them musicians. INSTRUMENTS: harp, lyre, kithara, aulos

from the same period and in the *Madonna with the Girdle* by Matteo di Giovanni.[10]

By the fifteenth century the motif had become so popular that it influenced the representation of other figures, such as the Muses. In antiquity, these goddesses had usually been shown seated or standing; only rarely were they dancing. For example, on a vase from the fifth century B.C., the Muses are seated or standing, five of them with musical instruments (Fig. 60). The classical musical activity of the Muses is singing in antiphonal chorus, as in Homer and later in Petrarch.[11] Around 1400, however, the *Libellus de imaginibus*

[10] Marle, *Italian Schools of Painting*, IV, 165.

[11] Roscher, *Lexikon der Mythologie*, Art. "Musen" (O. Bie); *Odyssey*, XXIV, 47; Petrarca, *Africa*, III, 167–73:

> Hic Graecis Italisque optanda poetis
> Dulcis odorifere lauri viridantis in auro
> Umbra novem placido refovebat tegumine Musas.
> Illas carminibus varioque manentia cantu
> Sidera mulcentes alterna voce putares.

The Greek and Latin poets wish for a pleasant shade, laden with the odors of laurels, to protect the nine muses "whom you would think are with their poems and different songs in alternating voices arresting the stars." This idea goes back to one expressed by Virgil, *Aen.*, x, 696. Furtwängler-Reichhold, *Griechische Vasenmalerei*, Ser. II (1907), Pl. 99; C. Lenormand, *Élite des monuments céramographiques* (1844–61), Pl. 86, Munich, Antikensammlung, Glyptothek.

deorum mentions, among the attributes of Apollo, the "laurel tree . . . under which the Muses nine perform their round" and dance around Apollo singing their melodies. In an Italian manuscript of about 1420, nine dancers are shown performing a round beside Apollo (Fig. 61).[12] The text says that Apollo holds a kithara in his hand, but in the drawing his instrument is a rebec. According to the text, the muses dance around Apollo, but in the illumination they dance at his feet. Raphael followed the tradition of antiquity in his *Parnassus*, but Mantegna and Giulio Romano (Fig. 62) let the Muses perform a round.[13]

Singing Angels

Representations of singing angels were initially less important than those of other musical angels, and there appear to be reasons for their relative neglect. There are figures of angels holding scrolls with a

[12] F. Saxl, "Rinascimento dell'antichità," *Repertorium der Kunstwissenschaft*, 43 (1922); E. Panofsky, *Hercules am Scheidewege, Warburg Institute, Studien*, Vol. 18 (1930), Pl. vi; J. Seznec, *La survivance des dieux antiques* (1940), p. 147.

[13] F. Knapp, *Andrea Mantegna* (*Klassiker der Kunst*) (1910), Pls. 59, 61, 62; E.v.d. Bercken, *Malerei der Renaissance in Italien* (*Handbuch du Kunstwissenschaft*, 1927), p. 36, Fig. 32.

FIG. 61. Apollo seated on a throne with a round of the Muses; a fifteenth-century Italian illumination. INSTRUMENTS: rebec (cythara)

FIG. 62. Giulio Romano, *Il Ballo d'Apollo con le Muse*

text inscribed, a way of expressing singing, as well as telling or saying. However, depicting the act of singing itself, the opened mouth, might make an unfortunate impression, especially in sculpture. Indeed, in Romanesque sculpture this feature had a pejorative connotation. Puffed cheeks and lips were reserved for monsters, and especially for Satan. Perhaps this is why singing angels appear somewhat later than music-making or dancing angels. The earliest, so far, are the fourteenth-century angels found in Bohemia.[14] The singing angels by Gozzoli in the Riccardi Chapel are well known, as are the angels on Van Eyck's Ghent Altarpiece.[15] (The particular problem of the symbolism of Ghent singers is discussed in Appendix IV.) Mantegna included singing *putti* in three of his Madonnas, and there are singing *putti* and angels on the tribunes in the Cathedral of Florence.[16]

[14] A. Friedle, *Mïstr Karleniska Apokalypse* (Ivar, 1950), Pl. 2.

[15] Marle, *Italian Schools of Painting*, xi; L. v. Puyvelde, *The Holy Lamb* (1947), pp. 70, 81; E. Panofsky, *Early Netherlandish Painting* (1953), i, Pl. 150.

[16] P. Schubring, *Die italienische Plastik des Quattrocento* (*Handbuch der Kunstwissenschaft*, 1912), p. 71, Fig. 73; Luca della Robbia, Cathedral of Florence; see also p. 70, Fig. 71, *Madonna with Six Angels*, Kaiser Friedrich Museum, Berlin; H. W. Janson, *The Sculpture of Donatello* (1957).

FIG. 63. Mary in Glory; illumination from a fourteenth-century manuscript called Caleffo dell'Assunta. INSTRUMENTS: double end-blown flute, vielle, lute, psaltery

Singing angels often appear in groups of three, sometimes among other groups playing on instruments but more frequently by themselves. In an illumination of the Adoration by Niccolo di Ser Sozzo Tegliacci (Fig. 63),[17] we have two groups of angels, one with instruments and the other singing. In the *Mary in Glory* by Giovanni di Paolo, Mary appears in a mandorla formed by cherubim.[18] There is a whole orchestra of angels playing in her honor, and among them, on both sides, trios of singing angels. In the illumination for the Annunciation in the *Très riches Heures* at Chantilly, a trio of singing angels appears twice, once within the main picture and once in the margin at the bottom.[19] There are also angels playing on instruments in both locations, but they do not form groups. A group of three angels singing from a music book is to be found in the Nativity in the *Très riches Heures* at Chantilly (Fig. 64), in the Madonna from the Saint Omer Altarpiece by Simon Marmion,[20] and in a Madonna from the Van Eyck school. Groups of three, singing from a scroll, appear in the Nativity pictures by the Master of Flémalle [21] and by Multscher,[22] in an Adoration scene from the Ortenberger Altar,[23] in the *Madonna with Violets* by Lochner,[24] to mention only a few. This trio also appears in a number of later paintings, such as Borgognone's *Adoration of the Christ Child* and his *Madonna with Saints*, where there are two trios of *putti* singing from books.[25] As late as the sixteenth and seventeenth centuries, singing angel trios appear in the Assumptions by Sabbatini and by Lanfranco, along with

---

[17] Bernath, *Die Malerei*, Fig. 424; Marle, *Italian Schools of Painting*, II, 601; the manuscript, a collection of government documents, is called *Caleffo dell'Assunta*.

[18] Marle, *Italian Schools of Painting*, IX, 456.

[19] Panofsky, *Early Netherlandish Painting*, II, Pl. 36, Fig. 80.

[20] G. Ring, *A Century of French Painting* (1949), Pl. 99, cat. no. 171, National Gallery, London.

[21] Panofsky, *Early Netherlandish Painting*, II, Pls. 88–89. See also Fig. 233, Jacques Daret, *Nativity*.

[22] Heidrich, *Die alt-deutsche Malerei*; Kaiser Friedrich Museum, Berlin.

[23] Altar aus Ortenberg, Mainzer Werkstatt, *ca.* 1420–30, Darmstadt Museum; G. Dehio, *Geschichte der deutschen Kunst*, Vol. II (1921), Fig. 432; F. Burger, *Die deutsche Malerei* (*Handbuch der Kunstwissenschaft*, I, 1917), Pl. xxv.

[24] Burger, *Die deutsche Malerei*, Cologne Museum; see also the Madonnas by Gossaert in Palermo and Lisbon, M. Friedländer, *Altniederländische Malerei*, VIII (1934), Pl. 2; Wolgemut, *Nativity*; Heidrich, *Die alt-deutsche Malerei*, Pl. 88.

[25] Bercken, *Malerei der Renaissance*, p. 54, Fig. 56.

FIG. 64. Nativity, with three angels singing on the roof; illumination by Pol de Limbourg in *Les très riches Heures du Duc de Berry*

players of instruments in both instances. They appear unaccompanied in Spada's *Vision of Saint Francis*.[26]

The singing angels do not always seem to inhabit heaven, though sometimes they are in clouds. Often they appear to act as messengers from heaven. It is noteworthy that they are so often grouped in threes, a number which inevitably connotes the Holy Three, the Holy Trinity, though the choice of a trio may also have been due to the fact that this was the usual arrangement for the part songs of the fourteenth century.

[26] C. Ricci, *Geschichte der Kunst in Nord-Italien* (1911), Fig. 754, Modena Gallery.

ANGEL ORCHESTRAS

The heavenly dancers and singing angels described above were eventually outnumbered by the representations of angels playing musical instruments. Indeed, these representations are so numerous that one can trace only some of the more important forms and traditions here, and touch only on the major problems involved. With few exceptions, all these representations of musician angels are meant to illustrate music and song in the praise of the Lord, of Christ, and of the Virgin in the highest heaven. There are a very few exceptions, where the angels appear as divine inspiration, as in the vaults of Offida (Fig. 65) and of Kampill near Bolzano.[27] Here, the holy men are depicted in the act of writing their works. In Offida, above each prophet an angel is playing on a musical instrument. In Kampill, angels are kneeling and playing in front of the Church Fathers. Thus, angels have now taken over the role assigned to the Muses in pagan works.[28]

The traditions of the angel orchestra range from representations based on the old, structured vision of the cosmos to those in which all divisions into spheres have been dissolved and angels fill the whole heaven. The structure of the cosmos may be clearly visible or it may be discernible through a more or less veiled division in several layers or groups. The groups may either represent all the nine orders or only sections; all the orders or only a selection may be recognized through their emblems, or sometimes the musician angels alone are distinguished by their instruments. The angels may just hold the instruments in their hands, or they may be represented performing, or dancing, as well as singing and playing. The figures of the angels may be differentiated from the crowds of the faithful and the blessed or they may be identified with them.

However, apart from the exceptions where the music gives inspiration, the representations of musician angels can only be interpreted as expressing celestial music and harmony, and a state of bliss. They subscribe to the old Platonic tradition of identifying musical and cosmic harmony. In the paintings after 1300 or so, the cosmos is not al-

[27] See Marle, *Italian Schools of Painting*, VIII, 359; for Kampill, see Burger, *Die deutsche Malerei*, II, 297, Fig. 245; A. Colasanti, "Per la storia dell'arte nelle Marche," *L'Arte*, x (Rome, 1907).

[28] E. R. Curtius, *Europäische Literatur und lateinisches Mittelalter* (1948), pp. 233–50.

FIG. 65. Detail of the vault of Santa Maria della Bocca at Offida. INSTRUMENTS: psaltery, positive organ, lute, bowed rebec, double flute, harp

ways represented in full, as nine spheres. To the contrary, all the orders of the angels are generally placed in the highest heaven, or paradise. In the earlier written sources, such as Capella, the pagan deities were the movers of the spheres. Now the angels take their place, and at the same time are gathered in the highest sphere of heaven. Ultimately, as ensuing chapters will show, the pagan deities and forces rejoined the music-makers, but for several centuries, until about 1500, the angels starred in this role.

Starting in approximately the fourteenth century, angels became increasingly identified with the blessed, whereas in Dante's *Paradiso* they were still to be understood as separate entities. In earlier representations of the Last Judgment from the Romanesque period, the blessed were shown, to one side, as emerging from their graves and lifting the covers of their coffins. Mâle [29] and other scholars concluded, therefore, that the outlook of the twelfth and thirteenth centuries was more pessimistic, and that people then visualized the state in hell as more frightening, perhaps excluding any happier hereafter. But it seems to me that it was not that the state of bliss was doubted, but simply that the painters and sculptors had not yet found a form for expressing the vision of paradise. In the literary sources, such as the writings of Saints Bernard, Bonaventure, and Thomas,[30] one reads that light and music are the characteristics of the highest heaven. But how was music to be represented as long as the playing of instruments was considered sinful? Even Dante, in his grandiose vision, still mentions only singing and dancing, not instrumental music.[31] Heavenly music-makers with instruments had been shown in a few exceptional instances, such as the Beatus manuscripts. There they were a sign of the beauty of heaven, as also in the derived Romanesque sculptures. But it must be borne in mind that the new music, the *ars nova*, made its appearance in the thirteenth century, and that it was not until the fourteenth and fifteenth centuries that instrumental music came into its own as an art.[32] Attitudes toward instrumental music were changing, too, so that Johannes Tinctoris, who lived at the time of the flowering of the Burgundian court, could write in his *Complexus effectuum musicae* (*On the Effects of Music*), "If the painters want to picture the happiness of the blessed they paint angels with different musical instruments. This would not be permitted if the Church did not think that the happiness of the

---

[29] *L'art religieux du XIIIe siècle* (Paris, 1919); M. Meiss, *Painting in Florence* (1951); Panofsky, *Early Netherlandish Painting*, p. 74.

[30] Mâle, *L'art religieux de la fin du moyen-âge en France*, p. 477, names Saint Bernard and Saint Thomas without giving the exact source; Panofsky, "Abbot Suger de St.-Denis," *Meaning in the Visual Arts* (1955), pp. 130ff.; W. Schöne, *Über das Licht* (1954); M. Meiss, "Light as Form and Symbol," *Art Bulletin*, XXVII (1945), 175ff.

[31] Dante mentions musical instruments only as comparison, *Paradiso*, XII, 118; XIV, 118; XX, 24.

[32] J. Wolf, *Geschichte der Mensural-Notation* (1904); G. Reese, *Music in the Middle Ages* (1940), pp. 202f. and 324f. with rich bibliography.

FIG. 66. The Lord in Glory in the Celestial Jerusalem; twelfth-century illumination from Saint Augustine's *Civitas Dei*. INSTRUMENTS: oval and guitar-fiddles, bowed rebec

blessed was enriched by music." [33] All these ideas and impressions are found integrated in the paintings from about 1300 on.

Paradise is sometimes represented as part of the highest heaven, the Empyreum. It has been noted that in Fra Angelico's *Last Judgment*, paradise is a beautiful garden adjoining the highest heaven, where the celestial court sits, flanking Christ's mandorla. In Fra Angelico's painting, *Christ in Glory*, the scene is laid entirely in the highest heaven; [34] the angels attending Christ are grouped as in the old frescoes, as if they were standing in different spheres, but the last scene shown is the Empyreum. In a later version of the Last Judgment, the construction of the hierarchy is more compact, and there is not the slightest doubt that the scene is the highest heaven; the other sections pale in comparison with the mandorla, which is flanked by the celestial court and the musician angels. This arrangement became typical for representations of the Coronation of the Virgin, where usually only the central scene is shown: Christ crowning the Virgin, surrounded by musician angels.

The *Civitas Dei* also was adapted to this form. [35] For Augustine, the City of God was a spiritual community of the faithful; by the time in question it had become a celestial city, the heavenly Jerusalem, surrounded by walls like a medieval town. A very early representation occurs in a twelfth-century manuscript of the Canterbury school (Fig. 66). The walls form the frame of the illumination, with four high columns or towers. In four layers, the apostles and saints attend the heavenly court. On the highest tier, the Lord, in a mandorla, is flanked by six angels playing instruments: three stringed instruments with bows on the right and on the left, a wind instrument, a dulcimer and a harp. [36] This motif was especially popular in the illuminations of the French manuscripts of the *Civitas Dei* (Fig. 67). Usually the Lord was placed in the center, flanked by the celestial court, surrounded by walls; musician angels appear above in the clouds or, more often, in the framework and margin borders. The scene is the highest heaven, Dante's Empyreum.

[33] E. de Coussemaker, *Scriptores de musica* (1867), II, 504.

[34] F. Schottmüller, *Fra Angelico*, Pl. 25, Accademia, Florence; Pl. 5, National Gallery, London; Pl. 140, Kaiser Friedrich Museum, Berlin.

[35] A. de Laborde, *Les manuscrits à peinture de la Cité de Dieu* (Société des bibliophiles français, Paris, 1909).

[36] Florence, Bibl. Laurenziana, MS. Plut. 12, cod. 17, fol. 2; C. R. Dodwell, *The Canterbury School of Illuminations* (Cambridge, 1954), Pl. 17a; Hammerstein, *Die Musik der Engel*, Fig. 55.

FIG. 67. The Lord in Glory in the Celestial Jerusalem; fifteenth-century illumination from Saint Augustine's *Civitas Dei*. INSTRUMENTS: shawms, lutes, harps

A number of representations, however, adhere more to the older tradition that distinguished separate spheres. In an Italian manuscript from about 1400, the illumination to the text *Santa Trinità* (Fig. 68) shows one arc with stars, denoting the dome of heaven or the firmament. Above is the figure of Christ. Two angels stand where the arc meets the border of the illumination; they are playing on a psaltery and a bowed instrument. These figures are tall compared with the arc, and it may be that the illuminator was inspired by a model in a church where an arch was flanked by the figures of two angels. The *Mary in Glory* by Geertgen [37] or his school shows Mary

[37] Now in the van Beuningen Collection, Holland; M. Friedländer, Zu Geertgen tot Sint Jans; *Maandblad voor beeldende Kunsten* (Amsterdam, August 1949); H. Gerson, *Van Geertgen tot Frans Hals* (1950), Pl. 12.

surrounded by three circles of angels (see Fig. 81); however, the place of the scene is the highest heaven. In representations of the Adoration of the Lamb, the influence of the old tradition is even stronger, for a division into the parts of the cosmos, sometimes as on a chart, prevails. The Ghent Altarpiece divides scenes into distinct panels where the musician angels have their definite place.

It has been mentioned that in the Beatus manuscripts, where the

FIG. 68. The Lord in Glory; fourteenth-century illumination. INSTRUMENTS: psaltery, bowed fiddle or vielle

FIG. 69. Coronation of the Virgin; fourteenth-century fresco in the Cathedral of Venzone. INSTRUMENTS: 3 psalteries, 2 lutes, 2 tambourines, portative organ; 2 busines, lute, vielle, drum (?) nakers, portative organ; 2 guitars, fiddles, tambourine, psaltery, bowed rebec. Foto Technograph UDINE

musician angels appear for the first time, they stand side-by-side with the musician Elders; yet at first it was the Elders who carried on the tradition, the angels as musicians being a later development. Where the angels appeared beside the Elders, the latter were often placed in a group and played on musical instruments, while the angels showed the emblems of their orders but did not make music. For this combination we have a good and elaborate example on the Royal Portal at Chartres (see Fig. 47).[38] Fortunately, there is one work in which the two sections of the heavenly orchestra, the Elders and the angels, meet; and both are included as musicians in the hierarchy of the highest heaven. It is a fourteenth-century fresco, a Coronation, in the Cathedral of Venzone in northern Italy (Fig. 69).[39] In the center, Christ is crowning Mary; above them there are angels with wind in-

[38] Et. Houvet, *Cathédrale de Chartres* (1926).

[39] L. Coletti, "Sull'origine e sulla diffusione della scuola pittorica Romagnuola nel trecento," *Dedalo*, xi (1930/31), 291, 301; possibly of the fourteenth century.

struments, and Christ and Mary are flanked by rows of angels, with
those in the front row carrying musical instruments. On the left of
the center section there are three angels with lute, psaltery, and a
wind instrument; on the right, three angels with a wind instrument, a
portable organ, and a double drum. Above the group of Christ and
Mary, and above the musician angels on top, there are angels, elderly
men (perhaps the apostles), and youthful figures, all without music.
On the farther sides, in separate sections, appear the Elders, identified by their crowns and beards, and they make music. The left-hand
group has two tambourines, a portable organ, two lutes, and three
psalteries; the right-hand group has what might be identified as a
tambourine, a psaltery, three bowed instruments of different sizes
(one with a curved neck), a harp, and a portable organ. This fresco is
the only example I have been able to find which combines the tradition of both groups working together as musicians.

When angels alone are the music-makers, the duty of playing on
instruments is sometimes assigned to only one of the orders, sometimes to several; yet there are instances in which all of the angels
play music. When only one order is playing, the instruments are
usually given to the group placed lowest or farthest from the center.
The Mary in Glory in the illumination by Niccolo di Ser Sozzo
Tegliacci from a Sienese manuscript shown above (see Fig. 63) [40] is
an early example. The Virgin in the mandorla is supported by the
inner circle of the angels; the orders of the cherubim and seraphim
form two rows on top. Then follow, in descending order on each side,
groups of adoring figures, singing angels, and, finally, angels with
musical instruments (psaltery, lute, vielle, and flute).

This arrangement, with the music-making assigned to the lowest
order of angels, appears in numerous representations. In the *Assunta*
by Masolino (Fig. 70),[41] the Virgin is in a mandorla formed by
cherubim and seraphim. Both orders are shaped like swallows, with
human heads with halos. An outer circle is formed by the other
orders, with the angels carrying the emblems of their status—shields,
orbs, lances, scepters—the Virtues holding banners inscribed *virtues;*
and at the bottom, there are four angels with psaltery, lute, vielle,
and portable organ. In the Coronation by Leonardo da Bisuccio (Fig.
71),[42] in a mandorla, Christ is crowning the Virgin and they are

---

[40] See n. 17 above.

[41] Marle, *Italian Schools of Painting*, IX, 279.

[42] *Ibid.*, VII, 147–50.

FIG. 70. Masolino, *Assumption of the Virgin.* INSTRUMENTS: lute, portative organ, vielle, psaltery

FIG. 71. Leonardo da Bisuccio, Coronation of the Virgin; fifteenth-century fresco in San Giovanni a Carbonara at Naples. INSTRUMENTS: 4 busines, vielle, portative organ, vielle, lute, shawm, harp, psaltery, portative organ

being blessed by the Lord. The angels frame the mandorla in a broad band. The corners, outside of this frame, are filled by groups of the saints, patriarchs, and donors. The angels themselves are divided into distinct groups. The innermost bands are formed by cherubim and seraphim. The outer circle has an arrangement different from the Sienese and Masolino pictures: the angels are divided into four sections, and their position follows the line of the mandorlas so that the upper group forms a kind of steeple and has a counterpart of two groups of angels at the bottom. The groups at both top and bottom carry palm branches or fold their hands in prayer. The two middle sections of angels are musicians, with the singers in the higher rows and the angels playing on instruments in the lower row; the lower orders are on the sides.

Angels without instruments were not always identified with a particular order. Thus, the Coronation by Giusto da Padova [43] shows the Virgin flanked by adoring angels without emblems, but in their midst, to both left and right, there are two lute players and a tambourine player. In the *Coronation* by Caterino and Donato Veneziano [44] groups of angels appear above and below the Virgin. In the group above, the angels carry a lute, a bow instrument, a portable organ, and again a lute; below, between two adorants, there is an angel with a portable organ.

Frequently, however, angel orders are clearly distinguishable. In a Coronation by Bernardo Daddi,[45] two corresponding trios of musician angels are each playing on an organ, a herald trumpet, and a stringed instrument. To either side of the throne there are two rows of saints, and the highest positions are occupied by the higher orders of the angels, ending with the cherubim. In a Madonna by the same master (Uffizi), four angels are playing at the foot of the throne, and at the sides are groups of singing angels. In a Coronation by a master of the school of Daddi, we have several groups of angels on the sides, with the bird-like cherubim and seraphim grouped around the heads of Christ and the Virgin, and orders with scepters and lances below these. Yet farther below there are two groups of saints, and at the

[43] *Ibid.*, IV, 165, Coronation tryptich, National Gallery, London.

[44] Ricci, *Geschichte der Kunst*, Figs. 85, 86; Marle, *Italian Schools of Painting*, IV, 61, Venice, Querini Stampaglia, and 63, Venice, Accademia.

[45] Bernath, *Die Malerei*, Pl. 155, Fig. 363, Altenburg Museum; another version in Berenson, *Italian Painters*, Fig. 130, National Gallery, Washington.

bottom in the middle, four angels with herald trumpets and two kneeling angels with a vielle and a portable organ.

Arrangements vary considerably. In a Coronation of the Sienese school (*ca.* 1450),[46] the Virgin is surrounded by the celestial court, the mandorla supported by cherubim. Angels form two upper circles, the lower ones making music; at the left can be seen a wind instrument, drum, vielle, and a kind of lute, the mandorla; at the right four wind instruments. Below in a round appear a double aulos, an organ, and a vielle. In the *Coronation* by Lorenzo Veneziano (Milan, second half of the fourteenth century), two angels with organs are kneeling at the foot of the throne. Above, two angels are holding a curtain over Christ and the Virgin. Behind and above the throne, in a semicircle, are two rows of angels with different instruments, and singing angels appear in the background. In the *Last Judgment* by Zanobi Strozzi di Benedetto (1412–68),[47] a pupil of Fra Angelico, Christ is surrounded by circles and flanked by four rows of angels. At His feet there are in the center two organ players, then three long straight trumpets on the left, and on the right a tambourine and one short and two long herald trumpets. There are other instruments in all of the groups, but not with all the angels. The row before last at the top centers around a portable organ on the left and a lute on the right, a combination which should be remembered. There are two Coronations by Paolo Veneziano (fourteenth century), with musician angels.[48] In the version at the Brera, there are two organs, above and below the group of Christ and Mary, and three lines of musicians below them. The instruments to the left are a bladder pipe (a kind of bagpipe), a lute, a recorder, a tambourine, and an organ; in the middle row there are three angels on each side, two of whom can be recognized as singing; the instruments are a psaltery, a bowed instrument, and a lute; on the right, a recorder, a harp, one short and two long wind instruments, and an organ appear. In the version formerly in Sigmaringen and now in the Frick Collection, two angels with portable organs stand beside Christ and the Virgin; above the throne there is a group of angel musicians: four angels with tam-

---

[46] Kaiser Friedrich Museum, Berlin, *ca.* 1450, W. Hausenstein, "Die Malerei der frühen Italiener," *Das Bild. Atlanten zur Kunst*, 3/4 (1922); a very similar arrangement in the *Madonna with the Girdle* by Matteo di Giovanni, National Gallery, London, see Fig. 80.

[47] Marle, *Italian Schools of Painting*, x, 173.

[48] *Ibid.*, iv, 6, 13; Bernath, *Die Malerei*.

bourine, herald trumpet, lute, and bladder pipe on the left; four
angels with a psaltery and three wind instruments on the right; and,
in the middle, three singing angels and three with instruments—lute,
psaltery, and vielle (Fig. 72).

Thus it seems there were a variety of solutions rather than any
strict rules for placing the musician angels, especially in the Coronation and Assumption paintings. However, it may be said that when
there is a hierarchy with several circles or layers, the allotment of
musical instruments to the angels in the lower level or in the outer
circle seems to prevail. Mary in Glory is more often surrounded by
circles; in the Madonna pictures, the throne is usually flanked by
groups, or musician angels sit on the steps of the throne. In the earlier Madonna paintings by Cimabue and Giotto, the angels stand at
the sides of the throne to support it.[49] Later, this function of support
is often given to the higher groups, while the lower ones have the
musical instruments. In Donatello's Padua Altar,[50] the Madonna is
in the center and the musician angels on the base. Sometimes the
musician angels stand behind the throne, and the instruments are
placed beside the head of the Madonna, as noted above in the Coronation pictures by Paolo Veneziano. More often, the place for
the performers is at her feet. The Madonna pictures are essentially
a concentration of the vision of Mary in Glory, and the usual two
or three musician angels on the steps are a reflection of the richer
circles or rows of musician angels which appear in Assumption and
Coronation pictures. The background of the throne can only be interpreted as the highest heaven, even if very often it is not specifically indicated, and the angels must be visualized on this background.

Most of the representations of musician angels originated in Italy.
Neither in France nor in the northern countries is their appearance so
general. Yet some specific traits of the French conception are worth
mentioning. French works tend to show the Empyreum not as a
dome of clouds but as similar to real cathedrals and cities. It has been
noted that the *Civitas Dei* in French manuscripts has the form of a
walled city.[51] The different approach of the French masters may be

---

[49] G. v. Vitzthum, *Die Malerei und Plastik des Mittelalters in Italien* (*Handbuch der Kunstwissenschaft*, 1924); Cimabue, pp. 248ff., Figs. 200 and 201;
Giotto, p. 263, Fig. 212.

[50] Janson, *The Sculpture of Donatello*, Vol. 1, Pl. 257.

[51] Laborde, *Les manuscripts à peinture de la Cité de Dieu*, Pl. 127.

FIG. 72. Paolo Veneziano, *Coronation of the Virgin*. Copyright The Frick Collection, New York. INSTRUMENTS (from left to right): portative organ, tambourine, busine or herald trumpet, psaltery, vielle, lute, mandora, bladder pipe, shawm, psaltery, busine, shawm, portative organ

illustrated with an illumination from Fouquet's *Chevalier Hours*.[52]
Here, in the *Madonna in the Church* (Fig. 73), Mary is seated in a
cathedral portal or arched niche which has three voussoirs of adoring
angels. She is attended by angels in the position and costumes of
choir boys. The illumination of the Holy Trinity from the same
Book of Hours also sets the scene in the interior of a cathedral.
Twelve circles of angels surround the Trinity. Cherubim and seraphim, the former characterized by six feathered wings, the latter by
the color red, as of fire, form two circles around the Trinity. Rows of
figures follow, like the voussoirs of a portal, starting at the bottom
with saints and patriarchs and the like, and changing to angels in
adoring postures as the row rises. Neither illumination suggests an
outdoor image of the highest heaven so much as the interior of a
cathedral.

The work of the French masters also differs from the Italians in
that the French angels are busier with practical duties as servants and
pages, such as carrying the crown and the train of the Virgin's man-
tle, as shown, for example, in the Coronation illumination of the
Berry Hours.[53] In Fouquet's *Chevalier Hours*, angels serve Saint
Michael like pages, and one is supporting his wings while he is fighting the dragon.[54] A third characteristic of the French is that they
often place musician angels in the arches of buildings. Thus, two
angels with bowed instruments (mandorla and vielle), appear in the
frame of the Bargello Diptych (French, *ca.* 1390),[55] on the upper
left part of the architecture. Musician angels appear in the architectural border of a drawing of Saint Jerome in his study by Pol de
Limbourg, where they may be understood as signs of inspiration
(Fig. 74).[56]

One further French illumination worth noting is from the
fourteenth-century manuscript of Dionysius in the Bibliothèque
Nationale (Fig. 75).[57] At the bottom, Saint Denis is shown writing

[52] K. Perls, *Jean Fouquet* (1940), p. 57, Fig. 25, and plate between pp. 56
and 57.

[53] *Les belles heures de Jean de France*, ed. Jean Porcher (1953), Pl. xxx,
fol. 30.

[54] Perls, *Jean Fouquet*, p. 73, Fig. 41.

[55] Ring, *A Century of French Painting*, Pl. 1.

[56] Bernath, *Die Malerei*, Fig. 267; Ring, *A Century of French Painting*, p.
27, Fig. 13.

[57] H. Martin, *Légende de Saint-Denis* (1908).

FIG. 73. Etienne Chevalier adoring the Virgin; from the *Heures d'Etienne Chevalier*. INSTRUMENTS: 2 recorders, cornette or *Rauschpfeife*, psaltery, vielle, lute

FIG. 74. Detail from Saint Jerome in his study; illumination by Pol de Limbuorg which appears in a fragmentary manuscript of the *Bible moralisée*. INSTRUMENTS: transverse flute, harp, nakers, lute, vielle, portative organ

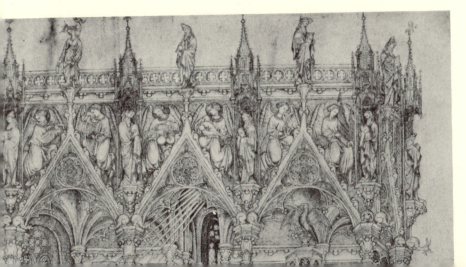

FIG. 75. Saint Denis at his desk, writing his book on the Hierarchy; illumination in a fourteenth-century manuscript of *De Hierarchia*. INSTRUMENTS: vielle, shawms, 2 portative organs, 2 guitars

his book. Above him, in nine arcs, appear the nine orders of the angels, three angels on each side. In three of these nine rows or arcs, the angels have musical instruments. The instruments are identical on both left and right sides of the arcs. In the lowest circle, each trio has a plucked instrument, a wind instrument, and a percussion instrument; in the fifth circle, a psaltery, an organ, and a tambourine; and in the ninth circle, cymbals, shawms, and vielles. In the arc second from the bottom, there are two cymbal players on each side, in addition to an angel with censers. The rest of the angels either hold censers or crowns, or they are adorants. This is the old tradition of the structure of the heavens in nine spheres with Dionysius's nine orders of the angels, but the orders have not the usual emblems and, contrary to the theory of the hierarchy, three of the orders are musicians.

When discussing singing angels, we noted the frequent appearance of a trio of singers as messengers or as a sign from heaven. Groups of

FIG. 76. Hieronymus Bosch, roundel from the painting *The Seven Cardinal Sins*. INSTRUMENTS: psaltery, busine, harp

FIG. 77. Detail from
the Ortenberger Altar.
INSTRUMENTS: harp, lute

three music-making angels occur in all kinds of scenes, but they may always be regarded as messengers from heaven, whether they appear in clouds or on earth. For example a group appears in the clouds in the Saint Omer Altarpiece [58] by Marmion. Such a group is built into the hierarchy of Bosch's *Seven Cardinal Sins* (Fig. 76). Christ enthroned is flanked by adoring angels, and four adoring angels kneel before Him while saints look on from the right. On the left, the blessed are seen entering paradise through a door, where they are recieved by Saint Peter and defended against Satan by Saint Michael. In the center foreground, three angels are making music on a psaltery, a wind instrument, and a harp. In Cranach's *Flight into Egypt*,[59] two angels are playing on pipes beside the Christ-child, and there are similar angel musicians in the Adoration of the Child [60] on the Ortenberg Altar (Fig. 77). Four music-making angels are leaning against a column, playing and singing, in Bramantino's *Nativ-*

[58] Ring, *A Century of French Painting.*
[59] Heidrich, *Die alt-deutsche Malerei*, Pl. 158; Kaiser Friedrich Museum, Berlin.
[60] See n. 23 above.

ity; [61] a similar group appears beside the Christ-child in Piero della Francesca's *Nativity*.[62]

In the course of the sixteenth century, the image of a structure of heaven gradually dissolved. In Signorelli's painting in the cathedral at Orvieto, the elects upon entering heaven are greeted by musician angels on clouds, playing tambourines, lutes, a guitar, a harp, and a vielle.[63] In pictures of the Assumption, a theme now more popular than the Coronation, Mary is seen soaring or flying upward into the clouds, sometimes greeted or supported by angels. Relatively few of these angels are musicians. Thus, in Titian's *Assumption*,[64] one of the *putti* holds a tambourine and one a small pipe; in Sabbatini's *Assumption*,[65] a group of angels seems to be singing, one with a harp, another a plucked instrument (only partially shown). In the *Assumption* by Lanfranco,[66] three angels are singing and one has a lyra da braccio. In the *Assumption* of Annibale Carracci, one angel has a pipe and a viola da braccio. The orchestration is comparatively elaborate in a painting, *Paradise*, by Lodovico Carracci in San Paolo, Bologna (Fig. 78),[67] where angels in several groups are playing on wind, string, and percussion instruments; there is also a chorus singing in the background and one angel conducting. In the lower left of the picture are saints and, above, one angel is swinging a censer; yet no distinct layers are discernible. Indeed, in none of these paintings is there any suggestion of a systematic structure of spheres or orders.

However there are some paintings as late as the sixteenth century in which one can recognize a certain structure of the parts of heaven, though not of the order of the angels. In the cupola at Saronno by Gaudenzio Ferrari (Fig. 79), as well as in the so-called *Paradise* by Tintoretto [68] in the Louvre, there are three strata. In

[61] A. Venturi, *North Italian Drawings of the Quatrocento*, Vol. 1 (1930), Pl. 34; Suardi called Bramantino, Ambrosiana, Milan.

[62] K. Clark, *Piero della Francesca* (1951), Pls. 125–28.

[63] R. Hamann, *Die Frührenaissance der italienischen Malerei* (1909), Pl. 87.

[64] H. Tietze, *Titian* (1950), Pl. 35.

[65] Ricci, *Geschichte der Kunst*, p. 387, Fig. 739; Accademia, Bologna.

[66] *Ibid.*, p. 397, Fig. 752; Pitti, Florence.

[67] A. Voss, *Die Malerei des Barock in Rom* (1924), Pl. 152; Dresden Gallery.

[68] Detlev v. Hadeln, "Die Vorgeschichte von Tintoretto's Paradies im Dogenpalast," *Jahrbuch der preussischen Kunstsammlungen*, Vol. 40 (1919), pp. 119ff., with sketch for the Louvre painting. K. Geiringer, "Gaudenzio Ferraris Engelkonzert," *Beethoven Zentenarfeier* (1927).

FIG. 78. Lodovico Carracci, *Paradise*. INSTRUMENTS: portative organ, cymbals, lute, recorder, cornette, triangle, gamba, harp, lute, trombone, shawm

FIG. 79. (OPPOSITE PAGE) Gaudenzio Ferrari, *Assumption of the Virgin*, sixteenth-century cupola painting in the cathedral at Saronno. The painting shows conductor, 18 singers, and 61 instrumentalists. A detailed list of the instruments in K. Geiringer, *Gaudenzio Ferraris Engelkonzert*

both paintings, the crowd of musician angels is assigned to one circle of clouds, and they are so conspicuous that the other sections seem veiled, almost hidden, in the background. Tintoretto's *Paradise* is a Coronation, and in the famous dome at Saronno, Ferrari has painted an Assumption in which the highest heaven is divided into three separate spheres. On top, at the apex, the Lord appears in a circle formed by seraphim, who are shown as heads with flames and rays instead of the bodies—a sign that these angels are born anew every day out of the celestial fire. A second, lower sphere is formed by a round of dancing *putti*, and the third and largest sphere is occupied by musician angels. The figure of the Virgin, above the console of the organ, is almost obscured in the crowd; she is crowned by two *putti* and supported by four.

Let us go back and compare some typical paintings of the Coronation and the Assumption from the fifteenth through the seventeenth centuries. In Fra Angelico's *Death and Assumption of the Virgin*,[69] the Virgin appears in the clouds; the scene, typical for Fra Angelico, is seen against a horizon. Three layers are recognizable in terms of groups of angels: in the lowest there are kneeling, supporting, or adoring angels; in the middle there is a dancing round, and in the upper, groups of angels with musical instruments.

A representation typical of the middle of the fifteenth century is Matteo di Giovanni's (*ca.* 1435–95) *Madonna with the Girdle* (Fig. 80). In the center, Mary is seated on a throne flanked by cherubim. Above is Christ, also surrounded by cherubim and flanked by two groups of patriarchs and apostles. At the sides of the throne are two groups of six angels, arranged in two rows. The higher ones are singing; the three in the lower rows are playing on instruments—on the left, lute, tambourine, double aulos; on the right, shawm, cymbals, and an S-shaped trumpet. Below, a round of angels is dancing and at the same time playing on instruments: portable organ, nakers, two bowed instruments, a harp, and a lute. Toward the end of the fifteenth century there is Geertgen's *Mary in Glory* (Fig. 81);[70] here the Virgin also appears in the sky, surrounded by three concentric circles of angels. The innermost is formed by the heads and wings of angels, who are identified as cherubim and seraphim by the colors red and blue. In the middle circle the angels hold the objects of the Pas-

[69] See n. 34 above.

[70] See n. 37 above. E. Winternitz, "On angel concerts in the 15th century," *Musical Quarterly*, 49 (1963).

FIG. 80. Matteo di Giovanni, *Madonna with the Girdle*. Reproduced by courtesy of the Trustees, The National Gallery, London. INSTRUMENTS: lutes, tambourine, double flute, shawm, cymbals, S-shaped trumpet, psaltery, nakers, portative organ, vielle, harp

FIG. 81. Geertgen tot Sint Jans, *Mary in glory*. INSTRUMENTS (from top counter-clockwise): lute, shawm, vielle, handbell, pipe and tabor, hurdy-gurdy, jingle bells, clappers, coiled trumpet, bagpipe, set of seven small jingles on a rope, positive organ, clavichord, krummhorn, dulcimer, double shawm, claviciterium

FIG. 82. Master of the Saint Lucy Legend, *Mary, Queen of Heaven*. National
Gallery of Art, Washington, D.C. Samuel H. Kress Collection. INSTRUMENTS
(from left to right): portative organ, shawm, harp, shawm, vielle, shawm, lute;
(above): harp, dulcimer, lute, 3 recorders

FIG. 83. Detail from Tintoretto, *Coronation of the Virgin*. INSTRUMENTS: clavichord, harp, lute

sion. In the other circle, the angels have musical instruments. Thus, here the hierarchy of angels is similar to the arrangement in the cupola. As noted above, there may be a link with the illumination in the Scivias manuscript (see Fig. 40), which shows nine circles, of which the inner ones correspond to the Geertgen painting, though there are no musical instruments.

A good example of the hierarchy represented in the form of layers is provided by the *Mary, Queen of Heaven* by the Master of the Saint Lucy Legend (Fig. 82).[71] The Virgin appears between earth and paradise, supported by eight angels. At the bottom there is the landscape of Bruges which is typical for this painter. At the top is the Holy Trinity, surrounded by groups of singing and playing angels, inside a circle of dense clouds. Further, there are three groups of musician angels: three in mid-air, beside the Madonna, with a lute, a portable organ, and a wind instrument; then four angels singing, with sheets of music in their hands, forming a semicircle in the clouds above the head of the Virgin; and then, still higher, on the level of the dense circle of clouds bordering the Trinity, four angels with musical instruments—harp, dulcimer, and three recorders. The form of this painting is derived from the arrangement on the triumphal arches. There are three levels, the lowest at the side of the Virgin

[71] Gerson, *Van Geertgen tot Frans Hals;* the Flemish Master of the Saint Lucy Legend (fl. 1480–89); S. W. Kenney, *Walter Frye and the Countenance Angloise* (New Haven, 1964).

having the typical group of three angels with lute and organ; the figures of the Trinity and the surrounding angels are much smaller, in order to depict the distant height of paradise.

From the sixteenth century there is the Tintoretto painting generally called *Paradise*,[72] but actually a Coronation of the Virgin. The scene consists of six or seven strata, all in the clouds. On the highest level, Christ is crowning Mary, both flanked by apostles. On lower levels of clouds there are groups of the blessed, and then, on the lowest cloud (Fig. 83), centered in the painting, there is an orchestra of angels assembled around a keyboard instrument. Directly above and seemingly behind this orchestra, there are angels grouped like a choir.

Finally, from the seventeenth century there is Mignard's[73] cupola decoration in the Val-de-Grâce church in Paris, also generally referred to as a *Paradise*. It shows three not very distinct layers with musician angels, all in the clouds.

It is characteristic of all these Coronation and Assumption representations that the scene is set in the sky, usually in clouds, and there is a hierarchy of blessed and of angels. No particular number of spheres or layers can be established, although three seems to be the most usual arrangement. Nor does there seem to be any set number of angels making music.

The paintings that might be termed *Paradises* more appropriately than Tintoretto's and Mignard's have certain noteworthy characteristics of their own. Generally, the scene is not placed in the clouds, or, at least, only part of it, and the hierarchy is distinctly separated into several groups. An early example of this type is Jacobello del Fiore's *Coronation* (Fig. 84),[74] which is thought to have been modeled on the *Paradiso* by Guariento. The whole hierarchy is arranged in and around an architectural core. In the top center Mary and Christ sit enthroned on an elaborate base; below are the four evangelists, and still lower seven musician angels. On each side there are three columns of saints and angels, but no clouds.

---

[72] See n. 68 above.

[73] N. Pevsner, *Barockmalerei in den romanischen Ländern* (*Handbuch der Kunstwissenschaft*, 1928), p. 320, Fig. 236; Paris, Val-de-Grâce; A. de Champeaux, "L'art décoratif dans le vieux Paris," *Gazette des Beaux-Arts*, ii (1890), 405, without illustration.

[74] Marle, *Italian Schools of Painting*, vii, Fig. 355; Colosanti, "Per la storia dell'arte nelle Marche."

FIG. 84. Jacobello del Fiore, *Coronation of the Virgin*. The angelic orders in vertical rows are recognizable by their emblems: orbs, scepters, shields, crowns, censers. INSTRUMENTS (from left to right): psaltery, vielle, psaltery, portative organ, harp, tambourine, lute

Then there is the Adoration of the Lamb on the Ghent Altar,[75] a theme that seldom recurred in either painting or sculpture after the illuminations to the Beatus manuscripts of Revelation. Van Eyck's paradise is here a beautiful garden. The Lord, the Virgin, and Saint John are placed on separate panels high in the architecture. At the same height there are, again on separate panels, two groups of angels, one singing and one with musical instruments (see Fig. 173). (These singers present a rather special problem, which is discussed in Appendix IV.) Van Eyck's paradise, then, is not in the clouds. Its

[75] Puyvelde, *The Holy Lamb*; Panofsky, *Netherlandish Painting*.

visualization as a beautiful garden corresponds to Dante's earthly paradise. The groups of the saints, judges, the righteous, and such, form a kind of celestial court.

The representations of the City of God,[76] the heavenly Jerusalem, also belong in this category of images of paradise. They usually depict the celestial court, the architecture of the city, and a landscape; however, sometimes the highest strata are in clouds, and sometimes there are angels in the clouds. More often, though, angels appear in the marginal and architectural frame of the pictures. This trait, the relegation of angels to an outside stratum, to another region, leads logically to the last group or kind of musician angel to be considered —angels who appear not so much as a group or in a hierarchy but by themselves, in a tradition that has its origin in and is inspired by the Psalms.

Angels of the Psalter

A final general category of representations of musician angels is formed by those related to the Psalms. The boundaries of this group may seem arbitrary in specific instances, but there is nonetheless a useful distinction to be drawn between the angel musicians of heavenly bliss discussed above and those related to the Psalms. The latter fill an essentially different role, that of replacing or representing the faithful in praising the Lord, and have relatively slight connections with the concepts of music of the spheres.

The Psalms played an important part in Christian liturgy from the very beginning, and today about nine-tenths of the liturgy is drawn from the Psalter, not so much in the form of whole psalms as in isolated verses. The texts of the Psalms were thus ever present to the clergy and the community, and singing and praising the Lord with music are constantly mentioned in the Psalms.[77] Singing and playing on psaltery and harp are mentioned with greatest frequency, and the last Psalm (150) gives a detailed list of the instruments to be used to praise the Lord: trumpet, psaltery, harp, timbrel, stringed instruments, organs, and cymbals. Of course, it is not known exactly what

[76] Laborde, *Les manuscripts à peinture de la Cité de Dieu*; angels in the clouds, Pls. 12 and 70; the celestial court, Pls. 60, 69, 72.

[77] E. Nikel, *Geschichte der katholischen Kirchenmusik* (1908), pp. 88ff., with quotations from Saint Augustine on Psalms 42, 70, and 150; B. Finesinger, "Musical Instruments in the Old Testament," *Hebrew College Annual*, III, (1926), with quotations from Jerome, Isidor, and Chrysostome.

most of the terms originally meant. "Organ" is certainly not an accurate translation, because there were no organs used by the Biblical peoples.[78] And different translations name quite different instruments.[79]

In the Psalms it is not the angels specifically who are said to be singing and playing, but the multitude of the faithful that is called upon to sing the praise of the Lord. It may be recalled that one of the Gnostic books attributed singing to the angels only during the night.[80] The duty of singing during the day was to be performed by the faithful. Thus, in the earliest illuminations to the Psalter (the Utrecht Psalter, ninth century), it is not angels but the companions of David who play instruments. In the visions of the Lord in the Utrecht Psalter, adoring angels stand beside Him, while in the lower strata humans play instruments (Fig. 85).

Later, musician angels began to appear in conjunction with the faithful in Psalter illustrations, and it might be noted that while this development is analogous to the angels' joining the dance of the

[78] *Ibid.*; W. O. Oesterley, "The Music of the Hebrews," *Oxford History of Music*, Vol. VII (1929).

[79] *Petrus Apokalypse*, see Dieterich, *Nekyia* (1913); Hekataios, quoted by Dieterich, *ibid.*; *Hexameron* of Ps. Epiphanius, see Trumpp, *Das Hexameron des Pseudo-Epiphanius* (1882), p. 221; Enoch, xxxix, 12, quoted by O. Wulff, *Cherubim, Throne und Seraphim* (1904), pp. 6, 23.

[80] Utrecht Psalter in the Library of Utrecht University; facsimile, London, 1875: fol. 18b, Ps. 32; fol. 25b, Ps. 42; fol. 26b, Ps. 45; fol. 27a, Ps. 46; fol. 37b, Ps. 72; fol. 48a, Ps. 80; fol. 54a, Ps. 91; fol. 56b, Ps. 96; fol. 63, Ps. 107; fol. 76a, Ps. 134; fol. 81b, Ps. 145; fol. 83a, Ps. 149; fol. 90b, 91b for additional psalm.

FIG. 85. Illumination from the Utrecht Psalter for the 150th Psalm. INSTRUMENTS: lyres, krotalon, organ, horns or oliphants

FIG. 86. Bosses in the north transept of Westminster Abbey, showing King David with his harp and angel musicians. INSTRUMENTS: psaltery, harp, guitar-fiddle, cymbals

blessed in paradise, it seems to have started somewhat earlier. The earliest example I have found is in the Majestas illumination of a Psalter manuscript supposed to have come from Gloucester in the thirteenth century.[81] Here, in the border, there are six musician angels who seem to be more or less integrated into a kind of hierarchy. On the highest level, there are two with bowed instruments, plus two singers. In the lower stratum there are four harp players.

The illuminations of the Queen Mary Psalter [82] are full of musicians, both angels and mortals. The angels are shown both in celestial scenes and in events taking place on earth. In the illumination of the Lord in Glory, four pairs of angels flank the mandorla. Three of these pairs play instruments, as follows: harp and psaltery, two stringed instruments, one with a bow, and two wind instruments. All the illuminations show the instruments being played, not just held, and one can tell that the artist must have known how these instruments were used.

Single musician angels also seem to antedate grouped heavenly musicians in works of art in churches. Individual musician angels began to appear in windows and sculpture in the fifteenth century, often as a series either in lunettes on the same window or separate small windows, or spread out on the bosses. No specific number of

[81] Staatsbibliothek, Munich, Clm. 835, fol. 29; the text on the scrolls: *Te Deum* and *Gloria in Excelsis*; Hammerstein, *Die Musik der Engel*, Fig. 56.

[82] British Museum, Royal MS, 2B VII; facsimile edition by G. F. Warner, 1912.

musicians seems to have prevailed in this kind of presentation; their quantity evidently depended on the number of places they were intended to decorate.

This type of angel is to be found in England, France, and Germany. One of the earliest specimens is the "choir of angels" in the north transept of Westminster Abbey, dating from about 1250 (Fig. 86).[83] There is a total of twenty-four angels, of which eleven carry objects used in the liturgy and the rest play musical instruments. As far as the instruments can be recognized, there are five strings, two winds, and five percussion instruments. The stringed instruments can be designated, though some of them seem rather fictional, as a lyre, a cithera (plucked and played with a plectrum), a viol with bow, a psaltery, and a harp. The wind instruments are a single and a triple kind of pipe; the percussion instruments are cymbals and tambourines. From a somewhat later date (fourteenth century) are the single angels with musical instruments (including a portable organ) at Saint Edmunds-Saint Mary and Exeter (Fig. 87).[84] At Gloucester, single angels appear on the bosses, some with the instruments of the

[83] C. J. Cave, *et al.*, "A 13th Century Choir of Angels in the North Transept of Westminster Abbey," *Archeologia*, Vol. 84 (1935), Pls. 10–12.

[84] C. J. Cave, *Roof Bosses in Medieval Churches* (1948), Fig. 54.

FIG. 87. Detail of the minstrels' gallery in Exeter Cathedral. INSTRUMENTS: vielle, recorder (?), lute, bagpipe, harp

Passion and six with musical instruments: bagpipe, portable organ, harp, trombone (busine), vielle, and shawm.[85] In the Lincoln Cathedral (second half of the thirteenth century), a choir is decorated with angels, including a number of musicians. Some are shown to be singers by their scrolls. The instruments used are several harps, a stringed instrument with a bow and one to be plucked, winds, among them a double aulos, and one percussion instrument. In the middle is a winged King David with harp and crown.[86] In Germany there are a number of fourteenth-century musician angels in glass paintings; there are five angels (dating from 1335) at the Cisterciensi monastery in Bebenhausen, in stained glass lunettes in the refectory, who are playing a harp, a double aulos, a vielle, a plucked instrument (similar in form to the one in the Westminster cycle), and another bowed instrument. Glass lunettes in one Eustachius window in the dome at Erfurt show angels playing against a patterned background.[87] In France, the appearance of such musician angels in glass windows is so frequent that Mâle speaks of hundreds of them.[88] Like the few examples given here, they support the generalization that all kinds of instruments are played by this type of angel and that the instruments shown are of the period in which the work in question was executed.

For the most part these angels appear on a neutral background. However, at Thann, in Alsace, there are windows where musician angels appear once on a background of stars and clouds (Fig. 88), and once on stairs in an architectural background.[89] They also are from the fourteenth century. In the Saint Mary and Saint Anne window, four angels leaning on a stair railing sing, two using a choir book; four others play a bowed instrument, two pipes, and a drum. In the other, the Genesis window, among stars and clouds, angels play two pipes, a shawm, a drum, a bagpipe (bladder pipe), a tromba marina, and cymbals. In another fourteenth-century window, now in the Münster Museum, an angel plays a bowed instrument against a

[85] *Ibid.*, Figs. 107–12.

[86] Hammerstein, *Die Musik der Engel*, Figs. 57–60; E. Prior and A. Gardner, *An Account of Medieval Figure Sculpture in England* (1912), p. 266. snake for a lyre.

[87] The information on these stained windows and the photographs thereof come from the Institute at the Stuttgart Technische Hochschule. Professor Hans Wentzel and Dr. Eva Heye helped me most generously, for which I wish to express my sincere thanks.

[88] Mâle, *L'art religieux de la fin du moyen-âge en France*, p. 477.

[89] See n. 87 above.

FIG. 88. Genesis window in Saint Theobald at Thann, Alsace. Instruments: nakers, shawms, slide trumpet, tenor shawn, nun's fiddle, rattles

background of organ pipes (Fig. 89). Perhaps, even if these figures are most often represented on a neutral background, and even if there are no visible clouds or spheres, they should be imagined as playing in the heavens or as messengers from heaven (which may shed some light on how such paintings as Altdorfer's *Nativity*, with the round of angels in the loft of the cathedral, originated).[90]

A link to the Psalms is perhaps more definite where musician angels decorate the balconies for choirs or for the organ. Among the most famous examples are the figures in the Exeter Cathedral[91] (Fig. 87), Memling's paintings for an organ setting (details of which are shown in Figs. 90a & b), and the works of Donatello and Luca della Robbia, shown in Figs. 58 and 91.[92] The decoration of

[90] Heidrich, *Die alt-deutsche Malerei*, Pl. 154.

[91] Exeter, see C. J. Cave, *Medieval Carvings in Exeter* (1953); Gardner, *English Medieval Sculptures* (1951); K. Voll, *Memling* (*Klassiker der Kunst*) (1909), Pls. 120–22.

[92] A. Marquand, *The Brothers of Giovanni della Robbia* (1928); *Luca della Robbia* (1940); Janson, *The Sculpture of Donatello*, 1, Pl. 163, figures from the musicians' tribune; Pls. 259–63, musician *putti*, Padua; Pl. 313, singing *putti*, Padua.

the singers' balcony in Exeter Cathedral is dated about 1350; it consists of twelve angels standing in Gothic niches with the following musical instruments: lute, bagpipe, recorder, vielle, harp, pan's pipe, herald trumpet, portable organ, guitar, shawm, tambourine, and cymbals. The musician angels of Memling's organ decoration are placed in the clouds, in heaven, and beside the figure of Christ as Pantocrator, who is also flanked by three singing angels on each side. The composition is divided into three panels. The side panels show groups of five angels, one group with psaltery, tromba marina, lute, trombone, and recorder; another with herald trumpet, trombone, portative organ, harp, and vielle.

Both Della Robbia's and Donatello's panels were planned for the same place, the Cathedral of Florence, and at approximately the same time, around 1430–35. Della Robbia decorated his balcony with ten panels. For the front, there are four panels in the upper row and four beneath the columns; then there are two for the sides. If there were any doubt that these groups are related to the Psalms, it would be cleared by the inscription on the border of the balcony, which cites the opening phrase of the last five Psalms: *Laudate*

FIG. 89. Fragment from a fourteenth-century glass window from Mark, West-phalia. INSTRUMENTS: vielle

FIG. 90a and 90b. Memling, Christ and angel musicia
sels. INSTRUMENTS: psaltery, nun's fiddle, lute, slide t

Dominum. The two side panels show five and seven singers, and it
may be that these numbers have allegorical meaning. The five singers
would correspond to the five sacred tones (the notes do, re, mi, fa,
sol) of the Magnificat, the seven to the movers and singers of the
seven spheres. Though the figures have no wings, they might be presumed to represent angels, as they are standing on clouds. The four
panels in the upper front row show a combination of playing and
dancing figures. The order of the instruments follows the list in the
150th Psalm. Beneath we read the inscriptions: *tuba, psalterium et
cithara, corda, tympanum, organum, cimbali benesonantes,* and *cimbali iubilationis.* There are 76 musicians, dancers, singers, and players. All the instruments were in use in the fifteenth century.

Donatello decorated the counterpart to Della Robbia's balcony. He
made the upper row a continuous round of dancing and singing *putti*
with wings. On one panel of the lower row, two *putti* play the tambourine and cymbals. Donatello used similar motifs in three other
works: two *putti* on the baptismal font at Siena play tambourine and
horns; a round of dancing and singing *putti* with tambourine and

cymbals appear on his outside pulpit at Prato; and his twelve panels
for the altar in the Santo at Padua have singing and playing *putti*. At
Padua, two panels show pairs of *putti* singing from books; the instruments are three stringed instruments (one of them a little viol with
bow, a pochette, and a lute and a harp), percussion instruments (tambourine and cymbals), and wind instruments (twice the double aulos,
and thrice recorders).

The number of the performing angels in the works I regard as inspired by the text of the Psalms is not uniform; the figures are not
always portrayed as angels. The maidens and youths of Della Robbia's balcony might equally well belong to a work on a secular theme.
The musician *putti*, too, look as if they were taken from a joyful
piece of pagan sculpture and were, rather, *eroti* or *amoretti*. In the
English works and on the German glass windows, however, the musicians are definitely angels; here they have taken over the role of the
faithful from the texts of the Psalms. With a few exceptions the
background does not show any sign of cosmic spheres. That the place
where the music is performed is heaven is sometimes suggested by

the clouds on which the dancers and musicians are standing, and once by clouds and stars in the background. Thus there is occasionally a weak reflection of the traditional structure of heavenly music.

The angel musicians deriving from the Psalms have the loosest connection with the cosmic spheres. Yet it is possible, as noted above, that such sculpture and painting might have been seen by Dante, who integrated these figures into his vision of paradise which, in turn, influenced later representations. From the fourteenth century on, musician angels are regularly seen surrounding the Virgin, and this form became so prevalent that the Assumption paintings by Tintoretto and Gaudenzio Ferrari have survived under the title *Paradise*.

FIG. 91. Luca della Robbia, detail from the so-called Cantoria. INSTRUMENTS: lutes

ANGELS' INSTRUMENTS—REAL OR IMAGINARY?

The painters of celestial concerts were free to assemble all the instruments they wanted, and it is obvious that very often the artists did not intend to depict reality. Therefore, the questions generally asked by musicologists—are the instruments which we see real ones, is this a real orchestra—are too simply formulated. Real instruments can be shown side by side with invented ones. Realism, illusion, and symbolism can be interwoven.

This field as a whole is tangential to the main topic of this study, since it is properly part of *musica instrumentalis* and not of *musica mundana* or *musica humana;* but a few points are worth touching on here. A study of two ninth- and tenth-century manuscripts indicates a mixture of sources for the instruments (see Appendix V). In the Beatus illustrations, the instruments seem to show some forms drawn after reality and some forms apparently in imitation of classical models. In the Utrecht Psalter there is also a mixture of contemporary and antique instruments, with the latter predominating. Of course, from the representations of contemporary instruments conclusions may be drawn concerning the practice of music-making at the time. However, one must be very careful. The problem is that one must know beforehand what to expect.[93] The knowledge to be drawn from the picture has to be supplemented by the text if a text accompanies the illustration, and has to be further combined with the information that can be gathered from reports of performances of the time. Then only can one apply the findings from what is observed in the paintings.

The same problem exists for representations both of single instruments and of ensembles. Can one speak of angel orchestras if this term is understood in the modern sense? For instance, I am convinced that an illustration such as the one for the 150th Psalm in the Utrecht Psalter is not an image of actual music-making of the ninth

---

[93] For example, the instrument of one of the elders at Fenouillard (tenth century) has open or drone strings, and similar strings appear on the viola da braccio of Raphael's Apollo (sixteenth century). To rely on observation alone can lead to major blunders in interpretation. One specialist on the history of instruments, C. Sachs, mistook the rod which David carries in the Utrecht Psalter (Psalm 108) for the bow of a stringed instrument, and a Cretan goddess's snake for a lyre.

FIG. 92. Details from Gaudenzio Ferrari, *Assumption of the Virgin*

or tenth century, when only music in unison was known. Even the Beatus ensembles, where all players have exactly the same instrument, are unlikely to represent reality when there are as many as twenty-four persons. In Gaudenzio Ferrari's ensemble (detail in Fig. 92) one can count more than seventy instruments, some of them completely imaginary. Shall we consider this a picture of music-making in the sixteenth century?

As related to reality, I would like to point out several characteristics which can often be observed in the representations of angel orchestras. First, there is the trio combination of harp, lute, and a bowed instrument. These are the types that appeared, though usually separately, in the Beatus manuscripts. This trio is found in a number of other works, including one in which David and his companions are performers. The latter is a twelfth-century sculpture in the baptistry at Parma, a work attributed to Antelami, a sculptor probably appren-

ticed in Provence. This would help to confirm the theory that instrumental music wandered from Spain and Provence to the northern
countries, northern France, and northern Italy. The second point is
that often in the two groups framing the figure of the Virgin the lute
appears on one side, and on the other there is a bowed instrument or
a portative (which came into use about 1200).[94] Thus, this pairs an
instrument which carries the tune with an instrument to provide
chords in accompaniment. Both the combination of the trio and the
pair in question can be imagined as ensembles of the *ars nova*. A third
scene which seems a plausible reflection of actual music-making is one
in which one type of instrument appears in different sizes. This sort
of ensemble playing is known to have been popular far into the seventeenth century and still exists today in our quartet. There are such
sets of instruments in the frame of the Landino illumination of the
Squarcialupi Codex.[95] Another example is the famous painting of
the angel concert from Matthias Grünewald's Isenheimer Altar.
(This provides, incidentally, an interesting case of a complex relationship; one's first impression is that of a huge orchestra, yet there
are actually only three viol players.)

For the problem of reality versus illusion in orchestras, there is the
excellent material E. Bowles has assembled, especially in his article
on musical instruments in civic processions during the Middle Ages.
Bowles collected descriptions from the fourteenth century onward,
and especially from the fifteenth century. He quotes from poetic
works and chronicles. The poets mention many instruments without
specifying whether they were played simultaneously. In the reports
contained in the chronicles, we read of a few musicians accompanying
the king or prince, or, if the scribe mentions many instruments, he
adds that they are sounding from all over the town, from all the
towers and gates, or that the procession passes a number of places
where different groups of musicians are set up. According to these accounts, groups of singers and instrumentalists performed on floats in
processions, or passed before balconies and stages erected for the occasion on which certain scenes were represented. Sometimes figures
from classic myths are mentioned, but more often we hear of our old

---

[94] H. Hickmann, *Das Portativ* (1936).

[95] The *Squarcialupi Codex*, Pal. 87, Bibl. Laurenziana, Florence, fol. 121v,
ed. Joh. Wolf (St. Louis, 1957), p. 197; M. Agricola, *Musica instrumentalis
deudsch* (1529); S. Virdung, *Musica getutscht* (1511).

acquaintances, the angels and the Elders. Such scenes are also included in some of the mystery plays. In a miracle play of the In-
carnation, given at Rouen in 1474, the real musicians played from behind the figures of angels. In 1485, at the entry of Charles VIII into
Rouen, figures representing the twenty-four Elders, in white brocade
and with crowns, held different instruments, while the town musicians stood behind them and played the music. In 1461, Louis IX, on
his way from Reims to Paris, passed tableaux on erected scaffolds. On
one, three sirens sang motets and bergerettes, while musicians beside
them played "grandes mélodies." One of the reports mentioned by
Bowles provides an interesting account of a scene of the twenty-four
musician Elders; the Elders are described as having all kinds of instruments, but the actual music was made by musicians standing behind the group in the scene.[96]

Thus there are instances both in paintings and in the reports in the
chronicles where reflections and descriptions of actual music-making
are discernible. And, admittedly, something can be learned from
them concerning both single instruments and ensembles. But in the
main, the question of whether or not these are representations of real
performances seems put in the wrong way. It is perfectly possible
that the representations were not so much imitations of an existing
reality as the inspiration which led the composers to create the reality.
In his cupola painting, Ferrari depicts real instruments and imagined
forms. Some groups of his orchestra seem to represent real ensembles, combinations of instruments for which we have reports by several chroniclers. We see also some groups in which instruments of the
same kind but in different sizes are shown. Such ensembles are documented in the contemporary treatises on musical instruments. From
the fifteenth century we have numerous descriptions of actual ensemble performances and descriptions in which the instruments are
listed.[97] In the sixteenth century, small orchestras are mentioned for

[96] E. Bowles, "Musical Instruments in Civic Processions," *Acta Musicologica*
(1961); L. Traube, *Vorlesungen und Abhandlungen*, Vol. 3 (1920), p. 302.
Also, there is a little-known miracle play, still annually enacted in Spain, in which
children dressed as angels take part, singing. A set of the stage directions has
survived from the fourteenth century, but unfortunately no copy is available in the
United States. Both Pedrell and Anglès reported that the music includes old
Provençal songs. It is a pity that the music has not been recorded.

[97] G. Thibault, "Le concert instrumental dans l'art flamand au XVe siècle et
au debut du XVIe," *La Renaissance dans les provinces du Nord*, CNRS (1956);
Thibault, "*Le concert instrumental au XVe siècle*" CNRS (1955).

the accompaniment *in intermedii* of a group of comedians from Padua in Ferrara and in Florence in 1560. Two famous orchestras existed in Ferrara in the sixteenth century, one at the court and one in the convent of Saint Vito. Of the latter we have enthusiastic reports by Artusi, Guarini, and Bottrigari.[98] They mention that a nun conducted from a gravicembalo, list the many instruments, and emphasize the effect of the harmonious playing together. Later follow the reports by Pietro della Valle about the orchestras used by the Camerata in Florence about 1600. In the seventeenth century the famous orchestra, often regarded as the first modern institution of its kind, was the Vingt-quatre Violons du Roi, the string ensemble under Lully. And I wonder whether the number twenty-four is not a last reminder of the musician Elders.

[98] H. Bottrigari has written about it in his "La Mascara overo Della Fabrica dei Teatri," a treatise which exists in manuscript only in the library of the Liceo Musicale, Bologna, Cat. 1, 43. H. Bottrigari, *Il Desiderio*, ed. K. Meyer, *Veröffentlichungen der Musikbibliothek Paul Hirsch* (1924), Introduction.

IX Renaissance and Humanism

EARLIER CHAPTERS have described how, in the vision of celestial music, the angels took over as performers and how the place for celestial concert became more and more restricted to the highest heaven, as well as how greatly the vision of paradise was influenced by Dante's *Divine Comedy*. Ultimately, the angels replaced the Muses as movers of the spheres and the Elders of the Revelation and the faithful of the Psalms as musicians. With the coming of the new art of instrumental music, the angels changed more and more from dancers and singers to instrumentalists.

However, the former forces of celestial music did not completely disappear. They continued to be represented, especially in the illustrations of theoretical books, and, eventually, under the influence of the Renaissance and Humanism, these forces came again to the fore. The trend was manifested in many different ways. A typical example are Ripa's books,[1] in which a number of allegorical figures and emblems are given for one and the same idea, and the artist has the liberty of choice. Cartari, on the other hand, gave to his two figures of Zeus emblems from different ideologies, a lyra-viol as the symbol of the ruler of the music of the spheres, and thunderbolts (Fig. 93).[2] There is a particularly good document for the fusion of the angels with the figures of the *parthenoi* and Muses, the *putti* and *eroti*, in the decoration of the Malatesta chapel at Rimini (1447–56).[3] Here the musician angels look like Muses, and the Muses like angels. The third chapel of Saint Francis at Rimini is decorated with the figures of the Muses (eight) and the liberal arts (seven), grouped in parallel with the figures of the seven spheres, as follows:

[1] Ces. Ripa, *Iconologia* (1613) and *Nova Iconologia* (1618).

[2] V. Cartari, *Imagini delli dei de gli antichi* (1571); T. Seznec, *The Survival of the Pagan Gods* (1953), Pl. 148, Fig. 92; A. Gilbert, *The Symbolic Persons in the Masques of Ben Jonson* (1948).

[3] C. Ricci, *Il tempio Malatestino* (1925); for the relation to San Bernardino di Siena at Perugia, see Ricci, p. 309; A. Warburg, *Gesammelte Schriften*, p. 453.

Thalia	lowest sphere (earth)	
Clio	Luna	Grammar
Calliope	Mercury	Dialectic
Terpsichore	Venus	Rhetoric
Melpomene	Sol	Music
Erato	Mars	Geometry
Polyhymnia	Saturn	Astronomy
Urania	Fixed stars	Arithmetic

There are also music-making *putti* in one of the other chapels. Agostino di Duccio, one of the creators of the Rimini sculpture, was familiar with the traditional representation of musician angels. They appear on the façade and the portal which he made for Saint Bernardino at Perugia.[4] Here, eight angels with wings, playing on musical instruments, surround the saint who, in a mandorla, seems to be flying up to heaven. The frame of the mandorla is formed by little flames, the symbol of the seraphim. If one compares Agostino di Duccio's figures of standing angels from the portal (Fig. 94) with his

[4] P. Schubring, *Die italienische Plastik des Quattrocento* (*Handbuch der Kunstwissenschaft*, 1912); San Bernardino di Siena, 1380–1444, Franciscan orator and saint.

FIG. 93. Zeus in his two aspects; sixteenth-century woodcut from Vincenzo Cartari, *Imagini delli dei degli antichi*. INSTRUMENTS: lyra-viol

FIG. 94. Agostino di Duccio, detail from the portal of the Church of Saints Andrea and Bernardino, Perugia. Instruments: triangle, nakers

FIG. 95. The Muse Clio, from a relief by Agostino di Duccio for the Tempio Malatestiano at Rimini. Instruments: busine

figure of Clio from Rimini (Fig. 95), they look very much alike, except that Clio has no wings.

The parallel of the Muses and the spheres is the old one from Capella's *De Nuptiis*. The group of the liberal arts is set in correspondence because of the obvious identity of the number seven for the spheres and the sum of quadrivium and trivium. There is a similar relationship in the famous woodcut (Fig. 96) from Gafori's *Practica Musica* (later incorporated into his *Teatrum instrumentorum*).[5] Here the following elements correspond: the planets, the spheres, the Muses, and the sounds and intervals of the scale. It is a table that goes back to the era when the orders of the angels were not included in the cosmic structure. The chief symbols in the table—the segments, the figures in the medallions, the *tituli*—represent the pagan tradition traced in earlier chapters. The segments of the spheres are identified with the ruling deities and turned by the Muses; the names of the tones and intervals indicate the distances of the orbits of the planets; all this is familiar from the earlier sources. The additional signs and figures—Apollo, the three Fates, the serpent, and the elements (around the earth)—show a fusion of ideas that goes back to Plato's vision with Christian symbols. Apollo is shown here as Pythicos, as Helios, and as Musagetes. As Helios he is identified with the sun and the light. As Pythicos he has vanquished the serpent and puts his feet on it as a sign of victory, just as Christ or the Virgin step on the monster representing Satan or on the mouth of hell. The three-faced head of the serpent is an old symbol for the three aspects of time: past, present, and future. The three Fates were identified with the three phases of time, and we remember that the three Fates in Plato turned the spindle around which the spheres rotated. Beside the seated Apollo, there are three figures with the names of the Fates.

The four elements surrounding *terra* in Gafori's table are perhaps the most novel addition; they reflect the outcome of the comparison of the macrocosmos and the microcosmos, of universe and man, an idea mentioned above with reference to the writings of Silvestris and Alanus. This theory was later elaborated by Johannes Kepler and Robert Fludd. Fludd, principally a physician, was interested in all kinds of speculative philosophy, and in his books he tried to construct

---

[5] Warburg, *Gesammelte Schriften*, pp. 271, 412; E. Panofsky, "Titian's Allegory of Prudence," *Meaning in the Visual Arts* (1955).

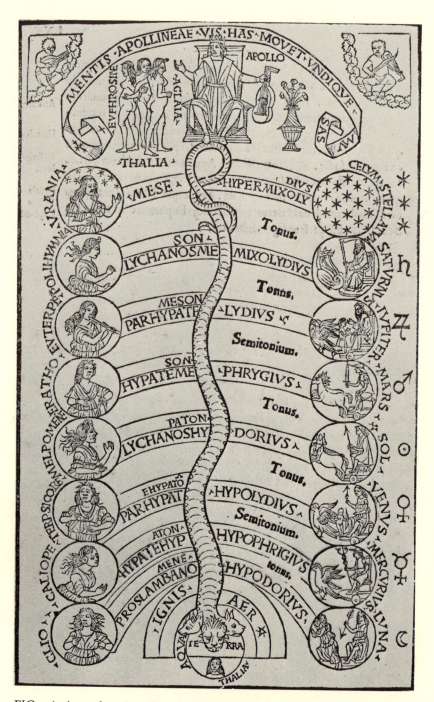

FIG. 96. A woodcut from Franchino Gafori, *Practica Musicae utriusque cantus* (1508). INSTRUMENTS: lute, bowed rebec, lute-type instrument, pipe

a scheme of the harmony of the cosmos.[6] In his charts, the musical intervals and scales play the role of the *tertium comparationis* between the two kinds of cosmos and provide a link between the two poles of the universe, God and man. Fludd's books must have been quite popular, because a number of editions were published during his lifetime. Five of the many illustrations to Fludd's works seem worth discussing at some length.

The title page of *De templo musicae,* which may or may not have been chosen by Fludd himself, shows Apollo and the nine Muses. They are not framed in a structured cosmos. Apollo is seated under a laurel tree with a lyre in a form modeled after Roman prototypes, while four of the Muses hold musical instruments of Fludd's day; they are not playing. Apollo can be seen alone on one of the other plates illustrating the temple of music, but in a minor role, and neither the Muses nor Apollo appear in the other charts. This seems to reflect an ambiguity that also made itself felt in the poetry of the time.

The role of the Muses has been studied in detail by E. R. Curtius,[7] who followed their history from the first centuries of our era up to the eighteenth century. He found them largely invoked as givers of inspiration, at the beginning of poems or at the beginning of the climactic parts of larger compositions. After the model of Homer, almost all epics began with their invocation, but as the Christian era advanced, Curtius found varying compliance with this. Strict believers like Aldhelm or Florus rejected their power and replaced them with figures from the orbit of the Christian faith; at the other extreme, some simply adopted the classic figure as it was. There were yet others who molded the Muses' character along the lines of allegories developed by Christian writers. There are writers who had a Muse inspire the poets of the Old Testament. Muses were mentioned in

---

[6] R. Fludd, *Utriusque Cosmi Historia* . . . (Oppenheim, 1617); *Monochordi Mundi Symphoniacum* (1622); Tractatus, No. 2 in *Utriusque Cosmi Historia.* See also his *De anima intellectualis scientia* (2nd edn., 1704).

[7] E. R. Curtius, "Die Musen im Mittelalter," *Zeitschrift für romanische Philologie,* Vol. 59 (1939), pp. 129ff.; Vol. 63 (1943), pp. 256ff.; E. R. Curtius, *Europäische Literatur und lateinisches Mittelalter* (1948), pp. 232ff., 241ff., 248ff.; sources for Curtius: Dante, *Inferno,* II, 7 and XXXII, 10; *Purgatorio,* I, 8 and XXIX, 37, 42; *Paradiso,* II, 9 and XII, 7. A. Krause, *Jorge Manrique,* Publ. of the University of California at Los Angeles in Language and Literature, Vol. I, No. 3 (1937); H. G. Lotspeich, *Classical Mythology in the Poetry of Spenser,* Princeton Studies in English, Vol. 9 (1932).

liturgical hymns, especially in the songs of southern France, where the form of the *sequentiae* developed and where our Western music ultimately originated. In his *Divine Comedy*, Dante invokes the inspiration of the Muses, but in his *Monarchia* and the treatise *De volgari eloquentia* he invokes the Lord and Christ. Even when a poet denies and rejects the power of the pagan Muses the conflict becomes apparent, as in the dirge on the death of his father by Jorge Manrique (1440?–78), "where the worn topic of the rejection is revived in the words of a real poet":

> I do not invoke the Muses
> Like the masters, the poets, and the sages;
> Their tales are schemes;
> In their gardens grow poisonous plants.
>
> I praise the One, my poem is devoted to Him alone
> Who abased Himself to the world;
> But the world did not recognize His light.

Tasso in his *Gerusalemme liberata* rejects the classic Muse and invokes the heavenly muse who dwells among the heavenly choirs. Spenser has three forms of invocation in his *Faerie Queene*, once the Muses in general, once Clio, as the force yielding knowledge, the daughter of Phoebus and Mnemosyne and at the same time the sacred child of Zeus—that is, as the classic goddess—and later he again asks the aid of the "Muses." Milton invokes a heavenly muse derived from the forces which inspired the Old Testament. He knows two kinds of muses, the classic and the Christian. But it is in Spenser that the form of invocation at the beginning is especially relevant. It is the Holy Virgin, "chief of nine," who is asked for help, and Spenser leaves it undecided whether he means the Holy Virgin as the leader of the nine orders of angels, in the role which Dante assigned her, or as the leader of the classic Muses. When the classic Muses are called upon, generally Urania is singled out as the mover of the cosmos, the role she has played since Capella's day. In Calderón, the fusion of the classic and the sacred Parnassus is completed. *Divinas letras* and *humanas letras,* the Bible and the wisdom of the classic authors, are united through the sacred numbers. In Calderón's *Sacro Parnaso*, Faith asks the Gentiles and the Jews to read from the Scriptures. The Jews answer with the verse of Psalm 68:25. "The singers went before, the players on instruments fol-

lowed after; among them were the damsels playing with timbrels."
For Calderón these musician maidens and players of timbrels were
identical with the Muses, and Christ was their leader, the *musagete,
el verdadero Apolo*.[8]

Another interesting illustration from Fludd's books is the representation of his *Templum musicae*.[9] This is a structure so laden with allegorical references that it is difficult to interpret all of them. On the
left, there appears a kind of campanile crowned by a figure of Time, a
winged figure with a scythe. Below there is a clock with the symbols
of the musical rests and the letters of the tones, then, further down,
Apollo Helios with a lyre, then yet lower a chart of the tones with
the Greek Γ for the lowest sound, and, at the bottom, a lute. The center tower, crowned by a cupola, has an arch with ten spheres or voussoirs. Columns beside the windows are decorated with musical instruments: harp, cornett, and organ (left) and viol and two lutes (right).
Six steps standing for the hexachord of tones (fa, sol, la, re, me, ut)
lead to the windows; at the bottom, Pythagoras's experiment with
the hammers may be seen through an arch. Within the latter scene,
on the right, there is a kind of portico with six columns, inscribed
with the signs of the clefs; on the wall behind, at the far left, are the
tones of the musical system, starting at the bottom with the Γ; farther to the right, at different heights corresponding to the clefs on
the columns, are the syllables of the hexachords. The base on which
the portico stands is a wall on which the rhythmical values of the
notes are inscribed. The portico has a frieze with three arcades, with a
set of seven organ pipes in each, reminiscent of the organ on the
Ghent Altar with its twenty-one pipes. As suggested above, this number, which does not correspond to the usual form of organ used in the
fifteenth century, and certainly not to that of the seventeenth, was
probably a symbolic expression for the compass of three octaves, for
the three kinds of music (*mundana, humana, instrumentalis*), and,
finally, for the Trinity.[10]

Three other charts illustrating Fludd's main text and theory are of
even greater interest. The first is the chart of the "internal numbers
and harmony of the human being" (Fig. 97). Around a circle repre-

[8] Curtius, *Europäische Literatur*, p. 249.

[9] Facsimile in J. Hollander, *The Untuning of the Sky* (1961), plate following
p. 242.

[10] Grossman, *Die einleitenden Kapitel des Speculum Musicae von Johannes
de Muris* (1924), pp. 23 and 52.

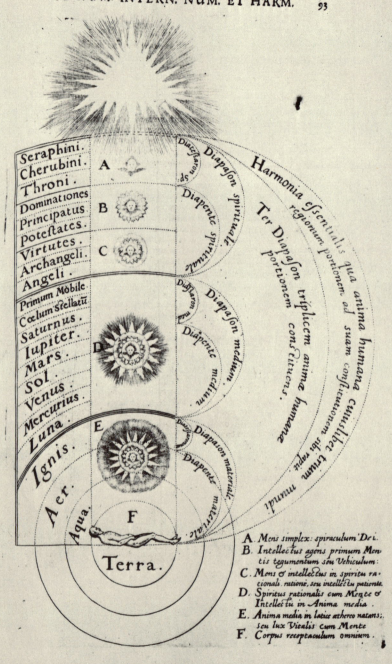

FIG. 97. Diagram from Robert Fludd, *Historia utriusque cosmi* (1617)

senting the earth, in which a man is lying on his back (*corpus recep-taculum omnium*), are three circles representing the other elements. Above the circle of fire there is erected, on the left, a scale of the spheres, with the *coelum stellatum* and the *primum mobile* at the top and, above, the nine orders of angels, topped by the "seraphini" (a word which points to an Italian source). On the right are half-circles with the different musical intervals; the whole combined gives the compass of the triple octave, "harmonia essentialis qua anima humana cuiuslibet trium mundi regionum portionem ad suam constitutionem sibi rapit" (the essential harmony comprising the three regions of the cosmos of which the human soul grasps one part corresponding to her constitution). The three octaves are the spiritual, the medial, and the material, corresponding to the realms of the angel orders, the spheres of the planets, and the elements. In the middle, in a column resting on the human form, are the orders of angels in rosettes formed by rays of light and clouds, and, at the very top, a triangle of light for the Trinity. Such rosette emblems were typical for the Rosicrucian sect. As noted earlier, the chart corresponds exactly to the one found in the manuscript of hymns from the twelfth century, except for this middle column and for minor differences of form—notably that the names of the tones and the intervals were given in classic Greek terminology in the earlier work.

The second chart from the same treatise contains the same elements, but the outer form is somewhat changed (Fig. 98). Everything is arranged around a musical instrument called the monochord, then in use for measuring the musical intervals. On the string are the names of the tones, and since the whole chart must be read from right to left, the lowest sounds appear on top. In a row on the left, the intervals are indicated; then, in the next row, the numbers of the sound waves, and then the larger intervals. To the right of the instrument, there are the names and signs of the elements and the spheres, this time to be read from the bottom up, starting with *omega* and the earth. Above the earth are the four elements, then the spheres, with the sun in the middle, and, on top, two sections for the orders of angels "corresponding to the fifth and the fourth." At the very top stands the *alpha* or *aleph*, the Lord, "the *monas* from whom everything proceeds and to whom everything returns."

The third chart, *Meteoro graphicum* (Fig. 99), demonstrates the relation of the stars and the weather to human moods and emotions. It contains no musical terms or symbols; however, in the top row

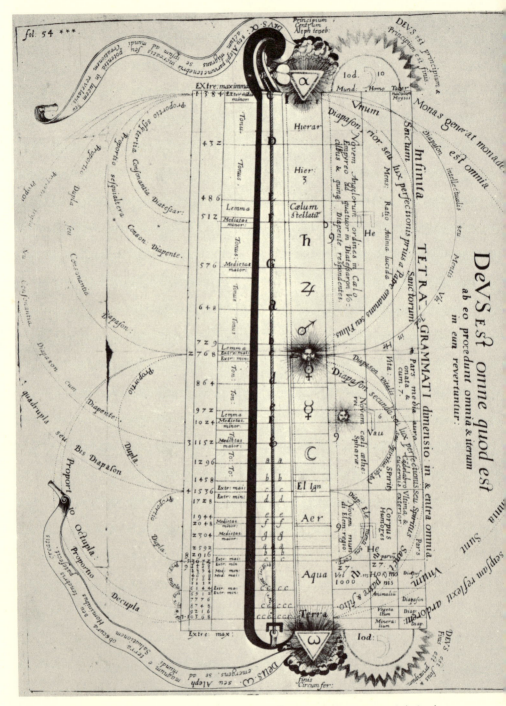

FIG. 98. Diagram from Robert Fludd, *Historia utriusque cosmi* (1617)

there are five angels on either side of the emblem of the Lord, each standing on a sphere. The inscriptions read *primum mobile,* the sphere of the fixed stars, then Saturn, Jupiter, Mars, Sol, Venus, Mercury, Moon, and the Elements. On the upper spheres, above the heads of the figures, are inscribed the names of the orders of the angels, with *animae* for the tenth figure. Each angel is standing beside a palm tree, and the trees are inscribed in Latin and Hebrew with the names of the Virtues. Of the three charts, the first is the most traditional; in the others the spheres and their music are related to human temperaments and moods.

Fludd's treatises provide a comprehensive elaboration of the theory of the music of the spheres. The cosmos, music, and the orders of angels are set into relation with each other and with the spiritual forces in man. The figures of the pagan orbit are not included in his scheme. In Gafori's chart, on the other hand, the relation of the spheres, music, and the Muses was set forth without including the order of angels.

For a final summary of the theoretical handling of the music of the spheres, it is apt to refer to one last book from the second half of the seventeenth century, a work which provides a survey of all the problems, even though it discusses them without elaborating a clear structure. This is the *Museum Historico-legale Bipartitum,* by Carlo Pellegrini, published in Rome in 1665.[11] The cosmic aspect is treated in its first part, and in the second, the relation of the orders of angels to the spheres. Pellegrini's book is a veritable encyclopedia for our topic; in it all the laws for the music of the spheres discussed above are set forth, as well as theories on the origin of the music, a survey of the different kinds of music, *mundana, humana, instrumentalis,* and also *harmonica* and *organica.* Pellegrini discusses the music of paradise, the role of the angels in moving the spheres and performing heavenly music. He does not elaborate in the precise way that Fludd did, nor does he give exact charts. He quotes freely from a great variety of sources, from the classics as well as from authors of the early centuries of our era. Of greatest interest is his list of heavenly musicians: the sirens, the angels, and the Muses; and it should also be noted that he identifies the song of the Muses and the song of

---

[11] Carlo Pellegrini, *Museum Historico-legale Bipartitum. In cujus primo libro sub praestantia Musices involucro diversae disciplinae praelibantur. In Altero vero quaedam de Angelis, Caelis, Planetis, Anima et Elementis* (Rome, 1665).

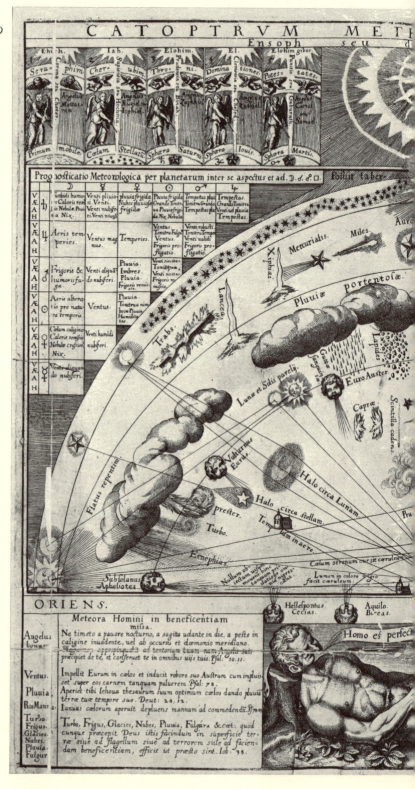

FIG. 99. Diagram from Robert Fludd, *Philosophia sacra et vere Christiana se*

the angels. Here, then, the circle of history is closed and the two branches of heavenly music are joined. From this time forward when the music of the spheres is mentioned, be it by Milton, Shakespeare, or Goethe, ideas are only repeated.[12]

[12] F. Erckmann, "Sphaerenmusik," *Zeitschrift der Internationalen Musik-gesellschaft*, Vol. 9 (1908), p. 417; L. Curtius, "Musik der Sphaeren," *Deutsches Archaeologisches Institut, Römische Abt., Mitteilungen*, 50 (1935–36); Warburg, *Gesammelte Schriften*, p. 417; Th. Reinach, "La musique des sphères," *Revue des études grecques*, XIII (1900), 432ff.; Ch. Tolnay, "The Music of the Universe," *Journal of the Walters Art Gallery*, VI (1943).

X Two Offshoots of the Idea of the Music of the Spheres

Two OTHER FIELDS where the influence of the idea of the music of the spheres was strong and remained palpable well into the nineteenth century are musical drama, or opera, and the illustrations for music books, especially their title pages. This does not, it should be noted, apply to medieval drama, in which, despite the frequent inclusion of angel choirs or a solo sung by an angel, I have yet to find a reference to cosmic structure or the music of the spheres. From the seventeenth century onward, music of the spheres was represented, not so much as a whole structure, but in the aspect of the planets as rulers of the spheres. The early music dramas and ballets were designed for performance at court, usually for a special occasion, such as a royal birthday or wedding.[1] It was a popular notion that the planets ruled man's fate and character, and, therefore, the planets were regularly called upon to shower their benefices upon the individual or the couple in question.

One of the most complete and elaborate examples available is the ballet *Von der Zusammenkunft und Wirkung der sieben Planeten* (*The Meeting and Influence of the Seven Planets*), performed in Dresden in 1678 in honor of the visit of the brothers of John George II of Saxony.[2] A splendid report of this fête was published, along with engravings of different scenes. Each planet arrived on a machine; each time, the scene represented a different landscape, and each planet came with a different entourage. They sang or spoke, introducing themselves and recounting what good they intended to do for Saxony; then their companions performed a ballet. The cast included a whole army of allegorical figures. The seven planets were accompanied by Nimrod when they appeared together; the Muses, too, were included, as were the Virtues. No clear plan is apparent,

---

[1] A. Solerti, *Musica, Ballo e Drammatica alla Corte Medicea* (1905); A. Warburg, *Gesammelte Schriften*, pp. 261, 394.

[2] R. Haas, *Die Musik des Barocks* (*Handb. d. Musikwissenschaft*), p. 177; S. T. Staden, *Seelewig und der VII Tugenden, Planeten, Töne oder Stimmen Aufzug*, 1657.

and evidently the allegories were chosen with a view to the tastes of the people before whom the ballet was performed.

In most of these ballets or masques the concepts of cosmic structure are quite vague and the relevance to our topic exists merely through the use of the same figures. In addition to the planets and the Muses, one encounters Harmony, who appears in a work by Ben Jonson as a male with a crown and a halo.[3] The figures lose their defined character, become interchangeable, and no longer hold a specific place in the structure of the cosmos. There seems to be only one exception, one where a set of scenes was devised to illustrate "music," in the famous *intermezzi* performed at Florence in 1589 for the reception of Christine of Lorraine, who was to become the wife of the Grand Duke Ferdinando I.[4] Warburg has assembled all the documents referring to these scenes—the reports by Rossi, Bardi, and others, the accounts of the technicians, the drawings for the costumes of the singers—so that we have an idea of the plans as well as of the actual performance. The subjects of the *intermezzi* were:

1. *L'Armonia delle sfere*
2. *La gara fra Muse e Periedi*
3. *Il combattimento pitico d'Apollo*
4. *La regione de' Demoni*
5. *Il canto d'Arione*
6. *La discesa di Apollo e Bacco insieme col Ritmo e l'Armonia*

All six scenes are related to music, but it will suffice here to explain only the first in detail, as it is the only one directly concerned with our topic.

First, however, it is necessary to have some idea of how the whole series was planned and why it was planned in this way. The performance of these *intermezzi* has often been described as the beginning of the musical form of the opera; it has also been said that a revival of the antique drama was planned, and that it was here that the new monodic style and the modern recitative were created. Warburg was therefore astonished to find that the music which was sung in the interludes followed the old form of the madrigal, along with the new form of solo singing with the accompaniment of instruments. The actual history of the *intermezzi*, however, is rather different. Songs to be

[3] A. Gilbert, *The Symbolic Persons in the Masques of Ben Jonson* (1948).
[4] Warburg, *Gesammelte Schriften*, "I costumi teatrali per gli intermezzi del 1589."

performed by a single voice to the accompaniment of one instrument originated with the troubadours and developed in a number of countries. Indeed, singing with the accompaniment of lute or viol became very popular and was, in the sixteenth century, an absolute necessity in the education of a courtier. The real innovation of Bardi and his associates was that they studied the Greek authors and endeavored to find evidence of the classical Greek music drama and to imitate it. In these attempts they had several forerunners, such as Vincenzo Galilei, Girolamo Mei, and especially Hercole Bottrigari, who as musicologist gave lectures on the "history" of music at Bologna, where a professorship *ad lecturam musicae* had existed since 1450.[5] All their attempts were rather futile because almost no documents of Greek music have survived, in contrast to the fields of architecture and the visual arts. Their chief source of inspiration was Plato's report in the *Republic* which, as argued in an earlier chapter, is less a report on actual music than a speculative vision. The efforts of Bardi and his academy had less influence on the development of specific musical forms, such as the recitative, than on the whole approach to the problem of the *drama per musica*, the drama with music. In this respect the *intermezzi* of 1589 were important because they connected a series of single scenes through the common factor of music.

Let us now consider to what degree the scenes, or, more particularly, the first—the representation of *L'Armonia delle sfere*—corresponds to Plato's vision. The drawing for the scene, by Agostino Carracci,[6] shows in the center a female figure with a halo and a spindle in her right hand, seated on a throne that rests on clouds; around the base of the throne there are three dancing figures. Three layers of clouds are seen, and above, the heaven with stars. There are figures in the clouds, all of whom are women in Roman costume. On the lower level of the clouds are standing, left and right, six figures; in the middle row there are four on each side, seated; and, above, two groups of seated figures. However, there are no emblems and no musical instruments. To supplement this general sketch, we have drawings of details of *L'Armonia doria, Necessitas colle Parche, nugola con Diana, Venere, Marte, Saturno,* other drawings showing *Mercurio, Apollo, Giove e Astrea,* and five further drawings for the

<hr>

[5] H. Bottrigari, *Il Desiderio,* ed. K. Meyer, *Veröffentlichungen der Musikbibliothek Paul Hirsch* (1924), Introduction, pp. 8, 12, *passim.*

[6] Warburg, "I costumi teatrali," p. 261.

Sirene delle dieci sfere. From Rossi's explanation one learns that the
figure in the center of *L'Armonia delle sfere* represents Ananke as
well as Harmony, and, at the same time, the Doric scale or *L'Armonia doria.* The justification given for identifying these three is
Plato's text, interpreted as follows: Ananke, necessity, rules the cosmos and the sirens sing on the borders of the spheres; their song
results in harmony, a harmony which cannot be other than the harmony of the cosmos which is, in turn, the result of Ananke's rule.
Rossi continues: "And because the same Plato says in another place
in his *Republic* that the Doric is the best among all the other scales
(*armonie*) . . . the Doric was chosen." [7] (In Capella's *De Nuptiis*
the Doric scale is identified with Zeus.)

In this first scene, the character representing the Doric scale was
not to be heard but to be seen, as the singer descended on a cloud to
join the other scales in a Doric temple. After she has disappeared into
the temple, the ten sirens arrive and introduce themselves with the
following madrigal: "We who while singing make the heavenly
spheres smoothly turn, have left paradise for this happy occasion."
Thus Bardi and the poet Rinuccini, hard as they tried to be authentic,
inserted the idea of the Christian paradise into their vision, and their
sirens have their usual abode in paradise, like the angels and the
blessed. After the sirens have left, three clouds appear, with the
goddess of Necessity and the Fates on the one in the middle, and the
planets and Astrea on the others. Behind these clouds the heroes of
ancient legends are to be seen (their portraits appeared in Jupiter's
castle in *De Nuptiis*). From the clouds, but apparently not visible to
the audience, instruments are heard which accompany the singing by
"Harmony," as Ananke is now called, and the three Fates, who are
here called by their right names, Lachesis, Clotho, and Atropos (elsewhere in the description Atropos is replaced by Thalia). While the
heroes remain in the clouds, the planets descend and join Harmony
and the Fates in various songs. Rossi compares the heroes to the
blessed in Elysium, and he calls Ananke, or Harmony, *madre neces-
sità,* Mother Necessity. From the list of performing artists it becomes
evident that there are more than ten sirens. To the classic spheres of
the planets, three more have been added, bringing the total to ten,
and there is the further addition of the Empyreum with three sirens.
Singing is mentioned in this first *intermezzo,* but no dancing; the

[7] *Ibid.*, p. 394.

only action is the up-and-down movement of the machines representing the clouds. But in the third *intermezzo,* where Apollo's battle with the serpent is represented, Rossi speaks of a kind of ballet, in which the battle is danced, and of a chorus representing the Delphic people, who move as did the Greek chorus. One gathers from these descriptions that Bardi quite certainly studied the writings of the Greek and Roman authors; Horace is mentioned by Rossi as one of his sources. Warburg has found influences of others, such as Lucian. However, though Bardi tried to follow classic customs exactly, he did not avoid yielding to Christian influence. His heaven is the *paradiso.* Necessity or Harmony becomes the mother of this heaven, the *Mater Coelorum.* The heroes of Elysium are staying in the highest heaven, or Empyreum. I mention these facts not to minimize Bardi's merit, but to point out that in the sixteenth century the two heavens could no longer be separated. The cosmos with the spheres as it appears in Carracci's drawing is not different from heaven as it appears in the scenery for a sacred opera, *San Alessio,* by Stefano Landi (Fig. 100). Here there are three strata, two of clouds and one at the level of the saint, and the angels in the clouds play musical instruments. It might be noted that even as late as the nineteenth century, Goethe, at the end of his *Faust,* divides heaven into three regions, lower, middle, and highest, and that for him, too, paradise is ruled by the *Mater Coelorum.*

As for the identification of the place where the heroes are gathered, it is significant to compare the changes which the story of Orpheus and Eurydice underwent. The two poles of development are represented by the version given in Alessandro Striggio's libretto for Monteverdi's *Orfeo* and in the opera by Gluck. Monteverdi's drama ends in a tragic vein and the chorus is sung by "spirits" not otherwise identified. There is no mention that Orpheus while in the underworld implores help from above, from heaven. In Gluck's work, where the libretto is by Calzabigi, the story has a happy ending; Elysium is located in the underworld and is the abode of the heroes and heroines.[8] In Bardi's *intermezzo,* Elysium was in heaven, and in Greek mythology it was situated at the end of the world toward the west. The farther away in time from Plato, the more confused ideas become. Elysium, Empyreum, and the highest heaven sometimes are

---

[8] New edition of Gluck's *Orpheus* in *Denkmäler der Tonkunst in Oesterreich,* Vol. 44a.

identical, or sometimes belong to different worlds or parts of the cosmos. In a play entitled *Orfeus*, for a wedding festival at the Danish court in 1648, devils kill the animals which have been attracted by the music and then kill Orpheus, who is carried to heaven by four angels.[9]

The illustrations on the title pages of music books are an excellent and very rich source for tracing the influences of the ideas of heavenly music, even far into the nineteenth century. Little has been published on these illustrations so far, and no statistics are available.[10]

[9] *Triumphus Nuptiale Danicus. Festbericht von der Hochzeit Christian I von Dänemark mit Magdalena Sybilla, Herzogin von Sachsen Jülich Cleve*, Copenhagen, in *Verlegung Jürgen*, 1648.

[10] K. Meyer, "Musikillustrationen des 15.–17. Jahrhunderts," *Philobiblon*, Vol. 10 (1938), pp. 205, 278ff.

FIG. 100. Engraving by Colignon after G. J. Bernini for S. Landi's religious opera *San Alessio* (1634)

Even so, it seems that many, perhaps half, of the title pages are adorned with the group of Apollo and the nine Muses. They appear in all kinds of costumes, either in classic garb or the dress of the period. For an example of how baroque these designs can be, the reader might refer to the title page of Dedekind's *Aelbianische Musenlust* (1657), the Elbian (from the river Elbe) Delight of the Muses or the Delight of the Elbian Muses. This is a landscape showing the river, and two hills in the foreground. On one hill are the nine Muses, playing contemporary instruments; Apollo sits on the summit of this hill, holding an antique lyre. On the other hill sit the poets of the artist's day, playing identical instruments. In the sky there is Pegasus.[11]

The custom of using the word "Muses" or "Muse" in music-book titles was very common. From 1558 to 1569, Scotto and Gardano and others in Rome published three *Libri delle Muse,* collections of madrigals for four and five voices.[12] Collections of spiritual songs also used the name of the Muses. Michael Praetorius's famous collection has the title *Musae Sioniae—Muses from Zion.*

The figures of the Muses were also shown as being in heaven. The title page of a book of music for the lute (1701) by Wenzel Ludwig von Radolt (Fig. 101) [13] depicts the composer with Minerva beside him. A ladder formed by the musical notes of the scale leads to heaven, where the Muses appear playing on instruments. The ladder or gradus has been popular in titles of music books. One of the best-known books of exercises for the piano, still in use today, is the *Gradus ad Parnassum* by Clementi. The scales with their Greek names, and not only the Doric scale, are illustrated on the title pages of Denis Gaultier's collection of music for the lute, *La Rhétorique des Dieux.*[14] In the background, the names of the modes are inscribed on a Renaissance façade; in the foreground *putti,* some with wings and some without, are making music in scenes representing episodes from Gaultier's life. (The illustrations are by Abraham Bosse.) The rather frequent combination of real and mythological figures is also found on the title page of the *Currus triumphalis musicus*

---

[11] Haas, *Die Musik des Barocks,* p. 167, Fig. 90.

[12] E. Vogel, *Bibliothek der gedruckten weltlichen Vokalmusik . . . 1500–1700* (1892); new edition by A. Einstein in *Notes of the American Music Library Association* (1945), 11, 63, 154ff.

[13] R. Haas, *Die Musik des Barocks,* p. 261, Fig. 163.

[14] *Ibid.,* p. 121, Fig. 66.

FIG. 101. Engraving by Hoffman & Hermundt after Waginger. Frontispiece of W. L. von Radolt's lute book *Allertreueste Freundin* (1701). INSTRUMENTS: lyre, plucked lute, triangle

(1648) by Andreas Rauch.[15] There the groups appear in the clouds; on top, the reigning emperor appears in a carriage drawn by two eagles and attended by the virtues of good government; on the side and below, in two ranks, there is an entire orchestra, the figures partly costumed as courtiers and partly dressed as angels or Muses.

Numerous title pages show yet stronger ties to the representation of heavenly music described in earlier chapters. Five examples will be cited here as especially informative and typical. On the title page of Praetorius's *Musae Sioniae,* a title he adopted for the second part of his *Syntagma Musicum* (1620), a group of church musicians are seen assembled around an organ. Above, on two balconies, there are two groups of singers and musicians; then on top, in clouds, the symbol of the Lord is in the center, and beneath it is the Lamb on Mount Zion. These figures are flanked by the symbols of the Evangelists, on the left by angels playing on different instruments, and on the right by the Elders, all playing harps and one with a crown, providing, all told, an elaborate juxtaposition of celestial and secular instrumental music.

[15] *Ibid.,* p. 184, Fig. 108.

On the title page (Fig. 102) of the first part of the *Kleine geist-liche Concerte* by Heinrich Schütz [16] (1636), there is an oval medallion on top showing five angels seated on clouds, one in the middle singing from a book, two with wind instruments, two with a lute and a harp. Flanking the script of the title in the center of the page are Harmony and Measure.[17] A panel across the bottom of the page shows, again in clouds, the Lord, the Lamb, and the emblems of the

[16] *Ibid.*, p. 177, Fig. 102.
[17] These figures also appear on the title page of Galle's *Encomium Musices*.

FIG. 102. Engraving of the twenty-four Elders with their harps on the title page of Heinrich Schütz, *Kleine geistliche Concerte* (1636). INSTRUMENTS: harps, lute, cornettes (?)

Evangelists; then, on the sides, the twenty-four Elders with crowns and harps. A *titulus* above the angels reads *Misericordias Domini in eternum cantabo*. The two figures of Harmony and Measure, or Rhythm, which have also been encountered in Bardi's *intermezzi*, were a common feature on the title pages of music books until well into the twentieth century. They adorned the title pages of the popular collection of classical music by the publishing house of Peters.

There is an almost excessive implication of allegorical meaning in the titles and on frontispieces of song books by Johann Rist,[18] most of which were published by von den Sternen at Lüneburg (northern Germany) around the middle of the seventeenth century. The cover of the *Sabbathische Seelenlust* (*Sabbatical Delight of the Soul;* 1651) shows a globe representing the cosmos, surrounded by three spheres and a band with the signs of the zodiac. On it, a female figure is seated holding a pan's pipe in one hand and in the other an antique lyre; she is *Musica*, or a Muse, and she is crowned with laurel. At the top of the page, beside a symbol of God—a triangle with an eye in a disc—there are heads of *putti* with wings, the cherubim, and beneath them two winged *putti* carry a scroll inscribed with notes and the Thrice Holy. *Musica mundana* and *musica celestis* are here confronted. A somewhat simpler title page is that for Rist's collection, *Musicalische Fest Andachten* (*Musical Festival Devotion or Prayers,* 1655). Beneath the symbol of the Lord, surrounded by cherubim, the script of the title is flanked by three *putti* on each side; five have instruments (three viols, a harp, and a lute), and one is singing from a book.

The title page of Part I of Johann Eccard's *Preussische Fest-Lieder* (1642) is divided into two parts.[19] In the lower section a medallion is set in an idyllic landscape and flanked by two figures which may again represent Harmony and Measure; in the medallion itself, *Musica* and a group of five female musicians playing other instruments sit before an organ. The upper section shows clouds, with the symbol of the Lord in the left corner and a group of angel musicians playing to His praise on the right.

Lastly, as an appropriate concluding example, there is the title page for *Canon Angelicus* from Athanasius Kircher's *Musurgia* (1650), where not only the title page but the musical composition is

[18] Haas, *Die Musik des Barocks*, p. 123, Fig. 70.
[19] F. Blume, *Geschichte der evangelischen Kirchenmusik* (*Handbuch der Musikwissenschaft*), p. 87, Fig. 33.

FIG. 103. Frontispiece engraving by F. Baronius after Paul Schor for Athanasius Kircher, *Musurgia* (1650). INSTRUMENTS: kithara, pans pipe, triangle, cymbals, tambourine, S-shaped lyre (?), portative organ, shawm, lute, keyboard instrument, flutes

an expression of heavenly music (Fig. 103). Many of its features are the same as those in the illustration for Rist's *Sabbathische Seelenlust.* In the center of the page there is a globe, representing the cosmos, with three spheres and a band with the signs of the zodiac; the figure of *Musica* or harmony is seated on the globe, a pan's pipe in one hand and an antique lyre in the other. Below, in a landscape with a view of the sea, appears on the left the figure of Pythagoras, on the right the figure of *Musica,* and in the middle the scene of Pythagoras's experiment, located in a forge. Above, in the clouds beside the triangular symbol of the Lord, there are nine groups of heads of *putti,* the nine orders of the angels; beneath, two six-winged angels, cherubim, hold a scroll with the motif of the canon to the text of the Thrice Holy, *canon angelicum 36 vocum in 9 choros distributus.* The text on the band around the globe is a quotation from Job 39. The solution of the canon is given later by Kircher in the text.

Kircher's composition has an interesting companion piece or forerunner from the sixteenth century, a *Salve Regina* by Robert Wilkinson (Figs. 104a and b).[20] It is written for nine parts, and each part is allotted to one of the angelic orders. In the manuscript each part begins with an illuminated capital letter representing a group of three angels holding a scroll on which the name of the caste is written: Quadruplex—Seraphim; Triplex—Cherubim; Primus Contratenor—Dominaciones; Tenor—Potestates; Primus Bassus—Angeli; Medius —Troni; Secundus Contratenor—Principatus; Inferior Contratenor —Virtutes; Secundus Bassus—Archangeli.

This is the order in which the parts occur on the two pages shown in Figs. 104a and b. The order of their pitch, from low to high, is the usual one, with the variance that the cherubim and seraphim and the angels and archangels are interchanged. At the bottom of the second page, at the end, we read the following stanza:

> Antiphona hec Cristi laudem sonat et Marie
> Et decus angelicis concinit ordinibus
> Qui sunt Angeli erunt (?) Archangeli. Et ordo sequitur
> Virtutes: que potestatus; tunc principat(us) alter.
> Post dominacionesque . . . adde tronos cherubinque
> Et seraphyn junges que loca summa tenent.

[20] From the *Eton Choirbook,* ed. F. Harrison, *Musica Britannica,* x (1956).

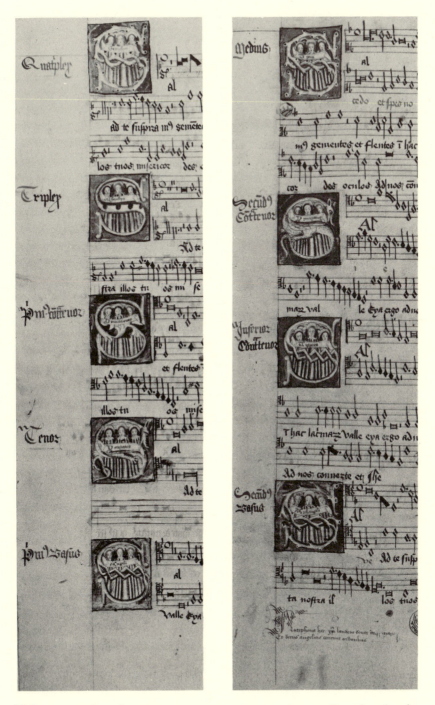

FIG. 104a. and 104b. Historiated initials with the nine angelic orders for the composition of the *Salve Regina* by Robert Wilkinson in the Eton Choirbook

This antiphon is in honor of Christ and the Virgin
In adoration the angelic orders are singing.
They are the angels and the archangels, and the following
  orders:
The virtues and the powers; then the princes;
Then the dominations, add to these the thrones and the
  cherubim,
And unite the seraphim who hold the highest places.

Thus, in this composition, too, it is not the harmony of the universe, the planets, but the celestial order of the angelic choirs that is set in parallel with the parts of the music.

TWO

MUSIC AND DEATH

FIG. 105. Frontispiece engraving for J. Rist, *Musikalische Kreuz-Trost-Lob-und Dankschule* (1659). On the left music as symbol of sin, on the right as sign of bliss. INSTRUMENTS: lute, rattle, harp

Introduction to Part Two

THE SECOND PART OF THIS STUDY will trace the history of the symbolic relationship music has with death. This relationship is at once more complex and less familiar than the connection between music and harmony. It is more complex because the basic concepts involved are in themselves more problematic, the whole topic being, of course, connected with the varying ideas of death evolved by the different religions.

As an opening illustration, there is the frontispiece of a seventeenth-century Protestant hymnbook (Fig. 105), which aptly combines the different symbolic aspects with which this part of my study will be concerned. On the left side, the human soul is represented as a youth beset by death in the form of a skeleton, by Satan, a horde of monsters, and a figure carrying a lute and a wine glass. The lute here symbolizes music's seductive capacity for leading to sin. On the facing page, the saved soul is standing between two angels, one holding a crown and the other a palm frond. The youth, about to be crowned with a wreath from heaven, is playing on a harp, and the decorative figurehead on the harp itself is singing. Here music symbolizes resurrection. Thus these pages provide a confrontation of symbols similar to that of the Halberstadt monument discussed in the first part of this study (see Figs. 3 and 4)—albeit in the more florid style of the seventeenth century—and represent the three aspects of our topic: the use of music as a symbol of death, a symbol of sin, and a symbol of resurrection.

These concepts will be treated separately, however closely connected they are fundamentally, for the sake of clarity in tracing their development. The sagas, rites, and customs concerned are, of course, based on the ideas that the various cultures formed as to the significance of death. Obviously, it is beyond the scope of this outline to discuss the whole history of the subject. Hence the treatment of ancient times will concentrate solely on the aspects that are relevant to understanding later forms, forms which cannot be explained without reference to their early forerunners in the Egyptian and Near Eastern civilizations.

All the religions which are of importance for our topic recognize in the human being the duality of soul and body. In death, then, this union is thought to be severed, and the question arises as to what constitutes the substance of the soul which leaves the body. In some religions the soul is identified with breath (*spiritus*); it appears, in fact, that this identification is the chief reason for using music as a symbol for death. The religions under which the essence of life is placed in another part of the body, such as in the blood or the liver, do not use music as a symbol of death. Some beliefs do not elaborate on the separation of soul and body at the moment of death, but use breath as the symbol of the beginning of life and of giving life, as in Genesis and Ezekiel. If at death the soul, understood as breath, is separated from the body, the soul takes to the air and is often visualized as a bird or a bird-like being. This bird-like figure may stand for the soul itself or for a psychopomp, whose role is to lead the soul through air. Alternately, the soul *is* air, the *pneuma*, the *ruah* of the Hebrew text of the Bible. This medium—breath, air, *pneuma, ruah*—is readily related to music, especially to the use of wind instruments. Some early Christian sects made the *pneuma* the center of their dogma, though the Church Fathers denied it a major role; and in the sacrament of Communion the communicants partake of the body and blood of Christ, not of the *pneuma*.

The other essential question that arises is, what is the soul's fate after it has left the body? Various solutions are offered by the different creeds. Some allot the soul a specific abode. Some make a basic distinction between a fortunate and an unfortunate fate. Such a distinction was made in Babylonian myths and in the Persian religion, and while Old Testament teachings are not explicit in this regard, the Christian religion has the basic difference between heaven and hell. When the soul was to go to a specific abode, a guide was usually thought to be needed, and several religions elaborated theories that certain rites had to be performed in order to find these guides. Should the soul fail to meet its guide, it could become homeless and dangerous. These beliefs found their expression in some funeral customs such as the practice of wild and noisy chants and dances, intended to chase away the evil spirits of the homeless souls. These ideas were expressed in early Roman rites and have survived in fairy tales. Such practices retained importance in the later periods, during the Middle Ages, and must inevitably be mentioned in any discussion of the origin of the Dance of Death, though this fifteenth-century phenomenon seems to have been motivated by other ideas.

The figures which will be presented as major symbols of death connected to music remain outwardly the same over the centuries—the hybrid bird-like, or, later, fish-like figure, the Muse, the savior or giver of life, and the skeleton—but these figures acquire different meanings in different periods. Major changes occur in crossing the threshold from the archaic to the classic and Hellenistic periods in the Graeco-Roman orbit; a second great change occurs with the rise of Christianity, and a third in the fourteenth century. These changes are the result of shifts in attitudes toward the problems of death and life after death.

For instance, in ancient Egypt the bird-like figure Ba had no connection with music; rather, it stood for the soul as breath. But in Homeric mythology, Ba became the malevolent siren which leads man to death through music. For the Greeks in the archaic period, death was the fate of every person; the guide to the underworld was Hermes, and the dead led a shadow-like life there. It was punishment not to be able to enter Hades; there was no resurrection, and the only positive way of individual survival after death lay in being remembered by one's survivors, whose duty it was to preserve the memory of the dead. In the classic and Hellenistic periods, however, the soul was able to leave Hades to be integrated into the eternal motion of the cosmos. The siren became a guide for the soul, and was often represented on tombstones as musician and psychopomp. In this period the Muse, too, became a psychopomp assigned to lead the soul from Hades to the specific sphere of the universe appropriate to the merits of the person. The Muse was able to perform this duty in view of her knowledge of music and was therefore frequently represented as a musician on sarcophagi.

The third great figure of classic Greek mythology related to death and music is Orpheus, whose myth originated in the sixth century B.C. The two aspects of his legend that are relevant here are his power to tame and to bring to life through music. Both reflect the enchanting power of music, and both can have a positive or a negative effect or aim. Orpheus stands for the positive: bringing to life in nature, liberating from Hades, bringing to life again, and leading to eternal life. His attributes were divided up in early Christian ideology and conferred on two opposite figures, Christ and Satan. The abode of the soul in afterlife became heaven or hell, two opposite realms. As symbol of resurrection, Orpheus was replaced by Christ the musician, playing a harp; Christ remained the symbol of resurrection but His playing gained the new meaning—the spheres of the cosmos were harmonized by the harmony of the strings of His instrument. The enchanting power of music with which Orpheus tamed and appeased was given to Satan, and turned to a negative end. In Christian ideology Satan does not liberate souls from the underworld through music, but ensnares and tempts the living to sin and to eternal perdition in hell.

For many centuries, Satan was usually identified with death in Christian imagery, but in the fourteenth century death seems to have lost this connotation. Death now came to meet persons of every way of life. In representations of the Last Judgment, up to and into the fourteenth century, one sees Satan leading the damned to hell on one side and Christ or His servants, the angels, leading the blessed to paradise on the other. But the Dance of Death, in the fifteenth century, uses the realistic approach; the crowd is not divided, and death, in the figure of a skeleton, comes to every man and leads him to the grave. This form for death had been known in antiquity, without any moral connotation, but in the Christian era death as skeleton had often been identified with Satan. In the form of the *Totentanz* of the fifteenth century, however, this identification was dissolved, and the skeleton stands simply for death.

Developments in the period between 400 and 1400 are not easy to follow, because part of the tradition had to go underground as a consequence of the teachings of the Church Fathers. However, some events and some forms are traceable and can be recognized as links between antiquity and the fifteenth century. After about 1400 many of the earlier figures reappear, and most have acquired different significance. Just as the sirens and Muses, who turned the wheels of the cosmos, returned in the form of musician angels, so the figure of Orpheus, the musician savior, reappears as Christ the musician in the treatises of the mystics of the fifteenth century and plays music to lead the blessed souls, to join the dance in heaven. The siren, the musician psychopomp of the Hellenistic monuments, reappears now half-human and half-fish (rather than bird), as Melusine, Lorelei, or Ondine, in the fairy tales. She returns, indeed, as a malevolent spirit, often bringing destruction through music, hence as the siren of the *Odyssey* or the Satan of the Middle Ages. Thus, though the interweaving of doctrines, myths, and symbolic figures is complex, it is possible to discern certain parallels among the figures related to music and death, and it is hoped that the outline will grow in clarity as ensuing chapters trace in more detail the history of music's connection with death, sin, and resurrection.

XI

Music as
a Symbol of Death
in Antiquity

MUSIC'S VARIED ASPECT in relation to death, its connotation in some contexts of good, in others of evil, has roots far in the past. The evidence, of course, is scattered, and in many instances our knowledge is insufficient for any clear assurance in interpreting the exact role that music was believed to play. One may readily contrast the presumably beneficial chants for the dead of ancient Egypt and the benevolent soul-bird Ba with the evil intent of Homer's sirens. Even for Egypt, however, some questions remain open, and the significance of musical figures and symbols in the tombs of other early civilizations is still less certain. Hence this chapter can, at best, assemble the fragments of evidence and suggest the possibilities that seem relevant to later, more familiar developments.

ANCIENT NON-GREEK CIVILIZATIONS

The early tombs of a number of cultures have been found to contain objects apparently provided for the dead to use in afterlife. These objects have sometimes included musical instruments, such as the remains of a harp found in a neolithic tomb and the famous inlaid harp in the tomb of Ur.[1] Further, many tombs have contained little clay figures of musicians, frequently of female instrument players (Fig. 106). No comprehensive study of the meaning of these items has yet been made, but the most usual interpretation has been that they were intended to enable the dead to continue their former customs in afterlife. Hence the tombs which contain musical instruments have generally been explained as tombs of musicians, or the little orchestras as imitating the customs at the courts where musicians belonged to the retinue of a ruler.[2] Yet I wonder whether the frequent

[1] W. Galpin, *The Music of the Sumerians* (1937); C. L. Woolley, *Ur of the Chaldees* (1954).

[2] C. Hentze, *Chinese Tomb Figures* (1937); one such little orchestra in the Metropolitan Museum, New York; a harp from a Neolithic tomb mentioned in A. Delatte, "La musique au tombeau dans l'antiquité," *Revue archéologique*, 4ᵉ

FIG. 106. Clay figures from a Chinese tomb; seventh century. The Metropolitan Museum of Art, Rogers Fund, 1923. INSTRUMENTS: lute, clapper, harp

occurrence of musical objects in tombs, especially the presence of the little orchestras, might not be equally plausibly attributed to the role of musicians as psychopomps. It is not difficult to believe that the figure of the female musician psychopomp which became so prevalent in Hellenistic times may have had a long, undocumented ancestry. The point, of course, is hardly subject to proof, but the possibility is worth consideration.[3]

Ancient Egyptian remains do not, however, bear this thesis out. Their psychopomp figure, Ba, does not seem to have been directly connected with music, despite his identity with breath. And, while music evidently figured prominently in Egyptian funeral ceremonies, the nature of its role remains unclear.

As is well known, the Egyptians had elaborate death rites. "Their lives seem to have been a continuous preparation for death," and the

---

série, 21/22 (1913), pp. 318, 324; W. Deonna, "Croyances funéraires," *Revue de l'histoire des religions*, 60 (1939), p. 53; W. Helbig, *Führer durch die öffentlichen Sammlungen in Rom*, II, 3 (1913), 217, harp in a tomb on the Via Tiburtina.

[3] A comparative study of the gifts to the dead in tombs has still to be made.

FIG. 107. Drawing by C. Wilkinson after a fresco in the tomb of Djesre-Ka-Re-souhe, showing an Egyptian funeral procession. The Metropolitan Museum of Art. INSTRUMENTS: bow harp, Egyptian lute, double flute, kithara

afterlife was seen, as depicted in the pyramids, as a continuation of life on earth.[4] Pictures of ancient Egyptian festivals sometimes show dancing and music-making, and the usual instruments are the harp and the flute (Fig. 107). The pictures of funerals, however, usually show percussion instruments (Fig. 108). This might point to an apotropaeic aspect of the funeral rites, since percussion instruments might be assumed effective in warding off evil spirits.[5] However, there is a report from the second millennium which does not seem to bear out this hypothesis. It concerns a high official, Sinuhe, who had to flee and live in exile in Canaan until he was called back by Sesostris I (1971–28 B.C.). The king's letter reads: "Return to Egypt that you may see again our court where you grew up. . . . Think of the day when you shall be buried; here you shall be anointed and

[4] L. Curtius, *Antike Kunst, Handbuch der Kunstwissenschaft*, 1, 43, 225.

[5] H. Bonnet, *Reallexikon der aegyptischen Religions-Geschichte* (1952); A. Wiedemann, *The Ancient Egyptian Doctrine of the Immortality of the Soul* (1895); E.A.W. Budge, *Egyptian Heaven and Hell* (1906); H. Kees, *Totenglauben und Jenseitsvorstellungen der alten Aegypter* (1956), interprets the text of the Book of Death in an apotropaeic sense, in opposition to Budge.

enveloped in bandages . . . you shall be accompanied on the day of your burial. The coffin shall be gilded and its top of lapis lazuli; you shall be put on a bier. Oxen will draw the carriage and singers shall open the procession, and the [dwarfs'] dance shall be performed at the door of your grave. The funeral prayers shall be chanted for you and the necessary sacrifices performed on the altar." Thus this description of the customs does not suggest magic, though the dwarfs' dance may have originally been a magic rite and have lost this meaning by the time of Sesostris I.[6]

It has been suggested that the use of music at funerals in modern Egypt corresponds to the ancient customs.[7] Today, the musical part

[6] Berlin, Staatliche Museen, Hieratische Papyri, v (1909), *Die Erzählung des Sinuhe* ed. A. H. Gardiner; G. Maspero, *Les Mémoires de Sinouhit, Recueil de travaux* (1916), pp. 32–36; J. B. Pritchard, *Ancient Near Eastern Texts Relating to the Old Testament* (1950), pp. 18ff., does not translate the term *muu* as "dwarf"; if *muu* means dwarf, as it has been translated by W. Keller (*Und die Bibel hat doch recht* [1955], p. 68), this might explain the occurrence of numerous statuettes of dwarfs among Egyptian remains (see Curtius, *Antike Kunst*, p. 90).

[7] J. Bonwick, *Egyptian Belief and Modern Thought* (1956); H. Frankfort, *Ancient Egyptian Religion* (1948); H. Kees, *Der Opfertanz des aegyptischen Königs* (1912); P. E. Kahle, *The Cairo Geniza* (1947); Kahle, "Die Totenfeier im heutigen Aegypten," *Festschrift Herrmann Gunkel* (1923); H. Schaefer, "Darstellung einer Beisetzung im alten Reich," *Zeitschrift für ägyptische Sprache*, 41 (1904), p. 66.

FIG. 108. Relief with an Egyptian funeral scene. INSTRUMENTS: krotala, tambourine (?)

of the rites is performed in the house of the dead, not in a procession or near the grave. The modern ceremony has two parts: one is a dance, called the Nadb, performed to the accompaniment of tambourines (the use of percussion instruments may itself be seen as a survival of old customs). The other part, the Adid, consists of songs sung by a professional singer. The texts of these songs are eulogies of the dead, enumerating his virtues, deeds, etc. Everything is sung to the little motif:

The texts are stereotype and collected in a book which provides the songs for all walks of life. The texts for the funeral rites of ancient Egypt, which have come down to us in the famous *Book of the Dead,* are quite different in both form and meaning. They are invocations to the gods, whereas the modern songs are based on Islamic belief and belong to a civilization in which the hero is highly estimated. Thus today's texts praise the dead, continuing a practice which can be traced back to ancient Greece, though, as will presently be noted, its purpose there was more to commemorate than to glorify.

The one figure in Egyptian mythology that is relevant to our subject is the soul-bird Ba, who represents the soul which leaves the body as breath in the moment of death. At the same time, Ba was the psychopomp and guide of the soul. Ba was thought to have the form of a bird with a human head. It was a benevolent spirit, helping the dead along his journey through the other world, a journey which would be successful if the dead were properly initiated and knew the right prayers to open the several doors along the way. In the end, "he will be among the living ones and see Osiris every day, and have air in his nostrils." [8] Thus Egyptian belief identified life with breath, and Ba was the symbolic figure for the life of the individual person during his life on earth as well as in the hereafter. In one manuscript of the *Book of the Dead,* Ba is shown returning to the tomb through a shaft to bring a present to the mummy.[9] On a relief from Sakkara, Ba is drinking from the fountain of life under a tree in the other world. On a number of urns for ashes, Ba appears sitting on the funeral bier to wait for the soul of the dying (Fig. 109). Although the

[8] Budge, *Egyptian Heaven and Hell,* p. 13.
[9] Budge, *The Papyrus of Ani,* Facsimile, 1913.

FIG. 109. Small Egyptian ash urn, with the soul-bird Ba at the deathbed waiting for the soul of the dead; ninth dynasty

figure of Ba has no known direct connection with music, the idea of Ba has, as shall be shown, influenced several later creeds and figures.

The information to be gathered from the ancient works of Mesopotamia is rather scanty. Where music is represented, the occasion bears no relation to death or funerals, but this may be because no tombs have survived intact.[10] There was one figure in Babylonian mythology that is relevant. The figure of the monster guarding the castle of perdition [11] is an ancestor of the gruesome angel of death (who appears, for example, in a fifteenth-century work at the Pisa cemetery), if my exposition of the influence of the winged lion and similar hybrid figures on the development of angels in the first part of this study is valid.

The Old Testament, while not explicit in describing the after life, has relevance to our topic because of the story of the creation of man

[10] Curtius, *Antike Kunst*, p. 225.

[11] P. Jensen, *Die Kosmologie der Babylonier* (1890), p. 235; A. Jeremias, *Die babylonisch-assyrische Vorstellung vom Leben nach dem Tode* (1887); Jeremias, "Hölle und Paradies," *Der Alte Orient*, 1 (1900); A. Mortgal, *Tammuz, Der Unsterblichkeitsglaube in der altorientalischen Bildkunst* (1949); J. de Morgan, *Mémoires de la délégation en Perse*, VII (1905), Pls. XXVII, XXVIII.

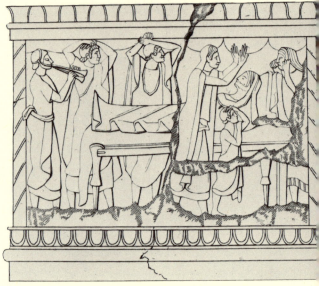

FIG. 110. Etruscan funeral scene from a mural in the Tomba del Morto a Corneto; fifth century B.C. INSTRUMENTS: double aulos

in Genesis, in which life was instilled into a form of clay by the breath of the Lord. The idea that breath, *pneuma,* is identified with life seems a particularly direct link in the connection of life and death with music. A wind instrument, sometimes, indeed, of clay, is brought to life by the breath of the player, and a tune "dies away" if the breath lessens and finally stops.

Easily, however, the most intriguing civilization from the point of view of this study is the Etruscan.[12] Great art treasures have been found in Etruscan necropolises, their cities of tombs, and numerous musicians and dancers are represented. Despite recent progress in discovering more about the Etruscan religion, present knowledge remains incomplete and rather vague. Whether the musicians and dancers are meant to show customs of ordinary festivals or are pictures of funeral rites is not always clear. One painting seems definitely to show a funeral ceremony: five persons move around a bier, with mourning gestures, while one figure plays a double aulos (Fig. 110). But as for the many other works on the walls of the tombs, it is

[12] M. Pallottini, *Etruscologia* (1947); F. de Ruyt, *Charun, démon étrusque de la mort* (1934); Ruyt, "Les traditions orientales dans la démonologie étrusque," *Antiquité classique,* 5 (1936); R. Enkling, "Lasa," *Deutsches Archäologisches Institut, Römische Abt. Mitteilungen,* 57 (1942), Pl. 1; Enking, "Culsu and Vano," *ibid.,* 58 (1943), pp. 48ff.; F. Messerschmidt, "Das Grab der Volumnier bei Perugia," *ibid.,* Vol. 57 (1942); J. D. Beazley, *Etruscan Painting* (1947); G. Hanfmann, *Altetruskische Plastik,* 1 (1936).

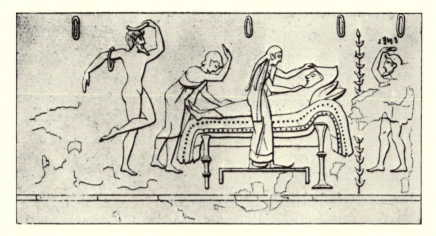

FIG. 111. Drawing after a painting in the Tomba del Morto a Corneto; fifth
century B.C.

FIG. 112. Mural in the Tomba del Triclinio at Tarquinii; fifth century B.C.
INSTRUMENTS: lyra

not certain whether the figures of musicians are connected, essentially, with the myths or rites for the dead.[13] The dances shown usually look very lively (Figs. 111 and 112) and I feel that one must

[13] J. Martha, *L'art étrusque* (1889), p. 181, Fig. 145; F. Weege, *Etruskische
Malerei* (1921), Tomba del Tifone, Pl. 48, Vulci, Tomba Bruschi, around 200
and 150 B.C., Corneto, Tomba del Morto, Fig. 215; G. Micali, *Italia avanti il
dominio dei Romani* (1821), Pl. 34; Micali, *Monumenti inediti*, (1844), p.
137, Pl. XVI, 1; E. Paribeni, *Studii Etruschi*, XII (1938), 71, 91, Pl. 34;
A. Maiuri, *Painting in Italy* (1959).

consider them to have been, probably, stamping dances performed at funerals for apotropaeic purposes.[14] The reason for this suggestion is that the Romans had similar rites and they, in turn, are known to have derived many of their ideas and customs from the Etruscans.

Almost equally little is known of the early Latin religion, prior to the period when the figures of the gods became largely based on the pattern of the Greek Olympus. Fragmentary evidence, however, suggests certain affinities with Etruscan practices. In the organization of their religion, the ancient Latins had four castes of officials or priests.[15] They had the *auguri* and *pontifices*, i.e., the seers and the planners of the calendar and technical matters. The third and fourth castes, the *tubicines* and the *saltatores*, were both guilds of musicians, players in bands, and dancers. The participation of the two musician guilds was a requirement for all festivals, the public games, the *ludi*, and especially for funeral processions.

The only Roman song which has come down to us from this period is a hymn in honor of Mars, then their highest god.[16] Its text, in ancient Latin, is:

> Enos, Lases, invate!
> Ne velue rue, Marmar, sins incurrere in pleores
> Satur fu, fere Mars! Limen sali! staé berber!
> Semunis alternei advaocapit conctos!
> Enos, Marmar, invato,
> Triump!
>
> (*To the god*):
> Help us, Lases
> Not death, nor ruin, Mars
> Let come over us.
> Be satisfied, cruel Mars!

---

[14] Virgil, *Aeneid*, 6, 644, "Pars pedibus plaudunt choreas et carmine dicunt"; Horace, *Odes*, 1, 37, 12, "Nunc pede libero pulsando tellus"; R. Eisler, "Orphisch-Dionysische Mysteriengedanken," *Vorträge der Bibliothek Warburg* (1925), 395.

[15] T. Mommsen, *Das Weltreich der Caesaren* (1933), pp. 501ff., 525; on the philological aspects, G. Hermannsen, *Studien über den italienischen . . . Mars* (1940); F. Cumont, *Apotheosis and Afterlife in Roman Paganism* (1922); Cumont, *Les religions orientales dans le paganisme romain* (1929).

[16] Mommsen, *Das Weltreich der Caesaren*, p. 525.

(*To the group*):
Jump on the threshold, stay, stamp on it!
(*To all the companions*):
To the Senones:
First you, then you
Call all:
Help us, Mars
Jump!

This is a song for a rite including a jumping and stamping dance, and, as the *saltatores* had to take part in the funeral processions, one may suppose that their dances there, as in the above hymn to Mars, had apotropaeic meaning. The role of the *tubicines*, the players on brass instruments, in the processions need not be explained as symbolizing life and death. The *tubicines* were essentially heralds and hence attended to the practical business of calling the procession together.

To return to the Etruscan works, there are also other figures, not musicians, where a symbolic relation to death seems persuasive.[17] These are winged figures that appear on sarcophagi, usually surrounding a portrait of the dead (Fig. 113). The male figures are

[17] *Mostra dell'arte e della civiltà Etrusca* (1955), Nos. 314, 315, Pl. 52; C. C. v. Essen, *Did Orphic Influence on Etruscan Tomb Painting Exist?* (1927).

FIG. 113. Male figures with large wings on the so-called "Season" sarcophagus, *ca.* 300

generally naked and do not always have wings. The female figures,
as mentioned in the first part of this study, look like angels. Possibly
both types symbolize the soul of the dead. There are also winged figures, with human heads but animals' bodies. These sphinx-like figures
are also seen on Roman sarcophagi and are related to another category of beings, to be discussed presently, of which the sirens of Greek
mythology are the best known.

Harpies, Sirens, and Muses in Homer's Greece

One is on somewhat safer ground concerning the civilization and
mythology of the Greeks, the source of three of the major figures
connected with music and death: Orpheus, the sirens, and the Muses.
While the surviving representations of these figures as musicians date
from Hellenistic times and the myth of Orpheus probably originated
as late as the sixth century b.c., the figures of the sirens and the
Muses were known to Homer, and the roles that they were cast in
during the archaic period are of particular interest in view of their
subsequent metamorphosis into musical psychopomps.

From the ideas of death and descriptions of funeral rites that occur
in the *Iliad* and, especially frequently, in the *Odyssey*,[18] it appears
that there was no special god of death. Each god was able to kill
through his particular attribute: Zeus with the thunderbolt, Neptune
with the trident, etc. Apollo and Artemis are invoked in the *Odyssey*
to bring a painless death with their arrows. Hermes was related to
death because he was the god of sleep, regarded as the brother of
death, and because he guided the dead to the underworld. Hermes
did not kill.[19] Gorgo, one of the Furies, was the spirit in Hades who
threatened perdition.

Hades was the term for the locale as well as for the god who was
the ruler of the underworld; but he was not a god of death. To die
was the common fate of man, and in Hades the dead lived a kind of
shadow life. The essence of life was not breath, but blood. As Ulysses
nears the entrance to Hades, the dead still have their bodily form,
and Ulysses is able to recognize them.[20] But this form is only the
shape of the former person, no "muscles and nerves," and no con-

---

[18] *Odyssey*, i, 291; ii, 223; v, 124; xi, 172, 199; xv, 408.

[19] S. Eitrem, "Hermes und die Toten," *Christiania Videnskabs-Selskabs
Forhandlinger* for 1909, No. 5; Eitrem, *Beiträge zur griechischen Religions-
geschichte*, iii, *Christ. Vidensk. Sels. Skrifter, Phil. hist.* (1917 and 1920).

[20] *Odyssey*, xi.

sciousness. The dead acquire memory only after they have tasted the blood of sacrificed animals; only then are they able to remember their former life.

Hades was the usual abode of the dead, heroes and ordinary persons alike. It was ill luck to be deprived of light and activity, but it was not punishment to be in Hades. On the contrary, it was a kind of punishment if the dead could not enter Hades. Thus the shade of Elpenor,[21] Ulysses' young companion, "not very clever and not very courageous," who falls to death on the isle of Circe, waits for Ulysses at the entrance to Hades. Elpenor cannot enter Hades until the necessary rites for his burial have been performed. He therefore implores Ulysses to bury him with his armor and to erect a monument.

From the Elpenor episode one gathers that, according to the ideas of Homer's period, the spirit of a person lived after death through memory, that is, he lived if he was remembered. The same point is emphasized in the *Odyssey* in the story of Menelaus on Pharos.[22] When Menelaus, returning from Troy, is forced to sail back to Egypt and hears that his brother Agamemnon has been murdered, he erects a monument to his brother on the island of Pharos, so that his memory will be preserved. When Telemachus, Ulysses' son, laments his fate, he wishes to know whether his father is alive or dead,[23] for if he knew that his father were no more among the living, he could erect a monument to him and the memory of both the father and the surviving son would thereby be honored. Thus these and other incidents make it clear that in early Greek belief it was the duty of the survivors to preserve the memory of the dead.

The importance of preserving the memory of the dead is a key to distinguishing the sirens from the harpies, with whom they are often identified.[24] Harpies are mentioned by Homer in the *Odyssey* in two noteworthy contexts. Penelope prays either to be killed by Artemis's arrow or to be seized and borne off by harpies, out of the knowledge

---

[21] *Odyssey*, xi, 51ff.; xii, 10–15.

[22] *Odyssey*, iv, 582.

[23] *Odyssey*, i, 235.

[24] E. Buschor, *Die Musen des Jenseits*; Roscher, *Lexikon*, "Harpias," col. 1842; Virgil mentions harpies at the door of Hades, *Aeneid* 6, 289; the monument of Xanthos in the British Museum is erroneously named *Monument of the Harpies*. The psychopomps on the side walls are sirens; this error also occurs in Andrea del Sarto's so-called *Madonna of the Harpies*, Berenson, *Italian Painting* (1952), Pl. 222; the figures on the small pedestal are sirens.

of mankind, so that she may be delivered from her sorrows. Telemachus complains that his fate is bitter because he does not know what has befallen his father; the harpies may have carried him out of the remembrance of the Achaeans. The harpies, evil spirits, were believed to appear suddenly like birds of prey, seize their victims, and carry them off to unknown regions. The harpies did not kill, nor did

FIG. 114. Odysseus sailing past the Sirens; drawing after a Corinthian vase; fifth century B.C. Courtesy, Museum of Fine Arts, Boston, Pierce Fund

FIG. 115. Three sirens hovering over the boat of Ulysses; a fifth-century B.C. red-figured amphora

they bring their victims to Hades. They annihilated the memory of a person.

It is possible that in the archaic period the sirens and the harpies were not clearly separated. Their outward appearance was similar, both were imagined as birds or bird-like beings, and, in the one place where sirens appear in the *Odyssey*, they are described as playing an equally evil role. In Ulysses' adventure the sirens sing enchanting songs so that the traveler stops to listen and is attracted to their island, where he is killed. They flatter Ulysses as the great hero of whose deeds they have heard and they promise to spread his fame. They promise to preserve fame and memory, but it is only a pretence to snare the passerby. It is not clear that Homer made any strong distinction between the sirens and the harpies, though his sirens do kill their victims. Homer does not describe their appearance as bird-like, and says only that they sing with sweet voices. Of course, it is possible that in Homer's time the term siren was applied to evil spirits, singers and killers, whereas by the classic period their role had completely changed.

The tradition of the archaic period nonetheless survived in later images of the Ulysses adventure.[25] Representations from the fifth century B.C. are extant in vase painting and sculpture on sarcophagi, making it possible to follow how the figure of the siren changed. Among the earliest are two vase paintings, one in Boston and one in London (Figs. 114, 115). Both show the scene of the boat, with Ulysses tied to the mast. On the Boston vase there are three sirens, birds with the heads of women, perched on the rock of the island, and two enormous bird-like vultures attacking the crew in the boat. On the London vase the boat is passing between two rocks. On each rock there is a singing siren, a bird with a human head, and a third siren seems to be falling from the rock into the ocean. This may refer to the popular tale, not told by Homer, that the sirens are doomed if someone is

[25] P. Courcelle, "Quelques symboles funéraires du néo-platonisme latin. Le vol de Dédale—Ulysse et ses sirènes," *Revue des études anciennes*. 46 (1944); Ch. Picard, "Néréides et sirènes. Observations sur le folklore hellénique de la mer," *Annales de l'école des hautes études de Gand*, 2 (1938); Frz. Müller, *Die antiken Odysseusillustrationen* (1913); *Encyclopedia Cattolica*, "Sirene"; Roscher, *Lexikon*, "Seirenei"; sarcophagi, see Buschor, Die Musen des Jenseits, Fig. 60; Cumont, *Recherches sur le symbolisme funéraire* (1942), Pl. 35; with reference to vase paintings, see G. Weicker, *Der Seelenvogel* (1902), pp. 162, 178; Martha, *L'art etrusque*, Fig. 253; Buschor, *Die Musen des Jenseits*, Figs. 36, 38, 39, 44.

FIG. 116. Male musician siren on a fifth-century B.C. black-figured Lekythos

able to withstand their magic song. Other early vases show Ulysses only, tied to the mast, with one or several sirens in the form of birds with human heads, playing instruments (Fig. 116). To be able to play, they have hands and arms in addition to their wings. Later representations on sarcophagi show the whole scene, but the sirens are depicted as three female musicians with musical instruments (Figs. 117 and 118).

As noted, Homer, in the *Odyssey,* did not explicitly describe the sirens as bird-like beings. However, there must have been such a tradition, because it is thus that they appear in a number of representations of the Ulysses adventure. This hybrid form, bird with human head, has been mentioned in the works of the Hittites and Babylonians.[26] It was frequently used in Greek design from the seventh

[26] *Odyssey,* XII, 41ff.

FIG. 117. Roman sarcophagus showing sirens, human figures with bird legs; third cent

FIG. 118. Etruscan ash urn with musician sirens; fifth century B.C. Instruments: pans pipe, lyre, wind instrument

century B.C. on and is a characteristic of the Corinthian style. The figure often appears as the handle on amphoras and craters. It may have
a female or a male, bearded head. Only once, on a fifth-century vase,
is the designation "siren" given,[27] and these figures do not appear
with musical instruments prior to the sixth century B.C. Presumably,
not all of these bird figures should be regarded as representing
sirens.

On the other hand, there are several other winged but not bird-like
figures in Greek mythology who can appear with musical instruments, e.g., Nike, the goddess of victory, and Eros.[28] Though their
appearance is reminiscent of the musician sirens, these figures generally have no relation to death and should not be confused with sirens.
The famous Nike of Samothrace was represented as a musician, and
Eros appears with a harp or cithara in a number of paintings. Neither
Nike nor Eros appears as a musician on Hellenistic tombstones. If
such figures have the monumentality of the Nike of Samothrace, or

[27] Buschor, *Die Musen des Jenseits*, Fig. 34, Attic vase in the Louvre;
Weicker, *Der Seelenvogel*, p. 124.

[28] A. Furtwängler, *Eros in der Vasenmalerei* (1874); Roscher, *Lexikon*,
"Eros."

if, as was often done on vases, names are added, the meaning is clear. But there are numerous representations where the winged figure is small in comparison with its surroundings, and no names are inscribed. Here, a definition is difficult and depends on the interpretation of the whole scene. If, for example, the little figure has no musical instrument and accompanies a warrior going to battle, it may represent a *nike* as well as a symbol of death (Fig. 119). Even if it has a musical instrument, the interpretation may not be plain. Often these figures have been explained as Eros, in places where I would prefer to understand them as soul-birds or psyches. On several vases we see a little music-making winged figure in a scene with women grouped around a stepladder (Fig. 120). This picture is now interpreted as showing a festival for Adonis which took place on the roofs of the houses. In the accompanying texts, scholars have described the little figure as Eros.[29] I would like to suggest that it might instead be understood as a soul-bird related to the meaning of Adonis as a symbol of resurrection.

[29] Corpus vasorum antiquorum, British Museum, facs. 6, III, Ic, p. 8, Pls. 96–97; H. Metzger, *Les représentations dans la céramique du IVᵉ siècle* (1951), pp. 94ff., Pl. VII, 5; to Miss Milne of the Metropolitan Museum of Art, New York, sincerest thanks for giving me this information.

FIG. 119. The soul-bird above dying Prokris; red-figured amphora from the fifth century B.C.

FIG. 120. Drawing from a fourth-century Greek vase depicting a festival for Adonis. INSTRUMENTS: double aulos

Finally, to complete the review of the archaic Greek figures related to music and death, it is necessary to mention the Muses and, in anticipation of later developments, the nereids. The Muses appear in Homer's work in several roles: as guardians of the order of the cosmos, as the chorus at feasts of the gods, and, in connection with death, as music-makers at Achilles' funeral, where they are said to have sung in antiphonal chorus. The nereids also attended Achilles' funeral, but not to make music. The *Odyssey's* account describes how they arrived, accompanying his mother, the goddess of the sea, with such a great roaring noise that the Achaeans were initially frightened into fleeing.[30] Thus for Homer, the nereids apparently had no specifically musical role, though they are clearly the ancestresses of the many hybrid, fish-like musician figures that were later variously connected with death.

[30] *Odyssey*, XXIV, 47.

XII

Later Greek Concepts and the Hellenistic Period

IN LATER GREEK IMAGERY, the connection of both the sirens and the Muses with music and death continued and was, indeed, elaborated and reinforced. But the nature of the relationship underwent a distinct change. Homer's evil, luring sirens survived within the Ulysses legend, but outside the context of this specific tale, sirens became helpful spirits, no longer identified with harpies but, rather, with the gracious Muses.[1]

The radical shift in the sirens' role was a facet of new currents in Greek thought, notably the more elaborate view of the universe generally associated with the Pythagoreans. As indicated in the first part of this study, the cosmos came to be seen as a complex and harmonious mechanism of stars and planets turning on spheres, and, corresponding to this image of the cosmos, theories as to the fate of man's soul after death became more sophisticated. Hades was no longer the single, terminal abode of the dead, but merely the first repository of the soul, which might subsequently rise to a higher sphere.

In some traditions, the Pythagorean underworld itself was divided into several spheres, like the cosmos. An inscription by Didymos (Imperial period) on a Roman tombstone for a young woman named Khoro mentions seven parts of Hades,[2] saying that her soul will enter the seventh circle of Hades, which is the abode of the purest souls. Existence in Hades, thus, was still not considered punishment, though ethical criteria had entered into consideration for the soul's graduation to higher places.

These new concepts were reflected in changes in the roles of two of the musical figures with which this study is concerned. The rulers of both the motion and the harmony of the cosmos were thought to be the Muses or, as for Plato, the sirens, who turned the spheres and sang for each its appropriate note. In the context of death, the Muses

[1] G. Weicker, *Der Seelenvogel* (1902); E. Buschor, *Die Musen des Jenseits.*
[2] I. Levy, *La Légende de Pythagore de Grèce en Palestine, École des hautes études, sc. hist. et phil.,* fasc. 250, 1927.

and hybrid siren figures that appear on so many Greek and Hellenistic tombs and sarcophagi may thus be seen as benevolent psychopomps, capable of guiding souls through the spheres precisely because of their knowledge of music.

A third major figure of the Hellenistic period is Orpheus. In a development which seems essentially separate from the siren-Muse tradition, Orpheus provided a more obvious pre-Christian symbol of resurrection, and a symbol reflecting the good purposes of music's power to entice.

THE BENEVOLENT SIREN

There are a number of written sources, dating from the seventh century B.C. and later, to document the role of the musician-siren figures on tombs. There are, for instance, verses which suggest the vision recorded later by Plato in the *Republic,* the image of the sirens sitting on the spheres of heaven, singing the musical scale which results in the harmony of the cosmos.[3] Alkman (earlier than 600 B.C.), the great lyric poet, likened the song of a young girl to the beautiful "song of the sirens, the Muses," thereby identifying the sirens with the Muses.[4] As noted in the first part of this study, Plato's image virtually substitutes the sirens for the Muses. That the musician figures on the steles actually represent sirens is made quite explicit by the words of a tombstone epigram from about 300 B.C. The text reads:[5]

> Slabs of stone! and you sirens! and you urn of grief
> Which preserves the poor remains of ashes for Hades!
> Salute the wanderer as he passes my hill, whether he be
>   from far away or from my own town.
>
> I was buried here soon after my wedding—and tell him
>   also that my family comes from Tenos.
> I was called Baukis by my father, and the epigram
> Inscribed for me on the stone is by my companion Erinna.

[3] Plato, *Republic,* in Loeb Classics, II, 404–405.

[4] *Poetae lyrici Graecae,* ed. Th. Bergk (1853), Alkman, Frgs. 7 and 15; *Lyra Graeca,* ed. Edmonds in Loeb Classics, I, 56ff., No. 1, Maidensongs (Bergk 15), "Hagesichoras, she may not outsing the Sirens, for they are gods"—p. 67, Frg. 14 (Bergk 7).

[5] E. Staiger, *Griechische Epigramme* (1946), pp. 70ff.; E. Peterich, *Fragmente frühgriechischer Lyrik* (1948), p. 41, Alkman, Frg. 94.

(The stone):

I belong to Baukis, the recently married.

If you approach the tombstone where so many have wept,

Tell Hades he should not have been so envious.

If you look at the beautiful figures they will inform you
about the cruel fate of Baukis,

That with the same torches that lighted the wedding songs,

Her brother lighted the pyre for the funeral,

And you, Hymen, had to tune the festive wedding songs

To the threnodic sounds of the mourning chants.

Thus the opening words, supposed to be spoken by the dead girl, are an invocation to the parts of the tomb, including the figures of the

FIG. 121. Winged musician siren on a Greek stele from about the fourth century B.C. INSTRU-MENTS: harp

sirens on the monument, to salute the wanderer who passes by. Other aspects of this little poem are of interest with regard to the different attitudes of the classic and Hellenistic period concerning Hades. First, however, some examination of the typical forms for the musician sirens that appear on tombstones seems warranted.

Music-making sirens often crown Greek steles [6] (Figs. 121 and 122). Frequently the main, lower part of the monument shows a scene of the dead surrounded by members of his family or accompanied by a servant. This is especially typical of the steles of the

[6] Roscher, *Lexikon*, "Seirenei"; Weicker, *Der Seelenvogel*; Courcelle, "Quelques symboles funéraires du néo-platonisme latin. Le vol de Dédale— Ulysse et ses sirènes," *Revue des études anciennes*, 46 (1944); F. Cumont, *Recherches sur le symbolisme funéraire* (1942).

FIG. 122. Detail of a Greek stele, showing a musician siren with a kithara; fourth century B.C.

FIG. 123. Musician sirens, human figures with wings and bird tails on a fourth-century cup. Courtesy, Museum of Fine Arts, Boston, Pierce Fund. INSTRUMENTS: kithara, double aulos

fourth century.[7] In these scenes, the room is often divided in two by a column, and in the triangle on top one or two sirens play on the cithara. The sirens usually have bodies of birds, with wings and tails, plus arms with which to play their instruments. They always have human faces. On the steles they are generally female figures, whereas on the *lekythoi* (the pitchers for oil used at the funerals), there are sometimes male music-makers in a similar setting, in a room divided by a column. In contrast, on a wooden sarcophagus from Egypt, only the lower part of the legs of the siren have the form of a bird. On some cups that are probably late Etruscan (Fig. 123), the sirens look like angels and tails are only suggested.

There are also monuments where there is a larger space for the section with sirens, and whole groups of them are shown. On a sarcoph-

[7] P. L. Couchoud, "Interprétation des stèles funéraires attiques," *Revue archéologique*, 5ᵉ serie, 18 (1923), p. 249; A. Delatte, "La musique au tombeau de l' antiquité," *Revue archéologique*, 4ᵉ serie, 21/22 (1913), pp. 318, 324.

agus from Belevi,[8] for example, there is a long frieze of sirens, including one playing on a kithara (Fig. 124). On the tombstone of Metrodoros of Chios,[9] above a battle scene there are four siren music-

[8] Buschor, *Die Musen des Jenseits*, p. 67.

[9] A. Brueckner, "Zum Grabstein des Metrodoros v. Chios," *Deutsches Archäologisches Institut, Athen, Abt. Mitteilungen*, 13 (1888); F. Studniczka, "Aus Chios," *ibid*.

FIG. 124. Human figures with bird legs; detail of a sarcophagus from Belevi, Asia Minor; third century B.C. INSTRUMENTS: kithara, aulos (?)

FIG. 125. Winged musician sirens with bird legs on a frieze in a tomb from about the third century B.C.

makers, two with rattles, one with a tambourine, and one with an aulos (Fig. 125). Here one is seen in profile and three from the front; their upper bodies are naked and human, but they have wings and bird-like tails and legs.

On a number of steles and monuments the sirens do not appear as musicians but in the pose of a mourning woman, with one arm lifted above her head as if putting ashes on her hair (Fig. 126). Frequently the sirens are shown carrying small human figures, representing the souls of the dead.[10] These winged figures carrying human beings may have come to Greece from other civilizations. Such figures are used as the feet of an Etruscan bronze *ciste* of the fifth century B.C., and they appear on the so-called Monument of the Harpies (Fig. 127)—from the fifth century—which was found at Xanthos in Lykia, in eastern Ionia, as well as on several other monuments. Though

[10] Weicker, *Der Seelenvogel*; *Messerschmidt*, "Das Grab der Volumnier bei Perugia," *Deutsches Archäologisches Institut, Römische Abt. Mitteilungen*, 57 (1942).

FIG. 126. Mourning sirens on a Greek stele; fourth century B.C.

FIG. 127. Winged female figures with bird legs; detail from the so-called Monument of the Harpies from the Mausoleum at Xanthos; third century B.C.

these figures are called harpies today, it seems unlikely that they represent evil spirits, for they carry the little human figures with the loving care of a mother for her child. They apparently have the noble duty of taking the souls to heaven, a duty which otherwise belongs to the Muses.

The musician siren generally appears on top of the tombstone, either alone or in pairs. However, on a Hellenistic stele found in Piraeus, the arrangement is reportedly different: at the bottom there are two tritons blowing on horns; above, in the centerpiece with the figure of the dead, "his left hand . . . rests on the head of a siren, smaller in size, which is standing beside him. The siren is playing on a kithara." [11]

There are also variations on the hybrid form of the siren, which have different names. From antiquity there is an excellent example in the figure of a woman with a fish-tail and an inscription reading

[11] G. Lippold, *Gemmen und Kameen* (1922), p. 6.

skylas, meaning Scylla.[12] Then there is a curious Roman mosaic from Aunale in Algeria, in which a nereid rides on a dolphin and Eros sits on the tail playing on a huge harp. In a scene from *Ezekiel* at Dura Europos (Fig. 128), the prophet is shown with a group of blessed, while to the left there are winged figures fitting the heads to the corpses. Three more are flying toward the prophet and the place where the dead lie dismembered.[13] All the winged figures have human forms. And there are many later hybrid forms, including what one author calls a "scorpion bird-man with Di(mono)chordium" on the thirteenth-century choir stalls of Basle cathedral,[14] and the figure called *Melusine* in a 1491 edition of *Der Ackermann von Böhmen*.[15] The latter is a combination of the two hybrid forms, with wings and a fish tail, but does not play an instrument.[16]

All the siren figures are evidently intended to represent them in a role essentially identified with that of the Muses, that is, as psychopompoi who guide the souls of the dead. The only characteristic which these figures have in common with their evil forerunners is that they are winged and able to charm with their music. The great difference is that now they lead to rest and bliss, and not to destruction.

Buschor, the great scholar,[17] recognized the fundamental change in the character of the siren between the archaic and the classic period, from that of siren-harpy to that of siren-Muse. But he insists on calling the sirens on steles "Hades Sirenen" and Muses of the underworld, and he sees Hades as a kind of hell, which Hades was not, either in the archaic or in later periods. I do not feel that the evidence which Buschor cites to justify his terms is convincing. If, in the *Antiope* of Euripides, Helen calls the sirens to help her with the funeral songs, one can take this as an identification of the Muses with

---

[12] "Inventaire des mosaiques de la Gaule et de l'Afrique," *Institut de France, Acad. des Inscr.*, Vol. 3 (1925), Algérie; also Lippold, *Gemmen und Kameen.*

[13] M. E. du Mesnil du Bouisson, *Les peintures de la synagogue de Doura Europos* (Scripta Pontifici Inst. Bibl. LXXXVI, 1939) Pl. XLIII; this illustration of Ezekiel, 37. 11ff., supports our contention that in Dura there was a cult emphasizing the dogma of immortality and resurrection.

[14] H. Waterbury, *Bird Deities in China* (1952), p. 60.

[15] A. Schramm, *Der Bilderschmuck der Frühdrucke*, Vol. 19, Strassburger Drucker (1936), Figs. 545, 554 from the *Ackermann von Böhmen*; Fig. 347 from *Melusine*, both printed by Knoblochzer in 1491.

[16] E. Buschor, *Die Musen des Jenseits* (1944).

[17] *Ibid.*, pp. 62, 69.

FIG. 128. Drawing of angels assembling the bones of the dead for resurrection; after a fresco in the so-called Synagogue at Dura Europos

the sirens. As noted above, Homer told of the Muses singing at the cremation of Achilles, so that there seems to have been a tradition that the Muses sang at funerals. Buschor's quotation from a fragment of Sophocles, where Ulysses says that the sirens sing the songs of Hades, can also be interpreted in the same way, as signifying merely that the sirens sing funeral songs, not necessarily that they live *in* Hades.

Finally, there is a quotation by Buschor from Plato's *Cratylus* which surely has another connotation. Here Plato has Socrates say that Hades, the ruler of the underworld, is so eloquent that even the voluble sirens are not a match for him.[18] It is in *Cratylus* that Socrates admits that his explanations of the etymology of the names of the gods sometimes are meant as jokes. Hades is here described as a caricature of a Sophist, of a person who has stronger powers of persuasion than most other people. This is a traditional idea. For instance, in one of the popular epigrams by Anyte of Tega, Hades is called the god who is hard to persuade,[19] and the idea that Hades is a "Sophist"—and that the Sophists are condemned to live in Hades—occurs also in the legend of the *nekyia* of Pythagoras, in which he

[18] Plato, *Cratylus*, 403 E, in Loeb Classics, Vol. 6, 72–73.
[19] Staiger, *Griechische Epigramme*, p. 39.

meets three kinds of foes on his trip to the underworld, among them the Sophists.[20] Indeed, all Buschor's references lose their weight when one realizes that, for Buschor, the underworld Hades has the wrong connotation. While it is true that Pythagoras and Plato made Hades a kind of place of lower grading, it was, nonetheless, not the hell of Christian ideology. After all, the seventh sphere of Hades was the abode of the purest souls. Nor was the ruler of the underworld seen as a monster like Satan.

The Psychopomp Muse

As noted above, the Muses appeared in the *Odyssey* as the deities who guarded the order of the cosmos, who formed the chorus at the feasts of the gods, and sang at the funeral of Achilles.[21] The role of the Muses in relation to death expanded similarly to that of the sirens. By the time of Pythagoras and Plato, the Muses had become psychopomps, like the sirens. They acquired this role because the cosmos was now visualized as a huge globe formed by the spheres of the planets, and the Muses were seen as the turners of the spheres, which were thought to emit musical tones. Thus when souls were supposed to be able to rise from Hades to other and higher spheres, according to their merits, the Muses provided able psychopomps in view of their knowledge of the order of the spheres and their musical abilities. This is one reason that they appear so often on sarcophagi of the Roman period, indeed, so frequently that there is a special classification called "sarcophagi of the Muses."[22]

[20] Levy, *La Légende de Pythagore*; A. Ruegg, *Die Jenseitsvorstellungen vor Dante* (1945).

[21] *Odyssey*, xxiv, 47.

[22] Roscher, *Lexikon*, "Musen" (Bie); F. Cumont, *Apotheosis and Afterlife in Roman Paganisme* (1922); H. I. Marrou, "Croyances funéraires," *Revue de l'histoire des religions*, 60 (1939), p. 53; Marrou, Μουσικός ἀνήρ, *Etudes sur les scènes de la vie intellectuelle figurant sur les monuments funéraires romains*, *Thèse complément* (Grenoble, 1937); V. Macchioro, *Il Simbolismo nelle Figurazioni Sepulchrali Romane. Memorie della R. Acad. d'Arch. Lettere e Belle Arti.* (Soc. Reale di Napoli), 1, 2 (1911) 9; Jamblique, *Les mystères des Egyptiens*, tr. Pierre Quillard (1948); Curmont, *Recherches sur le symbolisme funéraire*, p. 291, Fig. 65, sarcophagus (Berlin); Pl. 25, sarcophagus (Lateran); p. 297, sarcophagus (British Museum); Pl. 27, sarcophagus (Ancienne Coll. Simonetti); Pl. 28, sarcophagus (Vatican, Belvedere); Pl. 29, sarcophagus (Naples); Pl. 30, sarcophagus (Rome, Mattei and Farnese); Pl. 32, sarcophagus (Louvre); Pl. 34, sarcophagus (Vatican); Pl. 35, sarcophagus (Metropolitan Museum of Art, New York); Pl. 35, sarcophagus (Mus. Termi, Rome); Pl. 40, 1 (Vatican).

There are three typical scenes in which the Muses appear on sarcophagi: as a group of the nine Muses, generally on the front slab of the sarcophagus, with all or several playing musical instruments; a single Muse playing the kithara or the aulos; a Muse with a scroll or book, beside a portrait of the dead person.

For the first type, where the whole group of nine appears, the theory that they represent psychopomps offers one satisfactory explanation. They will take care of the dead person and lead him to his proper sphere. There seems to have been a long tradition for this idea, with an elaborate theory of the correspondence of the spheres, the musical tones, and the fate of the dead. There is, for instance, an anecdote—told by Jamblichus, one of Pythagoras's biographers—concerning Philolaos, Pythagoras's first important pupil.[23] Since Jamblichus, who lived in the fourth century (A.D.), gives as his source Apollonius of Tyana, who lived around 100 B.C., the tradition apparently extends over a considerable span of time. The story tells of a shepherd who once paused to rest near Philolaos's tomb. The shepherd heard singing in the tomb and told Eurytos, one of Philolaos's pupils, whereupon Eurytos asked: "In what key did he sing?" The soul of Philolaos was supposed to be on its journey of purification through the spheres or heavens, and depending on the key in which he sang, Eurytos could tell which sphere his teacher had reached. Because knowledge of the pitch of the spheres was necessary for this trip, the Muses were believed to be logical guides.

There is a further possible explanation for the Muses' appearance on sarcophagi, a reason which seems to me not only to apply in cases where they appear as a group, but also to yield the best explanation for the sarcophagi on which a Muse is seen with a scroll. The reason is that it was the task of the Muses to preserve the memory of the dead.[24] As mentioned above with reference to the archaic period, this was an issue of major importance. The Muses, as the daughters of Zeus and Mnemosyne, would therefore be appropriate figures to

[23] Delatte, "La musique au tombeau," pp. 318ff.

[24] "Mnemosyne," the Greek word for memory; mentioned as goddess by Hesiod; L. H. Gray, ed., *The Mythology of All Races* (1916), I, 238ff., Chapter, "Greek and Roman," by W. S. Fox; titulus for the first time on red figured *lekythos*, fifth century, Fig. 9, reproduced from *Monumenti antichi*, Vol. XVII, Pl. 26; Cicero, *Paradoxa stoica*, II, 18: "Mors est terribilis iis quorum cum vita omnia extinguntur, non iis quorum laus mori non potest," quoted by Cumont, *Recherches sur le symbolisme funéraire*, p. 254.

FIG. 129. *Putti* with the emblems of the Muses on the front of a third-century sarcophagus. INSTRUMENTS: kithara

FIG. 130. Roman-Christian sarcophagus from about the third century, with two psychopomp musician muses at the left and right corners. INSTRUMENTS: lute-like instrument, Roman fingerboard instrument

appear in this role on sarcophagi. The importance of preserving the memory of the dead was the same for any person, even for a child, and in Fig. 129, a sarcophagus of an infant, there are nine children with the emblems of the Muses.

This explanation seems particularly adequate for the type where one Muse appears with a scroll. This scene is quite often represented on the ends of the sarcophagus, while the group of eight or nine Muses appears on the front. Marrou and Cumont have inferred that this figure with the scroll occurs only when the sarcophagus is for a "musical" person (that is, according to Greek terminology, a well-educated person), and that the scene represents a heroization.[25] I

[25] Marrou, *Études;* Cumont, *Recherches sur le symbolisme funéraire.*

FIG. 131. Two psychopomp muses on the front of a third-century Roman sarcophagus. One is holding a kithara; the other, who is standing beside the dead man, is holding a book

FIG. 132. Front of a third-century sarcophagus, showing a funeral rite; two female figures with large wings carry the sphere with the bust of the dead. INSTRUMENTS: double aulos

feel that this is too narrow a concept. The book or scroll which the Muses hold in their hands is the Book of Life, in which the daughter of Mnemosyne engraves the data on the dead to be remembered.

Several explanations have also been offered for the scene showing a music-making Muse (Fig. 130) which sometimes appears as a counterpart to the Muse with the scroll or book (Fig. 131). All the suggestions seem plausible enough: the dead person was supposed to have been a musician, and the figures on the sarcophagus correspond to his profession; the instruments represent gifts offered to the dead by survivors. If the musician figure is playing an aulos, the instrument was said to be a sign of mourning.[26] The aulos was probably used in funeral rites. Thus in a scene on a Roman sarcophagus, a winged aulos player appears between two female figures with wings (Fig. 132). It is also true that the aulos is mentioned in several texts of the period as a sign of mourning. However, the aulos was used for joyous occasions as well, at weddings, by shepherds, etc. The figure of the Muse with a kithara has been explained in the ways cited above and, additionally, by Quasten[27] as a symbol reflecting the pleasures the soul would meet in the other world.

For both instruments, however, I prefer somewhat different solutions. The kithara is, I feel, a symbol of resurrection, not only as a reference to the music of the Elysian Fields but in the sense in which it appears later as the instrument of Orpheus and Christ.[28] As to the aulos, why can it not be explained on the sarcophagi as a symbol of both death *and* resurrection, based on the theory of the *pneuma* outlined earlier? This idea may seem complex and not readily grasped because it implies that the aulos and the *pneuma* are symbols for death as well as for life, for resurrection, which is possible only after death, and overcomes death with eternal life. This double and oppo-

[26] S. B. Finesinger, "Musical Instruments in the Old Testament," *Hebrew Union College Annual*, III (1926); "Halil," probably the aulos, is mentioned for mourning, Jer. 48:36; but also for festive occasions, I Sam. 10:5; Isaias, 5:12; 30:29; I Kings 1:40.

[27] J. Quasten, *Musik und Gesang in den Kulten der heidnischen Antike und christlichen Frühzeit* (1930); Quasten, "Die Leierspielerin auf heidnischen und christlichen Sarkophagen," *Römische Quartalschrift*, 37 (1929).

[28] The kithara appears on numerous Christian seals as the instrument of Christ and a symbol of resurrection; O. Wulff, *Altchristliche und byzantinische Kunst* (*Handbuch der Kunstwissenschaft*, I).

FIG. 133. Musician Nereids and Tritons on the front of a second-century sarcophagus

site solution is analogous to the use of the torch as a symbol, which when lighted, means life, and when turned downward and extinguished, stands for death.[29] I feel that this explanation offers a better solution than those postulated on the mournful sound of the instruments, and I prefer to interpret the use of both instruments as signs of resurrection. This solution, furthermore, opens the way to regarding the aulos-playing Muse as bringing life again to the soul, preparing the soul for its trip through the spheres. Both Muses and sirens, then, lead the immortal soul from Hades to the spheres of heaven.[30]

As a branch of or variant of the Muses, the nereids also often appear on sarcophagi (Fig. 133). These figures, half-human, half-fish, are seen performing as psychopomps who guide the souls of those who are privileged to enter forever the Elysian Fields, that abode of ever-pleasant climate, without rain or snow. Elysium was visualized as an island separated from the earth by the river Oceanus, and it was the nereids' task to carry the soul across this ocean.[31] Thus, on the water, they replaced the sirens and Muses of the air, and presumably, this is the reason why they appear frequently on sarcophagi and frequently with musical instruments, or with companions playing musical instruments.

THE FIGURE OF ORPHEUS

The figure in Greek mythology whose connection with resurrection is undoubtedly the most familiar is Orpheus. He, too, symbolizes liberation from Hades through music. However, his method of accomplishing the task was essentially different from that of the Muses; his success was not based on theoretical knowledge of the music of the spheres but on the power of music to enchant the soul as well as to pacify and enchant the rulers of the underworld.

It is irrelevant for this discussion whether or not Orpheus was an historical person, whether he should be considered a god or a priest, whether he was the founder of a religion, etc. Nor does it matter which tradition of the Orpheus myth is the best and most authentic,

[29] Claudianus, *Rape of Proserpina*, 375, in Loeb Classics, II; A. Ludwich, *Eudoxiae Procli Claudiani Carmina* (1897), p. 143.

[30] In Plato's *Phaido* the Muses lead to immortality; see also the inscription on the tomb of Asclepiades in Rome, cited in P. Boyancé, *Le culte des muses chez les philosophes grecs*, Bibliothèque des écoles françaises d'Athènes et Rome (1937), p. 281.

[31] C. Picard, "Néréides et sirènes: Observations sur le folklore hellénique de la mer," *Annales de l'école des hautes études de Gand*, No. 2 (1938).

because the two facets of his legend which are relevant here belong to all traditions. These are the legend that through his music Orpheus was able to attract and tame animals and to animate lifeless objects like rocks and trees, and the legend that Orpheus liberated Eurydice from Hades through music. Both illustrate music's power to bring to life, to animate. According to the second legend, Orpheus was supposed to have entered Hades and rescued the soul and person of Eurydice. Here a soul is liberated from death, and Orpheus is a symbol of resurrection.

The Orpheus tradition, as noted, seems to be quite separate from that of the Muses as a symbol of resurrection. Plato's account in *Phaedros* suggests that souls emerge from Hades, apparently by their own force, into a meadow located between Hades and the earth.[32] (This meadow recurs as the *prato* of Dante's *Divine Comedy*.) Here, according to Plato, the souls undergo judgment and are eventually guided by the Muses to their proper sphere. These ideas are reflected in a fresco from the temple in Marasa-Locris in Italy (Fig. 134); two youths on horseback, supported by two male triton-sirens, are seen emerging from the underworld into the meadow to be presented to the judging deity.

Whether the Orpheus myth was the basis of a religion, whether an Orphism originating from the myth became a religion, we do not know. Some scholars think that Orphism was identical with the cult

[32] Plato, *Phaedros*.

FIG. 134. Tritons supporting horses and riders who are emerging from the underworld; drawing after a fresco in the Temple of Marasa-Locris; fifth century B.C.

in Eleusis;[33] some think that it is identical with the beliefs of Pythagoras and his school,[34] and some scholars speak of Dionysian-Orphic rites.[35] All three hypotheses may be right. If Orphism was a religion, the chief dogma would have been the idea of the immortality of the soul and of resurrection, and the little that is known of the rites in Eleusis indicates that the idea of resurrection was its central concept. There is a surviving fragment of one of the hymns which implies that in Eleusis not only the rebirth of nature in spring was venerated, but the resurrection of the soul.[36] Persephone, the daughter of Demeter, goddess of agriculture and fertility, personified the seasons. She was supposed to live in Hades during the winter and to be resurrected every spring; this possibility of resurrection was apparently thought to be transmitted to initiates.

The text of the sole surviving fragment (dating from the seventh century B.C.) of the Eleusian hymns reads:

> Blessed is he among mortals who has seen them [the rites
>   of Demeter].
> He who is not initiated and does not take part in the rites,
> Once he is dead, has another fate, and must live in the
>   damp underworld.

Plutarch, later, reported a dance at Eleusis which symbolized the motion of the stars and the spheres.

The Pythagorean philosophy also expressed the idea of the immortality of the soul, but in the form of metempsychosis, a form different from that in Eleusis. Scholars who suggest a connection between the Pythagoreans and Orphism see a link in the texts of the small gold tablets, engraved with prayers,[37] found in Egypt and in the south of Italy, where Pythagoras taught. The plates are supposed to have been used as amulets by the followers of Pythagoras and possibly by

---

[33] Boyancé, *Le culte des muses*, p. 19; Dieterich, *Nekyia* (1913), pp. 64, 74.

[34] A. Boulanger, *Orphée* (1925), p. 18; W.K.C. Guthrie, *Orpheus and Greek Religion* (1935), p. 219; V. Macchioro, *Zagreus* (1930); R. Eisler, "Orphisch-Dionysische Mysteriengedanken," *Vorträge der Bibliothek Warburg* (1925); Plutarch, *Lives, Alcibiades* in Loeb Classics, IV, 98ff.

[35] E. Rohde, *Psyche* (London, 1925), p. 219.

[36] R. Eisler, *Weltenmantel und Himmelszelt* (1910); Quasten, *Musik und Gesang*, p. 63; A. Dieterich, *Nekyia* (1913), p. 64; the rites are mentioned in Arnobius, v, 1174, *Patrol. lat.* 53 and Lactantius, *Patrol. lat.* 7, 237.

[37] D. Comparetti, *Laminette Orfiche* (1910); A. Olivieri, *Lamellae aureae orphicae* (1915); Kern, *Orphicorum fragmenta* (1922).

the adherents of Orphism, if the two are related. On one of the tablets, two fountains are mentioned; the one called Lethe should be
avoided if the soul is bent on salvation.[38] The other fountain,
Mnemosyne, is desirable. Thus the archaic idea that man is immortal
through being remembered recurs. The soul gains immortality by
picking roses in the grove of the Muses. Sappho sings:

> If you die you shall be completely forgotten.
> No one will remember you; no one wants you here either
> Because you never picked the roses of the grove of the Muses.

Here again, fame and the Muse and Memory-Mnemosyne are related to life after death.[39]

The most popular and at the same time most complex theory is one
which connects the legend of Orpheus with that of Dionysus; [40] both
are said to have originated in Thrace. One tradition is that Orpheus
was the priest of the cult of Dionysus and the author of the sacred
hymns. The tradition of this connection is difficult to follow because
the figure of Dionysus appears in many different guises. Plato, for
instance, characterized Dionysus as the god who introduced and protected wine. In the Hellenistic world and the Roman Empire all
kinds of deities and civilizations were merged. After Alexander's conquests, the whole Middle East fell under Hellenic influence, and the
Greek gods, especially Dionysus, were fused with local deities.[41]

[38] *Ibid.*, p. 104; Dieterich, *Nekyia*, p. 84.

[39] Cumont interprets the figures with musical instruments on sarcophagi as
teachers of the musical arts and harmony; he is puzzled that only female
musicians appear beside the reading male figure, the sign of an educated man,
and that these duties are never reversed. He understands the figures as representing a couple or the female figure as an allegory of the educated man, but never
as a psychopomp. Marrou, *Études*, pp. 247ff., also wonders why the female figure
is always the musician, as he assumes that the figure of the Muse represents a
reflection of the deceased's former life. I regard all these sarcophagi as representing prospective, not retrospective, scenes; Peterich, *Fragmente*, p. 11.

[40] Boulanger, *Orpheé*; R. Eisler, *Orpheus the Fisher* (1921); Eisler,
"Orphisch-Dionysische"; G. Guidi, "Orfeo, Liber Pater e Oceano in Mosaici
della Tripolitania," *Africa Italiana*, VI, 3/4 (1935); Guthrie, *Orpheus and
Greek Religion*; V. Macchioro, *From Orpheus to Paul* (1930); V. Schultze,
"Orpheus in der frühchristlichen Kunst," *Zeitschrift für Neutestamentliche
Wissenschaft*, 23 (1924); J. R. Watmough, *Orphism* (1934); Wulff, *Alt-
christliche und byzantinische Kunst*, p. 71; K. Reinhardt, *Poseidonius, Orient
und Antike* (1928); H. Glück, *Die christliche Kunst des Ostens* (1923), Pl. 51;
Plato, *Kratylos*.

[41] N. Glück, *The Other Side of the Jordan*, American School of Oriental
Research (1940); Origen, *Contra Celsum*, see Chapter I, n. 21.

Also, for many centuries the only sources of information on this epoch were the writings of the Church Fathers, especially those who wrote against the pagan cults, such as Origen and Saint Augustine. Naturally, since their views were highly biased, they must be read with caution. Indeed, all too often they did not understand the pagan "superstitions."

Recent discoveries, however, are beginning to broaden our knowledge of this era.[42] Some evidence for a mixed cult fusing Dionysus with the local god has been found during excavations of remains of the Nabataeans or Sabaeans, now tentatively identified with the people ruled by the Queen of Saba in the south of Saudi Arabia, near the Yemenite frontier.[43] Their chief god, Durasis, was clearly modeled after Dionysus.[44] Further to the north, in Syria, a coin (of the fifth century B.C.) has been found which has Bacchus inscribed on one side and, on the other, Yahw, possibly to be identified with Jahve.[45] In Jerusalem this god was called Dionysus-Orpheus. In the same period at Alexandria, Orpheus was described as a pupil of Musaeus-Moses. There is also a seal of the third or fourth century with an engraving of a crucified figure surrounded by the inscription "Bacchos-Orpheos," with seven stars and a crescent moon above the cross (Fig. 135).[46]

[42] Plato, *Cratylus* in Loeb Classics, Vol. 6.

[43] R. Reitzenstein, *Poimandres* (1904), p. 166; Glück, *The Other Side of the Jordan;* Boulanger, *Orphée;* Macchioro, *Zagreus;* Eisler, *Orpheus the Fisher,* pp. 31, 56.

[44] T. Mommsen, *Das Weltreich der Caesaren* (1933), p. 525.

[45] Boulanger, *Orphée,* frontispiece.

[46] Eisler, *Orpheus the Fisher.*

FIG. 135. Seal cylinder, showing the crucified Orpheus-Bacchus-Christ; third to fourth century

FIG. 136. Orpheus with animals; a first-century Roman mosaic floor. INSTRU-
MENTS: kithara

The figure of Orpheus, whether as the center of its own cult or as
part of the cult of Dionysus, or, as I think, as the symbol of immortality, must have been very popular throughout the countries bordering
the Mediterranean from the fourth century B.C. until well into the
Roman imperial period—that is, into the Christian era. Numerous
representations of Orpheus in all kinds of media have survived.[47]
The most usual scene is that of Orpheus taming the animals (Fig.
136). Guidi distinguishes four variations of this scene.[48] One has a
landscape background, showing the rocks that Orpheus brought to
life. Another shows Orpheus without rocks, surrounded by the figures
of animals; a third shows only one or two animals. In the fourth,
Orpheus appears in a center panel, and animals or flowers or other
emblems are visible in other parts of the pattern. In most, Orpheus,
wearing the Phrygian bonnet, is seated and playing on an instrument.

The legend of a person able to attract or tame animals through
music is also referred to in several other civilizations. One of the
newly discovered frescoes from the Temple of Bel at Nippur shows a

[47] Wulff, *Altchristliche und byzantinische Kunst*, Part 1, 71, 145, and,
especially, 149.
[48] Guidi, "Orfeo."

FIG. 137. A goddess with cymbals leading a procession of musicians and animals: drawing after a frieze from a border-stone in the Temple of Bel at Nippur; seventh century B.C. INSTRUMENTS: long-necked lutes, tambourine

procession of musicians playing on instruments like lutes, with tame and wild animals (Fig. 137).[49] This work would belong to the Babylonian civilization of the seventh century B.C. In the music of modern India there exists a series of musical motifs—ragas—corresponding somewhat to our modes or scales. For each of them there is a typical illustration and a typical poem. The illustration for the *Todi Raga* (Fig. 138) shows a female musician who attracts animals, generally with a flute or a lute, though the poem makes no reference to the Orpheus legend.[50]

However, when a musician surrounded by animals wears the Phrygian bonnet, there seems little doubt that he represents Orpheus. For this reason, it would seem that the figure in the so-called synagogue in Dura Europos should properly be regarded as Orpheus.[51] This sanctuary is situated in what is now Syria, that is, in

[49] Eisler, *Orpheus the Fisher*, Pl. III; A. Jeremias, *Altes Testament und alter Orient* (3rd. edn.), Fig. 200.

[50] Information from a letter by Coomaraswamy, January 21, 1942; there is an anecdote about Puccini who attracted lizards by whistling while sitting in the early morning on the shore of one of the lakes in northern Italy.

[51] M. E. du Mesnil du Bouisson, *Les peintures de la synagogue de Doura Europos*, Pl. XXXIV.

the regions where Orpheus was popular and where mixed religions, fusions of Greek and local mythologies, once existed. The walls of Dura show scenes from both the Old and the New Testament, and a third cycle which is not related to either. In all the cycles, there are striking differences in the sizes of the figures, and it seems that the figures were probably scaled according to their importance in the legends. In one of the frescoes (Fig. 139) there is a large figure, a lyre-playing musician, with a Phrygian bonnet. Several animals seem to be attracted by his music, that is, they are shown moving toward him; among them, again comparatively enlarged, a lion. This musician figure was originally interpreted as King David, with the lion of Judah; more recently the scene has been given the caption "Christos-Orpheus." To me, however, the best and easiest way to explain the figure is to say that it is Orpheus, and that he appears large-

FIG. 138. Illumination from a sixteenth-century Rajasthani manuscript. Courtesy, Museum of Fine Arts, Boston, Ross-Coomaraswamy Collection. INSTRUMENTS: vina

FIG. 139. Musician with a Phrygian bonnet; drawing after a fresco in the so-called Synagogue at Dura Europos. INSTRUMENTS: kithara

FIG. 140. Orpheus the musician in the underworld pleading before Hades and Persephone; from a Greek vase found in southern Italy. INSTRUMENTS: kithara

sized to emphasize his importance in the religion once followed in the sanctuary, a religion centered on the idea of immortality and resurrection through music.

Representations of the other relevant scene of the legend, Orpheus in Hades, are not so numerous.[52] Orpheus appears, pleading before

[52] Eisler, *Orpheus the Fisher*.

Hades, on several vase paintings on amphoras found in southern Italy. These have been dated as from the fifth or fourth century B.C., which would coincide with the period in which the Pythagorean sect flourished. In these paintings, Orpheus is standing with his lyre beside a small temple (Fig. 140). Inside the temple on a throne sits Hades; Persephone stands beside him. Orpheus can be seen, on the left, holding a kithara. Eurydice or Hercules often appear as well in

FIG. 141. Orpheus the musician and listening animals; from the mural in the Casa di Orfeo at Pompeii. INSTRUMENTS: kithara

these paintings.[53] Orpheus appears with Eurydice on two reliefs, one in Armentum-Santangelo, where we see him with the lyre and the Phrygian bonnet and Eurydice with the soul-bird.[54] The relief of Orpheus, Eurydice, and Hermes now in the Naples Museum is probably the best known of all representations.[55] Orpheus appears twice in Pompeii, once surrounded by animals (Fig. 141) and once playing for the Muses and Hercules.[56] For a connection between Orpheus and the Muses, there is yet another document in the temple mentioned by Pausanias, reportedly erected on Helikon and dedicated to both the Muses and Orpheus.[57] Orpheus also appears on a sarcophagus and in a mosaic as a counterpart to the other mythical musician, Arion,[58] a connection which later became popular in the Middle

[53] Guthrie, *Orpheus and Greek Religion*, Fig. 17, p. 188; Quasten, "Die Leierspielerin," *Römanische Quartalschrift*, 37 (1929), Pls. VIII, IX.

[54] Roscher, *Lexikon*, "Orpheus," col. 1187; the name of Eurydice is connected with the figure and the legend of Orpheus from the fifth century on only; according to Dieterich (*Nekyia*), Orpheus goes to Hades "of course not in order to free his wife, but to obtain from Persephone a favorable fate for the initiated."

[55] L. Curtius, *Antike Kunst* (*Handbuch der Kunstwissenschaft*, I, 1925), 234, Fig. 407; L. Curtius, "Komposition," *Antike*, Vol. 8 (1932), p. 308.

[56] J. Bayet, "Hercule funéraire," *Mélanges d'archéologie*, École française de Rome, 39 (1922).

[57] Pausanias, I, 30, 2, cited by Boyancé, *Le culte des muses*, p. 265; Diogenes Laertius, quoted by Cicero, *De finibus*, V, 1, 5.

[58] Guidi, "Orfeo," Fig. 27.

FIG. 142. Second-century B.C. mosaic floor from a Roman villa in Chebbe, Tunisia. In the lower left and upper right segments are the two mythical charmers of animals: Arion and Orpheus. INSTRUMENTS: kithara

Ages. In Fig. 142 he appears with the kithara in the upper lozenge on the right; in the lower left is Arion on a dolphin.

Orpheus's relation to Hercules is based on the legend that Hercules, too, liberated a soul—Alcestis—from Hades and vanquished death. This is probably why Hercules is also sometimes represented with a musical instrument (Fig. 143); he appears thus in several works.[59] In 187 B.C., for example, Fulvius Nobilior erected a temple in Rome dedicated to Heracles Musarum, with statues of the nine Muses and a lyre-playing Hercules.[60]

Two works from imperial Rome, one preserved and one known from description, are also relevant, especially because they bring us to the threshold of Christianity. Alexander Severus, in his Hall of Fame, erected statues of Christ and Orpheus side by side, as symbols of resurrection; and on the Esquiline, near the Capitoline Hill, a statue of a musician surrounded by animals was found, a statue which very probably represented Orpheus. Further, near the place where it was found there stands a monument to the guild of the *tubicines*, mentioned above (p. 232).[61]

At the dawn of the Christian era, in fact overlapping the start of Christianity by several centuries, there were three major figures related to music and death: the siren, the Muse, and Orpheus. All three, as mentioned, connoted the idea of resurrection to some degree. Of even greater importance, in view of subsequent changes, one might emphasize that all three also connoted the use of music for beneficent purposes and that Orpheus quite specifically represented the use of music's power to lure and charm to gain an essentially positive end.

[59] Bayet, "Hercule funéraire"; Lippold, *Gemmen und Kameen*, p. 39; A. Furtwängler, *Die antiken Gemmen*, LVII, 10.

[60] Roscher, *Lexikon*, "Musen," Ch. 10, Allgemeine Übersicht der Musendarstellungen auf Sarkophagen.

[61] Quasten, *Musik und Gesang*, Pl. 8; Guthrie, *Orpheus and Greek Religion*, pp. 266ff. The Roman inscription mentions the *Collegium* under L. Pontius L. C. and L. Lucinius L. L; in another inscription the *Collegium tibicinum* is mentioned as taking part in the cult of the *Magna Mater*, *M.D.D. mag. curaverunt*; T. R. Palangué *et al.*, *The Church and the Arian Crisis*, tr. in *The Church in the Christian Roman Empire* (1953), II.

FIG. 143. First-century Roman cameo, showing Hercules the musician

XIII

The Christian Era
the Development of Early
Medieval Images

WITH THE SPREAD OF CHRISTIANITY, basic concepts of death and after-life underwent significant change, and these new concepts, combined with the negative attitude the early Church had toward music itself, had radical effects on the symbols and images with which this study is concerned. Unfortunately, the only sources for tracing the earlier phases of these developments are the undoubtedly biased writings of the Church Fathers. Yet certain inferences may be drawn, especially from the works of those authors who were educated in the classical tradition, such as Origen, Saint Gregory Nazianzen, and Saint Augustine, and the fate of the classical figures related to music and death may also be judged from the traces of their survival in early medieval work.[1]

As a broad generalization, it may be said that the various benevo-lent classical musician psychopomp figures went into virtually total eclipse during the long period prior to the thirteenth century. In-deed, the very idea of a musician psychopomp seems to have survived only in the perverted form of Satan, who used music as a lure to lead the soul to sin, thence to hell. Orpheus, on the other hand, survived with remarkable tenacity, both in his own figure and, in the early Christian era, in the guise of Christ in appropriate roles.

---

[1] F. C. Conybeare, *Myth, Magic, and Morals* (1909); T. R. Palangué *et al.*, *The Church in the Arian Crisis*, tr. in *The Church in the Christian Roman Empire* (1953), I, 580ff.; see also "Dependence on Greek Thought," p. 582; "The way to profit by Hellenistic Letters," by a bishop of Caesarea, attributed to Saint Basil, in *Collection des Universités de France* (1935); Origen, *Contra Celsum*; Saint Augustine, *Sermo de psalmo CXVI, Patrol. lat.* 38, 185; *De civitate Dei, Patrol. lat.* 41, 207, 181, 183, 221, 569ff.; Arnobius, *Adversus Gentes, Patrol. lat.* 5, 745ff., 1051, 1118, 1174, 1251; Lactantius, *De falsa religione, Patrol. lat.* 6, 192ff., 282, 405; Lactantius, *De origine erroris, Patrol. lat.* 7, 494; Tertullian, *De falsa sapientia philosophorum, Patrol. lat.* I, 304ff., 403, 437, 474, 574, 638, 643ff., 656, 692; Vol. 2, 649; E. Nikel, *Geschichte der Katholischen Kirchenmusik*; J. Quasten, *Musik und Gesang in den Kulten der heidnischen Antike und christlichen Frühzeit* (1930), pp. 171, 195, *passim*.

CHANGED CONCEPTS OF LIFE AFTER DEATH

The eclipse, survival, or mutation of the classical musicians of death was closely related to the new Christian vision of the soul's fate after death. Christianity's rapid spread has often been attributed to its simplicity and clarity. To be admitted to the old mystery rites, initiates had to go through complicated instructions, and membership was selective, whereas under Christianity every believer could become part of the community. The new ideas concerning death and afterlife offered two clear alternates, either the positive path into heaven through resurrection, or the negative fate of existence in hell. These concepts are more akin to the Babylonian and Persian myths than to Greek ideas,[2] but in contrast to the Babylonian castle of death and the Persian abyss, the Christian hell is filled with flames. Hell is ruled by Satan, the successor to the monster guarding the castle of death.[3]

The figure of Satan had appeared in the Old Testament, where Satan is first mentioned in the Book of Job and there called a child of the Lord.[4] His image became more and more gruesome as it developed in Gnostic writings,[5] and eventually, for Saint Augustine, Satan became the reason, the cause of death, *diabolus auctor mortis*. Satan's goal is to ensnare the living in his net, and the term *diabolus* may mean "all ensnaring net." To achieve this end, Satan uses all kinds of enticing devices, including the magic power of music. In hell itself there is no music, as there was none in Hades. In hell there is only noise.

In this radically different picture of the afterlife, there was no place for psychopomps, no role for the sirens or the Muses. It was only considerably later, as outlined in Part 1, that these figures in a sense reappeared in the form of angels, and only much later, in the thirteenth and fourteenth centuries, does one find angels carrying souls to heaven. The figure of the siren was not used by the Church Fathers, and when they mention the Muses it is not with reference to their temples, the Museums (*Museions*), or their rites, or their duty

---

[2] V. Macchioro, *From Orpheus to Paul* (1930); see also Part 1 of this book.

[3] J. Kroll, *Gott und Hölle, Warburg Institut, Studien*, Vol. 20 (1932).

[4] Job, 1:6, *passim.*

[5] A. Jeremias, "Hölle und Paradies bei den alten Babyloniern," *Der Alte Orient*, 1 (1900); see above Chapter XI, n. 12.

as psychopomps, but only to explain their name, their origin, their myth.[6]

The Survival of Orpheus

Orpheus, however, was to some degree accepted by the Church Fathers. He was praised as one of the greatest poets of sacred hymns, "theologi poetae in quibus Orpheus maximo nobilitatus," and recognized beside the Sybillae and the prophets of the Old Testament as having predicted the coming of Christ. At the same time, Orpheus was condemned by Saint Augustine as leading the sacrilegious rites of the heathen (*sacrilegiis praeficere soleat infernis sacris*).[7] Gregory Nazianzen, in several of his hymns, mentions Orpheus as the poet and the singer who enchanted nature and who could, through the eloquence of his music and song, tame wild animals and bring trees and rocks to life. The Orphic songs are called famous and popular among the ancients; but the members of the Christian community should repent and reject these songs inspired by insane demons. Gregory rejects the songs of Orpheus, together with those of Hesiod and Homer. Celebrated though they were, they are rejected because they never can penetrate to Christ. *Valete Musae,* he dismisses the inspiration of the Muses.[8]

It is reasonable to assume that if their criticism was strong, the Church Fathers must have felt the pagan cult worth combatting. The cult of Orpheus, therefore, must still have been influential in the fourth century, the time of Saint Augustine and Saint Gregory Nazianzen. Musical rites probably had an important part in the cult, and quite possibly it was to sever every link to this kind of rite that the use of music was restricted in the liturgy of the first and second centuries. Instrumental music was completely proscribed, and only the singing of psalms to limited tunes, really mere chants, was allowed. In his letter on the education of a Christian girl, Saint Jerome writes that she should know nothing about instrumental music ("virgo Christi, surda sit ad organa, tibia, lyra, et citara, cur facta sint, nesciat").[9]

---

[6] Arnobius, *Adversus Gentes, Patrol. lat.* 5, 787, 693, 988ff., 1048, 1231, 1631; Saint Augustine, *De doctrina christiana, Patrol. lat.* 34, 49.

[7] Tertullian, *De falsa sapientia, Patrol. lat.* 1, 403; Vol. 2, 649; Saint Augustine, *De civitate Dei, Patrol. lat.* 41, 572, 581.

[8] Gregory Nazianzen, *Patrol. gr.* 14, 95ff.

[9] Saint Jerome, *Epistula CVII ad Laetam, Corpus Script. eccl. Viennae* (1912),

On the other hand, the figure of Orpheus as musician and symbol of resurrection was initially, if briefly, taken directly over into Christian iconology. How otherwise can one explain the occurrence of the figure with the lyre and the Phrygian bonnet on Roman coins and in the early Christian catacombs in Rome? The figure seems, however, to have had a different though related significance. Under the influence of the Alexandrian and Neoplatonic schools, the allegorical interpretation of myths and poetry had developed and had been adopted by the Church Fathers. Christ is the symbol of resurrection per se. If Christ plays on the lyre, this instrument represents the cosmos, and Christ is the ruler of the cosmic harmony, the Pantocrator. The figure of Christ with the lyre, however, seems to have disappeared after the third century. Music became entirely evil in connotation and an attribute of Satan. Thus, whereas Orpheus had liberated the soul from Hades through music, Satan came to lead the soul through music to hell.

The other scene of the myth, Orpheus taming the animals, was also adopted and transformed into the figure of Christ the good shepherd,[10] with the original meaning thus retained. Apart from the fact that the lyre is omitted, the mosaic of Christ the good shepherd in Ravenna shows a scene identical to the typical scene of Orpheus among the animals.

The figure of Orpheus appears to have survived with notable vigor for a number of centuries after the new faith had been established. There is a commentary on the sermons of Gregory Nazianzen by Nonnus,[11] a cleric of the ninth century, in which Orpheus is criticized even more severely than by Gregory. In Nonnus's commentary, the sweetness of Orpheus's singing is characterized as black magic, his songs are related to the Homeric hymns on Zeus, Ceres, and the like, and Gregory is said to have condemned them for mentioning obscene and phallic traits of the gods, "Orpheus turpiter atque obscene profaneque configit" the myths of the gods. Gregory had mentioned

---

Vol. 55, p. 299, cited in Quasten, *Musik und Gesang* and K. Meyer, *Der chorische Gesang der Frauen* (1917), p. 10.

[10] Clausnitzer, *Die Hirtenbilder in der altchristlichen Kunst* (1904); M. Dibelius, *Der Hirt des Hermas* (1923); O. Wulff, *Altchristliche und byzantinische Kunst* (*Handbuch der Kunstwissenshaft*, 1, 1918).

[11] Nonnus. "Nonni collectio et repositio historiarum quarum S.P.N. Gregorius meminit in priore invectiva adversus Julianum imp."; first edn., Eton, 1610; *Patr. gr.* 36, 1027ff., 1042ff., *cap.* 76ff.

FIG. 144. A fifth-century Byzantine alabaster flask with Orpheus and listening animals. INSTRUMENTS: kithara

the Orphic rites in his sermon on the Sacred Light, and here again Nonnus's commentary is even stronger in the terms of its rejection. The pagan rites are defined as magic; neither the Orphic sacrifices nor mysteries should be adhered to, despite the fact that the Greeks had performed them in the name of wisdom. Orpheus's lyre should no longer be venerated, though once it had been thought able to influence the whole universe. By the very vigor of its criticism, Nonnus's commentary demonstrates that the figure of Orpheus was still very much alive in the ninth century.

One can also infer his popularity from the numerous representations in the visual arts. The scene of Orpheus taming the animals can be traced without interruption into the Romanesque period and the Renaissance. From the beginning of the fifth century there is a figure of Orpheus surrounded by animals, and holding an ancient kithara (Fig. 144). A quite similar figure appears on a twelfth-century capital at Torsac (Fig. 145),[12] and likewise on the Campanile at Florence by Della Robbia (Fig. 146).[13] In the latter, Orpheus wears the dress of the period, and the scene is an illustration of "Music" as one of the liberal arts. Frequently, one would not be able to distinguish Orpheus from his counterpart, Christ the good shepherd, were it not for the musical instrument which designates the figure as Orpheus. It should be noted, however, that after the year 1000, approximately, the figure of Orpheus ceases to appear on burial places or sepulchral vessels. His connection with the idea of death and resurrection seems

[12] T. George and A. Guerin-Boutand, *Églises romanes* (1928), Fig. 270; L. Gischia *et al.*, *Les arts primitifs français* (1939), p. 115, Fig. 91; W.K.C. Guthrie, *Orpheus and Greek Religion* (1935), Pl. 15; similar figures, ivory at Bobbio; Wulff, *Altchristliche und byzantinische Kunst*, p. 149, Fig. 141; from the castle at Knole, England, R. Eisler, *Orpheus the Fisher* (1921), Pl. 7.

[13] P. Schubring, *Die italienische Plastik des Quattrocento*, p. 74, Fig. 76; in Kinsky, *Musikgeschichte in Bildern*, attributed to Andrea Pisano; J. Schlosser, "Giusto's Fresken in Padua," *Jahrbuch des allerhöchsten Kaiserhauses*, 17 (1896).

FIG. 145. Orpheus with a lyre and listening animals on a Romanesque capital at Torsac-en-Charente; twelfth century

FIG. 146. Luca della Robbia, Orpheus the musician; on the Campanile in Florence. INSTRUMENTS: lute

to have faded and, instead, his figure is linked with Pythagoras among the companions of Musica, the art of music.

Other pagan rites also survived and were reflected in Christian liturgy, especially in the Eastern Church. As noted above, there was the hymn from the *Acts* of Saint John mentioned by Saint Augustine,[14] which described a dance representing the movement of the celestial bodies and invited the faithful to join it. The vision expressed here is reminiscent of the fragment of the hymn from Eleusis.[15] It seems possible that the song from the *Acts* was intended for a ritual dance similar to the kind performed at Eleusis.

More clearly recognizable is the relationship to the old rites in one

[14] E. Hennecke, *Neutestamentliche Apokryphen* (1904), p. 424.
[15] See above Chapter XII, n. 36, and G. Pfannmüller, *Tod, Jenseits und Unsterblichkeit* (1953), p. 17.

of the hymns by Saint Romanos, the *melodos* and great poet of the Byzantine Church. Romanos flourished around 700, a Syrian Jew who had converted to Christianity. He wrote the following Easter hymn for a chorus of women: [16]

> Why this fearfulness?
> Why do you hide your faces?
>
> Turn your hearts upward!
> Christ has arisen!
> Perform your dance
> And sing thus with us:
>
> The Lord rose to heaven,
> Candle of Light
> He is born!
> Bringer of Light!
> Desist from your mourning,
> Breathe again in bliss!
>
> Spring has come,
> Bloom you lilies,
> And carry the fruit.
>
> Do not perish,
> Come, all of you
> Clap your hands
> And let us speak:
>
> He has awakened who helps the fallen to
>   resurrection!

In this Easter hymn, spring—the revival of nature and of the flowers—is used to signify the resurrection of Christ, and there are obvious traces of the old fertility and spring rites typical of the Eleusinian festivals. It is quite probable that in the Byzantine Church a real dance was performed on this occasion. Such a dance, performed by ladies in Byzantine court dress, is depicted in an illumination to the

---

[16] F. J. Dölger, *Die byzantinische Literatur* (1948), p. 34; K. Dieterich, *Geschichte der byzantinischen . . . Literatur* (1909) (Die Literaturen des Ostens), p. 35; J. B. Pitra, *Analecta Sacra*, Vol. 1 (1876), 138; G. Cammelli, *Romano il melode* (1930); E. Mioni, *Romanos* (1937); M. Carpenter, "Romanos and the Mystery Play of the East," *University of Missouri Studies*, 11 (1936); P. Maas, "Das Weihnachtslied des Romanos," *Byzantinische Zeitschrift*, Vol. 24 (1923/24) and Vol. 38 (1938), pp. 156ff.; see also W. Otto, *Menschengestalt und Tanz* (1956).

famous Greek Psalter in the Vatican library.[17] The manuscript dates
from the ninth or tenth century; the illuminations are supposed to
have been modeled after earlier sources which might date from the
period of Romanos. Traces of pagan ideas also appear in Romanos's
famous Christmas hymn, in which the Virgin asks her son Jesus to
fulfill three wishes: "I invoke your forgiveness for the air, for the
fruit of the earth, and for all its inhabitants, forgive them all!" Here,
too, nature, fertility, and air and breath are connected with mankind.
Further, Christ is invoked to forgive, or purify and revive, nature
and air. Nature, Physis, had become one of the deities symbolizing
the center of life; one of the Orphic hymns was dedicated to Physis.[18]
This goddess, thought to be the essence of life, of revival and resurrection, was opposed by the Church Fathers, but, evidently disguised,
she survived in liturgical hymns. Finally, it might be noted that in
the liturgy of the Eastern Church of today, in the Easter service,
Christ is invoked as Christos-Helios.[19]

The Concept of the *Pneuma*

Another ancient concept, that of the *pneuma*, hitherto mentioned
in passing, also now becomes important with regard to Christian
ideology.[20] While the *pneuma*, as far as we know, had no equivalent
in either Greek or Oriental mythology, there were abundant prece-
dents elsewhere. A personification of air, Napischtu,[21] was among
the Babylonian deities. A cult of the air was mentioned once by
Firmicus Maternus as existing among the Assyrians and in Africa.[22]
The idea of breath or air as the central force of creation occurs in the
legend in Genesis. Under the Neoplatonic school, the *logos* and *nous*

[17] E. de Wald, *The Illustrations in the Manuscripts of the Septuagint*, III.
Psalms and Odes, II. MS. Vat. gr. 752, fol. 449v.

[18] Curtius, *Europäische Literatur*, pp. 114ff.

[19] In Homeric mythology Helios, the god of the sun, is a completely different
figure from Apollo. The fusion of Helios and Apollo was developed during the
Hellenistic era, probably under the influence of the cult of Mythras.

[20] D. C. Crump, *Pneuma in the Gospels*, Catholic University of American
School of Sacred Theology, 2nd. Ser., Vol. 82 (1954); H. Leisegang, *Pneuma
Hagion* (1922); P. v. Imschoot, "L'esprit de Jahve, source de la vie dans l'ancien
Testament," *Revue biblique*, 44 (1935).

[21] See Jeremias, "Hölle und Paradies."

[22] Firmicus Maternus, *De errore profanorum religionum*, cap. 4: "Item Aeris
apud Assyrios et Africanos populos nonnullos . . . ," *Patrol. lat.* 12, 989.

were similarly regarded as a central force in the universe.[23] The Church Fathers describe this *pneuma,* the *spiritus,* as resulting from the union of *Sophia,* wisdom, and *Anima,* which is equated with the spiritual part of the soul. This *spiritus* is sanctified and as *Spiritus Sanctus* becomes a part of the Holy Trinity. Saint Augustine defines "*spiritus,* whether divine or human . . . as what air is named in the sacred scriptures and what in Greek is called *pneuma.*" In this context he distinguishes it from breath—as *flatus* (Latin) and as *pnoe* (Greek). The material *spiritus* is air, is fire and flame. *Spiritus* of God and of man is the same. They are wed in the soul. By this *anima,* or soul, this *spiritus Dei,* by the breath or *pneuma* of the Lord, life was given to Adam.[24] One of the Oriental Christian sects, the Montanists, centered their dogma on the *pneuma,* since they considered it to be the strongest spiritual force.[25] One of the apocryphal books, the *Testament of Reuben,* outlines an elaborate theory distinguishing seven kinds of *pneuma* in man: the five senses, the faculty of procreation, and the faculty of speech.[26]

Pagan concepts also intruded into representations of the idea of *pneuma.* It was depicted in the form of *Aer* (air), as in an illumination in a twelfth-century Pontifical from the school of Reims (Fig. 147). The emphasis in this illumination is on the air as a source of music.[27] Air is the center of the three kinds of music which the medieval theory of music identified, *mundana, humana,* and *instrumentalis*—two kinds of heavenly music, in addition to real music. *Musica mundana* is represented with spheres, the circles of the

[23] A. Döring, "Wandlungen in der pythagoräischen Lehre," *Archiv für Geschichte der Philosophie,* v (1892), 523; P. Heinisch, *Der Einfluss Philos auf die älteste christl. Exegese* (*Alttestamentliche Abhandlungen,* Heft 1/2 1908).

[24] Saint Augustine, *Patrol. lat.* 38, 717, 923, 1466.

[25] "Montanists," Catholic Encyclopedia; "Montanisten" (Macedonier), by W. Moeller in Herzog, *Real-Encyclopedia*; N. Bonwetch, *Texte und Untersuchungen zur Geschichte der christlichen Literatur* (1914); A. Faggiotto, *L'eresia dei Frigi* (1924); P. Ch. Labriolle, *La crise montaniste* (1913); G. L. Finney, "Music, the Breath of Life," *The Centennial Review,* iv, 2 (1960); Tertullian, *Patrol. lat.* 68, and 2, 155, *cap. Pneumatici heretici,* 10, 53; 13, 807.

[26] Quoted from the apocryphal *Testament of Reuben, chap.* 2, in R. Eisler, "Orphisch-Dionysische Mysteriengedanken," *Vorträge der Bibliothek Warburg* (1925).

[27] E. v. Marle, *Iconographie de l'art profane,* p. 277, Fig. 341; H. Swarzenski, *Monuments of Romanesque Art* (1954).

FIG. 147. An illumination from the twelfth-century Pontifical Manuscript, showing *Aer* surrounded by mythical musicians. INSTRUMENTS: end-blown flutes, double pipes, short-necked fiddle, psaltery

cosmos. Air is shown surrounded by representatives of musicians, by the three mythical personalities Arion, Pythagoras, and Orpheus; then by the nine Muses, of which six have musical instruments; and finally by King David and his musician companions. Most of the figures represent actual music, or *musica instrumentalis*. The human figure stretching over the whole illustrates the connection of these figures and of Man with the spheres and the cosmic music which results in the *musica humana*. However, the most important aspect of this illumination, from the point of view of this study, is that here, as a matter of course, air is identified with music. Air may be envisioned here as a means whereby music is transmitted to the ear, or it may be understood as the force that gives life to musical instruments. It might be noted that it is air the element that is represented here, and not *spiritus*, the Holy Spirit. There is a contemporary illumination for the latter concept in the famous manuscript of Saint Hildegard, where a similar figure spans the spheres of the cosmos and is explained in the text as representing the vital force of the cosmos—life. The Saint Hildegard illumination, however, contains no references to music.[28]

The relation of air to music, of *pneuma* or *spiritus* to music, also has a bearing on why the figure of poetry is so often represented with a musical instrument. "Numen afflavit" is the inscription on Raphael's image of Poetry on the ceiling of the Camera della Segnatura. The figure holds a lyre in the classic Greek style. The term "inspiration" is so familiar that one no longer thinks of its origin in the word *spiritus*, air or breath. The *spiritus*, the *pneuma*, is instilled into the poet through music, and this inspiration through music is represented in numerous paintings, either through the figure of a Muse or an allegorical figure of Poetry holding a musical instrument.[29]

[28] Hildegard v. Bingen, *Wisse die Wege, Scivias*, ed. Maura Boeckeler (1954); J. Schomer, *Die Illustrationen zu den Visionen der h. Hildegard als künstlerische Neuschöpfung* (1937); H. Fegers, in *Das Werk des Künstlers*, I (1939); L. Baillet, "Les miniatures du Scivias," *Académie Inscr. Monuments et Mémoires*, Vol. 19 (Paris, 1911).

[29] K. Meyer-Baer, "Musical Iconography in Raphael's Parnassus," *Journal of Aesthetics*, VIII (1949); see also Filippino Lippi, *Parthenice*, Santa Maria Novella, Florence; Filippino Lippi, *Musica*, Kaiser Friedrich-Museum, Berlin; and Lor. Costa, *Parnassus*, Louvre, Paris.

FIG. 148. Flying musician sirens with fish tails; illumination from an eleventh-century *bestiaire*. INSTRUMENTS: harp, clapper, horn

SIRENS AND HARPIES

To trace the history of the figures of the sirens and the harpies dur-ing the Christian era, one must first turn to medieval bestiaries.[30] The transformation of the Muses into angels and musician angels has been discussed in the first part of this study, and this aspect of their development will become relevant again when the great change of imagery in the fourteenth century is considered. For the harpies and the sirens, however, the bestiaries, whose authors were more inter-ested in describing imaginary creatures than real animals, provide an abundant source (Fig. 148). In the bestiaries the harpies appear usually as four-footed animals with human heads and the bodies of winged lions or serpents. They appear in the form of a hybrid being reminiscent of Saint Augustine's description of Satan.[31] At other times they are shown in hybrid form, half-human but with fish-tails and wings, flying and playing on musical instruments.

The sirens appeared in two forms. Sometimes they were bird-like, as on numerous Romanesque capitals (Saint-Germain des Près, Saint-Julien des Pauvres, Notre Dame in Paris; Beigneux, Seine; Chars, Seine-et-Oise; Saint-Leu d'Esserent, Oise; Saint-Loup de Naud, Seine-et-Marne).[32] Or they appeared as nereids with human heads

---

[30] D. Jalabert, "De l'art antique et l'art roman: Recherches sur la faune et la flore romanes. II, Les sirènes," *Bulletin monumental*, 95 (1936), pp. 433ff.; C. R. Dodwell, *The Canterbury School of Illuminations* (Cambridge, 1954), Pls. 42ff.

[31] Saint Augustine; see n. 36, below.

[32] Jalabert, "De l'art antique et l'art roman," Figs. 4–7. Similar to the nereid is the monster Scylla, see G. Lippold, *Gemmen und Kameen* (1922), p. 6, and A. Furtwängler, *Die antiken Gemmen*, LVII, 10.

FIG. 149. Drawing after a stained glass window in the Lyons Cathedral, showing the soul-bird Kladrius waiting for the soul of the dead; see Fig. 109

and the bodies of fishes, with one or two tails. It is in this form that they have survived in legends and fairy tales. Both types were frequently represented as musicians, or accompanied by a musician companion, very often associated with Satan. Secular literary texts of the period mention the siren in similes to sweet singing; thus, Isolde's song is likened to the song of the sirens.[33]

The sirens of the Christian era seem to have completely lost their significance as psychopomps. Once again, they usually appeared as evil spirits, but in a sense different from the sirens of the *Odyssey*. The medieval sirens were often connected with the followers of Satan, among the symbols of voluptuousness and vice. However, Honorius of Autun,[34] in one of his sermons (for Septuagesima Sunday), lists them together with the pelican, the unicorn, and the phoenix, which are all positive symbols of purity and resurrection. Finding the siren among these companions suggests a survival of the idea of the siren-Muse and psychopomp.

The bestiaries also depict another bird, Charadrius or Kladrius

[33] M. Wehrli, "Der Tristan Gottfrieds v. Strassburg," *Trivium*, IV, 2 (1947), 98; *The Tristan and Isolde*, ed. I. Zeydel (Princeton, 1948), verses 4860, 4870, 8101; A. Dyksterhuis, "Thomas und Gottfried," *Wortkunst Untersuchungen*, ed. O. Walzel, Vol. 10 (1946).

[34] Honorius of Autun, *Spec. Eccles. Sermo in Ascens. Dom., Partol. lat.* 172, 958.

(Fig. 149), whose origin Mâle could not explain.[35] This creature appears in the cycle of animals symbolizing resurrection and is described as appearing at the bed of a sick person and being able to recognize whether the person will recover or die. In the latter case, it turns away from the dying. It seems probable that this figure should be construed as the medieval survival of the soul-bird, the Ba of Egyptian mythology (see Fig. 109).

THE FIGURE OF SATAN

The figure of Satan, of course, gained a prominent role in this period and underwent considerable change. The Hebrew word "Satan" means adversary; the Greek *diabolos* means hate or slander, or all-ensnaring net. The Latin "Lucifer" refers to the bringer of light, the highest angel, whose ambition and revolt were the reason for his fall. It is in this role that the figure appears in the apocryphal *Adam Apocalypse*, discussed in the first part of this study. In this Gnostic work, Satan is the "beautiful" angel, leader of the choruses of angels praising the Lord. After his fall, he is excluded from heaven, forced to live on earth, and eventually becomes the ruler of hell. In the Gnostic revelations and apocalypses, his figure develops as an increasingly terrible monster. Saint Augustine's figure of Satan seems to have been formed from all of these forerunners.[36] He calls him *diabolus*, the reason of death and the king of hell. In hell, he has his servants, smaller devils and monsters, but no music. Saint Augustine, in fact, does not mention any connection between Satan and music.

Nevertheless, music-making, especially instrumental music, was declared a vice and became an attribute of Satan.[37] As there was no music in hell, Satan used music to seduce souls into sin and entice them to hell, and Luxuria became his companion. Satan is represented in this role in Romanesque sculpture.[38] On a capital at Vézelay

---

[35] E. Mâle, *L'art religieux du XIIIe siècle* (1919), p. 57, Fig. 14.

[36] Saint Augustine, "Enarr. in psalmis 39, 1, diabolus biformis . . . leo et draco"; "hostis ille . . . leo fuit . . . modo draco est"; *ibid.*, 69, 2, "diabolus ille biformis est"; *ibid.*, 90, 9, "quemadmodum sit leo et draco," *Patrol. lat.* 36, 431, 867; 37, 1168; see also 36, 456ff.

[37] Jerome, "Epist. 54 ad Furiam," *Corpus Script. eccl. lat.* 54, p. 479; *Canones Hippolyti*, No. 12; Tertullian, and others, listed in Quasten, *Musik und Gesang*, pp. 169ff.; the edicts of the Church Councils, see *ibid.*, p. 171.

[38] E. Reuter, *Les représentations de la musique dans la sculpture romane* (1938), Pls. 26–30; Gischia, *Les arts primitifs*.

FIG. 150. Monster using music for the purpose of seduction; Romanesque capital at Sainte Madeleine in Vézelay; twelfth century. INSTRUMENTS: oliphants

(Fig. 150) a demon is seizing a woman while a *jongleur* makes music. On a capital at Anzy-le-Duc, in a scene of Luxuria, a demon is playing on an aulos. On the tympanon at Conques, two monsters torture a man, and one of the demons has a harp (Fig. 151).

All these monsters have wild hair, like lions' manes, and tails like serpents, showing the hybrid form mentioned by Saint Augustine as characteristic of Satan. There is an Etruscan chimera, a big bronze sculpture, a lion with a serpent as its tail and a horned head growing out of its back. It may have been this kind of figure that inspired Saint Augustine's vision. Satan appears as a hybrid monster in numerous representations of the Last Judgment in Romanesque and Gothic art, at Amiens, Vézelay, and other places. Generally the entrance to hell is shown as the mouth of a monster. Satan appears often with a host of little devils, always opposite Saint Michael,

FIG. 151. Tympanon of the
west portal of the cathedral
at Conques; twelfth century

where the condemned souls are gathered.[39] Sometimes the condemned are roped together, sometimes one of the monsters is tortur-
ing them or pushing them into hell.

Only twice, however, have I found such devils actually making
music. They appear once with a horn and a drum, in the *Last Judgment* by Lochner from the middle of the fifteenth century.[40] In an
engraving after Mantegna, of Christ in Limbo (Fig. 152), two
devils are shown blowing curved horns at the entrance to hell. These
monsters are flying, have wings and fish-tails, reflecting in their form
the tradition of the harpies or evil sirens. The medieval attitude that
music-making was a vice is perhaps more clearly reflected in the
fact that musicians were very seldom shown at the marriage at
Cana.[41]

Satan seducing through music also appears in several mystery plays
in the scene with Mary Magdalen; once Satan is dancing and singing, and once he is making music.[42] On the other hand, in the
liturgical play *Ordo Virtutum*, by Saint Hildegard, written around

[39] Mâle, *L'art religieux du XIII* *siècle, chap.* "Le Jugement Dernier."

[40] E. Castelli, *Il demoniaco nell'arte* (1952), p. 98.

[41] Examples for music at the wedding feast at Cana, in B.M. MS. Roy. 2 B
vii, fol. 168v; G. Warner, *Queen Mary's Psalter* (1912), Pl. 198; also on the
bronze door of the cathedral at Benevento; music at the Lord's Supper, here in
the form of the Adoration of the Lamb, in an English MS. of *ca.* 1230, see G.
Millar, *English Illuminated Manuscripts* (1926).

[42] H. Morf, *Aus der Geschichte des französischen Dramas,* Akademischer
Vortrag (Bern, 1886; Hamburg, 1887); E. Dreger, *Über die dem Menschen
feindlichen allegorischen Figuren auf der Moralitätenbühne Frankreichs* (1904);
S. Kozaky, *Danse macabre* (Budapest, 1935–44), p. 150.

1100, all parts are sung with the exception of *diabolus*, which is a speaking role.[43]

In representations of the Last Judgment, Saint Michael often holds a scale. Usually the balance goes up on the side of the condemned, yet in a few instances it is down on that side. Saint Michael has been connected with the idea of death not only as the weigher of the virtues of the dead, but also as a partial replacement of Mercury

[43] J. Gmelch, *Die Kompositionen der heiligen Hildegard* (1912); *Ordo Virtutum der heiligen Hildegard*, ed. M. Boeckeler (Eibingen, 1927).

FIG. 152. Engraving after Mantegna, showing winged Satans blowing horns at the entrance to hell. INSTRUMENTS: horns

in the role of psychopomp. There are several sanctuaries known to have been at one time dedicated to Mercury and later converted into churches of Saint Michael.[44] Saint Michael, however, has never been connected with music. Mercury, on the other hand, lost his character of psychopomp in the Christian era, but became an outstanding patron of instrumental music.[45] Medieval representations of Mercury and of his children show him in this role, stressing not so much musical ability as skill in making musical instruments. Still, it is possible that in the medieval figure of Mercury the earlier connection of music and death and some connotation of the psychopomp role survived.

THE SYMBOLISM OF PARTICULAR INSTRUMENTS

Finally, before closing the discussion of this period, it is well to touch on some aspects of the symbolic significance of the musical instruments. There is an outline on the subject by Gregory the Great, included in his commentary on the first book of Kings.[46] The text describes prophets and saints descending from heaven and carrying the following instruments: psalterium, tympanum, tibia, kithara (i.e., the psaltery, the drum, the flute, and the harp). Then Gregory goes on to explain what these instruments mean. The prophets carry the psaltery "because it prophesied the advent of the rule of heaven," and because "it signifies the coming of eternal bliss." Gregory derives the psaltery's meaning from its having been the instrument of King David. Theological reasons are given, but no reference is made to the musical sound of the instrument.

The tympanum "teaches us atonement for sin; it symbolizes atonement by the skin of a dead animal stretched over the frame; as the skin is punished, so shall we some day be punished for our sins."

With the kithara, the prophets will teach the faithful the music of

---

[44] Mâle, *L'art religieux du XIIIe siécle, chap.* "Le Jugement Dernier."

[45] Eitrem, "Hermes und die Toten," *Christiania Videnskabs-Selskabs Fordhandlinger* for 1909, No. 5; A. Hauber, *Planetenkinderbilder* (1916); E. Panofsky and F. Saxl. "Classical Mythology in Medieval Art," *Studies of the Metropolitan Museum,* IV (1933); Fig. 30, Hausbuch, *ca.* 1490; Panofsky, "Gothic and Late Medieval Illuminated Manuscripts," *Fine Arts Lectures,* University of New York (1935), p. 117; K. Kereny, "Hermes der Seelenführer," *Albae Vigiliae,* 1 (1944), approaches the topic from an angle not relevant to this book.

[46] S. Gregorii Magni, "In primum regum expositiones *libri IV,*" *Patrol. lat.* 79, cols. 291ff.; Remy de Goncourt, *Le latin mystique* (1919), p. 159.

heavenly bliss. They have taken part in the heavenly concert and bring their knowledge of heavenly music to the faithful.[47] The kithara symbolizes joy and resurrection. It might be noted that here the saints and prophets have a task similar to that of the Muses in Greek mythology, with the essential difference that the Muses produced the cosmic music themselves, while the prophets have acquired their knowledge from Christ, Who is the author of the heavenly harmony, and are the intermediaries through whom Christ brings the mind and soul of man into harmony with the cosmic concert.

This latter belief reflects the idea of *musica humana*, which is only tangentially relevant. It occurs for the first time in the work of Nikomachus, in the second century.[48] Nikomachus speaks of the harmony which lies intrinsically in the strings of the lyre, comes to life when the lyre is played, and perishes when the tune is ended. The strings are tense, and the relaxation and balance are brought about by the player. This thought was cherished by Saint Augustine (*De mus. lib.*, vi), and is mentioned by Synesius in his work *On Dreams* (*De Somniis*).[49] Synesius's kithara has seven strings for the seven spheres and is the instrument which Christ plays to effect and to symbolize the harmony of the cosmos.

To return to Gregory, the tibia is the symbol of death and grief; it makes sinners cry to attain the state of eternal bliss. According to the Gospels, the flute was played at funerals. Christ ejected the flute players (*tibicines*) from the temple because He was to erect the real Church. Hence the *tibicines* see themselves excluded from the eternal life for which they have hoped; therefore they mourn as if they were dead.

Gregory derives the symbolism of the instruments by various methods of allegory. The meaning of the psaltery is explained on dogmatic grounds. For the drum, the significance is established by reference to actual parts of the instrument. The symbolism of the tibia is constructed on old funeral rites, and for the kithara the old idea of cosmic music is used.

[47] The identity of Faith with music and harmony is mentioned by Paulinus of Nola, see E. R. Curtius in *Zeitschrift für romanische Philologie*, 59 (1939), p. 139.

[48] Nikomachus, *Arithmetica*, ii, quoted in Döring, "Wandlungen in der pythagoräischen Lehre," p. 526; Cicero, *Tusc.*, i, 19, 41.

[49] Synesius, *De Somniis*, cap. 3, quoted in P. Duhem, *Le système du monde* (1917), iv, 359; the *De Somniis* was translated by Marsilio Ficino.

All one can conclude from Gregory is that the flute was more often used for mourning and the kithara for joy and resurrection, parallels which are also mentioned in several other sources.[50] In works of art Orpheus, the savior, always plays a stringed instrument—a harp, a kithara, or a lute. However, lyre-players also appear on many Roman sarcophagi and also as emblems of inspiration. Nor is the flute exclusively used as a symbol of mourning. Further, there are realistic and technical factors which must be taken into consideration. As noted in Appendix v, the organ has played a different symbolical role in different periods, a difference based on attitudes of cult and religion. If originally the flute was the instrument best equipped to produce a mournful, wailing sound, its superior characteristics in this regard were eclipsed by the ninth-century invention of the bow for stringed instruments, an invention which enabled players to sustain a tone on strings and to make as lamenting a sound as on the flute. These remarks may suffice to inspire caution in evaluating the symbolic meaning of instruments. A certain instrument may have a certain meaning in a given context, but the relationship is never binding, not even during the same time period.

It should be noted that, by the end of the long period under discussion, Satan had become the central figure connected with music and death. The musician psychopomp figures of the Hellenistic era had faded and were now only to be found catalogued as curious monsters in medieval bestiaries. Orpheus's attributes were ultimately preempted by the figure of Christ. But the figure of Satan, represented as a fantastic monster, loomed large as a synonym for death itself, and in his hands, music had become a major symbol of vice.

[50] Quasten, *Musik und Gesang*, *chap.* vi; and Quasten, "Die Leierspielerin auf heidnischen und christlichen Sarkophagen," *Römische Quartalschrift*, 37 (1929).

XIV

Later Medieval Images: The Dance of Death

THE SIMPLE EARLY MEDIEVAL connection of Satan with death and of instrumental music with vice began to dissolve in later centuries, and, in the history of music's symbolic relationship with death, the fourteenth century, with its tragic experience of the plagues, represents a culmination of change. The earlier Middle Ages had indulged in allegorical thinking, such as that displayed in Gregory's discussion on the meaning of musical instruments. From the tenth century on, however, a trend toward factual thinking and realistic observation became evident in many fields. The new approach was reflected in the sudden appearance of musician angels playing on contemporary instruments. Music was thereby admitted to the heavenly concert and no longer restricted to Satan. Nor did death continue to be completely identified with Satan. This development, the separation of death and Satan, was enhanced by the great and tragic epidemics of the fourteenth century. If death could take massive toll, of saints and sinners alike, the identification of death with Satan became illusory. Survivors had seen whole families annihilated, they had seen the physical ravages, decaying corpses, and the innovation of charnel houses. It is understandable that after such experiences, death was imagined as a skeleton, and no longer as a monster.[1]

Death now became the topic of numerous poems and representations in the visual arts. The two outstanding forms created in which death appears in connection with music are the Dance of Death and the visions of the mystics. In the Dance of Death the skeleton is the chief figure; in the writings of the mystics, it is Christ, the savior from death, Who with music leads souls to join the dance of the blessed. Both forms are of the fifteenth century, and each is of sufficient interest to deserve its own chapter.

For an understanding of these developments, one needs some insight into the prevalent contemporary attitude toward death. A strik-

---

[1] R. Helm, *Skelett- und Todesdarstellungen bis zum Auftreten der Totentänze* (1928); M. Meiss, *Painting in Florence and Siena after the Black Death* (1951).

ing expression of the new ideas is to be found in Jorge Manrique's poem on the death of his father, written around 1440.[2] It is composed of three parts. In the first part, man is admonished to beware of ever-present death; death comes suddenly, at any time, and will come to every man. This part contains a list of the different estates of society, an assemblage which we shall see represented in what may be called the classic form of the Dance of Death.[3] The second part lists the treasures of the world with which man must part. Only spiritual riches will remain. The great heroes also had to die; but their "exemplary life of fame" means "eternal life of the spirit." This list of the heroes was traditional.[4] Manrique's poem has been described as typical of the transition from the Middle Ages to the Renaissance, and in this second section a new Renaissance attitude, the glorification of the hero,[5] becomes apparent.

Manrique also expresses an idea similar to that noted above as important in the early Greek mentality, the idea that it is essential to preserve the memory of the dead. Manrique admonishes: if you have lived like one of these great men, then the memory of your deeds and virtues will survive with your name. The third part of the poem consists of a dialogue between Manrique's father and Death. The discussion is that of two partners who stand on an equal level; the idea of death is rationalized. The form of this third section, the dialogue between death and his partner or victim, recurs exactly in the classic version of the Dance of Death. In none of the verses is death imagined as Satan or as a monster. This separation of the two figures was also to be observed in the visual arts, where the image of death became a realistic skeleton.

THE FIGURE OF THE SKELETON

The skeleton has been used as the image of death since ancient times, though not in all countries. And it is important to realize that the skeleton is a realistic representation of the dead, as opposed to the imaginary soul-bird or the little human figures carried by psychopomps. There is a report that at Egyptian festivals, guests were

---

[2] A. Krause, *Jorge Manrique and the Cult of Death in the Cuatrocientos*, Publ. of the University of California at Los Angeles in Language and Literature, 1/3 (1937); E. R. Curtius, *Europäische Literatur* (1948), pp. 245ff.

[3] S. Kozaky, *Danse macabre* (Budapest, 1935–44), p. 51.

[4] Curtius, *Europäische Literatur*, "Autorenkataloge," pp. 56ff., 251ff., 263ff.

[5] Krause, *Jorge Manrique*.

presented with small figures of skeletons to remind the party that *in media vita* death may be ever-present.[6] There are skeletons on some early works found in France and Italy, in regions influenced by the Etruscan and Gallic civilizations (Fig. 153). A roman mosaic (second century, from Ostia) shows a reclining skeleton, pointing with one hand to flames at his feet, at the bottom the motto "Know Thyself." The flames here have been interpreted as a symbol of hell, but I think they are more probably an indication of the cremation usual in Greek funerals. Skeletons appear in paintings on the walls of a tomb at Cumae and are also engraved on two ancient cameos, one of which shows a skeleton dancing to the tune of a piper. However, it should be noted that the figure of the skeleton was unknown to early Chris-

[6] Kozaky, *Dance macabre,* with detailed bibliography; Herodotus, Book II, *Euterpe,* tr. in *Ancient Classics for English Readers,* ed. W. L. Collins (1870), p. 47; P. Carus, "The Skeleton as a Representation of Death and the Dead," *Open Court,* 22 (1908); H. Goldman, "Two Terracotta Figurines from Tarsus," *American Journal of Archeology,* Ser. 2 (1943) p. 41.

FIG. 153. Musician skeletons on a second-century silver cup found in Boscoreale near Pompeii. INSTRUMENTS: kithara, flute

tian iconography as represented in the catacombs. The figure seems to have become popular only in the fourteenth century, as an allegory of the vanity of this world, as well as the image of death.

It has been noted that descriptions of death, as well as representations of the figure, are especially gruesome in France. In comparison with Manrique, Villon's approach is more grimly realistic.[7] An accurate picture of a decaying body is to be found in several works by the Master of King René (middle of the fifteenth century). One of these has the inscription *Le Roi Mort*, the dead king or King Death. A similar fresco was painted for King René in the cathedral of Angers, where his tomb was to be, and the same half-skeleton with a crown appears in the illuminations of two of his prayer books at the opening of the Office for the Dead. In the latter, the skeleton is shown standing before or emerging from the grave.[8]

A stone coffin as foreground or background generally indicates that the skeleton is intended to represent the dead person. The skeleton also may sometimes mean death itself, but never death equated with Satan, though what might be called a Satan-skeleton sometimes appears at the entrance to hell. Skeletons embracing all condemned souls replace the huge mouth of hell in a dyptich by van Eyck (Fig. 154) and in the painting of the Last Judgment by Petrus Christus (Berlin, Kaiser Friedrich-Museum), both fifteenth-century works.

Death as skeleton appears on the title page of Savonarola's *Ars Moriendi* (The Art of Dying), in the 1494 edition published in Florence (Fig. 155). Here, death as a skeleton is standing on a globe (the world), with hell beneath, and is confronting a youth. A scythe rests on his shoulder, and with one hand he points to *lagiù* (heaven) and with the other to *lazù* (hell) and a crowd of devils. In heaven, the Savior is seen surrounded by angels carrying small human figures, the souls of the dead. This is reminiscent of ancient works, such as the so-called monument of the harpies in the British Museum, with the difference that the psychopomps have now become angels.

The death skeleton appears here in the role of Saint Michael, yet

---

[7] Krause, *Jorge Manrique.*

[8] P. Wescher, *Jean Fouquet* (1947), p. 65, Pl. xi; G. Ring, *A Century of French Painting* (1949), p. 19, Fig. 8, King René; *King René, Book of Hours*, British Museum MS. Egerton 1070, fol. 55; *Grandes Heures de Rohan*, MS. BN. lat. 9471, V. Leroquais, *Les livres d' heures de la Bibliothèque Nationale* (1927), I, 281ff., Pl. xl.

FIG. 154. Jan or Hubert van Eyck, *The Last Judgement*. The Metropolitan Museum of Art, Fletcher Fund, 1933

not as a judge with a scale, but with the scythe as his emblem.[9] This attribute makes sense only in periods of great catastrophes like the plagues in the fourteenth and fifteenth centuries, when death reaps crowds. If death comes to an individual, death cuts down only one among many, and the scythe is not the appropriate emblem.

[9] A scythe or sickle is often the emblem of Father Time, an old man with an hourglass. E. Panofsky, *Studies in Iconology* (1939), III, "Father Time."

FIG. 155. The Lord surrounded by angels, some of them with trumpets, and winged Satans in hell; woodcut from Savonarola, *Ars Moriendi* (1494). IN-STRUMENTS: busines

FIG. 156. A pair of lovers hit by arrows of love and of death on a twelfth-century ivory cask

Psychopomp angels also appear in the so-called *Triumph of Death* by Traini on the Campo Santo at Pisa.[10] In this painting, the aspect of death and afterlife is oppressive. There is a host of black angels, huge figures with wide wings, and they give the threatening impression of rushing to seize the souls. However, they carry the souls upwards to heaven and resurrection. One of the angels, perhaps the leader, holds a scythe, the attribute of reaping death. In both the title page of *Ars Moriendi* and the painting on the Campo Santo, death is not equated with Satan, nor does it mean absolute perdition.

Death appears in an even friendlier guise on a French ivory of the twelfth century (Fig. 156). It shows two scenes from the story of Tristan and Isolde. The ivory plaque is divided into two parts; the left shows the pair of lovers, the right shows the death of Tristan. The two scenes are separated by a tower, on the rampart of which there is a winged figure with a crown. This figure holds arrows in both hands; one pointed toward the lovers, the other toward the dying Tristan. The figure is a fusion of Eros, of the angel of death, for it is winged, and of the *roi mort*, the king of death. Traces of Greek mythology, Christian ideology, and the ideas of the fourteenth century merge here. The composition of the scene, the tower with the

[10] Meiss, *Painting in Florence and Siena.*

winged figure on top, is also reminiscent of the form of the Hellenistic steles with the figure of the siren on top.[11]

Fifteenth-Century Examples of the Dance of Death

It was the new, non-Satanic image of death that appeared in the *danse macabre,* or Dance of Death, which is perhaps the most famous connection of music with death.[12] From the fourteenth century on, it is possible to find evidence that the form of the Dance of Death was widely known and was, indeed, such a familiar phenomenon that the terms "to perform" or "take part in" the *danse macabre* were used colloquially to mean "to die." Numerous representations of such dances are extant from the fifteenth century and later.[13]

Beginning in the mid-nineteenth century, much research has been done on the origins of the Dance of Death and its history. The explanations offered are highly varied and controversial. All theories agree, and I concur, that the fourteenth century was the time of origin, and that the terrible epidemics of bubonic plague were the influential factor in its creation. (I wonder, too, whether the strong modern interest in the problem of the dance of death is not due to the fact that the last generation and our own have had experiences similar to those of the fourteenth century, in the total wars in which millions have been annihilated and in the terrifying aspect of death suffered by a great number of people simultaneously.) I shall not endeavor to give a complete history of the Dance of Death, but will concentrate on aspects relevant to this study. Nor will I discuss all the various theories, beyond saying that, while each seems to have its

[11] R. Koechlin, *Les ivoires gothiques français* (1924), Vol. 3, Pl. 183, Fig. 1068 (London, Victoria and Albert Museum); Pl. 184, Fig. 1077 (Louvre, Paris); O. Falke, "Das Tristankästchen der Eremitage," *Pantheon,* I (1926), 75ff.

[12] The literature on the Dance of Death is huge. To cite only a few of the references: from the early period, G. Kastner, *Les danses des morts* (4 vols., 1852); a bibliography of the literature up to 1913 is provided by A. Dürrwächter, "Die Totentanzforschung," *Festschrift für Georg Hertling* (1913). From more recent publications: G. Buchheit, *Der Totentanz* (1926); Kozaky, *Danse macabre;* H. Rosenfeld, *Der mittelalterliche Totentanz* (1954); R. Eisler, "Danse macabre," *Traditio,* VI (1948), 187ff.

[13] N. Z. Davis, "Holbein's Pictures of Death," *Studies of the Renaissance,* III (1956); Holbein, *Der Totentanz,* Facsimile edn. by J. Springer (1907); H. Schramm, *Der Bilderschmuck der Frühdrucke,* Vol. 19 (1936).

good points, most make the mistake of overemphasizing one aspect or trying to include all forms where music and death have been similarly connected as related to the specific Dance of Death.

One may divide the development of the Dance of Death into two periods, comprised of the fifteenth and sixteenth centuries. Fully typical for the first period are the *Danse macabre* published by Marchand in 1486 and the so-called *Heidelberger Totentanz* published at approximately the same time by Knoblochzer.[14] For the second period, the sixteenth century, Holbein's version, later also called *Totentanz*,[15] provides a rich example.

In all versions of the Dance of Death the skeleton is the leader and is intended to represent death. The figures are shown either in a series of single scenes, where death confronts representatives of different ways of life and different age-groups, or the skeleton leads a kind of procession or pageant, a procession which sometimes takes the form of a round. In the type showing single scenes, there is sometimes an open grave before the dying person.

It is common to all representations that death is shown as a skeleton. This figure may hold or play a musical instrument, but more often does not. The figure is usually leading his partner quietly—very seldom is he in lively action, almost never is he dancing or fighting with his partner.

The title page of Marchand's edition of the *Danse macabre* reads: *Chorea ab eximio Macabro versibus alemanicis edita et a petro Desrey Trecacio . . . nuper emendata* (Dance in German verses edited by the outstanding Macaber [we shall, for the time being, let the term pass without further explanation], and newly published by Pierre Desrey of Troyes). The book opens with a picture of a cleric, the author, at a desk writing, assisted or inspired by an angel. Then follow, on facing pages, six skeletons: four have musical instruments (Fig. 157) and two carry shovels and pickaxes, the tools of grave diggers. Then follow scenes of death as a skeleton confronting representatives of the different estates, shown as pairs standing under arcades on lawns with flowers. The skeleton hardly touches the figures. They are standing or walking, but never dancing. Nor do they carry musical instruments in this context, but again shovels and

[14] *Dance of Death*, Paris 1490; a reproduction made from the copy in the Lessing Rosenwald Collection, Washington, 1945; Schramm, *Der Bilderschmuck*.
[15] Davis, "Holbein's Pictures of Death."

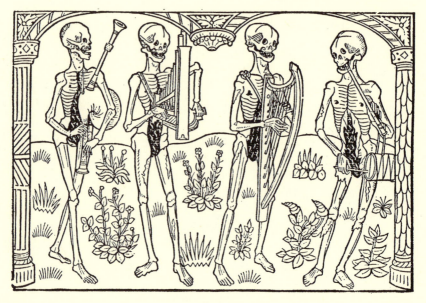

FIG. 157. Four musician skeletons: woodcut from Guyot Marchand, *Danse macabre* (1486). INSTRUMENTS: bagpipe, portative organ, harp, pipe, tabor

pickaxes. The Latin text above and below the illustrations lists the professions of those to whom death comes. At the bottom of each page there are short verses in French, also referring to the estates, and always headed "Le mort," to indicate that the verses are spoken by the dead.[16] The hands and feet of the skeleton are not bony, but look like the limbs of living people; also, the general structure of the bones is not shown distinctly, and the joints are only roughly indicated. Sometimes the skeleton wears a shroud.

There are eighteen such pairs. In the beginning of the series, high secular and clerical estates are confronted: the pope and the emperor, the cardinal and the king. Later, various lower secular estates are confronted: the astrologer and the burgher, the lawyer and the musician, etc. At the end, the author appears again, with a skeleton at his feet; a crown is lying beside the skeleton, and before it there is an open coffin. On the last page, the author is again shown sitting at his desk and writing. Except for the opening group of six skeletons and the picture of the musician, no musical instruments appear. Death

[16] It should be mentioned that the text reads "*le* mort," not "*la* mort," the masculine article referring to a male actor.

FIGS. 158–160. Woodcuts from the *Heidelberger Totentanz* (1485). FIG. 158. INSTRUMENTS: shawm, busine, trumpet. FIG. 160. INSTRUMENTS: snare drum

walks, stands, or leads, but does not dance except in the scene with the jester, where both figures dance. The title, though, contains the word *chorea*—dance.

In the plates of the German edition of the *Heidelberger Totentanz* (Figs. 158–160), the dance motif is stronger.[17] The title page reads "Come ye sires and servers, rush here from all estates, young and old, pretty or ugly, all must come to this house of dance." The woodcut under this text shows a kind of tent (Fig. 158); under it, half-seated on a bench, there are four skeletons playing shawms and trumpets, and in the foreground there are three skeletons apparently singing and two clearly dancing together. In ensuing scenes, death appears always as a skeleton and usually with musical instruments. The skeletons are clearly dancing or walking in lively steps. The figures of the dying are shown in their professional garb, all walking or standing, either on floors or hilly surfaces. As in Marchand's edition, the hands and feet of the skeletons are shown as bones but resemble those of living persons. The structure of the other bones, too, is not depicted realistically, but only suggested, as though on a costume.

Among the numerous other representations of the Dance of Death in the fifteenth century I found music-making in only three in-

[17] Schramm, *Der Bilderschmuck*, Figs. 618–58; *Altdeutscher Totentanz*, Facsimile edn. Wasmuth Kunsthefte, No. 2 (1920 and 1922).

FIG. 161. Skeletons with drum and pipe leading a procession of the dead, from the Klein-Basler Totentanz, a fresco found in Klingenthal near Basel. INSTRUMENTS: pipes, tabor, shawms

stances.[18] In the *Lübecker Totentanz* there is a procession of skeletons alternating with members of various professions. The skeletons beside the pope and the emperor are engaged in musical activity, one playing a pipe, the other dancing while holding an hourglass. In Schedel's *Buch der Chroniken,* as noted in the introduction to Part I of this study, there is a woodcut showing five skeletons, one of whom is just emerging from the grave, while the others dance and one plays a recorder. Schedel's skeletons have bony hands. In the *Oberdeutsche achtzeilige Totentanz,* there is music and dancing in the scene before the charnel house: one skeleton is lying in a grave, three are dancing around the grave, and one of them is playing on a drum. Dancing is also intimated in the *Lübecker Totentanz.* Only in a French woodcut, *Les loups ravissants,* is death shown as cruel, tripping people. Here death appears part flesh part skeleton, the skull and thorax alone being visible. This type of skeleton is also seen in the *Lübecker Totentanz,* the Basle *Totentanz frescoes* (Fig. 161), and the *Totentanz mit Figuren.*

HOLBEIN'S *Totentanz*

One generation later, between 1522 and 1526, Holbein created the cycle of woodcuts (actually cut by Hans Lützelburger) which was later called a *Totentanz* (Figs. 162–66).[19] He enlarged the usual

[18] Buchheit, *Der Totentanz,* and Rosenfeld, *Der mittelalterliche Totentanz;* Kozaky, *Danse macabre.*
[19] Davis, "Holbein's Pictures of Death."

FIGS. 162–166. Woodcuts from Holbein, *Les Simulachres et Historiées Faces de la Mort* (1538). FIG. 162. (*top left*) INSTRUMENTS: guitar
FIG. 163. (*top right*) INSTRUMENTS: xylophon
FIG. 164. (*middle*) INSTRUMENTS: tabor
FIG. 165. (*bottom left*) INSTRUMENTS: guitar-fiddle
FIG. 166. (*bottom right*) INSTRUMENTS: hurdy-gurdy, krummhorn, trumpet, busine, kettledrum

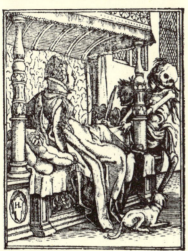

cycle of scenes with several not included in other publications. The
series has several additional scenes; it opens with a woodcut of Adam
and Eve; then follow twenty-nine representations of death confronting the various ways of life and three woodcuts for the different ages.
The cycle closes with three woodcuts: the charnel house, the Last
Judgment, and, finally, the coat-of-arms of death. The opening scenes
show how death came into the world according to the Book of Genesis, the woodcuts at the end show how death was overcome by Christ.
Death always appears as a skeleton, but in a variety of roles. Sometimes death is the killer, sometimes he carries out the functions of a
servant or helper, sometimes he is fighting the living as an opponent,
and sometimes he leads the person, almost like a good friend. The
emblems he carries are often those of the appropriate estate or profession; sometimes he holds an hourglass, or, infrequently, a musical
instrument. He is not shown dancing, not even in the scene before
the charnel house.

The scenes in which death carries or plays a musical instrument are
the following: the expulsion from Paradise; death with the peddler; [20] death with the old man and the old woman; with the
duchess and with the noblewoman. In the scene with the nun, her
lover plays on a lute, but the skeleton has no instrument. Death appears alone in only three of these scenes. In the others there is a pair
of skeletons, one functioning as killer and the other as music-maker.
A musician skeleton appears alone in the scene of death with the old
man and with the noblewoman. In the scene before the charnel
house, there is a full orchestra of skeletons with trumpets and horns,
a kettledrum, and a hurdy-gurdy. In the scene with the noblewoman,
death plays a little drum. The small drum and the pipe were the instruments of court pages. The other instruments shown in the
Holbein series are the xylophon, the viola da braccio, the tromba
marina (peddler), and the dulcimer.

The instruments are obviously used for a variety of reasons. The
little drum and the viola are simply an expression of the social customs of a certain estate, whereas the instrument in the scene of the
expulsion from Eden is the emblem of sin, and the figure of the
skeleton is both death and Satan. The lute which the lover plays
in the nun's scene is likewise a sign of sinful excess. In the scenes
with the old people, death plays a dulcimer and a xylophone, an

[20] Why there is a fight only in the scene with the peddler remains a puzzle.

instrument often played by the figure of death. The reason for the
latter is obviously acoustic, an imitation of the noise bones make rat-
tling together. The orchestra before the charnel house uses the instruments appropriate to a group of soldiers. The hurdy-gurdy was
then a popular instrument. The skeletons, indeed, are very similar to
the soldier-musicians that appear in the prayer book of the Emperor
Maximilian.

The woodcuts, which may have been influenced by the famous
anonymous Dance of Death frescoes at Basle, were completed by
Holbein in 1526. They were not accompanied by a text with dialogues, as in the earlier versions described above, but only by short
quotations from the Bible.[21] They were eventually published in
1538 at Lyons, under the title *Les Simulachres et Historiées Faces
de la Mort*, pictures and images of death, with no reference to dancing in the title. As noted, the front page of the *Heidelberger
Totentanz* invites people to come to the dance. Public dances were
held in dance halls at the time, and Holbein painted frescoes for such
a hall, also at Basle, with very lively dancing pairs of peasants.[22] Yet
in the illustrations of the *Totentanz* neither death nor his partners are
dancing. This fact should be noted because it will help later to explain the meaning of these dances of death. The form was so popular
by the end of the fifteenth century that Dance of Death scenes were
often used in the borders of Books of Hours (Fig. 167). The latter
scenes sometimes show musical instruments, but I have yet to find
any that depict dancing.

ORIGINS OF THE DANCE OF DEATH

The question obviously arises, how has this art form, or literary-art
form, come to be called the Dance of Death?[23] In the Heidelberg
book, death is making music in almost all the scenes, but generally,
and especially in the great frescoes, he is shown without a musical instrument. He is usually leading his partners quietly, as man wishes to
be led to his death. This attitude has changed in Holbein's woodcuts,
where death comes to inflict punishment and sometimes fights with
his victim, for Holbein's cycle was made under the impact of the

[21] Davis, "Holbein's Pictures of Death."

[22] P. Ganz, *The Paintings of Hans Holbein* (1950), Pls. 41–42.

[23] E. M. Manasse, "The Dance Motive of the Latin Dance of Death,"
Medievalia et Humanistica, fasc. IV (1944), 83; A. Tenenti, *La vie et la mort à
travers l'art du 15ᵉ siècle* (1952).

Reformation, when moral problems were vivid and important. But in all versions the skeletons usually stand or walk and are only rarely shown in livelier action. Skeletons really dancing, and apparently enjoying it, appear only once, on the title page of the Heidelberg version, in the scene before the tent of the dance hall. Much research has been devoted to the question of whether it is death or the dead who are dancing. The opinion, now, is that both may dance. Yet I would say that in the typical forms of the fifteenth and sixteenth centuries, no one is dancing.

FIG. 167. Woodcut border from *a hivre d'Heures* (1498), showing skeletons leading persons of different ranks to the grave

To some extent the form of the Dance of Death reflects the conventions of other literary forms of the period. The three major types are embodied in Manrique's poem.[24] To the first part of this poem, the warning of the coming of death, the name *Vado mori* is given, from its opening words, "you shall die." The second part, which lists the treasures which must be left behind, is called *Ubi sunt*, again from the opening words, "Where are they?" The third part, the dialogue between Manrique's father and death, is called *débat*, or discussion. It is primarily the form of this third part, combined with the form of the second part, which is used in the Dances of Death. In the Marchand edition, Mors, or death, is approaching his partner, telling him that he must die; then the partner tells why he is sad that he must leave, in a response that corresponds to the *Ubi sunt*. The list of examples of others, of whom it is said that they, too, had to leave, corresponds to the series of confrontations with the representatives of the various professions and estates. The form of the *débat* was also used in mystery plays, mostly of the allegorical type, where one figure discusses a problem with one or several partners.[25] Perhaps the best-known topic for this type of discussion is the dialogue between soul and body, or between the soul and the Savior. Often in this kind of play one figure remains on stage, while his partners in the discussion change; and there are several documents which show that the Dances of Death were performed in this way. A Flemish epic from the second half of the fourteenth century, *Madelghis Kintsheit*, also refers to a ring of figures: *"een de staen recht in een crans/als von doden luden en dans/waere gemalt bi mere ret"* "And they stood in a ring just like the skeletons in the paintings of the dance. . . ."[26] There is also a report that in Paris people went on Sunday afternoons to the Cemetery of the Innocents to see the Dance of Death, in paintings

[24] Krause, *Jorge Manrique*, pp. 103, 136; E. de Coussemaker, *Drames liturgiques* (1890); G. Cohen, *Nativités et moralités liègoises du moyen-âge*, Academie R. de Belgique, Lettres, Mémoires 4°, 2ᵉ serie (1953), Vol. 12.

[25] J. Bolte, *Drei Schauspiele vom sterbenden Menschen* (*1510–40*) (1927), Bibliothek des literarischen Vereins Stuttgart, Vol. 269/70; H. Morf, *Aus der Geschichte des französichen Dramas*, Akademischer Vortrag (Bern, 1886; Hamburg, 1887); E. Dreger, *Über die dem Menschen feindlichen allegorischen Figuren auf der Moralitätenbühne Frankreichs* (1904).

[26] Maugis d'Aigremont, *Madelghis Kintsheit*, ed. N. de Pauw (1889), quoted in G. Huet, "La danse macabre," *Le Moyen-Age*, Vol. 29 (1917/18), pp. 148ff.

and performed as a play.[27] In these performances, the figure of
death may have stayed on the stage throughout, while the sequence
of partners entered, discussed, and then left the scene, and, perhaps,
at the end all joined in a round, as it is represented in the paintings at
Lübeck or Clusone.

It is also curious that though the reports refer to a dance, no music
accompanies the printed editions of the Dance of Death. There is, as
far as I know, only one example of a song which might have been
sung for such a performance. It is a tune from a Spanish source at
Monserrat. It begins: We hasten to death, *Festinamus ad mortem.*
This song is known to have been sung by the pilgrims during the
nights when they were waiting to attend services. A similar tune
is said to have been sung before the famous statue of the Black Virgin
at Monserrat. The tenor of the text is that death comes suddenly and
skips no one, only Christ and the Holy Virgin can save one from
eternal death. The song has ten verses, and after each the first verse
is repeated.[28]

Ad mor-tem fe-sti-na-mus pec-ca-re de-si-
sta- - mus pec-ca-re de-si-sta- - mus.
Scri-be-re pro-po-su-i de con-temp-tu mun-
da- - no ut de-gen-tes— se-cu-li non
mul-cen-tur in va- - no iam est ho-ra
sur-ge-re a somp-no mor-tis pra- - vo.

[27] Guillebert de Metz, *Description de Paris* (1436), publ. by A. Mary as
Journal d'un bourgeois (Paris, 1929), p. 188; Eisler, "Danse macabre," p. 215.

[28] O. Ursprung, "Spanisch-katalanische Liedkunst des 14. Jahrhunderts,"
Zeitschrift für Musikwissenschaft, 4 (1921/22), p. 155.

It has been suggested that the musical form of the rondeau—a melody to be sung at round dances—is related to certain liturgical chants in which a certain formula is repeated. The words "vado mori" or "festinamus ad mortem" would have been appropriate repeated phrases or refrains for the Dances of Death. Hence there are tenuous grounds for connecting this song with an actual dance and with the dance of death, but research has only begun on this point, and it is still undecided whether the form was first used in the rondeau or in liturgical melodies.[29]

There is also a lack of information on the dancing itself. The term in English is "Dance of Death," in German it is *Totentanz*, or dance of the dead, in Spanish *danza della morte*, in French *danse macabre*. In attempting to account for its origin, scholars have ascribed influence, singly or collectively, to all the types of dances which relate music to death. It should not be denied that they may have had a vague connection. The idea of the dance of the blessed, which was frequently mentioned in the first part of this study, recurs in the writings of the mystics in the fifteenth century, which will be discussed in the next chapter. The magic dances of the souls of the dead emerging from their graves and dancing in the cemeteries, which survive in sagas and fairy tales, will also be dealt with presently. It is, however, my conviction that they have no direct relation to the *Totentanz*. In none of the examples of the *danse macabre*, either in the pictures or in the poems, is there any suggestion of a reference or link to the dance of the blessed or resurrection through music, nor do we find magic used to seduce or lure from life through music.

The most probable explanation, though I do not subscribe to all his conclusions, seems to be offered by Robert Eisler in his article on the *Danse macabre*.[30] Eisler started his research with an attempt to explain the term *macabre* and was able to prove that in the Syrian Arabic dialect, which is also used in the *Peschita* (the Syrian version of the Bible), the word means grave-digger. Thus, *danse macabre*

---

[29] Y. Rockseth, "Danses cléricales du XIIIe siècle," *Lettres, Mélanges*, III (1945; publ. 1947); H. Spanke, *Beiziehungen zwischen romanischer und mittelalterlicher Lyrik*, 1936; Spanke, "Das öftere Auftreten von Strophenformen und Melodien in der altfranzösischen Lyrik," *Zeitschrift für französische Sprache*, 51 (1928), p. 73; Spanke, "Das lateinische Rondeau," *Zeitschrift für französische Sprache*, 53 (1929/30), p. 113.

[30] Eisler, "Danse macrabre," p. 187; I cannot agree with Eisler's conclusion that this should be interpreted as a custom of Jewish gravediggers only, and Eisler seems to contradict himself when he refers to the Latin *fossores* and the customs of Syrian communities.

would mean the dance of the grave-diggers. This hypothesis is supported by the objects the skeletons frequently carry, the shovel and the spade. These tools appear as early as in the catacombs as the emblems of figures designated as *fossores,* the Latin word for grave-diggers. Further, the skeletons who are shown dancing appear beside graves or before the charnel house. On the frontispiece of the *Heidelberger Totentanz* they are seen before a *dantzhaus,* a tent, which could easily be interpreted as the dance hall of the grave-diggers' guild. Also, as Eisler noted, in almost all the representations the skeletons have hands and feet like living persons, the structure of the bones is not shown in a realistic way, the joints are only indicated, and the lines that separate the hands from the arms and the feet from the legs look like seams of a dress. In other words, the figures are drawn as if they were wearing skeleton costumes. To these observations, I would add that where the skeletons are seen dancing, they give the impression of dancing happily and having fun. They are grinning, but not in a sarcastic manner. There are reports that in certain places the grave-diggers annually performed such pantomimes and very likely they included dances.

From late in the nineteenth century there is an account of a strikingly similar dance performed by Tibetan Buddhists. Their religion has a god of death, Yama, and while Yama himself never appears as a skeleton, the actors in the dance are dressed as skeletons (Fig. 168). There are two benevolent skeletons, protectors of the cemetery, who try to drive away the ravens which come to feed on the corpses; they fight against nine evil skeletons who represent the souls which are lost and cannot find their appropriate place in the universe.[31] This dance is accompanied by noise instruments and by solemn chants which rise to a howl. Thus this rite echoes some of the ideas of the Neoplatonic school discussed above and also has traits related to old magic funeral dances.[32] On the other hand, the skeleton costumes and the kind of performance are strongly reminiscent of representations of skeleton dances such as those in the Schedel *Buch der Chroniken.*[33]

[31] B. Laufer, "Origin of Our Dance of Death," *Open Court,* No. 22 (1908), pp. 620ff.; P. Carus, "The Skeleton as a Representation of Death," *Open Court,* No. 22 (1908), pp. 630ff.

[32] E. F. Knight, *Where Three Empires Meet* (1893), photograph opposite p. 216.

[33] Hartman Schedel, *Buch der Chroniken,* Nuremberg, Ant. Koberger, 1493; facsimiles in Schramm, *Der Bilderschmuck,* Vol. 17 (1934), Pl. 258, Fig. 567.

FIG. 168. Skeleton dance, Tibet; nineteenth century

The custom of a grave-diggers' dance thus does not seem to be tied to any particular religious approach. The Dance of Death itself, whether in the Marchand or the Heidelberg version, or even in Holbein's cycle, makes no reference to dogmatic or explicit Christian concepts. The only slight allusion is in Holbein's woodcut of the Last Judgment. As noted, Holbein's version supersedes the classic form of the Dance of Death. He enlarged the cycle and added moral and ethical aspects which were not in the earlier versions.

From all the above, I am inclined to draw the conclusion that a performance by the guild of grave-diggers had probably long been traditional even before the fourteenth century. Then, with the

plagues, the problem of death and the duties of the grave-diggers became so important—and people became so familiar with the figure of
the skeleton—that the custom of the grave-diggers' dance came more
to public notice. From the expressions of the dancing skeletons shown
in the books and paintings, the intention of the performance was not
to warn, no *vado mori* idea, but to cheer the audience, to let them
know that we who should know, want you to know that, after all,
death is not a monster nor Satan.

XV

The Fifteenth-Century Mystics

THE IMAGES EXPRESSED or created by the mystic writers of the fifteenth century stand in sharp contrast to the rather practical approach to death discussed in the preceding chapter,[1] and seem to have more in common with far earlier models than with their contemporary, secular creation, the Dance of Death. In the mystics' visions, typically, Christ leads the "loving soul"—that is, the faithful and devoted soul—to heaven with music. Thus the figure of Christ the musician reappears after a hiatus of many centuries. As noted in Chapter III, the figure of the Savior with a kithara is found in very early Christian works. Later, however, possibly as a casualty of the Church's effort to suppress Orpheus and Orphism, it disappears, until revived by the mystics.

The movement of the Christian mystics began in the eleventh century. It was associated with the cult of the Holy Virgin, which was presumably encouraged by the relatively important position of women in the princely courts of southern France. The first great representative of the mystics was Bernard of Clairvaux (1091–1153), who wrote a famous commentary to the Song of Songs. Earlier writ-

---

[1] F. Schulze-Marginer, *Mystische Dichtung* (1925); W. Muschg, *Mystische Texte* (1943); L. Schreyer, *Deutsche Mystik* (1925); W. Oehl, *Deutsche Mystikerbriefe* (1931) (excerpts); W. Stammler, *Gottsuchende Seelen. Germanistische Bücher* (1948); J. Clark, *The German Mystics* (1949); K. Meyer, *Bedeutung und Wesen der Musik* (1932); A. M. Heiler, *Mystik deutscher Frauen im Mittelalter* (1929); Joh. Prestel, "Die Offenbarungen der Margaretha Ebner und der Adelheid Langman," ed. Ph. Strauch (*Mystiker des Abendlandes,* 1939); R. Banz, "Christus und die minnende Seele. Zwei spätmittel-hochdeutsche mystische Gedichte," *Breslau Germanistische Abhandlungen,* 29 (1908); Mechtild, "Das fliessende Licht," *Menschen der Kirche in Zeugnis und Urkunde,* Vol. 3 (1956), Buch 1, pp. 76ff., No. 44, von dem siebenfachen Weg der Minne. Von den drei Kleidern der Braut. Von Tanz; p. 92, Von der Schönheit der Engel. Alle waren gekleidet in dem Chore in leuchtendem Golde; Buch 2, p. 104, No. 20, Wie Schwester Hildegund im Himmel verherrlicht ist mit drei Mänteln und mit sieben Kronen und wie sie die neun Chöre loben; Buch 3, Vom Himmelreich und den neun Chören.

ers had already identified the bride of the songs with the Church, and
the lover with Christ. The influence of this idea is evident in the
legend of Saint Catherine, who becomes the bride of Christ. The idea
that intellect alone is not sufficient to understand religion, that not
everything can be taught, but that understanding is imparted by
grace and in personal contact with the Divinity, was elaborated in
several schools: in France, in the monastery of Saint Victor near
Paris; in Italy, notably by the order of the Franciscans; by teachers
like Occam in England, and by a series of writers in southwest
Germany.

The school of Saint Victor is important for the aesthetic theories of
the Middle Ages, but for the topic of this study the German mystics
have supplied the greatest contributions. These saintly teachers recorded their visions; their writings are not treatises, but reports of
their mystic experiences, set down in letters or diaries. They often
take the form of dialogues, of discussions between Christ and the
"loving" soul. Many of these revelations, *Offenbarungen* or visions,
express the idea of resurrection through music. The general outline
of this vision is stable: after death, the soul is afraid of not finding the
way to heaven and invokes Christ, the lover and bridegroom, to
guide it. Christ appears to the soul and leads it, often with music, on
the right path. Some quotations will best illustrate how the trial and
the salvation were visualized, and with what intensity. These writings have come down to us in manuscript and in print; some editions
are illustrated (Fig. 169), and sometimes the illustrations have been
published separately in woodcuts. Many of the writings are anonymous, and very often the images are repeated word for word.

FIG. 169. Single-leaf woodcut *Christus und die minnende Seele* (1501), showing Christ as musician, with fiddle and drum, leading the Loving Soul to Heaven

In one vision by Mechtild of Magdeburg, Christ is singing and playing, and the soul is dancing:

. . . So must du selber voraus-singen so springe ich in der minne	. . . Thus You must be the pre-centor And I shall join in the dance (literally: love)

Christine Ebner sings:

Es pfifet auch manger gar wohl das dem hörer suszer ist den dem pfifer, und die anderen tanczent mer danach den er selber . . . das ich den tantz eins warhaften lebens trett nach der suszen pfifen dein liebs Jesus Christ.	Many can pipe so well That the hearer enjoys it More than the player, and The others do more dancing, More than He does Himself . . . That I might dance the true dance Of Life, following Your sweet Piping, dear Jesus Christ.

It might be noted that, though Christ is here said to blow a pipe or flute, in the woodcut illustrations accompanying this text the instruments are the tambourine and a little drum.

Sometimes Christ is called the leader of the dance:

Do furt Jhesus den tancze mit aller magde schar.	There Christ leads the dance With all the maidens.

In an anonymous poem, "Dance in Heaven" and later in a corresponding scene by Suso, Christ is mentioned as playing music and leading the dance:

Die saiten chan er ruren	He knows how to touch the strings
Auz vreude in vreude furen Mit cherubim und seraphim Springet sie schon den rainen do-hin. Jhesus der tanzer meister ist, Zu swanzet hat er holen list Er wendet sich hin, er wendet sich her; Si tanzent alle nach seiner ler	To lead from joy to joy. With cherubim and seraphim The soul dances in the round. Christ is the leader of the dance, ... He turns this way and that; They all follow his lead.

The revelations of Mechtild of Magdeburg say that Christ "wil den himmel-reigen mit dir treten," that He wants to step the heavenly dance with the saint. Saint Gertrude says: "ego eas [virgines] praecedo in choro vitae aeternae" (I shall lead the saintly virgins in the dance of eternal life). Suso sings (in *Büchlein der Weisheit*):

Wol ym der des mynnespiel den freudentancz, in himelreych wunne an meyner seyten, an meyner schönen hant in frolicher Sicherheit Ymer ewiglich treten sol	Hail to him who in this loving game Shall dance the dance of joy, in the glory of heaven At my side, and on my hand; He will always tread, surely, In happy eternity.

In a text by Christine Ebner the Holy Virgin joins the dance:

Da sah sie einen Tanz im himmel da war Gott selber an und unsere Frau. Du Maria gest in vor die tenze dort in dem paradise.	There she saw a dance in heaven In which the Lord took part, as did Our Lady. You, Mary, will lead the dancing in paradise.

In a poem by Konrad of Würzburg the soul is asked to join the round and to dance with the Virtues.

Nu sendet si botten us, wan sie will tanzen, und sant umb den geloben abrahe . . . so wert da eine schone lobtantzen.	She [the soul] sends messengers when she wants to dance, she sends for the blessed Abraham . . . and there is beautiful and joyful dancing.
Sie tanzet unde singet. Ir Stimme susse clinget. Vor alle des hymels herrschaft.	She [charity] dances and sings. Her voice sounds sweet Before all the Lords of heaven.

In the anonymous poem "Christ and the loving Soul" the soul wants to dance with the blessed and with the saints "mit jubilierenden herczen," with joyful heart, a dance "nit geschaffen . . . als . . . in dieser welt," which is not of this world:

Myd den (Heiligen) wyl ich den spelen Unde treten in den dancz Ye scholt my helpen maken mynen leve eynen krancz.	I want to play with the saints And join the round You shall help me To make my life into a crown.

The "hymelische spilman," the heavenly musician, is calling her:

Hie wil er ir vor drummen	He wants to play and dance before her

and the soul follows Him:

Ich spring diner trumen nach	I follow your drum beat.
wer sy ye recht gehoret hat	Whoever heeded it well
We balt er von der welte lat	Oh, how soon he tires of the world
Und springt er an den rayen gut	And once he knows how to dance the round,
Den hast du selber in deiner hut.	So shall he be saved by You.

Or Christ should sing so that the soul can follow thus in the poem "Dance in Heaven". "Sometimes someone may play the flute so well that the listener has more pleasure than the player"; thus Christ will play:

das ich den tantz eines warhaften	That I shall be able to dance
lebens trett nach der suszen	The dance of real life to the
pfifen dein, liebs Jhesu Christ.	Sweet sound of Your pipe, dear Jesus Christ.

In another poem Saint Gertrude invokes Christ: "Cor tuum . . . sit animae meae ex corpore suo primum refugium . . . ut caelestem choream tecum intrem . . . non habens obstaculum" (Your heart shall be the first refuge after my soul has left my body, and it shall enter the heavenly dance with You and meet no obstacles).[2]

Thus, with minor variations, these revelations render the identical vision: Christ is the heavenly musician; he plays music, leads the round dance in heaven, and invites the soul to join; or he goes to meet the soul and induce it to come to heaven. The relation of Christ to the soul is often referred to as that of a bridegroom to his bride. All these visions are the expression of a simple belief: if the soul turns to the Lord, the soul will be able to join the heavenly chorus. They are also a reflection of the conditions of the period and offer hope that Christ will help the faithful to a better beyond.

It is interesting to note how many different components can be discovered in these visions. Traces of Hellenistic mythology combine

---

[2] Gertrude the Great (1256–1311, nun at Helfta, Thuringia), *Exercitia spiritualia* (Paris, 1875); *Revelationes Gertrudianae ac Mechtildianae* (Paris, 1875–77); E. Wolter, *Gertrudenbuch* (9th edn., 1920).

with contemporary concepts. Christ the musician appeared in the second century as a reflection of or substitute for Orpheus, but when Christ was described by the Church Fathers as playing on a seven-stringed lyre, this emblem designated Christ as the Pantocrator. Now, in the poems of the mystics, He seems to have been restored to Orpheus's original role of leading the soul with music to resurrection. There is no trace of how the figure of Orpheus-Christ, the Savior-musician, survived throughout the intervening centuries, and it can only be presumed that the tradition was carried on in popular legends and fairy tales, as were other traditions which will be discussed in the next chapter. Further, the idea of a round dance of the stars or the blessed goes back to far earlier concepts of cosmic music or harmony, whose history was traced in the first part of this study. The difference, again, is that it is Christ as musician who leads the dance. In the *Divine Comedy*, Christ leads a procession, but nowhere does Dante mention Him making music, though Dante's paradise is full of music.[3] Of course, some of the mystics' revelations may have been influenced by paintings of musician angels. But in these it is generally not Christ but the Holy Virgin who is the central figure. The legends of the Virgin, the motif of her coronation, with the Virgin surrounded by musician angels, had become popular in the eleventh and twelfth centuries, a trend probably fostered by the customs of the courts of southern France. Thus, the descriptions of the round dances, with a dance leader and accompanying music, can also be interpreted as a reflection of contemporary or recent habits. It is this combination of the old Orpheus tradition with the customs of the troubadours which makes the poems of the German mystics of the fifteenth century especially interesting. These visions also approximate the image of the dance of the blessed. Thus a variety of early ideas seems to have fused into a new image of Christ as musician, as leader of the chorus and dance in heaven, and as playing an instrument and attracting the faithful soul. Christ the Savior connected with music, though not as a musician Himself, appears in a curious miniature of the late fifteenth century. It is an illumination from an antiphonary made for King Matthias Corvinus of Hungary, sometimes reproduced in books on the history of music to demonstrate the practice of conducting.[4] The picture shows the interior of a chapel on the right,

---

[3] Dante, *Paradiso,* XXIII.

[4] R. Haas, *Aufführungspraxis der Musik* (*Handbuch der Musikwissenschaft,* 1931), Pl. VII. The manuscript is now in Budapest.

with singers standing before a lectern and singing from a choir book. On the left, there is a view of landscape, with the towers and roofs of a cathedral in the background, and the Lord in the clouds. In the foreground there is a cemetery, with Christ the Savior standing beside a coffin from which a man is arising. Thus the dead man rises and turns to Christ, to the accompaniment of the chorus singing in the chapel.

XVI

Survivals of Earlier Images

OF THE TWO MAJOR fifteenth-century images, the Dance of Death and the figure of Christ the musician represented in the poems of the mystics, the latter proved relatively short-lived. The mystics' vision soon merged into other traditions and experienced no further development per se, whereas the *danse macabre* had come to stay and has continued to engage both creative and scholarly effort into modern times.

FIG. 170. Pieter Brueghel the Elder, *Christ in Limbo*, showing Christ surrounded by musician angels. INSTRUMENTS: harp, guitar, bowed rebec, lute, krummhorn

Many far more ancient figures and images also survived in lively, if somewhat changed, form. Having led what might be termed a vigorous underground existence in oral tradition, recognizable descendants of the nereids and other early images began to reemerge in formal literature as nineteenth-century interest in folklore brought the publication of popular legends and fairy tales.

Later Versions of the Dance of Death

The Dance of Death survived both in the style of the first period, with death playing a neutral role, and in the form given it by Holbein, with added moral implications. There are examples in the form of the dance as a procession or divided into single scenes, in all kinds of styles and techniques.

The majority of the later representations have the traditional symbolic content, so it will suffice to describe in detail only those instances in which there are noteworthy variations. For example, there were two mid-sixteenth-century paintings by Pieter Brueghel. One of these which has survived in engravings, shows an elaboration of the scene before the charnel house. In it, *Christ in Limbo* (Fig. 170), the Savior is shown at the entrance to hell. According to an inscription beneath the engraving, a motto reads: "Stand firm and let the glorious king of the universe pass." [1] From the mouth of hell, depicted as the mouth of a monster, there emerges a crowd of men, not skeletons. They are proceeding toward Christ, who is floating in a mandorla shaped like a crystal globe. Christ is surrounded by nine angel musicians. It is impossible to identify all of the instruments, because some are hidden behind the figure of Christ, but one can see a guitar, a harp, and two krummhorns on the left, and a viol, a lute, and a music book (suggesting a singer), on the right. Christ himself is not playing. The musician angels might thus be understood as psychopomps in the retinue of the force of resurrection.

In the other painting, the *Triumph of Death*, Brueghel also depicts scenes before the charnel house. An army of skeletons is advancing toward the living and pushing them into the house of death. The building is not designated as hell; rather, it represents what was called *dantzhaus* on the frontispiece of the *Heidelberger Totentanz*, or the charnel house. Tne skeletons are armed with the covers of coffins, with the sign of the cross on them. On the roof of the death house, a skeleton is beating a big drum. The realm of the sinners is seen in one

---

[1] E. Castelli, *Il demoniaco nell'arte* (1952), p. 40, Pl. 142.

corner where, at a table, a figure carrying a lute appears among the companions and signs of Luxuria. Obviously, Brueghel used some features of other models, such as representations of the Coronation of the Virgin, and inserted them into the scene before the charnel house of the Dance of Death.

Though Brueghel shows music being played in front and on the roof of the house of death and near the mouth of hell, he was careful not to show music directly in hell; for him, too, this place is without music. In fact, there seems to be only one work in which musicians are seen in hell, and that is a painting sometimes called the *Garden of Lust,* by Hieronymus Bosch (Fig. 171).[2] As is usual in Bosch's work, the symbolic meaning of the instruments is so involved and obscure that I am unable to offer a full explanation. One possible general solution is that Bosch wanted to suggest the gruesome sound of untuned instruments. The group of instruments forming the center of the panel is shown beneath a huge pair of ears pierced by an arrow. On top of a hurdy-gurdy a man is turning a device which should grate on the strings. Apparently encased inside the body of the instrument, a woman looks out of the sound hole and plays a triangle. On the left, a harp grows out of a lute. A man is fettered to the neck of the lute by a huge, winding, snake-like creature, and a naked figure is spanned across the harp's strings in the position of someone crucified, as if the strings were overstretched and the pitch too high and shrill. A drum beaten by a monster has a hole in its casing through which a head emerges. A bassoon is sprouting out of the hurdy-gurdy muted by a person of whom only the arm appears. The music for the hellish concert is written in a book on which the lute is standing, and on the naked behind of a figure half-hidden by a lute. Add to this the figures forming a chorus singing from the book, some obscene gestures, a person squatting near the drum and holding his ears, and I do not think that we go too far wrong in describing the panel as a representation of a hideously dissonant concert. The sound that pierces the huge ears like an arrow is not music, but noise of hell. To have been able to paint this caricature of music, Bosch must have had a good knowledge of music and must have suffered from hearing it out of tune. His diabolic concert, however, does not otherwise appear to be a symbol of death or sin.

More in the traditional line and resembling Brueghel's engravings are two title pages. One was designed by De Bry for Boissard's *The-*

[2] M. J. Friedländer, *Die altniederländische Malerei* (1927), v, Pl. 75.

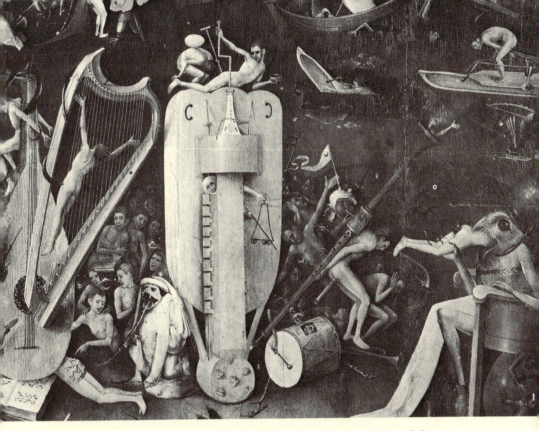

FIG. 171. "Music in Hell," detail from Hieronymus Bosch, *Garden of Lust*

atrum vitae humanae (1596) and shows various scenes of the Dance of Death, with death as a grave-digger at the bottom.[3] The other, the frontispiece to the *Theatrum mortis tripartitum* by J. Weichandt Valvasor,[4] published in Austria (1682), shows an elaborate scene before the charnel house in a typical baroque setting with landscape and ruins (Fig. 172). A crowned skeleton with scythe and hourglass sits on a mound of earth in front of the charnel house. Five skeletons are mounted on horses, a camel, and an elephant; two of the skeletons are musicians, with trumpet and drum. A skeleton on foot leads a lion. Toward the front, in the center, Adam and Eve appear; in the background Cain is seen killing Abel, and in the nearest foreground two men, not skeletons, are digging graves. The reflection of the old scenes in the Dance of Death is obvious; the scope of the representation is enriched by the additional figures symbolic of death.

The basic forms of the Dance of Death have remained stable up to the present day. Death always appears as a skeleton when the cycle is

[3] Copy in the New York Public Library.
[4] R. Eisler, "Danse macabre," *Traditio*, vi (1948).

FIG. 172. Frontispiece for J. W. Valvasor, *Theatrum mortis tripartitum* (1682); engraving after And. Trost by J. Koch

treated in a series of separate scenes with one partner. When the form is that of a pageant, the skeleton often appears only at the head of the procession. The figures of the dying appear either in the order of the Marchand edition, alternating secular and religious personages at the various levels of the social hierarchy, or the clerical dignitaries appear first as a group, followed by the secular dignitaries. The skeleton frequently has no musical instrument. In the sculpture of a Dance of Death executed for Duke George in 1534–37 (now in the Neustädter cemetery at Dresden), there are three skeletons, one at the head, one at the rear, and one in the middle of the procession. All of them carry the scythe and hourglass, and the leader has a trumpet.[5]

Though the tradition of the Dance of Death never seems to have been forgotten, its development received a fresh impulse in the middle of the nineteenth century. In 1852 Kastner[6] published his fine study, and in 1848 Rethel published his series of woodcuts, some of which are still popular today.[7] Rethel must have known and been inspired by Holbein's cycle. The best known of Rethel's woodcuts is death coming to the guard of the tower, a tower in which an old man is sitting in an armchair near a window. Death appears in the robe of a monk and manipulates two crossed bones as if playing a violin. Here death comes quietly and harmoniously. The scenes are more turbulent in two other woodcuts from the same series. In one, death has encountered soldiers, and a fight seems to have taken place since there are drums and trumpets on the stairs leading to a building that looks like a charnel house. In the other, death, the skeleton, appears at a performance of a *commedia dell'arte*. The musicians with their instruments are fleeing from a gallery; the score of the conductor is still open on the desk. Three actors are lying on the floor as if dead. A skeleton standing among them carries a loose mask over his arm and holds the crossed bones as if playing a violin.

But none of the examples is provided with musical accompaniment. As noted above, there is one song from Monserrat which may with some certitude be attributed to a mystery play or Dance of Death. Of course there are numerous songs, especially folksongs with French, German, and Italian texts, on the theme of death;[8] and in one of the motets of the Bamberg Codex[9] three well-known *tenores* with the initial word *Mors* are fitted together. But these latter do not essentially belong to the Dance of Death. However, one tune, with the title *Totentanz*, bears mentioning. The melody belongs to a party game which was played in German and Central European rural districts. One member of the party plays the role

[5] F. Boehme, *Geschichte des Tanzes in Deutschland* (1886), p. 46.

[6] G. Kastner, *Les danses des morts* (1852)..

[7] A. Rethel, *Auch ein Totentanz* (1848), 6 Pls.

[8] H. Stegemeier, *The Dance of Death in Folksong* (1939), lists the following songs: "Wol auf mit mir auf den Plan," "Rhaeto," "Ich geh herum in weiter Welt," "Ich stund an einem morgen."

[9] For two tenors, "Homo miserabilis" and "Mors" from the Bamberg Codex; see P. Aubry, *Cent motets du 13ième siècle* (Paris, 1908).

of the dead person and has to sit or lie completely still until all
the members of the opposite sex have kissed him or her. Then, the
"dead man" jumps up and joins the others in a round. The tune was
first published by Boehme in 1880, and he indicates no source,
though this was not his usual practice. One assumes that Boehme set
it down from oral tradition. He adds, "old melody," and for tempo,
"very slow." [10]

When modern research on the origin of the Dance of Death
started in the mid-nineteenth century, all kinds of forms and customs
similar to the game mentioned above were regarded as possibly related. The game in question is almost certainly a survival of an old
funeral or fertility rite, such as the festivals for Adonis or for
Tammuz, commemorating the death and rebirth of the hero.[11] Nothing is yet known about the role of music in these rites, nor about their
connection with what appear to be modern survivals; hence this
assumption must remain vague and cannot be confirmed. A number
of other popular dance customs were also cited as possible sources.
Among these were the dances in the cemeteries, whose existence is
documented by several Church Council decrees prohibiting them.[12]

[10] Boehme, *Geschichte des Tanzes*, ii, 186, No. 305.

[11] Mortgal, *Tammuz. Der Unsterblichkeitsglaube in der alten Bildkunst*
(1949).

[12] Decrees against such dances: Burchard of Worms, *Decretum* 10, 34; *Patrol.
lat.* 140, 838; Leo iv (847–55), *Homilia* (ed. Mansi), 14, 895; Robert
Grosseteste, *Manuel du pêcher* (quoted in Kastner, *Les danses des morts*, 1852);
Council of Exeter, 1287, Assemblée de Melun, 1579, *Rituale de Cahors*, quoted
in Boehme, *Geschichte des Tanzes*, pp. 16ff.; L. Lavater, *De spectris, lemuribus*

The decrees most frequently prohibit all dancing during the night, also the dancing in cemeteries, as superstitious merrymaking. Such customs as carnival and Halloween are clearly survivals of old rites, and in funeral rites the relation to the cemeteries is obvious. As noted above, in these apotropaeic rites the souls were supposed to come back, often as evil spirits who endangered the living. Persian Mazdaism more specifically taught that the *Fravashis*, the souls, were allowed to come back once a year.[13] The day of this festival is the forerunner of All Souls, or Halloween. The medieval dances in cemeteries, however, seem to have only a loose connection with such customs, though in the Tibetan play of the skeletons such connection seems obvious.[14]

Survivals of Ancient Figures in Fairy Tales

Even more apparent is the survival of old ideas and figures in our fairy tales. One hears of dances of the elves, singing sirens, ondines, and loreleis, of the playing of the Pied Piper, and finally the ballad "Das klagende Lied," the plaint and complaint. In fairy tales one can find and recognize most of the figures that have been explained above as symbols of the idea of death's relation to music. And one can compare them with the transformations traced thus far through the period of early Christianity and the decisive fourteenth century. Some aspects of the shape in which the figures appear today may have been acquired as recently as the eighteenth and nineteenth centuries. These recent changes are important, because they affect the forms in which the figures have become familiar to us from childhood. I shall try to explain these changes and mutations, as well as point out the characteristics which have been kept. Music, the magic power of music, is part of so many tales that the discussion here must be re-

---

et magnis . . . fragoribus variisque praesagionibus quae plerumque obitum hominum . . . praecedunt (1580), quoted in W. Fehse, *Der Ursprung der Totentänze* (1907), p. 41; F. N. Taillepied, *Traité de l'apparition des esprits, à scavoir des danses séparées, fantosmes, prodigues et apparitions merveilleuses qui précèdent quelque-fois la mort des grands personnages ou signifient changements de la chose publique* (Rouen, 1600), pp. 15, 175, quoted in Eisler, "Danse macabre," p. 198.

[13] N. Soderblöm, "La vie future d'après le Mazdéisme. Études d'eschatologie comparée," *Annales du Musée Guimet,* 9 (Paris, 1901); Soderblöm, "Les Fravashis," *Revue de l'histoire des religions,* 39 (1899).

[14] E. F. Knight, *Where Three Empires Meet* (1893).

stricted to selected examples where the figures or the proceedings or dramas have especial relevance to this study.

A convenient figure to begin with is Lorelei, this sprite—half-woman and half-fish—who sits on a cliff on the Rhine and lures fishermen to death with her singing. Related to the Lorelei figure are the ondines or Undinen. Obviously, all are followers and successors of the nereids. The nereids were first mentioned in this study as appearing at the funeral of Achilles, in the *Iliad,* in the role of mourning women. Later, in the Hellenistic period, they became the guides of the souls who were privileged to dwell, in afterlife, in the Elysians fields. To reach Elysium, one had to cross the Oceanus, the stream surrounding the earth, and for passage through the waters the nereids were the appropriate psychopomps, in place of the sirens,[15] a role in which they appear on a number of Roman sarcophagi. In Christian iconology, the nereids became equal to the sirens, and the hybrid fish-woman appears in medieval bestiaries and Romanesque sculpture generally as a symbol of sin, in the retinue of Satan: music-making had become a vice. It is in this form that the siren and the nereid survived.

The lore of elves and fairies had long been popular in English mythology and entered the literature with Spenser in the sixteenth century. Spenser has the Muses, the nymphs, and the fairies dance together.[16] The attention accorded to Ossian in the eighteenth century gave rise to the important Romantic movement in Germany. Interest turned to the study of the old tales, songs, and legends, which were collected and published in various editions. De la Motte Fouqué wrote the German novel *Undine;* both E.T.A. Hoffmann (1816) and Lortzing (1845) wrote operas entitled *Undine;* and Heine wrote his ballad "Lorelei" (1823–24).[17] Among these more modern versions of the old nereid, only the Lorelei uses singing—an old characteristic of nymphs and sorceresses—as a bait. In Homer it is

[15] See Chapter XIII, n. 32, on the figure of scylla as similar to that of the nereid.

[16] H. Lotspeich, *Classical Mythology in the Poetry of Spenser* (1932).

[17] "Lorelei" is not listed in the *Handwörterbuch des deutschen Aberglaubens,* ed. H. Bächtold-Sträuble, (1927–42), nor in J. Grimm, *Teutonic Mythology,* tr. J. S. Stally (1880), pp. 434ff., where Melusine is taken as the Celtic form of Merminne; the tale of Undine became popular after the publication of the novel by F. de la Motte Fouqué (*Undine,* ed. J. Dohmke, 1892, p. 327); he took the story from Theophrastus Paracelsus.

given to Circe as well as to Calypso; [18] both sing while weaving, and Circe sings to bewitch the passerby. In the same way, Lorelei ensnares fishermen passing on the river.

The function of this ondine is, of course, the opposite of the Greek nereid. The modern ondine has the nereid's shape, but instead of her original significance she carries the pejorative meaning that had been formed by the Church Fathers. The figure of the modern Lorelei, like the ondine in Lortzing's opera is quite different. In the opera, the plot centers on psychological factors. The sprites attempt to acquire human souls, but not by stealing them. [19] They try to gain a human soul by love, and fail; and it is the sprites themselves that meet a tragic end. They cannot attain real life and have to remain spirits.

The figure of Melusine, the heroine of several popular folktales, belongs among the female spirits who bewitch through their beauty. She does not use music as a charm, and her realm is not exclusively the water. However, in the 1491 edition of *Der Ackermann von Böhmen*, the popular poem dealing with the battle of body and soul, Melusine is represented with wings and with a fish-tail, a combination which has been noted above in the engraving after Mantegna showing devil-monsters at the entrance of hell (see Fig. 152).

The elves and fairies are related to the Loreleis in their activities, but their outward appearance is quite different. They do not have fish-tails and do not move in water, though they hover near swamps and moors. In the Danish legend of the *Ellerkonge*, the king of the elves, a knight riding in the evening is beguiled by the singing of the elves into joining their round, and thereby loses his life and his soul. [20] This old myth was used by Goethe in his well-known poem "Der Erlkönig," but altered and adapted to ideas of the nineteenth century. The king of the elves has become king of the alders, because these trees may look like human beings in the fog; this change does not

---

[18] *Odyssey*, v, 61ff.; x, 226ff.; W. Otto, *Die Musen und der göttliche Ursprung des Singens und Sagens* (1954).

[19] The modern approach also occurs in Giraudoux's *Ondine*.

[20] First published as "Erlkönigs Tochter" in J.G.F. Herder's *Stimmen der Voelker*, Reclam-edition 247; there Oluf refuses to dance with the elves and is killed by them. In another poem, "Elvershöh, ein Zauberlied" (*ibid.*, p. 244), two elves sing to ensnare the passerby, but the rooster crows and the man is saved.

affect the meaning of the legend. In Goethe's version it is not a lonely knight, but a father with a child riding at night, and it is the child who is ensnared by the elves and their king. The child, in fevered dreams, imagines that the elves are inviting him with their singing to join their round, and when the father protects him against their onrush, the elf-king touches the child's heart and he dies.[21]

The Danish ballad sees the elves as evil spirits who take the shape of beautiful maidens, a concept which links them to Homer's sirens and to the medieval figure of the siren. The idea that with their singing and dancing they draw the passerby into their round probably goes back to ancient apotropaeic dances performed to chase away the souls of the dead.[22] These rites were based on the notion that souls who could not find their place in the cosmos continued to hover about the earth, especially near graves. As noted above, such beliefs existed among the Romans and probably also the Etruscans. However, the Egyptian soul-bird, Ba, did not belong to this category of spirits,[23] for Ba had the mummy as the place to which it could return. It was in the beliefs which did not provide the soul such a definite, assigned place of return that it was thought the souls could become evil spirits. To cope with these, the dances were performed. Such dances seem to have survived continuously from Roman times, but unfortunately our knowledge about their existence during the Middle Ages is vague. The sole sources of information are the decrees of the Church Councils, invariably prohibitions, which connect this kind of dance with other revelries and tend to describe them as orgies, almost as vampiristic practices. However, the idea of a dance of dead souls who have been offended and take their revenge is so widespread in fairy

---

[21] E. Staiger, *Goethe* (1952), I, 345. Staiger feels that Schubert's composition, with its equal accomplishment to all the verses, is not as appropriate as Loewe's ballad, which provides an accompaniment differentiating between the beginning and the later verses. I do not feel that such a changing accompaniment is appropriate to the meaning of Goethe's ballad.

[22] See Manasse, "The Dance Motive of the Latin Dance of Death," *Medievalia et Humanistica*, fasc. IV (1944), 88ff.; Jaques de Vitry, quoted by G. Paris in *Journal des savants* (1892), p. 411.

[23] The Egyptian funeral dances seem to have lost this meaning by about 1900 B.C.; see, on the other hand, E. Panofsky, *Studies in Iconology* (1939), p. 183. I am inclined to interpret the possibility of Ba returning to the mummy as an expression of the idea of the immortality of the soul, not as a sign of magic.

tales that the tradition of the old magic rites must have survived virtually intact.

Goethe's poem "Der Totentanz"[24] provides an interesting example of the survival of old ideas in modern context. In this poem the caretaker of a tower near a cemetery watches the skeletons of the buried emerge from their graves and sees them perform a dance. For fun, he snatches one of the shrouds which the skeletons have laid aside. When the midnight hour is over, and the ghosts have to return to the graves, the skeleton whose shroud he has taken cannot find it, senses where it is, goes after the caretaker who is only saved by the clock striking one.

The poem combines characteristics from varied traditions. The image of a dance of souls in a graveyard may be a survival of ancient, pre-Egyptian and pre-Greek religions which remained alive in Etruscan and Roman customs. That music is used to evil purpose belongs to Christian ideology. The figures of the skeletons come from the *danses macabres* of the fourteenth century. There are, however, a number of differences from the original models: here the music-makers threaten to kill the watchman, whereas the sirens, Muses, and Orpheus did not kill, but liberated from death. This Christian concept of music put to evil use is changed in that it is not used to ensnare the caretaker. It should also be noted that here the skeleton, in effect, functions as a judge. Though the victim is more a minor offender than a sinner, the skeleton acts to revenge the theft of the shroud. This selective action is also different from that of the dancing elves, who take hold of every passerby, even an innocent child.

Finally, it might be emphasized that there is an important difference between Goethe's poem and the *danse macabre*. In the latter, death itself dances, rather than the souls of the dead. The distinction should be noted because Goethe's poem has often been counted as a relative of the *danse macabre*. The special combination of traditions makes confusion easy. The form which Goethe gave to the legend has remained popular and has been used for tone poems and ballets (for example, by Saint-Saëns, Liszt, and in the ballet *Giselle*). As far as I

---

[24] Goethe, *Gedichte*, ed. H. Viehoff (1870); the title is taken from Appel's *Book of the Spectres* (*Gespensterbuch*), 1811; the dance motive is also taken from it. The story, a Bohemian folktale, was told to Goethe in Karlsbad in 1813, see his letter to Riemer; for the same story in a Provençal poem, told by Damase Arbaud, see E. Carrington, "The Theft of a Shroud," *The Antiquary*, 1 (1882).

know, in all of these music represents an evil force endangering the living.

Another related fairy-tale figure is the Pied Piper, *Der Rattenfänger* or ratcatcher. Outside of the tale which concerns us here, the Pied Piper is a mischievous but not gruesome character who roams the country and has sweethearts in every town; but what he is said to have done in the city of Hamelin is frightening. The Pied Piper had worked several times for the city, destroying the rats; then the townspeople failed to keep their promise and did not give him his guaranteed fee. In revenge, he took his pipe and, instead of the rats, led all the children of the city into the river to drown. The story ends with the disappearance of the Pied Piper. The means of this medieval exterminator is music. It seems to be a fact, not just a legend, that it is possible to make some kinds of animals follow music, and of course, it is this characteristic which is at the bottom of one part of the Orpheus myth. Again, the big difference between the Orpheus myth and the story of the Pied Piper is that the latter uses his power to destroy and to kill rather than for resurrection.

Finally, one further story, from Grimm's fairy tales, belongs in this study: the tale of the Singing Bone.[25] Two brothers, one good and one bad, strive to kill a monster in order to win a princess. The good one succeeds with the help of a brownie; the bad one murders his brother, buries him, and takes the princess. Years later, a shepherd finds a white bone under the bridge where the corpse of the good brother was hidden. He fits it into his horn as a mouth-piece, and it starts to sing by itself, denouncing the murderer, who is then put to death.

Music here is not so much connected with death as a sign and cause of resurrection, bringing the truth to light and restoring the memory

---

[25] Grimm, *Kinder-und Hausmärchen*, No. 28, learned from oral communication in 1821; here it has the title "Der Singende Knochen" (The Singing Bone). The bone sings:

> Ach du liebes Hirtelein,
> Du blässt auf meinem Knöchelein!
> Mein Bruder hat mich erschlagen,
> unter der Brücke begraben
> um das wilde Schwein
> für des Königs Töchterlein.

Mahler has put the story into a dramatic setting in his cantata, "Das klagenede Lied," where *klagend* means both "accusing" and "mourning."

and the feat of the real hero. It is this relationship which I am especially concerned to point out, because it is the least popular use of music as a symbol. Though this idea is perhaps not widely understood, one has only to open an anthology of poetry to find on almost every page allusions to this concept of life created through music, be it with specific reference to the flute and breath or more general ones. Two quotations may suffice as examples. One line is taken from Hofmannsthal's "Spring Song," [26] which describes a wind in spring, listing the points through which the wind passes and stimulating new love and new life: "It was gliding through the flute with sobbing cry." And a verse from "Spruch," by Eichendorff: [27] "Everything has latent a song; things are dreaming and dreaming until you find the magic word, then they begin to sing." The poems of the German Romantics are especially rich in such images. In English poetry, it is more often the idea of breath equalling life that is expressed, as in George W. Russel's "The Great Breath," or "The Prayer" by H. C. Beeching, reflecting the ideas of wind bringing a tune to life in a musical instrument, of breath bringing life to a form of clay, signifying the life of history.[28]

[26] H. v. Hofmannsthal, "Vorfrühling," *Gesammelte Werke* (1924), I, 3.

> Es läuft der Frühlingswind
> durch kahle Alleen
>
> . . . .
>
> Er glitt durch die Flöte
> Als schluchzender Schrei
> An dämmernder Röte
> flog er vorbei.

[27] J. v. Eichendorff, "Spruch," *Eichendorffs Werke* (1891), I, 77.

> Schläft ein Lied in allen Dingen
> Die da träumen fort und fort,
> Und die Welt hebt an zu singen
> Triffst du nur das Zauberwort.

[28] *Oxford Book of English Verse* (1939), No. 911, "The Prayer" by H. C. Beeching:

> Spirit of Love and Truth
> Breathing in grosser clay
> The light and flame of youth
> Delight of men in the ray.

See also G. L. Finney, "Music, the Breath of Life," *The Centennial Review*, IV, 2 (1960).

Music and Death: A Summary

The basic concepts and figures connected with music and death have recurred throughout recorded history and remain alive in thought today, whether or not they are included in current dogmatic belief. This second part of my study has endeavored to follow their history from ancient times and to offer interpretations of some of the figures in which the symbolism of death's relation to music has found expression. Before going on to a final discussion of the influence on present-day thinking of the whole body of images covered in this study, including the traditions relating to harmony treated in Part I, it seems well to pause to recapitulate the main traditions relating to death.

Too little is known of the pre-Greek civilizations to allow specific interpretations and, therefore, apart from noting the few forms and figures clearly recognizable as precursors of later images, this study concentrated first on the major Greek figures: sirens, Muses, and Orpheus. The transformation of Homer's evil siren-harpy into a benevolent siren-Muse was noted, and the role of the sirens and Muses as psychopomps in the musical cosmos of later Greek philosophy was, I hope, demonstrated.[1] If my interpretation is valid, the sirens and Muses on tombstones and sarcophagi are thus ultimately, like Orpheus, symbols of resurrection, of resurrection as conceived by the Greeks.

Early Christianity adopted fragments of the Greek images, but its most conspicuous contribution was a radical change in the significance of music itself. Music, from the beginning of the Christian era to as late as the ninth century, became a negative force and an emblem of Satan. It was only with its gradual recognition in the ninth and tenth centuries that music could again become the attribute of benevolent figures such as the elders and angels.

In the fourteenth century the figures changed again, apparently reflecting the different attitude toward death engendered by the experience of the plagues. Of the new forms, the *danse macabre* is certainly the best known, and here the figure of death is no longer identified with Satan, as was the case in earlier Christian ideology. I have suggested that the texts of these Dances of Death are direct imitations of the *débats* used in the mystery plays and laments or me-

---

[1] For a similar transformation of the Furies to the Eumenides, see K. Reinhardt, *Aischylos als Regisseur und Theologe* (1949).

morials, such as Jorge Manrique's poem in memory of his father. For the origin of the figure of the skeleton and of dancing in connection with death, the quest seems to lead much farther back, to ancient Egypt of the second millennium. As the term *macabre* indicates, the more immediate origin was probably a dance of grave-diggers, a dance as it was performed in the thirteenth century, but this kind of dance may have been a survival of even older customs. It might be identical with the dance of the "dwarfs" mentioned in the Sinuhe report (nineteenth century B.C.), or it might be even more ancient, originating in a period when magic rites were performed at funerals.

Be that as it may, the Dance of Death has remained a lively concept to the present day. Its form, as observable from fifteenth-century examples, remained more or less stable, but the content had changed by the beginning of the sixteenth century. In the early versions, man is reminded that death is ever present, but no moral evaluations are involved—an individual's ultimate fate is not seen as depending on his moral worth. However, in Holbein's *Totentanz,* from the first quarter of the sixteenth century, death appears in several scenes as a judge, and it is in this role that death appears in the "Everyman" plays and in the modern Dances of Death. Thus the threatening part of the idea of death recurs, and the figure of death in later versions is, though not identical, more similar to Satan than the earlier natural death who was the same for all mankind.

The image of a dance leading to death also occurs in fairy tales, but as the expression of a different attitude: the magic power of music ensnares the living and lures them to death. Only in relatively few of the legends is death imposed as a punishment. These tales may possibly reflect the survival of old magic customs. The dances in cemeteries forbidden by the Church Councils may have been related to the dances mentioned in the fairy tales, though far too little is known about them to draw any firm conclusions. The official attitude of the Church concerning death is apparent in the Mass for the dead, the Requiem. The musical part of the Requiem calls for melodies of the most ancient type, for the most part psalm tunes.[2] Also the form of the liturgy, that is, the order of verses, points to ancient origins. The words of the Requiem Mass contain, in addition to the part identical with the *ordinarium missae* and the reading from the Gospel and prayers, verses from the apocryphal Jewish book of Esdras and the

[2] E. Nikel, *Geschichte der Kirchenmusik* (1908), pp. 142ff.

Dies Irae. The *Introitus* and the *Graduale* start with words from Esdras: *"Requiem eternam dona eis, Domine,"* and *"Lux perpetua luceat eis"*—"Eternal rest grant unto them, O Lord, and Let perpetual light shine upon them." Eternal rest and eternal light; no music and no dance of the blessed. Death leads to rest and is not a punishment. Implicitly, this is the attitude of the classic Dance of Death of the fifteenth century, and it is the attitude expressed in Schubert's famous song, "Death and the Maiden."

There is a sharp contrast of mood in the sequence, or the hymn *Dies Irae.* This text has tentatively been ascribed to Thomas of Celano, a companion of Saint Francis, hence to the thirteenth century, the period before the plagues. The hymn describes the Last Judgment and the horrors of hell, from which only Christ and the Holy Virgin can bring salvation. This hymn, too, ends with the invocation to Christ to bring rest, *"Pie Jesu Domine, dona eis requiem."*

The change in attitudes resulting from the plagues is strikingly reflected in the writings of the mystics of the fifteenth century. The mystics' vision simply omits the scene of the Last Judgment. Christ leads the round of the blessed, or he comes from heaven to meet the soul and lead it to resurrection. Music and dancing are no longer to be despised. There is singing and dancing in heaven, and Christ and the Holy Virgin take part in it. The image is highly similar to Dante's paradise, except that for the mystics Christ is also a musician.

Finally, one might again note the recurrence of the figure of the musician savior, the similarity of Orpheus to Christ with a lyre or viol. Both are symbols of resurrection connected with music and both are psychopomps, the difference being that Orpheus leads the soul from Hades back to earth, and Christ leads the soul to bliss in heaven. The idea that music can revive is persistent. For one last example, in the final act of *The Winter's Tale*, Paulina promises to bring the alleged statue of Hermione to life. "Let music play," music is heard, and the statue begins to move; Hermione is alive again.

Conclusion
Survivals in Contemporary
Musical Concepts

THIS STUDY HAS FOLLOWED the history of two basic concepts for which music has been a symbol: harmony and life. In both instances, it has become evident that their development into the patterns still known today reached a climax in the fifteenth century. There are survivals in later centuries, but in less concentrated form and often in peripheral branches of art, such as the title pages of music books. While the whole theory of heavenly music was elaborated in complete systems, such as the attempt made by Fludd in the beginning of the seventeenth century, the basic fifteenth-century images underwent no important changes, and it is essentially the influence of these images that is discernible in our music today.

Of course, when one speaks of musical symbols, the first things that come to mind are the forms and signs of musical notation: the notes, their varied heads and dots, the stems with their rhythmical differentiation, the staves, clefs, etc. They signify the sounds to be performed or heard; they form the technique of notation. These signs are called symbols *in* music, not symbols *of* music or music as symbol. In French and German these figures are called *signes* and *Zeichen*, which means signs, a more appropriate term than the English word "symbol." Of course, to some degree these signs have themselves become symbols, but it seemed advisable in this study to concentrate on the less obvious derivations.

As suggested at the beginning of this book, there are really two essentially different kinds of symbols *of* music. There are the gods and saints who have been considered inventors or patrons of music, and the abstract characteristics of music which have led to its symbolic use in connection with essentially nonmusical concepts. Of the first type of symbol, gods and saints, perhaps the best and most widely known are Apollo, Saint Cecilia, and Musica. When I originally became interested in this topic, it was my intention to trace the history of such figures in their varying modes and roles in symbolizing music. However, I very soon found that the history of these figure-symbols, which gives an impression of being almost self-evident, is very problematic and complex. Their validity as patrons of music was in many instances restricted to very short periods. The significance of their role underwent many changes and variations. They often acquired their characteristics from earlier figures and were themselves then succeeded by others. In looking for the reasons for these permutations, I found that either the meaning of the figure itself changed, or the actual conditions of music or of the whole social milieu made new personalities come to the fore.

Saint Cecilia, for example, became patroness of music around 1500, having had no previous relationship to music. She took over the role of two forerunners, the Muse and Musica, one of the seven liberal arts. The Muse, of course, had had a long tradition as patron of music, and Musica had been the symbol of a theoretical knowledge of music since the early centuries of the Christian era. The saint's appearance in the sixteenth century as patroness of music is to be explained by the structure of Renaissance society, in which the patron of art was an influential person. Further, liturgical music had by then acquired an importance in the service which music had not had during Cecilia's lifetime in the second century.[1]

All efforts to trace the history of such symbolic figures led inevitably to their predecessors. To explain the meaning of Saint Cecilia, one had to follow the history of the cycle of the seven liberal arts and the tradition of the Muse as a patron of the arts, a role which she did not acquire until the Hellenistic period.

It was in the course of trying to establish these trends of development that I was led far back into antiquity, and kept encountering the basic concepts of music which were at the bottom of the formation of the symbolic figures. That is, before these figures could be understood as symbolizing music and becoming allegories of music, some basic characteristics of music and even merely of sound had to be formed into symbols. These characteristic traits were personified and then attributed to contemporary deities who stood for or were symbols for similar concepts. This study has concentrated on three of these basic characteristics: music's obvious capacity for symbolizing harmony, the aspects that allow music to become a symbol of life or death, and its capacity as a luring force.

[1] K. Meyer-Baer, "Musical Iconography in Raphael's Parnassus," *Journal of Aesthetics*, VIII (1949); Meyer-Baer, "Saints of Music," *Musica Disciplina*, IX (1955).

These three aspects cannot be easily covered by a common explanation. Harmony originally meant "fitting together," and this concord can take place in many fields. Documents showing that cosmic harmony was identified with musical harmony are to be found as early as Pythagoras and Plato, and the idea appears to have already been a familiar one by that time. The recognition of the similarity of breath and life, with implications for breath as the cause of the melody produced in a wind instrument, can be documented in the Biblical myth of creation, which is much earlier. The problem of life and death, of a future life after death, has found different solutions in different religions; and music has correspondingly played various roles in these solutions, in the creeds themselves and in the rites that express them. Once the acoustic fact that breathing into a wind instrument brings a tune to life has become connected with the symbol of giving life with breath, these symbols are then used in myths and religions to represent life and death. The next step is that music, as a symbol of life and death, is attributed to specific figures who may already have been connected with the idea of life and death. Orpheus thus becomes a giver of life through music, and ultimately a savior from death. The sirens, the bird-like figures who sing, become psychopomps. They acquired this role with the development of the beliefs that soul and body are separated in death and that the souls have to travel through the air to their final abode in a musical cosmos.

Christianity adopted and changed both Orpheus and the sirens. Orpheus, who had been the center of a religion of resurrection, became Christ the musician early in the Christian era; the sirens later eventually became the musician angels. The figure of Christ as musician soon acquired additional symbolic meaning. His lyre came to signify the harmony of the cosmos, as well as the source of music that would lead souls to eternal life and bliss. Thus the two symbolic aspects were integrated. Another aspect of the figure of Orpheus was also adopted by Christianity, but, as were other aspects, this too was turned inside out. The influence of the Orpheus, who was able to lure and tame the animals with his music, had to be counteracted, and the Church Fathers transformed him into Satan, who lures people to sin and eternal death. This figure appears in Romanesque sculpture in the retinue of *Luxuria* as a monster with a musical instrument. However, the role of musician has apparently been a minor one for Satan. As the ruler of hell, where there is no music, he is restricted in the scope of his activity in the field of music. Only occasionally does one find musical instruments depicted in representations of hell.

The history of the basic symbolic forms thus shows continuous transformation. Every period develops new patterns. These new patterns are mixtures of known characteristics, adopted variously in identical or changed form. New images are formed under the influence of new kinds of music, and of new intellectual and cultural trends. The new influences are shaped into new patterns by great philosophers such as Saint Augustine and great poets such as Dante. They create new visions which, in their turn, become the models for later works of art.

The classic, or culminating, form of the vision of the music of the spheres seems to be expressed in the orchestras of angels in works of art of the fourteenth and fifteenth centuries. The idea of the relation of music and death found its classic expression in the *danse macabre*. The images seem to have reached their final maturity. It is in these forms that they have become familiar to our common understanding and have been used over and over again.

From the sixteenth century on, these images have been used in an eclectic manner; that is, the familiar features may appear in somewhat different combinations, but they nevertheless retain their original meaning. One example is Holbein's *Totentanz*, where the familiar symbols are employed indiscriminately, one beside the other. Another instance is provided by Mozart's popular opera, *The Magic Flute*. When one hears the opera performed, everything seems clear enough, but if one looks into the plot of the libretto, it is so inconsistent that one is forced to conclude that without an unconscious knowledge of the various musical symbols, no comprehension would be possible. The basic plot is the battle between the Queen of the Night, of the moon, and Zarastro, the High Priest of the Sun. However, the magic flute which saves Tamino and Pamina is a present from the Queen of the Night. The sound of this flute overcomes every threat. Playing on the flute enables Tamino to withstand the terror of water and fire which threatens to kill him. When played, the instrument becomes the symbol of life and, by means of Tamino's breath, has the power to tame the elements. This is clearly a variant of the Orpheus myth. The Queen of the Night's present to Papageno is also a musical instrument, a chime. In addition to this chime, Papageno, the representative of primitive man, has his pan's pipe. On the pipe

Papageno plays scales, but on his chime he can produce lovely tunes, and these tunes can render his enemies powerless by forcing them to dance, to become entranced and forget reality. Monostatos and his servants have to dance to Papageno's music and are driven away. And the magic instruments have not only the power to drive away, but also to attract. Papageno has lost his bride and in the last scene despairs of finding her again. He tries to call her with his pipe, but his attempts are in vain until he is told to use his magic chime. His pipe had no effect, but the melodies of his chime bring Papagena to him. This is a variation on another aspect of Orpheus, that music can attract and lure persons into the presence of the player.

Thus throughout *The Magic Flute* the use of music and musical instruments is influenced by the old beliefs which this study has tried to trace. Knowledge of these traditions was familiar to Mozart and to the poet who wrote the libretto, to Schikaneder, or whoever the author was. The traditions were equally familiar to his audience, to the extent of the rather fine point that artistic music would have a greater effect on the hearer than primitive music. It might be noted, however, that with all this complicated wisdom, the writer of the libretto did not succeed in creating a new vision.

Even more pervasive than the eclectic use of the old symbols are the traces of such influences in our own modern concepts of music. There are, for instance, two major items of terminology that do not seem explicable without these inherited ideas. One is the use of the terms "high" or "low" to designate the musical pitch, and the other is the use of the term "movement," or "motion," or *moto*. To take the high-low problem first, there are three characteristics which we ascribe to a musical tone. We say that the tone is loud or soft, that it is long or short, and that it is high or low. The terms "long" and "short" can be used for any kind of measurement in time as well as in space. "Loud" or "soft" can be applied to sound in general; a non-musical noise, too, can be loud. The terms "high" and "low," however, are elsewhere applicable to a different kind of grading. As a matter of fact, they were originally meant for measurement in space. High is above, and low is beneath. If we look more closely, there is nothing in music which is high that is above, or low that is beneath. On keyboard instruments the high tones are on the right and the low ones on the left. A child beginner will ask where are the high notes, and his teacher will say, on the right. The same is valid for stringed instruments which are put on a table for playing, such as a zither. On all the instruments which you hold in your hands, you must distinguish between tones farther away or nearer to you. Thus it is for the violin and the cello, and thus also for the wind instruments. The sound of the human voice is created by vocal chords in the larynx. We speak of a high voice or a deep, rather than a low, voice; but the vocal chords are longer or shorter, not higher or lower. On harpsichords and organs there are higher and lower manuals, but their sound does not differ in pitch, only in the color of the tones.

The realization of the fact that actually nothing is physically high or low in music, except the abstract and relatively modern conventions of notation, is disturbing, since we are so accustomed to these terms and their traditional use from quite early times. It should, however, be stressed that Plato did not apply the term "high" to a note; he called it "shrill." [2] Nikomachus, however, used the terms "high" and "low." [3] As outlined in the first part of this study, among the early writers on the theory of music there were two schools. One group assumed that the planets with the longer radii of orbit, that is, the planets farther away from the earth, would produce the higher tones. The opposite school attributed the highest tone to the planets with the shorter radii and with courses near the earth. Visualizing the orbit of the planets mapped as lines in the sky, we would refer to the farther planets as being higher than the nearer ones. It was the school that attributed shriller tones to the farther planets that prevailed. These theories were popular, and I feel that we must attribute this bit of modern musical terminology to the survival of this elaborated theory of the music of the spheres. This theory was used in practice by the conductors of singing in the early Church. The conductor demonstrated the course of the melody by lifting or lowering his arms, movements that were then set down in the early notation of neumes. From this eventually there developed the modern musical notation, where the heads of the notes are actually higher and lower on the staves, corresponding to their higher and lower pitch. Thus, over the centuries notation has hammered the concept of high and low into the minds of performers. So accustomed are we today to these terms that we would point to heaven to characterize a high note and point to the ground when speaking of a low or deep note. A conductor of a chorus will lift his finger if the singers are flat; or he will point to the ground to tell the singers not to sharpen the pitch. We

---

[2] Plato, *Timaeus* in Loeb Classics, Vol. 7, 157, 173, 213.
[3] C. Jan, "Die Harmonie der Sphaeren," *Philologus*, 52 (1894), p. 18.

feel it natural that the arrival of the dove from heaven in *Lohengrin* is accompanied by high sounds from the violins, and that the dragon, Fafner, living in a cave, sings with a deep bass voice. We may realize that the symbolic terms of high and low are here used to characterize the physical highness of heaven and lowness of the cave, but we are certainly not aware that this in itself is a survival of the theory of the *musica mundana,* or the music of the spheres.

An explanation of the terms "movement" and "motion" in music is more complex. Both words are defined in Webster's Dictionary as the "act of moving or changing position." In French we have two words, of which, however, *motion* is used less frequently than *mouvement;* in German there is only one word, *Bewegung.* Webster defines "motion" in its musical sense as "melodic progression, a change of pitch in the successive tones of a voice part." For the definition of "movement," Webster refers to this definition and gives four more explanations: "rhythm; time; tempo; and a structural division of an extended composition, as a symphony." "Progression" and "succession" are used as explanatory terms; both refer to a movement, to an order in which one thing follows or antecedes another; both are meant as happening in time and not in space. None of the definitions is applicable to what is actually moving in music or even in the performance of music. What is physically moving in music is the oscillation of the strings of an instrument or the column of air in wind instruments. What we see moving at a performance are the hands and arms of the conductor and the players. Neither type is meant when we speak of musical motion or movement. But what do we mean? In physics, "velocity" and "celerity" are defined as the time-rate of motion, and it is partly this time-rate which we experience as motion in music. The term "movement" for a section of a cyclical piece of music is derived from the fact that the titles of these sections generally indicate the tempo in which the section is to be performed. The French use the same word, *mouvement,* the Germans say *Satz,* which means sentence or section. The titles direct the tempo at which the piece should be performed, and the names of the tempi often refer to motion: *con moto, allegro con moto,* etc. The custom of indicating the tempo derives from the seventeenth century, and the most common tempi are *allegro, andante,* and *adagio.* If we examine the names we see that they denote quite different categories. *Allegro,* in Italian, means gay, *andante* means going, and *adagio* means slow. Slow is a measure of time; *andante* denotes a combination of measured time and physical motion, of walking; but *allegro* designates a mood, a state of mind or temperament. Other terms referring to time measurements are *largo* and *presto;* names designating moods are *agitato* and all titles which add *con espressione,* with expression.

One may ask, with the expression of what? We will not, and cannot, go into a discussion of the "what" that is expressed in music. Many theories have been proffered, ranging from the technical to the purely emotional explanation, yet the question has not been satisfactorily answered and the problem remains unsolved. What can be said is this: terms such as *con moto* refer not only to motion in a physical sense, but also, and, indeed, predominantly, to motions of the psyche or the soul, to emotions. The titles refer to the motion which we mean when we say we are moved. The affinity of music and moods, the effect of music on emotions, has always been recognized. The issue is reflected in a number of myths and rites. The Greeks clearly recognized this affinity: they called a well-balanced person a musical man, and Plato in his *Republic* decries certain scales as detrimental and recommends others as fortifying. The medieval writers elaborated the analogy even further into theories of *musica humana.*

Plotinus was the first to discuss the affinity of inner and outer motion.[4] To Plato and Aristotle, motion could be understood only if measured, and that with a stable kind of measurement. Plotinus abandoned this interpretation and led toward the modern dynamic interpretation by distinguishing two different types of motion, objective and subjective. Objective motion takes effect outside of us, subjective inside. Objective motion is bound to a thing and is effected in space. Subjective motion is internal and effected in time; it takes effect in the human soul. The soul is originally motionless; spiritual forces produce motion, that is, set the soul in motion.

Plotinus's theory recognized and analyzed the two kinds of motion without establishing any relationship to the *tertium comparationis,* music. It was about 150 years later that Saint Augustine took up the idea of the two kinds of motion and related them to music.[5] To Augustine, rhythm is the principle of our lives, and rhythm is mea-

[4] Plotinus, *Enn.*, II, 9. 5; V, 1. 2; C. Baeumker, "Witelo, ein Philosoph und Naturforscher des 13. Jahrhunderts," *Beiträge zur Geschichte der Philosophie des Mittelalters*, III/2 (1908).

[5] Saint Augustine, *De Musica, lib.* 6; K. Meyer-Baer, "Psychologic and Ontologic Ideas in Augustine's *De Musica,*" *Journal of Aesthetics,* XI (1953).

sured time. The very art of measuring is music, *ars bene modulandi*. We are able to measure rhythm and time because these qualities of motion outside of us correspond to qualities of the internal motion in our soul. External motion—Augustine is here following Plotinus—is perceived in space, internal motion can be realized only through sound, measuring time through the course or flow of sounds in poetry and music. Therefore, music is the link that establishes a harmonious relationship between the outer and inner worlds and life. A melody or tune is an image of motion. It comes to us through our senses and then is evaluated by our spiritual forces on the grounds of its affinity with the internal motions. The spiritual forces here at work are intellect (*ratio*), and memory, and the soul (*anima*). Augustine's description of the relation of the spiritual forces to music amounts to an exposition of the theory of *musica humana*, but he did not coin this term. Nor does he use the term *musica mundana*, though he relates cosmic music to the theory of sound and acknowledges numbers as means of measuring both the cosmic and musical harmony. The terms *musica humana* and *musica mundana* seem to have originated with Boethius, and the term "human microcosmos," corresponding to a celestial macrocosmos, can be traced back to Saint Gregory. The concepts of *musica mundana* and *musica humana* are based on the theory that the correspondence of microcosmos and macrocosmos is conditioned by an affinity between the internal and the external motions.

These theories are discussed in almost every treatise on music from medieval times until far into the seventeenth century. In almost every one of them, there are chapters on *musica mundana* and *musica humana*. In Jacques de Liège's encyclopedic *Speculum* (fourteenth century) there are two chapters on the *mundana* and one on the *humana*.[6] Music and motion are cited as the links that connect *musica mundana* and *musica humana*. Among the more elaborate charts of the theory available are those accompanying Fludd's books, published early in the seventeenth century.

In all these elaborate schemes, the basic outlines remained stable, but the theory changes as far as the question of the nature of the internal motions was concerned. There is no definitive answer to the problem in Saint Augustine or in any of the later writings, indeed not to this day; but what might be called a major change in speculation became manifest in the works of the philosophers of the fifteenth cen-

[6] W. Grossman, *Die einleitenden Kapitel des Speculum musica* (1924); H. Abert, *Die Musikanschauung des Mittelalters* (1905).

tury. By that time, music had changed considerably; the polyphonic style had become firmly established. At the same time, attitudes toward the fine arts in general had changed, and interest became centered on how the artist produces and creates, what forces are then activated, and how they correspond to the forces which one sets in motion to understand a work of art. Among the more original thinkers who tackled this problem was Nicholas of Cusa.[7] Typically, he used traditional ideas while expounding a new approach, but it is beyond our scope to describe his work in detail. Suffice it to say that Nicholas placed the center of creating and perceiving art in the human being, whereas his predecessors had based it on divine inspiration. He looked beyond the work of art to detect the forces in the artist and in the sensitive spectator. The total list that he offers, in different places in his work, amounts to about eight such forces, including the senses and the mental powers of reason, memory, and imagination. These forces originate in and lead back to their center in the soul. The two bridges linking these powers are intuition or rapture, and man's ability to form images. Nicholas of Cusa relates man's internal energy of the passions to the physical motion outside him and finds that motions outside are perceived best through the flow of sounds. From this outer course of sound, he turns to the inner self, the inner motions, i.e., emotions, which are innate and not impressions from the outside. The soul is governed by the emotions and passions which arise through contact with the senses. "These passions pass away, and sensuous impressions are beautiful only insofar as they mirror spiritual ideas or beauties."[8] Part of this beauty can be grasped through measurement, through *ratio pulchri*, such as are included in the theory of music. But there is more to a work of art. This can be comprehended only if one compares "the rich flow of sound with the parallel motion in the soul," for "enthusiasm is the moving force."[9]

Apart from this, he states that "signs derived from musical harmony" are used as allegories for religious and other ideas, that "those signs of joy derived from musical harmony . . . which came down to us from the writings of the Church Fathers as signs known to mea-

---

[7] K. Meyer-Baer, "Nicholas of Cusa on the Meaning of Music," *Journal of Aesthetics*, v (1947).

[8] *De venatione sapientiae, cap.* 5.

[9] F. A. Scharpff, *Des Cardinals . . . Nikolaus von Cusa wichtigste Schriften* (1862), p. 539.

sure eternal bliss, are only remote material signs which differ greatly from those spiritual joys that are not accessible to our imagination." [10] Nicholas uses the traditional concept of *musica mundana* here, but he understands that it is a sign, only a symbol; it is the idea which I have tried to explain in the first part of this book.

The theory of a bridge between the mental powers, the theory of image-forming, was not further elaborated by the followers of Nicholas of Cusa. The theory of the passions, however, was taken up by philosophers such as Giordano Bruno [11] and became in the late seventeenth and, especially, in the eighteenth century the famous and popular theory of the affects or passions, a musical theory still flourishing today. From the fifteenth century onward these passions and affects are understood to be the primary internal motions, and the affinity of these motions with musical "motion" is expressed in the use of the terms "motion," "movement," and *moto, con moto,* in music. This affinity, first recognized by Plotinus, then applied to music by Saint Augustine, has been discussed for many centuries and is the basis for the current use of the terms; it is a survival from the concept of *musica humana.*

Thus, in our contemporary musical terminology, the ideas of *musica mundana* and *musica humana* still survive in such terms as "high" and "low," "motion" and "movement." I have tried to follow the history of the continuous interchange of symbols—figures, signs, and other imagery—and music. Changes in the surrounding cultures have influenced changes in the symbols traced, but some basic ideas seem to be permanent and recur again and again. It seems apt to close with the verses about music which Lorenzo speaks near the end of *The Merchant of Venice,* and in which all of these basic ideas are summed up:

> LORENZO:
> How sweet the moonlight sleeps upon this bank!
> Here will we sit and let the sounds of music
> Creep in our ears: soft stillness and the night
> Become the touches of sweet harmony.
> . . . Look how the floor of heaven
> Is thick inlaid with patines of bright gold:
> There's not the smallest orb which thou behold'st

---

[10] *De docta ignorantia, lib.* III, *cap.* 10.
[11] K. Meyer-Baer, *Bedeutung und Wesen der Musik* (1932), *cap.* 3.

But in his motion like an angel sings,
Still quiring to the young-eyed cherubins;
Such harmony is in immortal souls;
But whilst this muddy vesture of decay
Doth grossly close it in, we cannot hear it.

[*Enter Musicians*]

Come, ho! and wake Diana with a hymn:
With sweetest touches pierce your mistress' ear
And draw her home with music.

[*Music*]

JESSICA:
I am never merry when I hear sweet music.

LORENZO:
The reason is, your spirits are attentive:
For do but note a wild and wanton herd,
Or race of youthful and unhandled colts,
Fetching mad bounds, bellowing and neighing loud,
Which is the hot condition of their blood;
If they but hear perchance a trumpet sound,
Or any air of music touch their ears,
You shall perceive them make a mutual stand,
Their savage eyes turn'd to a modest gaze
By the sweet power of music: therefore the poet
Did feign that Orpheus drew trees, stones and floods;
Since naught so stockish, hard and full of rage,
But music for the time does change his nature.
The man that has not music in himself,
Nor is not moved with concord of sweet sounds,
Is fit for treasons, stratagems and spoils;
The motions of his spirit are dull as night
And his affections dark as Erebus:
Let no such man be trusted. Mark the music.

Appendix I

Excerpts from First Chapter of Letter on Harmony
Addressed to Archbishop Rathbod of Treves by
Regino of Prüm *

That there is music in the motion of heaven has been recognized
and explained by the Pythagoreans. How is it, they said, that so fast
an engine as heaven is run so quietly and silently? And though the
sound does not reach our ear, it is impossible that so fast a motion
does not carry a sound, especially as the course of the stars functions
with such great adaptation and convenience that nothing else like it,
so combined and interwoven, is within our comprehension. Because
some courses are carried out higher and some lower, and, thus, all
turn through the same original impetus, the order of the courses
must follow different ratios. Therefore it is supposed that in the motion of heaven an order of ratios is contained. The consonance which
is at the bottom of all measurement in music cannot originate in
sound. Sound is not produced by an impulse or by striking. On the
other hand, a beat is not produced if no motion precedes.

Of the motions, some are faster and some slower; and if motion is
slow and uneven, a low sound is produced, but if quicker and more
intense, necessarily a high sound is produced. If a thing is not moved,
no sound arises. Therefore the musicians define sound as follows:
sound is percussion of air which comes uninterrupted to the ear. High
and low in sound are based on different motions.

Therefore the astrologers and the musicians say that between the
highest sphere and the circles of the seven planets all the musical
consonances can be filled in. They say that from Saturn to the heavenly sphere the highest sound is produced, from Earth to the lunar
circle the lowest. They assert that then from Saturn downward, at
every stage, a lower tone is produced, from Earth to the lunar circle
higher (ascending) tones, because what is more tense and faster necessarily produces a higher sound, as on the other hand, what is
slower, a lower one. Between the circles of Saturn and Moon,
through the whole vastness of the planets is produced the variety of
all sorts of tones and all musical consonances. All this has been—as

* Author's translation from text in Gerbert, *Scriptores de musica* (1831), I,
230ff.

349

Martianus has described in his book *De nuptiis Philologiae et Mercurii*—thought out in the sacred woods of Apollo, who as Helios is the moderator of heavenly music. For, so he [Capella] says, the outstanding elevations, that is, the branches that are higher, therefore the more distant, i.e., the vaster or longer, produce subtle and grace-ful sounds, that is, high tones. If he shook the branches near to the earth, such as the more inclined and humbler branches which are nearer the ground, then a rough and deep sound was produced. In the center, the middle parts of the same wood . . . sounded in a double concordance. Harmony is the united society of similar voices. Concordance is what fits best to the various tones, as we see in the organum. . . . He [Capella] mentions three consonances, the oc-tave, the quint, and the fourth. The octaves are consonant without interruption, that is, without connecting intervals. . . .

It must not be forgotten that the strings of an instrument are com-parable to the chords of the heavenly music. Among the tones, the musicians let the *hypate meson* correspond to Saturn. The *parypate* is likened to the sphere of Jupiter. They give *lichanos meson* to Mars. The Sun obtains the *mese*. Venus has the *trite synemenon*. Mercury rules the *paranete synemenon*. The *nete* is taken as an example of the lunar sphere. This follows Boethius. For Cicero expounds another order. In his *Somnium Scipionis* he asserts that what is high in nature is low in sound, and what is low in nature is high in sound. Therefore the highest course of the fixed stars, the circumference of which is the faster, is turned with a high and lively sound; the deepest and lunar sphere with the lowest sound. The ninth sphere of Earth is stable and rests always on the same place. Here Cicero imposes on the Earth si-lence, that is, immobility. Then, he allots the lowest sound, which is nearest to silence, to the Moon, so that the Moon is *proslam-banomenos*, which is the lowest tone; Mercury is *hypate hypaton*, the Sun *lichanos hypaton*, Mars *hypate meson*, Jupiter *parypate meson*, Saturn *lichanos meson*, the heavenly sphere *mese*. Thus the distance between the Moon and Mercury sounds as a whole tone. Between the Moon and Mars he states the consonance of the fifth, with the Sun the fourth and the heavenly sphere the octave. Thus we have in the motion of heaven the sum of the whole of music. This may be enough concerning heavenly music. Anyone who wants to know more about it, may read the above-mentioned *Somnium Scipionis* in the second book of the excellent philosopher Macrobius. We want to add only that not only the pagan philosophers but also the reliable teach-ers of the Christian faith confirm the celestial harmony.

Appendix II

EXCERPTS FROM THE HYMN
"NATURALIS CONCORDIA VOCUM CUM PLANETIS"
("NATURAL HARMONY OF THE TONES
AND THE PLANETS") *

1. The ratios of the planets are similar to those of the tones.
2. The divine order rises from Earth to Heaven.
3. According to Tullius [Cicero] the order rising from the lowest to the highest is the following:
4. Luna, Hermes, Venus, and Sol, Mars, Jupiter, and Saturn.
5. In a similar order one must modulate the tones.
6. One must begin with the Moon, which is nearest to the Earth.
7. From there Mercury is one tone higher.
8. By the interval of the tone, the musical order is apportioned.
9. The following space to Venus has the musical value of a half-tone.
10. Then the space to the Sun is filled by a fourth.
11. The way to the war-like Mars is limited by a fifth.
12. The interval to Jupiter is a half-tone.
13. To these the whole tone is added to reach Saturn.
14. The seventh tone reaches Heaven corresponding to the seven days.
15. For the notes the eighth completes the order of the octave.
16. Thus the order reaches from the low ones to the middle, to the high ones being the softest.
17. The double octave reaches Heaven. . . . [Here follow several symbolisms of the number seven.]
27. The nucleus (*nodus*) of the universe is the number seven.

*Author's translation is from text provided in J. Handschin, *Ein mittelalterlicher Beitrag zur Lehre von der Sphaerenmusik* (*Zeitschrift für Musikwissenschaft*), 9 (1927), p. 193, 202f.; see p. 80.

Appendix III

The Music in Dante's Cosmos

Dante's cosmos consists of the inferno (hell), purgatory (the mountain of purification), and paradise, with hell and paradise forming a double cone and each cone consisting of nine and ten layers, respectively. The inferno is largely irrelevant in the context of this study because angels seldom appear there and music is noise described in a way that cannot be described here. Of places for souls worthy of an afterlife in bliss, Dante has three. Elysium, for pagan heroes, is a beautiful meadow, but located at the highest stratum of the inferno. Dante called it *prato*, "lane" or "meadow," and mentions the name Elysium only in a reference to the *Aeneid*. The other two places are the earthly and heavenly paradises. The earthly paradise is located at the top of the mountain of purgatory, and it is here, on the last leg of the ascent, that angels are to be found; they start to sing only when Dante is approaching the earthly paradise, when he is standing on the border of Lethe. The layers in the *Purgatorio* are allotted to certain crimes, but to crimes of which the culprits can be purged. The angels that appear here represent the virtues that match the vices. For example, when Dante is in the layer of the misers, there is a great earthquake which frightens him into unconsciousness, and then he hears, comfortingly, the *Gloria in excelsis Deo*, shouted but not sung by the chorus of angels (Canto xx). Singing is mentioned once earlier in the *Purgatorio*, when Dante dreams that he hears the luring singing of the sirens. It is music of negative effect, and it is only in a dream that Dante hears it.

But in Canto xxvii, when Dante is approaching Lethe, just after he has heard the Provençal poet Arnaut *speak* his poem, Dante hears from the other bank of the river an angel singing *Beati mundo corde*. It might be mentioned that in the liturgy this text, one of the Beatitudes, is usually recited and not sung, while the *Gloria in excelsis* mentioned before as shouted is usually sung. It should also be noted that the term *cantando* may also stand for *commemorando* (Canto xxiii, 59). After Dante has met Beatrice, he constantly sees and hears dancing and singing. When he stands before the reprimanding Beatrice, broken, without tears and sighs, he can follow only the beginning of the comforting psalm *In te Domine speravi*, which the angels *sing*; that is to say, he stands numb "before the singing of those that continuously sing the music of the eternal spheres." He is unmoved even by the most celestial music, not overcome by it, but numb beyond feeling. After having confessed his sins to Beatrice, Dante drinks from Lethe and is admitted to the earthly paradise. On entering it he sees the triumphal procession of the Church (Canto xxii). Here the maidens representing the virtues—they are called nymphs—sing the 79th psalm in antiphonal manner (Canto xxxiii). After an invocation of Apollo as the divine virtue, Dante then enters the heavenly paradise. In the first two cantos the order of the spheres is explained, the graded order of the ten spheres, and the flight up higher and higher corresponds to the moral grading of the human being, who is more and more purified and perfected. The long development that produced this vision has been traced in this study; in Dante it seems so familiar that one hardly takes special note of it. The blessed appear in the sphere of the moon, and it is here, at the end of the third canto, that singing is again reported. The Empress Constance (mother of Emperor Frederic II) sings the *Ave Maria, cantando*. In the fourth canto, Plato's theories about life after death are discussed, and it may here be observed how Dante's ideas are formed out of a fusion of classic and Christian elements. In the sphere of Mercury, Dante meets the Emperor Justinian. They have a long talk, after which Justinian starts to sing the *Hosanna sanctus Deus*, and while singing he rejoins the round in which he had been dancing before he left it to talk to Dante. (The text of the song is a mixture of Latin and Hebrew words and demonstrates the fusion of Christian, Roman, and Talmudic tradition. In the *Talmud* Malachoth is the abode of the Lord.) One gathers from this scene that the blessed are continuously forming rounds to dance, and that when a person wants to talk he leaves the round, then afterwards resumes dancing, *volgendosi alla rota sua*. So far, that is, in the lower spheres of paradise, the figures who sing have solo parts; the dancers are in the background. In the next sphere, that of Venus, Dante observes the blessed forming two separate rounds, one slower and one faster, and he compares this twofold motion to the differentiated rhythm in a two-part song, where one note is sustained while the other proceeds. Here he meets persons who have come down from a higher sphere and left their circles. They sing a song in chorus, the *Hosanna,* and Charles Martell stands out singing alone the beginning of the canzone, *"Voi che intendendo il terzo cielo movete"*—the line from the *Convivio* which has been mentioned above (p. 126) and which is addressed to the angels moving the third sphere. In the following heaven, that of the sun (Canto x), the song of the blessed is such that it cannot be heard by or described to a human ear. It can only be understood by someone who actually is in this sphere. Here two circles of dancers are moving at a speed faster than Dante has ever seen on earth, and he likens the movement of the two circles to that of millstones, to show that they move in opposite directions. They are formed by members of the monastic orders of the Dominicans and Franciscans and surround Dante like a double rainbow, or like stars completing their courses. These blessed sing in honor of the holy Trinity and not in honor of Dionysus or Apollo. When one of them, Saint Thomas Aquinas, leaves his circle for a talk with Dante, and when he and later Saint Bonaventure resume their places again, the dancers and their singing stop for a moment, "as when in dancing there is a short rest as one movement ends and a new melody starts." In this sphere the dancers are singing, and they seem to sing several melodies. Before leaving the sphere of the sun, the song in honor of the Trinity is heard once more, and Dante discerns here one humble voice distinct from the chorus, that is, a solo voice against the background of the *tutti*. In the following sphere, that of Mars, Dante hears a song without being able to understand its beautiful unity, as someone not experienced in hearing polyphonic music is unable to follow the texture of the parts.

Here it is well to remember that the beginning of the fourteenth century saw the new polyphonic style, the *ars nova,* flourishing in Florence.[1] "As the viol and the harp, if all the strings are well tuned, make a sweet sound even to the listener who does not understand the notes, so there arose from the lights which appeared to me in the Cross [the blessed had formed the sign of the Cross] a melody which overwhelmed me without my understanding the text" (*Par.* xiv, 117–20). Dante could understand only a few words.

In the sixth sphere of Jupiter, Dante describes the blessed as performing a regular ballet. "As birds form figures in their flights, so the sparks which are the souls of the blessed sing and dance, forming the letters D and I and L" (*Par.* xviii, 73–76). Each sings his melody and turns to the place he must take, and then stops. Thus they eventually form the letters of the text *"Diligite justitiam qui judicatis terram,"* the sentence taken from Proverbs I.1 (in the Vulgate)[2]

---

[1] J. Wolf, *Geschichte der Mensural-Notation* (1904); G. Reese, *Music in the Middle Ages* (1940).

[2] Vulgata, Ratisb. 1929, *Liber sapientiae, studium pietatis,* 1–16; usually

which symbolizes the righteousness of the rulers who have been re-
warded for their good government. At the end, the blessed form the
letter M, and, remaining in their places, they shine like a golden
illumination on silver background. Later, the sparks dissolve again to
form different figures, finally an eagle, whose six eyes represent certain model rulers: David, Trajan, Hiskia, Constantine, William II of
Sicily, and Ripheus.[3] This eagle, "il segno del mondo"—that is, the
emblem of the emperor—starts to sing and he sings for the six men,
giving voice to all of them but in such a way that it sounds in unison.
In terms of musical composition this may mean that they sing in
unison, but since it is a song in several languages—Hebrew, Greek,
Latin, and possibly Italian—Dante may have been thinking here of a
composition typical of the *ars nova,* which often used texts in different languages for different parts.[4]

In the seventh sphere, of Saturn, the sphere bordering the crystal
heaven, Dante meets the souls of those who have lived in medita-
tion; there quiet reigns and no singing is heard. The groups are
differentiated not through sound or motion, but through greater or
lesser intensity of light. The whole atmosphere and mood here convey the impression of a general rest before entering the symphony of
the highest heavens.

Dante then reaches the heaven of the fixed stars, the crystal
heaven, and sees the triumphal procession of Christ led by the apostles and the Virgin. The archangel Gabriel is flying around the Virgin in a circle, forming a kind of nimbus. Both the apostles and the
archangels are singing, Gabriel with such sweetness that all human
song is like thunder compared with it, and the apostles sing the
Regina coeli with great sweetness. The blessed, sparks of heavenly
light, are dancing in rounds, some faster and some slower, moving
like the wheels of a clock, at different speeds. From one of these circles a figure detaches himself, singing so divinely that Dante is unable to describe it. He is Saint Peter, who has come to accept Dante's
confession. When Dante has finished, "the spheres resound with the
Te Deum, the melody which is sung up there" (Canto xxvi). As
Dante is about to leave the sphere of Saturn, the blessed, the whole

quoted as *Wisdom of Solomon,* i, i; however, the text in the King James Bible is
different.

[3] *Paradiso,* xx, 68; Ripheus is a Trojan prince mentioned in the *Aeneid,* ii,
339.

[4] Reese, *Music in the Middle Ages;* G. Adler, *Handbuch der Musikgeschichte*
(1924), pp. 152ff.

paradise, start to sing the *Gloria* and while singing they disappear over the golden ramp leading directly from the seventh sphere into the Empyreum. Dante follows them through the crystal heaven, and then to the seat of the *primum mobile,* the Lord, who is the force that starts all life and motion. From here, Dante looks into the Empyreum and observes there nine circles of light which are the nine orders of angels. The wider their circles the slower the movement, so that the three spheres nearest to God are rotating the fastest; they are also the brightest. All these circles move in the direction opposite to the movement of the spheres of the planets. But Dante, ascending from below, counts the orders from their nearness to God. The orders of angels disappear little by little from his sight *"poco a poco mio veder sostinse"* through the intensity of the light emanating from God when Dante enters the Empyreum. The Empyreum is a sea of light, and in it there appears the heavenly rose formed by the angels and the blessed; in its center is the Lord.

The crystal heaven and the Empyreum, the last two heavens, are the spheres of fire (there is also one other fire which Dante had to pass before entering the earthly paradise; this fire was the symbol for purification). In these last heavens light and music are everywhere; figures are described as sparks emanating from God; Dante sees more than a thousand angels (Canto xxxi, 131) giving honor by dancing and singing to the brightest light among them, the holy Virgin. He hears the souls of children singing with higher voices. Here again the archangel Gabriel approaches singing the *Ave Maria,* and "from all sides the heavenly court; that is the community of saints and angels, joins and continues the divine cantilena" (Canto xxxii, 94 *et seq.*). Dante finds Saint Anne honoring her daughter, singing *Hosanna.* Just as the distinction between time and space is no longer valid in the Empyreum, so light and sound cannot be separated. But while the intensity of light gains as it approaches more closely to God, the music does not gain in strength but in sweetness.

That there is continuous singing in the highest heavens of paradise in praise of God is not an original invention of Dante's imagination; as noted, the idea occurs as far back as the Psalms and the Book of Job; [5] but the intensity of the vision is exclusively Dante's.

---

[5] Job, 38, 7; E. Rohde, *Der griechische Roman,* p. 224, with quotations from Iambulus, Diodor, and Lucian; A. Dieterich, *Nekyia* (1913), pp. 36ff; K. Meyer-Baer, "Music in Dante's Paradiso," *Aspects of Medieval and Renaissance Music* (1966).

Appendix IV

A Note on the Singers
of the Ghent Altar

THE SINGING ANGELS of the Ghent Altar, shown in Fig. 173, constitute something of a puzzle in themselves. Of the eight angels, six
have notably strong facial expressions. These have been the subject of
much speculation and have even been characterized as grimaces. The
reason for their seeming reflection of different moods has not thus far
been understood, and I should like to propose a new solution.

Van Mander thought that he could recognize the pitch of the notes
being sung and that the tense expression of the two righthand angels
resulted from their straining to sing high notes.[1] But this does not
seem plausible, because the five outstanding and sacred notes are either
connected with the vowels *a e i o u*, or *a e u i a*, taken from the word
"alleluia." The shape of the mouths does not correspond to the pro-
nunciation of these letters. Besides, the sacred musical notes are sol,
fa, re, mi, do, having the compass of a fifth, and thus they would not
necessitate any forcing of high notes.

The mysticism of the five notes or words goes back to Saint Paul's
epistle to the Corinthians and was expounded in terms of musical
values in the twelfth century in the *Collectorium super Magnificat* by
the famous Charlier de Gerson.[2] He explained the five vowels and
the five notes as a sign of harmony: "The noble Apostle, the child of
the Gospel . . . said to the Corinthians: I had rather speak five
words with my understanding that I might teach others, then ten
thousand words in an unknown tongue. . . . This is the parable of
the mystic cantichord, or Song of the Heart, which the same Apostle
desires to be sung with the spirit, and to be sung also with understanding. In which song of the heart three things are found, as in
vocal song. Firstly, the subject of the song, which is called the Letter

[1] Panofsky (*Early Netherlandish Painting*, 1953), mentions "the somewhat
strained expression"; for the influence of Gerson's writings on the iconology of
the Master of Flémalle, see Meyer-Schapiro, "Muscipula Diaboli," *Art Bulletin*,
XXVII (1945), 182.

[2] Gerson, *Opera* (Strasbourg, Prüss, 1488), fol. 81 c, 81 kk3, 84 Nn v, 84 Nn
5v, 98 dd 4.

FIG. 173. (*left*) and FIG. 174. (*right*). Jan van Eyck, detail from the Ghent
Altar. Copyright A.C.L. Brussels

(in the sense of the letter of the law, in contradiction to the spirit). Secondly, the sound of the song, which is called Resonance. Thirdly, the figuring of the song, which is called Note or Mark (notation). The subject of the cantichord we term the holy and pure knowledge of all things divine and human. The resonance we call every moderate and well-ordered affection of the heart and spirit. The note or mark we figure according to the conception of the two preceding, so that to which of them the resonance of the affections is to be fitted may appear from the *letter* of the meditations. Upon this matter we will give a few verses, the purpose of which shall be further explained, and this by a triple set of five. Five words for the *letter: magnificus, largus, pius et justus, miserator.* Five affections for the harmony: *gaudia, spes, pietas, hinc timor, atque dolor.* The adaption of five vowels to the terms of the five affections: . . . The form is according to the five notes, sol, fa, mi, re, ut . . . ."

If one compares the strong facial expressions of the five angels in Fig. 173, it seems plausible that the two righthand figures were intended to show a negative and the two lefthand ones a positive mood or affection. The positive moods could well be determined as joy and faith (*gaudium, spes*), the negative as fright (*timor*) and grief (*dolor*). The angel in the center looking down might be understood as expressing compassion (*pietas, misericordia*). Facial expressions were generally depicted by the Van Eycks in a very restrained manner. The group of angels around the Lamb, those adoring and those with censers in front, seem to be completely absorbed in the duties they are performing. The four in the back with the instruments of the Passion show no expression of grief or sorrow, but two of them, with their eyes closed and their heads bent, have the same expression as the central figure of the singing angels and may express compassion. Gerson's book on the Magnificat was very popular in the fifteenth century and might well have been influential in this instance (perhaps coincidentally, the Annunciation forms the center of the outer panels in the Ghent Altar).

Some symbolism definitely seems to be expressed in the instruments of the group of angels in Fig. 174. The harp has twenty-four strings (as compared with the twenty-five mentioned as being usual by Machaut),[3] and there are twenty-four Elders; the viol has five

[3] G. de Machaut, *Le dit de la harpe,* verses 3 and 277ff.; verse 1/3, from

strings (compared to the usual four or six); [4] the organ has twenty-one pipes (compared to the usual fifteen). As the graduation of the organ pipes is even, this indicates three regular octaves, which may be understood as a symbol of the Trinity.[5] Of course, the number of strings and pipes was not completely uniform in the fifteenth century. However, the numbers here differ so consistently from the usual that it is reasonable to think that they are endowed with special meaning, and an allegorical explanation of the five singing angels seems to me persuasive.

Appendix V

REAL OR IMAGINARY INSTRUMENTS:
AN EXAMINATION OF THE BEATUS MANUSCRIPTS
AND THE UTRECHT PSALTER

TWO SETS OF WORKS from the ninth and tenth centuries—the group of manuscripts from Spain, the Beatus commentaries, and the group of manuscripts centered in the Utrecht Psalter, which is now ascribed to the Carolingian era and the school of Rheims—provide an interesting study on the problem of instruments. In the earliest copies of

---

K. Young, "The dit de la harpe of Guillaume de Machaut," *Yale Romanic Studies*, XXII (1943).

> Je puis trop bien madame comparer
> A la harpe et son gent corps parer
> De XXV cordes que la harpe a.

Verse 243:

> Or t'ay nommé i quateron de cordes? Que la harpe a
> et se tu t'i accordes
> . . . Honneur, Sens, Raison et Mesure.

Verse 277:

> Je t'ay nommé les cordes de la lire
> Dont il y a XXV tire à tire
> Et s'en y ay IIII mis par desseure
> Qui la harpe gouvernent à toute heure.

[4] Jerome de Moravia, *Tractatus de Musica*.

[5] H. Hickmann, *Das Portativ* (1936).

the Beatus, a kind of lute appears as the instrument of the angels and the Elders. It is an instrument with strings that are to be plucked, an almond-shaped body, and a neck and pegs. This instrument, drawn in a more-or-less realistic way depending on the technical knowledge of the illuminator, was new to the Occident and had come to Spain with the Arab invaders. Its name is derived from an Arab word. I shall use the term "lute" for convenience. Besides the "lute," there is an instrument of a similar but somewhat broader shape, played with a bow. A third instrument in the Beatus manuscripts is the harp.

The occurrence of these instruments has two different sources. The text of Revelation mentions harps and psalteries, as the words for the instruments of the angels and the Elders were usually translated. The harp in triangle form seems to have been in use from the Biblical period on; it remained one of the usual instruments of King David, who in turn became the allegorical figure of Church music.

The origin of the "lute" can be traced to central Asia, where a very similar instrument appears in the sculpture of the so-called Gandhara art, in works of the first century B.C.[1] It is one of the chief instruments shown in scenes of court life in Islamic art. This, or a similar instrument, is seen in many wall paintings and illuminations. Generally the oval-shaped stringed instrument is plucked, but it is also found being played with a bow. Where this technique originated remains a problem.[2] To define the form of the instrument is difficult because one cannot tell the shape of the sound box from strictly two-dimensional representations in which the instrument is seen directly from the front.

The lute became popular in Europe with the Arab invasion of Spain in the eighth century. Oriental influences, however, also came through Byzantium. In the imperial palace at Istanbul a mosaic floor (which seems to have been recently destroyed) showed a pastoral scene with a seated figure playing a lute, that is, an instrument with an oval soundboard and three strings to be plucked.[3] It also appears

---

[1] A. Foucher, *L'art greco-bouddhique du Gandhâra* (Paris, 1905–22); H. G. Farmer, "The Instruments on the Taq-i-Bustan Bas-Reliefs," *Journal of the Royal Asiatic Society* (1938), p. 405.

[2] A. Christensen, "La vie musicale dans la civilisation des Sassanides," *Bulletin de l'association française des amis de l'Orient*, No. 20 (Paris, 1936).

[3] G. H. Farmer, *Oriental Studies Mainly Musical* (1953), p. 61, calls it pandora; K. Schlesinger, "The Utrecht Psalter and Its Bearing on the History of Musical Instruments," *Musical Antiquary*, Vol. II (London, 1910), 18ff.; H. Dräger, *Die Entwicklung des Streichbogens* (1937), mostly for the later periods.

on the famous ceiling of the Cappella Palatina in Palermo, in varied forms, plucked as well as played with a bow, evidently modeled on Oriental sources.[4]

The explanation of the symbolic meaning of this instrument is complicated. Its appearance in the illuminations of the Beatus manuscripts as an instrument of heaven is definitely an innovation. Many Roman works show an instrument to be plucked that has a somewhat different form, with a small round body and a broad and sometimes very long neck. This instrument had become the attribute of Venus.[5] As the "lute" conquered Occidental music, the old Roman form of Venus's instrument took on the shape of the "lute." It is thus that it appears as the attribute of Venus and of Luxuria, and as the instrument of the lovers in the Gardens of Love.[6] The Beatus manuscripts must be regarded as the source for the lute as an instrument of heavenly music. Later it became the usual instrument held by the *putti* who sat on the steps of the throne of the Madonna. It might be noted that the form of the lute fits well into ornamental drawing, that it lends itself easily to representation. Be this as it may, the lute, coming from the Beatus manuscripts, remains one of the most popular instruments of the orchestras of angels.

Another important tradition can be traced to the Utrecht Psalter, and its illuminations warrant discussion, though they do not show angels performing music. In the Utrecht Psalter there is a distinct separation between the angels and other figures. The angels are always seen beside the Lord, and when a hierarchy is given, standing on a higher or the highest level. Music is performed by the faithful, the companions of David. David, if he is shown with an instrument, plays the harp, an instrument which belongs to this tradition as well. In addition to the harp, there are wind instruments, the lyre, possibly a kind of bagpipe (a bladderpipe), an instrument to be plucked, and the drum and an organ. What forms do these instruments have and where could models for them have been found? The lyre and the in-

---

[4] N. Monneret de Villard, *Le pitture musulmane al sofitto della cappella palatina in Palermo* (1950), "Liuto" on Figs. 200–206, 214, 217; E. Herzfeld, *Die Malereien von Samara* (Berlin, 1927), Vol. III, Pl. II.

[5] O. Fischel, *Raffael* (London, 1948), Vol. II, Pl. 80, Achilles in Scyros, Graeco-Roman sarcophagus relief, Louvre; Lateran Museum, Rome, sarcophagus, third century, see Fig. 130.

[6] Saxl, "Beiträge zur Geschichte der Planetendarstellungen," *Islam*, III (1912), Pl. 5, Fig. 6, *passim*; and see my Chapter VI, n. 18.

strument to be plucked point to models from antiquity. The instrument to be plucked has a long neck, a form found in Roman works. The elaborate, ornamented shape of this instrument and of the lyre suggests that the illuminator had not seen such an instrument in use. The form of the drum, with skins on both sides of a curved cylinder, appears also in Spanish manuscripts [7] among the instruments played at the feast before Nebuchadnezzar in the Book of Daniel. The similarity of forms to instruments from classical times is not surprising. Carolingian illuminators are known to have used such models.[8]

A most interesting point is the appearance of the organ, which appears for the first time in a Christian book in the Utrecht Psalter (ninth century). The organ did not originally take part in the liturgy. In pagan rites it had been the instrument of the *Magna Mater* and was therefore used at the circus games of which the goddess was the patroness.[9] The Church Fathers for this reason opposed its use.[10] However, it seems to have been used continuously at the Byzantine court and is mentioned in later centuries (around 500) in Spain and Italy.[11] In 757, the Byzantine emperor Constantine Kopronymos sent an instrument to King Pepin of France. This event was mentioned in all the chronicles of the time, a fact that demonstrates the novelty of this instrument, at least for France. This organ was probably erected at Compiègne. In 816 the Greek ambassador brought an organ to Charlemagne, and thereafter a number of organs were constructed in his empire, including one by Louis the Pious for Aachen in 820.[12] In England there must have been organs early in the eighth century, for Aldhelm speaks of the overpowering sonority

[7] Neuss, *Die katalanische Bibelillustration* (1922), p. 89, Pl. 32, Fig. 100.

[8] Buhle, *Die Musikalischen Instrumente in den Miniaturen des frühen Mittelalters* (1903), p. 4; A. Goldschmidt, *German Illuminations*, Vol. I, Pl. 68, title of Psalterium Aureum at Saint Gall; see also the illumination in the Bible of Charles the Bald (Paris, Bibliothèque Nationale); E. R. Curtius, *Europäische Literatur und lateinisches Mittelalter* (1948), p. 55.

[9] Thus on the Obelisk of Theodosius at Constantinople; Bottée de Toulemon in *Mem. de la soc. roy. des antiquités de France*, XVII (1844); I owe the information that the organ was the instrument of the *Magna Mater*, the patroness of the Circus games, to Professor K. Lehmann.

[10] Saint Jerome, *Epistula 107 ad Laetam, De institutione filiae, Patrol. gr.* 22, 871.

[11] Buhle, *Die Musikalischen Instrumente*, p. 57; H. Anglés "Early Spanish Musical Culture," *Aspects of Medieval and Renaissance Music* (1966), p. 4.

[12] Buhle, *Die Musikalischen Instrumente*, p. 58; H. Bittermann, "The Organ in the Early Middle Ages," *Speculum*, IV (1929), 390, and V (1930), 217.

of this instrument.[13] (It was because of this sonority that he opposes
it in his poem *De Virginitate*.)

Probably the illuminator of the Utrecht Psalter was inspired by the
organs sent to France from Byzantium and therefore put the organ in
the center of his illustration to the last psalm, in which all the instruments which should be used to praise the Lord are listed. In his
illumination, the faithful are divided into four groups on two levels.
Of these, the lower groups each have three singers and two horns;
the higher group at the right has a lyre, a harp, an instrument to be
plucked, and a drum; at the left we see a lyre and the forked rattle,
an instrument that was known from Roman works.[14] The organ
stands at the bottom in the center, and is played by two people; its
bellows are worked by four. Above in heaven, in a mandorla, is the
Lord, attended by six angels without instruments. In later psalters
the organ appears as the instrument of David,[15] but not of the
angels; the companions sometimes work the bellows.

Thus there are three sources for the instruments in the Utrecht
Psalter. The general kind of instrument—string, wind, or percussion
—was chosen following the text of the psalms. Forms were derived
from model manuscripts, probably on purpose with a view to representing instruments from earlier periods. No differentiation was
made between the Roman period and the period of the Bible and of
David. This custom continued to prevail for centuries and was still to
be seen in the seventeenth century.[16] The third source is reality; the
organ was drawn after the instruments which the illuminator had
seen in his own lifetime.

[13] Curtius, *Europäische Literatur*, p. 454.

[14] Goldschmidt, *German Illuminations*, Vol. i, Pl. 68; V. Leroquais, *Les
psaultiers manuscrits latins des bibliothèques publiques de France* (1940), p.
411, Pl. xxxv.

[15] David with an organ in the illuminations of MS. Pommersfelden (eleventh
century); Cambridge, Saint John's College and Trinity College (twelfth century); Belvoir Castle; Breslau University Library (thirteenth century); Buhle,
Die Musikalischen Instrumente, Pl. 14.

[16] Title of Mersenne's *Harmonie Universelle* (1636); Rubens, *King David*,
Städel Gallery, Frankfurt; the engravings for Galle's *Ecomium musices*; Jacques
Callot, *Mons Parnassus*, engraving for Salvadori's *Guerra di Bellezza*, 1616.

Index

Aachen, 363
Achilles, 18, 241, 251f., 328
Adid, 228
Adonis, 240, 326
Aer (Air), 230f., 279. *See also* breath
Agricola, Martin (1486-1556), 185
   n.95
Aischylos, 334n.1
Alanus de Insulis (*ca.* 1128-1202),
   122-27, 191
Albert the Great (1193-1280), 119f.
Alcestis, 268
Aldhelm (639-709), 193, 363
Alexander Severus, Emperor (222-
   235), 268
Alexander the Great (356-323 B.C.),
   18, 20, 260
Alexander of Ephesus (2nd cent.), 73f.
Alexandria, 73f., 261
Alfarabi (d. 950), 117
Algazel (1058-1111), 117
Algeria, 68, 250
Alkman (7th cent. B.C.), 243
Altdorfer (*ca.* 1477-1538), 136, 178
Ambrose, Saint (340?-397), 35
Amiens, 103, 112
Ananke, 12, 205f.
Angelic Orders 24f., 60, 78, 81,
   passim
   choirs of, 112, 383ff.
   colors of, 122
   emblems of, 39, 60, 106, 114,
     151
   names of, 18, 39, 60f.
   numbers, 16, 39
   in processions, 37
Angels
   of death, 297
   as heralds to Last Judgment, 45, 113
   human figures with wings, 50f., 53
   as movers of the spheres, 42ff., 51,
     120

   as musicians, 130, *passim*
   as psychopomps, 297
   as *putti*, 139, 180f.
   as tetramorphs, cherubs, 9, 15, 17,
     passim
   with tools of the Liturgy, 114
   with tools of the Passion, 107,
     114
   as winged messengers, 8
Angers, 294
Anima
   cosmic soul, 118, 123
   emotion, 345
   small human figures, 240, 248, 326
   See also breath, *intelligentiae, musica
     humana*
Anselm of Laon (d. 1117), 121n.24
Antelami (fl. 1178-96), 184
Anyte of Tega (3rd cent B.C.), 251
Anzy-le-Duc, 103, 285
Apocalypse of
   Abraham, 35
   Adam, 23f., 26f., 284
   Arda Viraf, 14, 32
   Baruch, 22
   Enoch, 22f.
   Jesaia, 23
   Joseph the Carpenter, 23
   XII Patriarchs, 40n.44
   Petrus, 23f.
   Reuben, 279
   Revelation, 25, *passim; see also*
     Bible
Apollo, 21, 28, 31, 68, 138, 191-95,
   204-209, 234, 337, 350
Apollonius of Tyana (1st cent.), 253
Apostolic Constitutions, 37
Apuleius (2nd cent.), 32
Aratos (*ca.* 310-245 B.C.), 73n.9
Archai, see angelic orders
archangels, 18, 24f., 51, 62, 286ff.,
   355f.

Aribo (11th cent.), 85n.35
Arion, 204, 267f., 281
Aristides Quintilian (1st to 2nd cent.), 34n.25
Aristotle, 13n.17, 16n.27f., 118, 123, 126, 344
Aristoxenos (4th cent. B.C.), 40n.44
Arnaut, Daniel (end of 12th cent.), 352
Arnobius (fl. 300), 259n.36, 270n.1
ars nova, 129, 354f.
Artemis, *see Odyssey*
Artusi (1545?-1613), 187
Ascensio, *see Apocalypse of,*
Assumption of the Virgin, 156-71, 182
Assur, 7, 53
astra animata, *see intelligentiae*
astrology, 200
Athanasius (*ca.* 298-373), 68n.50
Augsburg, Church of Saint Afra, 85
auguri, 232
AUGUSTINE (354-430), 261, 271-79, 340
   Civitas Dei, 64, 128, 147, 270, 272
   Contra Manichaeos, 32n.20
   De Doctrina Christiana, 272
   De Genesi, 35
   De Immortalitate, 33, 118
   De Musica, 33, 41, 289, 344f., 347
   Enarrationes, 173, 270, 282, 284f.
   Enchiridion de fide, spe et caritate, 40n.44, 118n.7
   Letter to Cerebrius, 36
   Retractiones, 33n.24, 118n.11
Aulnay, 103, 111
Autun, 103
Auxerre, 112
Averroes (1126-98), 117
Avesta, 9, 15
Avicenna (980-1037), 117, 119, 121

Ba, Egyptian soul-bird, 17, 221, 224f., 228, 330
Baal, 45
Babylonians, 7ff., 229, 238, 263, 271, 278, *passim*
Bacchus, *see Dionysus*
Bacon, Roger (*ca.* 1214-94), 120

Baghdad, 43
Bandinelli, Roland (fl. 1159), 121
Baouit, 51
Bardi (1534-1612), 204-207
Bargello Diptych, 158
Barlaam, monk (14th cent.), 94
Baruch (1st cent.), *see Apocalypse of*
Basilius of Caesarea (329?-379), 37, 119, 270n.1
Basle, 250, 302, 305
Beatus (d. 798), 87-101, 110, 115, 128, 130, 149, 172, 183ff., 360-64
Bebenhausen, 177
Beeching, Henry C. (1858-1919), 333
Belevi, 247
Bernard, *see Silvestris*
Bernard of Clairveaux (1091-1153), 116f., 145, 313
Bernardino, Saint (1380-1444), 189
bestiaries, 282
BIBLE
   Daniel, 90, 98, 100, 363
   Esdras, 335f.
   Ezekiel, 9, 15, 17f., 47, 54, 57, 119, 250
   Genesis, 220, 230, 278, 304
   Jesiah, 18n.36
   Job, 27, 271
   Lucas Gospel, 51
   Psalter, *passim*
   Revelation, 64, 87ff., 100, 119, 125, 128, *passim*
   Tobit, 18
Bisuccio, Leonardo da (d. *ca.* 1440), 151
Boehme, Franz Magnus (1827-98), 326
Boethius (480-524), 33, 41, 73-76, 80f., 126, 345, 350
Bohemia, 139
Boissard, Jean Jacques (1533-*ca.* 1600), 322
Bologna, 163, 205
Bonaventura (1221-74), 145, 354
Book of the Dead, 17, 228
Book of Hours, 141, 158, 305

Book of Life, 255
Bordeaux, 112, 114
Borgognone (ca. 1450-1523), 141
Bosch (ca. 1460-1516), 162, 322
Boscherville, 100, 109, 162
Bosse, Abraham (1602-76), 209
Botticelli (1446-1510), 134, 136
Bottrigari (1531-1612), 187, 205
Bramantino (*ca.* 1460-1536), 162
BREATH
    life, 228, 230
    pneuma, 279
    spiritus, 220, 279
    See also Aer
Brueghel, Pieter (*ca.* 1525-69), 321f.
Bruno, Giordano (1548-1600), 347
Bry, Theodor de (1528-98), 322
Buhle, 102
Burckhardt, Jacob, 129
Buschor, 250ff.
Byzantium, 64, 277, 361, 364

caelum, see coelum
Cahors, 110
Calderón (1600-81), 194f.
Calliope, 122
Calzabigi (1714-95), 207
Capella, Martianus (fl. 500), 29, 31-
    35, 76ff., 116, 123f., 129, 144,
    191, 194, 206, 350
Carboeiro, 103f.
Carracci, Agostino (1557-1602), 205,
    207
Carracci, Annibale (1560-1609), 163
Carracci, Lodovico (1555-1619), 163
Cartari, Vincenzo (*ca.* 1520-70), 188
Cassiodorus (*ca.* 490-583), 76
Catherine, Saint, 314
Cecilia, Saint, 337f.
Cefalù, 57n.31
Celsus, *see* Origen
Censorinus (3rd cent.), 73ff.
Centula, 38
Ceres, *see* Demeter
Chalcidius (4th cent.), 31f.
Charlemagne (768-814), 363
Charles the Bald (875-877), 101f.

Charles Martell (714-41), 353
CHARIOT
    celestial, 47
    of Kings, 17
    of the Lord, 36
Charlieu, 114
Chartres, 103, 106, 114f., 123, 128,
    150
Charun, 230n.12
cherub(im), 17, 29, 47, 57, 62, 81,
    90, 132, 158, 212, *passim*
Chios, 247
CHORUS
    angelicus, 38
    -group, 57
    musical, 18, 21, 27, 37, 40, 222,
        passim
    See also angelic orders
Christ the Musician, 69, 222, 291,
    313-19, 339
Christine of Lorraine (fl. 1589), 204
Christos Bacchos, *see* Orpheus
Christos Helios, 55, 278
Christos Orpheus, *see* Orpheus
Christus, Petrus (1446-*ca.*73), 294
Chrysostome, *see* John
Cicero (106-143), 21, 74ff., 80, 126,
    350f.
Cimabue (*ca.* 1240-after 1302), 156
Civate, 61
Civitas Dei, see Augustine
Claudianus (d. 408), 257n.29
Claudianus Mamertius (d. *ca.* 474),
    31, 118
Clement of Alexandria (d. *ca.* 215),
    23, 35
Clementi, Muzio (1752?-1832), 209
Clio, 191
Cluny, 106, 110
Clusone, 308
Codex Aureus, see manuscripts: Munich
    14000, Saint Gall
Coelum, 23, 81
Compiègne, 363
Compostella, 103f., 111
Conques, 285
consonances, musical, 85
Constance of Sicily (d. 1198), 353

Constantine, Emperor (306-337), 355
Constantine Kopronymos (719-775), 363
Constantinople, *see* Istanbul
Copenhagen, 208
Corneto, 231
Cornutus (1st cent.), 21, 27
Corvey, 38
Cosmas, *see* Kosmas
cosmology, *see* kosmos
Cranach the Elder (1472-1553), 162
crystal heaven, *see* heaven
Culsu, 230n.12
Cumae, 293
Cumont, 254
Curtius, Ludwig, 45
Curtius, Robert, 193
Cusanus (1401-64), 346f.
Cyrill of Jerusalem (*ca.*315-386), 36

Daddi (*ca.* 1290-after 1355), 154
DANCE
 of angels, 5, 130, passim
 apotropeic, 220
 of blessed, 5, 21, 130
 cosmic, 67
 of dwarfs, 227
 macabre, 221f., 291-312, 334f.
 of peasants, 305
 of *putti*, 180
Daniel, *see* Bible
DANTE, 10f., 258
 Commedia, 30, 40, 103, 116, 123-29, 134, 145, 173, 188, 194, 318, 336, 340, 352-56
 Convivio, 126
 Monarchia, 194
 De Volgari Eloquentia, 194
Daret, Jacques (fl. 1427), 141
David, King, 3, 57, 101ff., 132, 177, 184, 264, 281, 288, 355, 362
DEATH
 punishment, 218f., 291ff.
 salvation, 222ff.
 See also angel of, book of, Satan, skeleton
Dedekind (1628-*ca.* 1694), 209

Della Robbia, Luca (1399-1482), 134, 178-81, 275
Demeter, 259, 273
Dendera, 42
Desrey, Pierre (fl. 1500), 299
Diabolus, *see* Satan
Didymus (1st cent.), 242
Dieterich, 24
Diodor (d. after 21), 28n.32
Dionysios the Areopagite (6th cent.), 11, 20, 29, 38ff., 78, 115ff., 119ff., 130, 158, 161
Dionysus, 204, 259-62, 354
Dominationes, *see* archangels
Donatello (1386-1466), 156, 178ff.
Dresden, 203, 324
Duccio, Agostino di (1418-81), 189
Dürer, 90n.7
Dura Europos, 250, 263f.
Durasis, 261

Ebner, Christine (1277-1356), 315f.
Eccard, Johannes (1553-1611), 212
Eichendorff (1778-1857), 333
Eisler, Robert, 309f.
Elders, musicians, 87
Eleusis, 259, 276f.
Elenor, 235
elves, 328f.
Elysium, 5, 10, 16, 19, 21, 27, 31, 41, 68, 117, 124, 127, 206f., 256f., 328, 352
emotion, *see* motion
Empyreum, 30, 34f., 41, 79, 117, 119, 125, 127f., 130, 147, 156, 206f., 356
Enoch, *see* Apocalypse of
Eos, 10, 15
Ephrem of Edessa (315?-386), 36
Epiphanius of Cyprus, *see* Apocalypse of Adam
Erfurt, 177
Eridu, 13
Erinna (4th cent. B.C.), 243
Erlkönig, 329
Eros, 11, 15, 46, 50f., 68, 239f., 297
Esdras, *see* Bible

Etampes, 103
Eton, 215
Etruscan chimera, 285
Etruscan tombs, 55, 230, 232f., 246, 293
Eugenius III (1145-53), 124
Euripides, 250
Exeter, 176, 178f.
Eyck, Hubert van (d. 1426), 294
Eyck, Jan van (d. 1441), 139, 149, 172, 294, 357-60
Ezekiel, *see* Bible

Fates, 12, 16, 46, 191, 205f.
Favonius Eulogius (fl. *ca.* 400), 75
Fenouillard, 103
Ferdinand of Toscana (1549-1609), 204
Ferrara, 187
Ferrari, Gaudenzio (*ca.* 1471-1546), 163, 166, 182, 184, 186
Ficino, Marsilius (1433-99), 69n.51
Firenze, Andrea da (*ca.* 1343-77), 131
Firenze, *see* Florence
firmament, *see* heaven
Firmicus Maternus (4th cent.), 278
FLAMES
    HELL, 293
    Seraphim, 40, 62, 107
    Sun-Assur, 53
FLORENCE
    Campanile, 187, 204, 354
    Cathedral, 134, 139, 179f.
    Santa Maria Novella, 131
Florus of Lyons (d. *ca.* 860), 193
Fludd, Robert (1574-1637), 191, 193-99, 337, 345
Fouqué, de la Motte (1777-1843), 328
Fouquet (*ca.* 1415-*ca.* 1480), 158
Fra Angelico (1387-1455), 103, 132ff., 147, 166
Francesca, Piero della (1420-97), 163
Francis, Saint, 134
Fravashi, 327
Fronzac, 103

Fulgentius (fl. *ca.* 500), 31
Fulvius Nobilior (fl. 200 B.C.), 268
FUNERAL
    dance, 220, 227
    procession, 226f.
    rites, 255f.

Gabriel, *see* archangels
Gafurius (1451-1522), 83, 191, 199
Galilei, Vincenzo (1533-91), 205
Gaultier, Denis (*ca.* 1605-72), 209
Geertgen tot Sint Jans, (*ca.* 1465-95?), 148, 166, 170
Gela, 49
Genesis, *see* Bible
George of Saxony (1534-37), 324
Gerard of Cremona (*ca.* 1114-87), 120n.21
Gerson, Jean (1363-1429), 120, 357ff.
Gertrude, Saint (d. 1302), 316f.
Ghent Altar, see Eyck, Hubert and Jan van
Gilgamesh, 14
Ginza, 26
Giotto (1267-1337), 156
Giovanni di Paolo (1403-82), 141
Giusto da Padua, *see* Menabuoi
Glaber, Rodolfus (fl. 1000), 100
globe, *see* angels (emblems), Kosmos
Gloucester, 176
Gluck, (1714-87), 207
Gnostics, 20, 22, 26, 35, 271, 284
Goethe, 202, 207, 329ff.
Gorgo, 324
Gossaert (*ca.* 1470-1541), 141n.24
Gottfried of Strassburg (13th cent.), 283n.33
Gozzoli (1420-97), 139
gradual (Babylonian), 8
Gradus ad Coelum, 259ff., 313ff.
Gradus ad Parnassum, 209
Gregory the Great (*ca.* 540-604), 120, 288-91, 345
Gregory Nazianzen (*ca.* 329-*ca.* 390), 270, 272f.
Grimm Brothers, 332

Grocheo (fl. 1300), 76

Grosseteste (1175-1253), 120

Grünewald (*ca.* 1475-*ca.* 1530), 185

Guarini, Giovanni Battista (1537-1612), 187

Guidi, 262

Gundissalinus, Dominicus (12th cent.), 117

Hades, 221, 234f., 237, 242f., 245, 250, 252, 257ff., 271ff., 336

Hadrian, 67

Halberstadt, 3, 219

Halloween, 327

harpies, 235ff., 249, 282

HEAVEN
    bliss, 130, *passim*
    cœlum, 81
    crystal, 119, 125, 127, 355f.
    dome of, 42, 144
    firmament, 42
    and Hell, 3f., 219
    See also Elysium, Empyreum

heavens, number of, 21ff.

Hekateios of Abdera (*ca.* 300 B.C.), 21, 27

Henoch, *see* Apocalypse of

Hercules the musician, 266f.

Hermes, 10, 33, 46, 72ff., 81, 189, 199, 205, 221, 234, 287f., 353
    as psychopomp, 234

Herodotus (*ca.* 485-*ca.* 425 B.C.), 8, 43, 292

Hesiod (8th cent. B.C.), 272

Hildegard, Saint (1098-1179), 98f., 170, 281, 286

Hippolytos of Rome (d. *ca.* 236), 36

Hiskia (720-685 B.C.), 355

Hoffmann, E.T.A. (1776-1822), 328

Hofmannsthal (1874-1929), 333

Holbein (1497-1526), 299, 302, 304-311, 321, 324, 335, 340

Homer, 10f., 13, 34, 137, 193, 221, 224, 234f., 237f., 241f., 251, 272f., 328ff., 334

Honorius of Autun (12th cent.), 283

Horace, 207

Hugh of S. Victor, 120

INSTRUMENTS
    musical, identification of for terms, *see* captions of the illustrations and Appendix v
    of Passion, *see* angels

intelligentiae, 118 ff.

Iran, *see* Persia

Ishtar, 14

Isidor of Seville (7th cent.), 77n.24

Isolde, 283

Istanbul, 31, 363

Jaca, 103

Jacobello del Fiore (d. 1439), 171

Jacobus of Kokkinolaphos (11th cent.), 58f.

Jacques de Liège (14th cent.), 345

Jamblicus (4th cent. B.C.), 31, 253

Jerome (*ca.* 340-419), 119, 272

Jerome of Moravia (13th cent.), 85 n.35

Jerusalem, heavenly, 26, 64, 89, 117, 129, 173

Jesaia, *see* Apocalypse of

Job, 27, 271

Johannes Scotus, *see* John Duns Scotus

John the Baptist, 132

John Chrysostome (*ca.* 354-407), 37

John Damascene (*ca.* 676-749), 57, 119f.

John Duns Scotus (*ca.* 810-*ca.* 877), 78f., 120

JOHN the Evangelist, 172
    Acts of, 35, 38, 276
    Gospel, 20
    Revelation, 25f., 35, *passim*
    See also Bible

John of Gaza (5th cent.), 65f.

John George II of Saxony (1613-80), 203

John Sarascene (12th cent.), 38

jongleurs, 92, 100, 109f., 130, 285

Jonson, Ben (1573-1637), 204

Joshua scroll, *see* manuscripts: Vatican Lib. Ms. gr. 31

Julian the Apostate, Emperor (361-363), 14
Jupiter, *see* Zeus
Justin (d. 166), 36n.32
Justinian (527-565), 353

Kampill, 143
Kastner, G. (1810-67), 324
Katharists, *see* Montanists
Kepler (1571-1630), 191
Kircher, Athanasius (1602-80), 212-14
Kladrius, 283
Knoblochzer, Heinrich (fl. 1477-94), 299, 301, 305f., 310f.
Koja-Kalessi, 54
Konrad of Würzburg (d. 1287), 316
Kosmas Indicopleustes (5th/6th cent), 10, 57
Kosmos
 Babylonian, 7, 13, 15, 17f., 21, 44, *passim*
 Greek, 7, 10ff., 15ff.
 Hindu, 13n.17
 Persian, 7, 9, 13f.
 represented in circles, 67, 166, 170
 represented in layers, 62, 98, 100, 166

Lactantius (d. after 326), 270n.1
Landi, Stefano (fl. 1639), 207
Landino (*ca.* 1325-97), 185
Lanfranco (1580-1647), 141, 163
Laodicea, Councils of, 37
Last Judgment, 287, 304
Lethe, 260, 352
Lilith, 50
Lincoln Cathedral, 177
Linus, 34
Lios Monocus (9th cent.), 79
Liszt, 331
Lochner (d. 1451), 141, 286
Logia Chaldaea, 32
logos, 32, 118
Lorelei, 222, 327ff.
Lorenzetti, Ambrogio (14th cent.), 131

Lortzing (1801-51), 328f.
Louis the Pious (1226-70), 363
Lucian (2nd cent.), 27, 31, 207
Lucifer, 117
Lübeck, 302, 308
Lützelburger, Hans (fl. 1538), 302
Lully, J. B. (1632-87), 187
Luxuria, 97, 110, 284f., 322, 339, 362
Lyons, 114f., 305

macabre, see dance
Machault (1300-72), 359
Macrobius (4th cent.), 31, 75f., 350
Magna Mater, 363
Mahler, Gustav, (1860-1911), 332
Maimonides (1135-1204), 119
Majus, 88
Makrokosmos, 123f., *passim*
Mâle, 128, 145, 177, 284
Mander, Karel van (ca. 1548-1606), 357
Mani (3rd cent.), 32
Manrique, Jorge (*ca.* 1440-79), 194, 292, 294, 307, 335
Mantegna (1431-1506), 138f., 286, 329
Manuscripts
 Bamberg, Staatsbibliothek, Ms. Ed. N. 6, 325
 Berlin, Staatsbibliothek, Ms. theol. lat. 485, 57; Ms. theol. lat. 561, 90
 Boston Museum, Rajastanaut Ms., 264
 Budapest, Nationalbibliothek, Ms. S. B. Clm. 424, 318
 Chantilly, *Très riches Heures*, 141; Ms. 71. *Chevalier Hours*, 158
 Eton College, Ms. 178, 215
 Florence, Bibl. Laurenziana, Ms. Pal. 87, 185; Ms. Plut. I. 56, 60; Ms. Plut. 12 cod. 17, 147
 Hildesheim, Dombibliothek, Ms. U. I, 19, 96
 London, British Museum, Ms. 11695, 109; Ms. Egerton 7070,

MANUSCRIPTS (*continued*)
294; Ms. Royal 2. B. VII, 175;
Ms. Royal 6. E. IX, 122

Macon, Bibl. Municipale, Ms. 1,
148

Munich, Staatsbibliothek, Ms. Clm.
835, 175; Cod. Monac. arab.
464, 91; Cod. Monac. lat.
13601, 84; Cod. Monac. lat.
14000, 90, 96

New York, Pierpont Morgan Library, Ms. 429, 94; Ms. 644,
92; Ms. 742, 149

Paris, Bibliothèque Nationale, Ms.
fr. 166, 158; Ms. fr. 2090, 160;
Ms. gr. 1208, 59; Ms. lat. 1,
101f.; Ms. lat. 1118, 116; Ms.
lat. 7203, 82; Ms. lat. 8850, 96

Reims, Chapitre de Notre Dame,
Ms. 672, 279

Rome, Vatican Lib., Ms. gr. 31, 51;
Ms. gr. 699, 56f.; Ms. gr. 1162,
59; Ms. gr. 1613, 64; Ms. Reg.
lat 1790, 138

Saint Gall, Cod. 22, 102

Siena, Archivio del Stato, Ms.
Caleffo dell'Assunta, 140

Utrecht, University Lib., Psalter,
102f., 174, 183, 360-64

Vienna, Staatsbibliothek, Cimel. B.
4. IV. 22, 51

Wiesbaden, Staatsbibliothek, Hildegard Codex, 99

Marasa-Locris, 258

Marchand, Guy de (fl. 1483-1509),
299ff., 307, 311, 324

Marius Victorinus (4th cent.), 75

Marmion, Simon (d. 1489), 141, 162

Marrou, 254

Mars, 232f., 354

Martianus, *see* Capella

Masolino (1383-*ca*. 1447), 151, 154

Master of Flémalle (d. 1444), 141

Master of Saint Lucy Legend (fl.
1480), 170

Matteo di Giovanni (*ca*. 1435-95),
137, 166

Matthias Corvinus, *see* manuscripts:
Budapest

Maugis d'Aigremont (*ca*. 1350), 307

Maximilian, Emperor, 305

Maximus Confessor (580-662), 120

Mechtild of Magdeburg (d. 1285),
315f.

megiddo, 17, 54

Mei (1519-94), 205

Melusine, 222, 250, 329

Memling (*ca*. 1440-95), 178f.

Menabuoi, Giusto Giovanni (fl. 1363-
93), 275n.13

Menelaus, *see* Odyssey

Mercury, *see* Hermes

Mersenne, Marin (1588-1648), 364
n.16

Metrodorus (3rd cent. B.C.), 247

Michael, *see* archangels

microcosmos, 123f., passim

Mignard, Pierre (1610-95), 171

Milton, 194, 202

Mithras, 9, 14, 23, 26, 28, 46, 65

Mnemosyne, 194, 235, 237, 253, 255,
260

Moissac, 97, 100, 102f., 109f.

Montanists, 279

Monteverdi (1567-1643), 207

Montserrat, 308, 324

MOTION
cosmic, 15-19, 31f., 47, 242
emotion, 344
their correspondence in music, 343
See also musica humana

Mount Zion, 10, 89, 210

movers of the spheres, *see* angels, *intelligentiae*, muses, sirens,

Mozart, 340f.

Multscher (*ca*. 1400-*ca*. 1467), 141

MUSES
as guardians of cosmic order, 18f.,
30, 33, 241, 252
as movers of the spheres, 21, 31f.
as musicians, 21, 34, 138, 241
nine, their number, 16, 21
as psychopomps, 250-55, 334
sarcophagi of, 252f.

musica humana, 8, 33, 41, 76f., 135, 183, 195, 199, 279
musica mundana, 12, 76f., 125, 183, 195, 199, 279, 345
musical examples, 308, 326
musical intervals (consonances), 34, 70ff., 85
Mystics, 222, 291, 314

Nabataeans, 261
Nadb, 228
Napischtu, 278
Naples, 51, 151, 267
Nebuchadnezzar, 90, 363
nekyia, 251, 267, *passim*
Neoplatonists, 20, 27, 31, 35, 278, 310
nereid, 13, 241, 251, 257, 282, 321, 328
Nicaea, 51
nike, 37, 50f., 239
Nikephoros Gregoras (14th cent.), 73
Nikomachus (2nd cent.), 72, 289, 342
Nimrud, 50, 53
Nippur, 263
Nonnus, (9th cent.), 273f.
Notker, 76n.22
nous, 118, 123f., 278
NUMBERS, SYMBOLIC
  3 Fates, 18n.37, 32, 34n.36
  Persian kosmos, 9ff., 77
  Trinity, 27, 77, *passim*
  5 sacred musical notes, 357ff.
  7 planets, 7 *passim*, 351
  spheres, 7 *passim*, 351
  spirits, 89
  angelic orders, 16, *passim*
  9 Muses, 16 *passim*, 78
  10 heavens, 16, 22, 121

Occam, William (d. 1347), 314
Oceanus, 10, 257, 328
Odyssey, 17, 223, 234-38, 284
Offida, 143
Oloron-Sainte-Marie, 104, 111
Olympus, 10, 15, 35, 232
Ondine, 222, 327f.

Oracula Chaldaea, 23n.19
orbs, *see* archangels, kosmos, spheres
Origen (*ca.* 182-252), 15, 35, 65, 261, 270
Ormazd, 23
Orosius (5th cent.), 126
ORPHEUS, 34, 243, 257-70, 272-75, 281
  as musician, 68f., 222, 274, 332
  as symbol of resurrection, 77, 221f., 243, 257f., 270, 273, 332, 339
  -Christ, 256, 264, 313, 336
  -Dionysus, 259f., 262
  and Euridice, 77, 207, 266f.
  and sirens, 236ff.
Orphic Hymns, 65n.42
Orphism, 258, 260
Ortenberger Altar, 141, 162
Orvieto, 163
Osiris, 228
Ossian, 328
Ostia, 293

Padua, 181
Palermo, 88f., 362
Palmyra, 45
Paolo, Giovanni di (1403-82), 141
Paradise, 63, 125, 147, 166, 182, 207, 304, 356
PARIS
  Cemetery of the Innocents, 307
  Notre Dame, 103f., 109, 282
  Val-de-Grace, 171
Parma, 184
Parthenay, 99, 103
Paul, Saint, 22, 128, 357
Paulinus of Nola (354?-431), 69n.51
Pausanias (2nd cent.), 267
Pellegrini, Carlo (fl. 1665), 199
Penelope, *see Odyssey*
Pépin of France (751-768), 363
Persephone, 259, 266
PERSIA, 271
  Kosmology of, 7, 43, *passim*
  musical instruments, 361
Perugia, 189

Peter, Saint, 131, 162, 355
Petrarch, 137
Petrus Lombardus (d. *ca.* 1160), 121
Philo (1st cent.), 21, 36, 47, 118
Philolaos (5th cent. B.C.), 253
Physis, 124, 278
Piacenza, 68
Pied Piper, 327, 332
Pindar (522-442 B.C.), 21
Pisa, 229, 297
planets, *see* kosmos, numbers, spheres
PLATO (427-347 B.C.), 13f., 18, 20, 24, 118, 126, 242, 339, 344
   Axiochos, 20
   Cratylos, 251
   Epinomis, 20
   Phaido, 68
   Phaedrus, 11, 15, 46, 258
   Republic, 11f., 15ff., 18f., 31, 71, 75, 127, 191, 205f., 242f., 339, 344
   Timaeus, 32, 70-75, 117, 342
Pleydenwurff (d. 1494), 3
Plotinus (3rd cent.), 30, 32, 118, 344f., 347
Plutarch of Chaeronea (46?-*ca.* 120), 27, 259
pneuma, 220, 256, 278ff., 281
pnoë, 279
Poimandres (1st-2nd cent.), 32n.22
Pol de Limburg (d. 1416), 158
Pompeii, 267
Pons de Thomières, 110, 130
pontifices, 232
Porphyrius (3rd cent.), 30f.
Poseidonius (1st cent.), 27, 30
potestates, *see* angelic orders
Praetorius (1571-1621), 209f.
Prato, 181
primus movens, 119, 127, 197, 356
Principatus, *see* angelic orders
Proclus (410-485), 30f., 118
Prudentius (d. 413), 69n.51
PSALTER
   David, *passim*
   Queen Mary, 122
   Utrecht, 102f., 174, 183, 360-64

PSYCHOPOMP
   Ba, 17, 221, 224f.
   Christ, 222f.
   Hermes, 234
   Muses, 250-55
   Orpheus, 77, *passim*
Ptolemaeus (fl. 150), 73f.
Puccini, 263n.50
putti, *see* angels
Pythagoras, 11f., 15f., 22, 24, 28, 44, 195, 214, 242, 251f., 259, 276, 281, 339, 349

Quasten, 256
Quintanilla de las Viñas, 54

Radolt, 209
Raphael, 138, 281
Rathbod of Treves (d. 917), 79, 349
Rauch, Andreas (fl. 1621-51), 210
Ravenna, 43, 65, 273
Regensburg, S. Emmeran, 83
Regino of Prüm (fl. 900), 76f., 79, 349
Reichenau, 96
Remigius of Auxerre (9th cent.), 34n.25
René, King (1409-90), 294n.8
Requiem, 335
Rethel (1816-59), 324
Reuben, *see* Apocalypse of
Revelation, *see* Bible
Rimini, 188
Rinuccini, Ottavio (d. 1621), 206
Ripa, Cesare (1560?-1623?), 188
Ripheus, 355
Ripoll, 103
Rist (1607-67), 212-14
Romano, Giulio (1492-1546), 138
Romanos (fl. 700), 277f.
ROME
   catacombs, 273
   Esquilin, 268
   San Prassede, 53, 62f.
   Santa Maria Antiqua, 62, 96, 100
   Santa Maria Maggiore, 51
Rossi, Sebastiano de' (fl. 1585-89), 204, 206f.

Ruah, 220
Russel, George W. (1867-1935), 333

Sabbatini, Andrea (16th cent.), 141, 163
Saint Denis, 128, 158
Saint Edmunds-Saint Mary, 176
Saint Gall, 102
Saint Julien des Pauvres, 282
Saint Jumien, 103
Saint Martial, 122
Saint Omer, 162
Saint Pons de Thomières, 110, 130
Saint Riquier, 38
Saint-Saëns, 371
Saint Victor, school of, 314
Sakkara, 228
saltatores, 232f.
Samara, 89
Santiago, *see* Compostella
Sappho (6th cent. B.C.), 260
Saracens, 87ff.
sarcophagi of Muses, 252
Saronno, 139, 191
Satan, 3, 25, 85, 117, 139, 191, 219, *passim*
Savonarola, 294
SCALE, musical, 12
    Doric, 34, 205f., 209
    Greek, 71ff.
    See also kosmos, *Gradus ad Parnassum*
Schedel, Hartmann (1440-1514), 3, 302, 310
Schikaneder (1748-1813), 340
Schubert, 336
Schütz, Heinrich (1585-1672), 211
Scylla, 250
Sedulius (5th cent.), 69n.51
seraphim, 24, 62, *passim*
Ser Sozzo, *see* Tegliacci
Seuse, *see* Suso
Sevilla Cathedral, 136
Shakespeare, 202, 336, 347f.
Sidonius Apollinaris (5th cent.), 32
Siena, 136, 154f., 180
Signorelli (1441-1523), 163
Silvestris (fl. 1150), 122-25, 191

Simplicius (6th cent.), 31
Sinuhe, 226f., 335
SIREN, 122, 282, 284, 328
    evil spirit, 234-37, 250, 334
    mourning, 248
    musician, 12, 16f., 48, 243-49, 283f.
    psychopomp, 221f., 242, 271, 339
skeleton, 4f., 221, 291-94, 304
Socrates (469-399 B.C.), 251
Sol, 54
Sophia, 125
Sophocles, 251
Soria, 103
soul, see *anima*, breath, *spiritus*
soul-bird, *see* Ba, Kladrius, siren
Spada, Leonello (1576-1622), 142
Spenser, Edmund (1552-99), 20, 194, 328
SPHERES
    Heavens, 21ff.
    kosmos, 7ff., *passim*
    movers of the, 7, *passim*
    See also heaven, crystal, Empyreum, wheels
SPIRITUS
    breath, life, 279, 281
    Eros, 15
    Sanctus, 279, 281
    seven in Revelation, 89
    soul, 279
Suger of St. Denis, 116n.1
sun disc, 54
Suso, Heinrich (*ca.* 1300-66), 315f.
Swithbert, Saint (d. *ca.* 713), 79
Synesius (*ca.* 400), 289
Syrial, 25
Syrianus (*ca.* 380-*ca.* 438), 118

Tasso (1544-95), 194
Tarquinii, 231
Tatios, Achilles (fl. 300), 73
Tegliacci, Ser Sozzo Niccolo di (fl. 1334), 141, 151
Telemachus, *see Odyssey*
Tertullian (*ca.* 150-*ca.* 230), 270n.1, 279n.25

Testament, *see* Apocalypse
tetramorph, 9, 57, 62
Thalia, 34
Thann, 178
Theodosius, Emperor (379-395), 363n.9
Theon of Smyrna (2nd cent.), 73n.9
Thomas Aquinas (1225?-74), 116f., 119ff., 145, 354
Thomas of Celano (*ca.* 1200-*ca.* 1255), 336
Throne of the Lord, *see* chariot
Throni, see angelic orders
Tibet, 310, 327
tibicines, see *tubicines*
Tinctoris (*ca.* 1446-1511), 145
Tintoretto (1518-94), 163, 166, 171, 182
Titian (1487-1577), 163
Tivoli, 67
Tombs
    paintings, 230ff.
    offerings to the dead, 225
Toro, 102
Torsac, 275
Traini (fl. 1320-64), 297
Trajan, Emperor (98-117), 335
Tristan, 297
tritons, 249, 258
trumpets at the Last Judgment, *see* angels
Tubal, 3
tubicines, 232f., 268, 289
Tunisia, 267

Udalschalk, Abbot (1125-49), 85
Ulysses, 234f., 237f., 242, 251
Ur, 224
Urania, 33, 78, 124, 189, 194
Uta of Niedermünster (11th cent.), 83
Utrecht, *see* manuscripts: Utrecht, Appendix v

Valle, Pietro della (1586-1652), 187
Valvassor, J. Weichardt (1641-93), 323
Vano, 230n.12

Veneziano, Caterino and Donato (fl. 1362), 154
Veneziano, Lorenzo (fl. 1356-79), 155
Veneziano, Paolo (fl. 1333-58), 155f.
Venice, San Marco, 60f., 69
Venus, *see* Luxuria
Venzone, 150
Vermonton, 103
Vézelay, 284
Villon (1431-*ca.* 1463), 294
Virdung (fl. 1530), 185n.95
Virgil, 21, 34, 76, 127, 352
Virtutes, see angelic orders

Waginger, Johann Caspar (fl. 1701), 209
Wagner, 343
Warburg, 204, 207
Westminster Abbey, 176f.
Wheels, symbols of
    motion, 47
    seraphim, 57
    spheres, 57
Wilkinson (fl. 1490-1504), 214f.
William of Conches (*ca.* 1080-*ca.* 1150), 71n.4
William of Sicily (d. 1189), 355
Winged figures
    human, 50, 233
    hybrid, 17
    nike, 37, 50, 239
    sun disc, 54
    tetramorph, 9, 57, 62
    See also angels, Assur, Eros
Wolgemut, Michael (1434-1519), 3

Xanthos, 248

Yama, 310

Zanobi, Strozzi da Benedetto (1412-68), 155
Zeus, 23, 31, 33f., 72ff., 81, 125, 129, 188, 194, 199, 205, 234, 253, 273, 350, 354
Ziggurat, 8
Zion, *see* Jerusalem, Mount Zion
Zoroaster, 9n.9